THE POETICS OF BIBLICAL NARRATIVE

PUBLISHED VOLUME

Robert W. Funk, *The Poetics of Biblical Narrative*

THE POETICS OF BIBLICAL NARRATIVE

Robert W. Funk

SONOMA, CALIFORNIA

Library of Congress Cataloging-in-Publication Data

Funk, Robert Walter, 1926–
The poetics of Biblical narrative / by Robert W. Funk.
p. cm. — (Foundations & facets. Literary facets)
Bibliography: p.
Includes index.
ISBN 0–944344–04–6 (pbk.) : $19.95
1. Bible. N.T. Gospels—Language, style. 2. Bible. N.T. Acts--Language, style. 3. Narration in the Bible. 4. Fiction--Technique. I. Title. II. Series.
BS2555.2.F86 1988
225.6′6—dc19 88–12466
CIP

Printed in the United States of America

Contents

Preface

The Poetics of Biblical Narrative is an eccentric work. A preface, consequently, should be allowed to fulfill its proper function and place the body of the book.

Beginnings lie somewhere in the upper reaches of sentence grammar. During a sabbatical year in Canada, courtesy of Wilfrid Laurier University in Waterloo, Ontario and the American Council of Learned Societies, I found myself attracted to the mysteries that lay in the organization of discourse beyond the limits of the sentence. Once a week I took the train to Toronto and spent the day with H. A. Gleason, Jr., at the Linguistics Centre at the University of Toronto. Alan proved to be an electrifying prod. His own *Architecture of Language* was then in progress, and he allowed me to try out some of my green ideas on his graduate seminar.

My work on parables as narrative had inflamed my interest in the properties of narrative discourse. Structuralism was in the air, and my background in linguistics furnished fodder for an excursion into uncharted terrain.

Guides for the journey were few and hard to come by. First honors must go to Vladimir Propp's *Morphology of the Folktale* (original publication 1928). In a tantilizingly short section entitled, "Auxiliary Elements for the Interconnection of Functions" (71–74), Propp asked: How are the "functions" (read: events) connected with one another, in a sequence, in order to form a narrative? If these auxiliary elements, as he termed them, could be isolated and categorized, I reasoned, we would have a rudimentary grammar of narrative.

While engaged in the exploration of this territory, I came across Seymour Chatman's book, *Story and Discourse*, published in 1978. I welcomed this work with considerable enthusiasm because it reenforced my waning confidence in what I was about. Then the work of Gérard Genette came to my attention (*Narrative Discourse*, 1980) and I knew I was in the presence of a kindred spirit. Shlomith Rimmon-Kenan's compact book, *Narrative Fiction*, came along still later (1983) and my anxiety level over direction sank to a new low: a clear and distinct trend had set in and I was not alone.

My copies of Propp, Chatman, Genette, and Rimmon-Kenan are worn and feathered. Nevertheless, it would be misleading to aver that this study belongs in that august company. My course, determined much earlier, is more particularized, more text oriented, than theirs, or any other work on narratology, with the exception of Propp's pioneering study. I have tenaciously stuck to my grammarian's last and fashioned shoes for following the marks of formal grammar and linguistics at every turn. While I have learned much from these and other colleagues, I have struggled to let the data teach me wherever and whenever I could, particularly when the data throw light on, or modify, theory. And that brings me to a second identifying characteristic of this work.

This work, like my *Hellenistic Greek Grammar,* is based on an absolutely fresh compilation of textual data. The Greek grammar went unrecognized for what it was, viz., a new compilation of syntactical data, based on 3,000 actual sentences taken from extant Hellenistic texts. In addition, the Greek grammar was organized around new categories, some borrowed from modern linguistics, others invented at the behest of recalcitrant data. The *Poetics* was conceived in the same spirit and with the same goals: It is based on data derived from actual texts; it empties out into grammar and contemporary theory at some established points but mostly at newly conceived loci. It therefore requires to be viewed as a venture into largely unexplored country.

Naming newly discovered mountains, rivers, species is exhilarating. In this role I had the congenial help of many students at the University of Montana, who found that original research was more stimulating and pleasurable than rote learning. I endeavored to instill in them two cardinal rules for the intellectual explorer. The first is: two examples of the same phenomenon constitute a pattern, three examples warrant a rule. The second is: patterns and rules must be readily teachable to second and third parties, who must be able to get the same results with their analyses as the original discoverer. If a method does not produce common results, it is flawed.

Several generations of students have assisted in the development of this poetics of narrative. They have analyzed numerous texts of their own choosing with this method and arrived at results comparable to my own. So far, so good. We now come to the ultimate test: will a codification of the poetics in written form prove to be as functional for a wider audience as it was for students in the classroom?

A final placing word: I am painfully aware that the observations this poetics contains are but a small beginning in a truly colossal enterprise.

Narrative Diagramming

Narrative discourse may be diagrammed much like sentences in traditional sentence grammar. For this purpose a new set of symbols is required. The following is a summary of the diagrammatic system devised for this study.

1. Narrative discourse takes the form of a series of more or less discrete *actions* or *happenings* (§1.39) expressed by narrative statements. Certain actions or happenings are grouped together in units or clusters representing what may be termed an *event*. An event constitutes the fundamental *narrative segment* (§1.43; cf. §1.23).

An event is represented in the diagrammatic scheme by an egg:

The narrative segment in narrative grammar is the equivalent of the sentence in sentence grammar: the basic unit. Correlatively, the event denotes an agent performing an action or a patient subject to a happening.

2. Each narrative segment (and sequence) has a focusing introduction (code: INTRO) and defocusing conclusion (code: CON) (§§1.46–49; cf. §3.6, 25). The symbol for the focusing process is the wedge looking right:

The symbol for the defocusing process is a wedge looking left:

3. The narrative segment consists of a focusing introduction (INTRO), a defocusing conclusion (CON), and a nucleus (code: NUC) (§1.48). The nucleus (NUC) is what occurs between INTRO and CON. When diagrammed fully, each narrative segment or event will consist of these three interrelated parts:

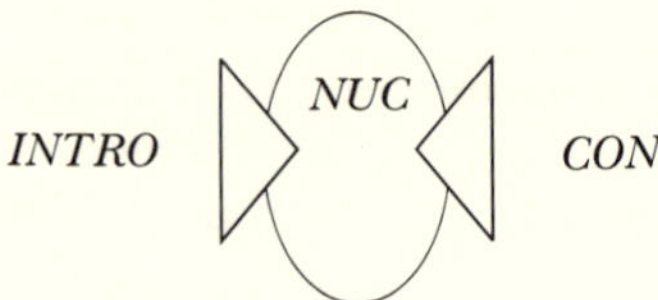

In this study, narrative segments occurring in sequences (see §0.5 below for a definition of sequence) are usually represented as simple eggs (focusing INTRO and CON are omitted); in sequences wedges normally represent the INTRO and CON to the sequence, rather than to the segment.

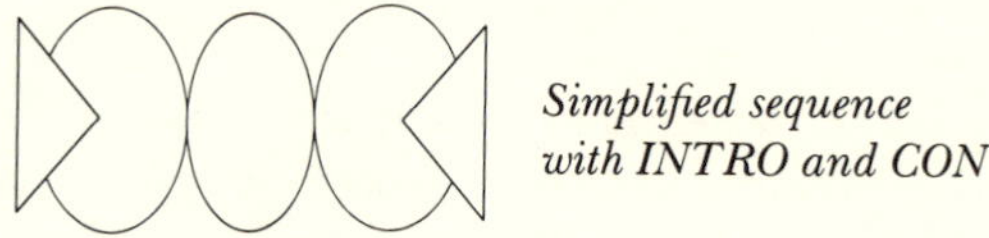

4. Narrative segments are related to each other—to the segment that precedes and the one that follows—at different levels. Overlapping eggs indicate that the relationship is extremely close, for example, in a scene with one or more subscenes.

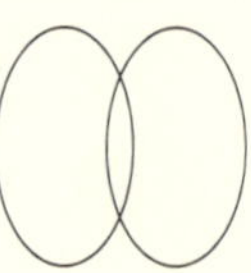

Touching eggs represent the "normal" sequential relationship:

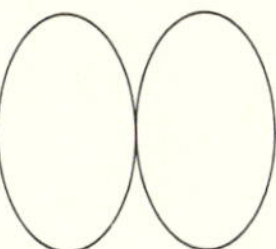

Segments that are relatively discrete and lack a close connection are separated by a space and connected with a "narrative" line, indicating that the segments are linked but at a greater remove.

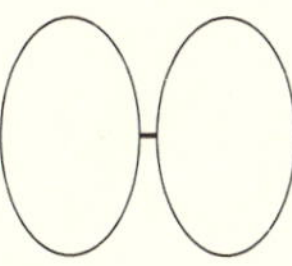

5. Narrative segments or events have a hierarchical structure in narrative discourse. Accordingly, segments are grouped into *sequences*. The boundaries of a sequence of segments are marked in diagramming by square brackets:

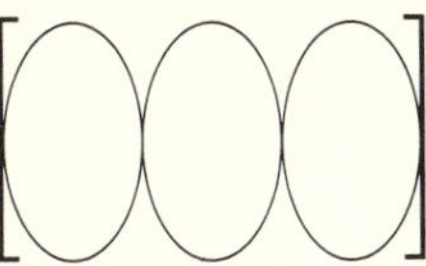

6. Linked sequences are separated from each other by a space and the brackets connected by a "narrative" line:

7. Major breaks between sequences and sequences of sequences are denoted by a vertical bar:

8. Where required, the end of a narrative may be marked with a period.

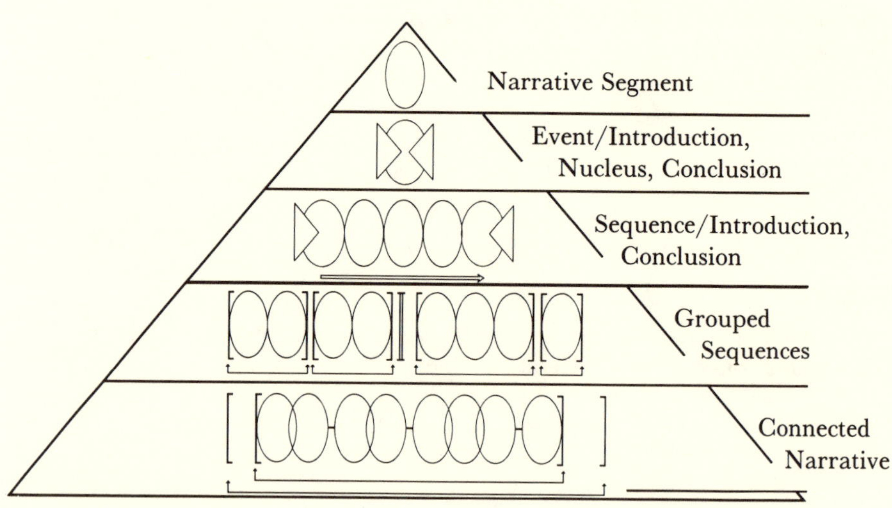

Table of Narrative Codes

1. The Focalizing Process

Participants:	P	participant
	CP	continuity participant
	TP	theme participant
	A, B	individual participants
	id	identification (and qualification)
Locale:	*ls*	local setting
	lc	local connective (with link to preceding narrative)
Time:	*ts*	temporal setting
	tc	temporal connective (with link to preceding narrative)
Focalizers:	*f*	focalizer
	pre-f	pre-focalizer
	f-recip	reciprocal focalizer
	pos	position

kinds of focalizers:

arr	arrival someone arrives or comes forward someone is brought, sent, or called persons meet (mutual arrival) someone finds someone
perc	perception someone sees something someone hears something someone finds something (i.e., perceives it) someone tastes something
perc-prec	perception precipitator a sound signal (cry, rush of wind, earthquake) a visual signal (vision, flash of light)
dia	dialogue
attn	attention getting devices
aa	action anticipator (telegraphs action)

2. *Kinds of Action*

	a	action (character is agent)
	h	happening (character is patient)
	s	status statement
	desc	description
	iter	iterative

3. *Marks of Segmentation*

With reference to participants:	P*set*	introduction of a new set of participants
	P*id*	the formal introduction of a new participant
	P*nomchg*	change in nomenclature for a participant
	P*nom*	reuse of noun (rather than pronoun)
	P*reid*	the reidentification of a continuing participant
With reference to time:	*ts*	a temporal notice
	tchg	an explicit temporal shift
	a:retro	reference to a preceding action as past
With reference to place:	*ls*	a locale notice
	lchg	an explicit shift in locale
	dep	departure (often marks segment end)
With reference to focalizers and action initiators:		any new focalizer or action initiator

4. *The Defocalizing Process*

Participants:	*pe*	participant expansion
	pc	participant contraction
	id:term	terminal identification
Locale:	*lchg*	locale change
	le	locale expansion
Time:	*tchg*	temporal change
	te	temporal expansion
	termt	terminal time
Action:	*dep*	departure
	dis	dismissal
	termf	terminal function
	ae	action expansion
	afore	action forecast (a future action anticipated)
	a:term	termination of action
Other Devices:	*pre-def*	pre-defocalizer (e.g., dismissal, followed by dep)
	recap	recapitulation
	rep	report
	constop	conversation stopper
	pershift	shift in perspective
	com	commentary of narrator

Table of Narrative Codes
Listed Alphabetically

a	action (character is agent)
aa	action anticipator (telegraphs action in INTRO)
A, B	individual participants
ae	action expansion
afore	action forecast (in CON)
a:retro	reference to preceding action as past
arr	arrival
a:term	termination of action
attn	attention getting devices
com	commentary of narrator
constop	conversation stopper
CP	continuity participant
desc	description
dep	departure
dia	dialogue
dis	dismissal
f	focalizer
f-recip	reciprocal focalizer
h	happening
id	identification
id:term	terminal identification
iter	iterative
lc	local connective (with link to preceding narrative)
lchg	an explicit shift in locale
le	locale expansion
ls	local setting
P	participant
pc	participant contraction
pe	participant expansion
perc	perception
perc-prec	perception precipitator
pershift	shift in perspective
P*id*	the formal identification of a new participant
P*nom*	reuse of noun (rather than pronoun)
P*nomchg*	change in nomnclature for a participant
pos	position
pre-def	pre-defocalizer
pre-f	pref-focalizer
P*reid*	the reidentification of a continuity participant
P*set*	introduction of a new set of participants
recap	recapitulation
recip	reciprocal (always used with focalizer)
rep	report
retro	retrospective
s	status statement
tc	temporal connective
tchg	an explicit temporal shift
te	temporal expansion
term	terminal
termf	terminal function
termt	terminal time
TP	theme participant
ts	temporal setting

1

Poetics and the Narrative Text

• 1 •

SENSES OF THE TERM NARRATIVE

The object of this study is the narrative text. So simple a statement would appear to require no further elucidation. To isolate the narrative text in a few well chosen phrases is not, however, an easy matter, nor is it a simple exercise to locate the narrative text in relation to other parties to, and elements of, the narrative transaction. The first step is thus to explore the terminological ground in an elementary way.

1. Narrative as discourse. The term *narrative* is used to refer to three different things. The first and perhaps most common reference (1) is the narrative expression, written or oral, that constitutes a story. In this sense, narrative refers to the linguistic medium, to the words and sentences spoken or written in telling a story. It is becoming widely accepted to employ the term *discourse* to denote this sense of the term narrative. Gérard Genette has written a book called *Narrative Discourse* because it treats the grammar of the narrative text (he explores only the written narrative). Shlomith Rimmon-Kenan prefers the label *narrative text* or, more simply, *text* for this sense of the term narrative.[1] Narrative discourse, narrative text, and narrative expression are synonyms: all three refer to the linguistic vehicle of the story.

2. Narrative as story. Narrative may also be taken to refer to (2) a series of events, real or fictive, that are the content of the discourse.[2] Narrative in this sense refers to what is told, to the actions and actors portrayed in the discourse, rather than to the words or statements of the expression. It is the subject of the story in contrast to the medium through which the subject is expressed. The words on the page or the sounds intoned are not the same entity as the events being narrated: there are no roads or houses or love scenes or heartbreak in the text; those things are in the story, so to speak. And so, narrative in the sense of the series of events to which the narrative refers—the referents of the narrative—is now commonly termed *story*. Seymour Chatman has written a book entitled *Story and Discourse* in which narrative as discourse and narrative as story constitute the fundamental distinction.[3]

3. It may be objected that the term story is commonly used to refer to the

1. In her book, *Narrative Fiction*. See especially 3f.

2. If the events are fictive, the narrative is said to be fiction; if the events are actual, the narrative is said to be historical.

3. Even here clarity is difficult. Story is sometimes taken to refer to an abstraction or hypothetical series of events; in other instances it denotes an actual continuum of events, a series in real life. This distinction will be the subject of further exploration below, §§2.29–37.

narrative expression, to the narrative discourse; it is therefore confusing to use the term exclusively in the second sense to refer to the referents of the narrative. This objection does not, perhaps, take into account the correlative common ambiguity that results: story often carries either sense and may be used equivocally to refer to both. A reporter may ask, "What is story?" and have in mind a report on an event or series of events, actual or fictive. Any response, of course, will have to take the form of discourse, since a story cannot be told without words (or some other medium of communication). However, the reporter may have in mind the question, "What is the real story?" In that case, the reporter is suggesting that some accounts being given do not match each other or the actual series of events; to use the current terminology, discourse does not match story. The common use of the term would itself seem to require the distinction between the first and second senses.

The distinction between discourse and story is a useful one in biblical studies. Indeed, this distinction has been at the base of much controversy since the rise of historical criticism, beginning already in the eighteenth century. The question often posed is whether there is any discrepancy between kerygma (a summary statement of the gospel) and history, or between the gospels and the events they report. Historical critics have pressed the question, What is the real story? Apologists for the faith have tended to argue that the biblical text tells the "real" story and is therefore not fictive.

4. Narrative as performance. Finally, the term narrative may also be understood to refer to (3) the act of narrating, to the telling itself as an event. The analogy in drama would be the *performance*. On cold winter evenings at the university, students often gather to hear poets give a *reading*. And at the children's library on Saturday mornings, the librarian *tells* stories. All of these acts are discourse being performed; the discourse is itself an event. They are not the events to which the discourse refers, nor the texts of stories, but the telling as act. In this sense, narrative is a verb: to narrate.

5. Summary. There are thus three senses of the term narrative: narrative as discourse, narrative as story, and narrative as narration. To substitute another set of terms, narrative as discourse is the tale itself, narrative as story is what is told, and narrative as narration is the telling.[4]

THE TEXT AS THE INTERSECTION OF THE NARRATIVE TRANSACTION

The three senses of the term narrative do not exhaust the elements involved in the narrative transaction. Two other elements require recognition and exploration.

4. The terminological question will be explored further in chapter 2, §1.

6. Storytelling mediates the act of one party, the narrator, whether author or merely performer, to a second party, the reader or listener, for whom the term *narratee* seems especially appropriate.[5] The act involved is a communication. The medium of the communication is of course language, but language in the form of narrative discourse. Storytelling also embraces a fourth element, as sketched earlier, viz., what the story is about, its referents. Just what is included in those referents turns out to be a very complex issue, to be explored subsequently.[6] Meanwhile, it need only be said that the referents are the story.

It is perhaps obvious to say that the relationship between narrator and narratee is made possible by the narrative text. It is equally obvious that the story becomes accessible to the narratee only when put in the form of a narrative text (or some other narrative medium).[7] Indeed, it can also be said that the story is equally inaccessible to the narrator except as narrative text. In short, the connections between and among the three termini, if one may put it that way, are provided exclusively by the narrative text. The text is the intersection of the narrative transaction, as represented by figure 1.

The Narrative Transaction

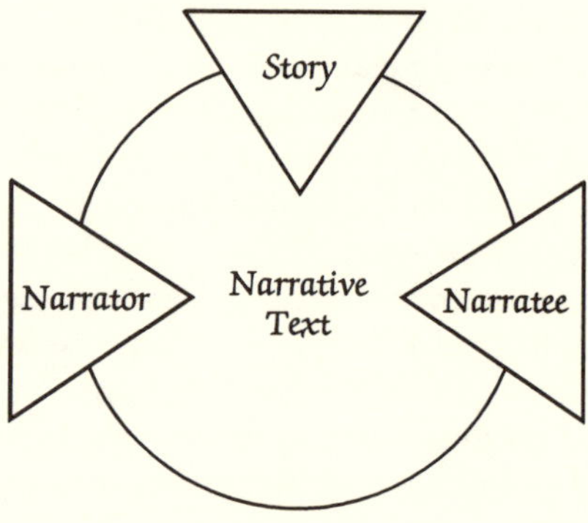

Figure 1

7. It is important to emphasize that it is only through the text that the reader (and critic) have access to the story or to the narrator. Of the various

5. Narrator and narratee are explored in chapter 2, §§4–10 and §§11–18, respectively.

6. The complexities of story are probed in chapter 2, §§19–52.

7. This qualification is necessary, of course, because there are other narrative media, such as film, pantomime, dance, comics, and the like. However, since this study is concerned with the linguistic medium, the reference is understandably shortened.

components belonging to the narrative transaction, only the narrative discourse, the text, is directly available to the reader or critic.[8] For this reason alone, it is crucial to learn as much as possible about the medium through which story must pass, that is, about the constraints imposed upon narrative and narration: To what "rules" must the storyteller subscribe in order to be able to tell a story? Only by identifying and isolating such constraints can the critic hope to understand the kind of filter or screen the narrative text erects between story and narratee, between narrator and story, and between narrator and narratee. As the necessary intersection of the narrative transaction, the text is the net that permits certain things to pass through while restricting others. The text is therefore a key to new advances in discerning the nature of the narrative transaction.

THE GOALS OF A NARRATIVE POETICS

8. Poetics, grammar, and narratology. The key role played by the text as the intersection of the narrative transaction is the reason this study focuses on the narrative text rather than on the narrator, narratee, or story. The objective of this investigation is to develop a poetics of narrative discourse based on clues provided by the surface features of a limited corpus of texts.

In its root sense, *poetics* has to do with everything involved in the creation or composition of (literary) texts, and not just of texts written in verse, although the use of the term poetry to refer exclusively to verse suggests a more limited range. In its modern sense, now well established among literary critics and linguists, poetics treats the formal properties of literary texts. *Narratology*, for which this new term was coined, is a subdivision of poetics: narratology is concerned with the formal properties of a special kind of discourse or text, viz., narrative. A narratology of biblical narrative did not seem to be a felicitous title, so it was determined to retain the more inclusive word and call this work a poetics of biblical narrative.

A poetics could also be called a grammar. Grammar is currently a less glamorous word, although in its larger sense, a grammar consists of the principles of any science or art, which is a reasonably good definition of a poetics in its literary sense. In a more specific sense, of course, grammar refers to the constituent elements of a natural language (the study of which is called morphology) and their organization into larger units of meaningful discourse (treated under the heading of syntax). A poetics of narrative would thus amount to a morphology and syntax of narrative discourse.

9. Narrative competence. The ability to represent story in narrative discourse, whether fictional or factual, appears to be native to users of natural

8. Similar claims are made by Rimmon-Kenan, *Narrative Fiction*, 4; Genette, *Narrative Discourse*, 27f.; Hrushovski, *Segmentation and Motivation*, 2.

languages. Every speaker can tell a story. The ability to form coherent narratives is analogous to the ability to form an almost unlimited number of novel but grammatical sentences. The analogy suggests that native competence has a grammatical base, just as sentential competence does. In short, there must be such a thing as a narrative grammar, parallel to but extending beyond sentence grammar.

If narrative competence is native, narrative grammar would be nothing more than making explicit what the narrator and narratee already know but know subconsciously. Narrative grammar is raising to the conscious level what narrators and readers of narrative practice each time they tell or read a story. This perhaps makes the process of creating a narrative grammar sound easier than it in fact is. Yet a substantial beginning has been made in recent years by scholars in a variety of disciplines toward establishing the lineaments of a narrative grammar or poetics. We shall be drawing freely on those contributions, but we shall also be adding our own to the growing body of explicit knowledge.

10. Supersentential grammar. In the investigation of language, linguists have noted that traditional grammar is sentence grammar. In the ancient world to rise above the level of the sentence meant to pass from grammar to rhetoric.[9] The chasm between sentence grammar and rhetoric, however, was considerable. In modern times, to rise above the level of the sentence is to pass over to literary criticism. Although a revival of rhetoric seems to be underway, the gulf separating literary criticism and rhetoric from sentence grammar remains enormous.

Linguists began to explore the "grammar" of language above the level of the sentence early in this century. Progress has been slow. Nevertheless, some important gains have been made and discourse structure has become an important wing of the linguistics movement, culminating in structuralism in the post-war period. Out of structuralism narratology has developed, but in a new form: narratology is perhaps recovering more of its linguistic roots than was apparent in structuralism. Moreover, narratology seems to have made a new alliance with literary criticism, at least in certain sectors.

The issue is whether linguistic technique can be employed to develop a grammar of discourse above the level of the sentence. Were that possible, the result would be a supersentential grammar. In any case, it is clear that discourse, narrative discourse in particular, is marked by recurrent features, which can be isolated and recorded as regularities. Regularities form the basis, when collected and systematized, of a discourse grammar. If the regu-

9. In Greek grammars, a final section is often devoted to figures of speech and thought, which is a gesture in the direction of rhetoric. Cf. Blass-Debrunner-Funk, *A Greek Grammar*, §§485–96.

larities so organized apply to narrative and only to narrative, the grammar would be a narrative grammar.[10]

11. In setting out the principles that govern the composition of narrative texts, narrative poetics abstracts away from the features of particular texts, and attempts to isolate and systematize the features that characterize all narrative texts. Poetics then formulates hypotheses regarding the structure of narrative texts, hypotheses that must be tested and verified against a larger body of data.

This study is oriented to the palpable text. As a result, hypotheses are formulated on the basis of the clues residing in the text continua of a specific corpus of texts. For the purpose of formulation, only two or more examples of a given phenomenon are required. The hypothesis can then be tested by reference to other texts in the corpus. Should the features so isolated appear in the balance of the corpus, it is assumed that the same features will be found in other narrative texts as well. Of course, the possibility always exists that further data will prompt the investigator to modify the original hypothesis to accommodate new evidence. As the data base is extended to other types of narrative texts and expanded into other historical periods and geographical regions, the need for revision will undoubtedly grow.

The final test to which a narrative poetics of this type must submit is the test of repeatability. My own version of this test consisted in teaching students the rudiments of the system; in asking them to assemble their own compendium of narrative texts derived from any source whatever; and then in comparing the results of their analyses with my own. The convergence of results was extremely high; where we did not agree initially, further investigation often revealed that one or the other of us had made a mistake in the analysis. Occasionally, we found it necessary to modify or amplify the grammar.

12. The corpus of texts includes a generous number of biblical narratives, mostly shorter ones, since the overarching aim of the study is to lay the foundations for a poetics of biblical narrative. For balance, or for control, other narrative prose texts are included in the data base. It did not seem wise to set biblical stories, which are folk literature for the most part, alongside sophisticated modern literary texts.[11] Instead, I have selected other texts of a similar or closely related type for comparison. In a few instances, texts some-

10. Cf. Rimmon-Kenan's discussion and reference to the work of A. J. Greimas in *Narrative Fiction*, 9.

11. It would seem to be an error of major proportions to assume that modern prose fiction is subject to the same categories of criticism as ancient prose narrative. Yet many recent forays into this field have made precisely that assumption. It is sounder to establish the lineaments of ancient prose narrative before, or in connection with, the development of literary-critical rubrics, rather than attempt to apply modern categories to ancient texts, without review and revision.

what higher on the literary ladder have been considered. In the main, however, the compendium of stories may be described as folk materials.

Hansel and Gretel seemed more appropriate as a control than Henry James, for example, or a Western like Shane more immediately apposite than Shakespeare. But the reasons for looking to folk and popular narrative texts were also methodological: the narrative grammar of such texts is less complex than the grammar of modern prose texts at their best, for instance as represented by Leo Tolstoy or Herman Melville. In laying the groundwork for a grammar, the simple, highly repetitive features of folk and popular texts offered a firmer purchase on the fundamentals and permitted the investigator to avoid the intricacies of a Marcel Proust.

POETICS, LINGUISTICS, AND INTERPRETATION

The goals of a narrative poetics were defined in a preliminary way in §§8–12. We must now enlarge on that definition in order to locate this study within recent and current poetics and narratology, and in relation to linguistics, structuralism, and literary criticism.

13. Poetics as bridge. In attempting to define what might be termed the approach of poetics to literary texts, we will do well to consult a durable pioneer in the field, Tzvetan Todorov. He begins with an admittedly simplified bifuration of the field of literary studies generally: one branch, he writes, "sees the literary text itself as a sufficient object of knowledge; the other considers each individual text as the manifestation of an abstract structure."[12]

The first of these approaches is exemplified in critical operations that parade under the names of exegesis, commentary, *explication de texte*, close reading, interpretation, or just plain criticism. Hermeneutics could also be grouped with these practices as the systematic statement of the principles of interpretation. What these approaches have in common is proximity to the particular text: commentary elucidates the individual elements of a given text, while interpretation translates the text into another set of statements that presumably represent its meaning.[13] In every case, the predominant focus is on the individual text.

The second of these approaches aspires to the scientific, by which is meant "the establishment of general laws of which this particular text is the product."[14] This mode of study brackets the autonomy of the individual text and seeks instead to relate the particular to another realm of knowledge con-

12. *Introduction to Poetics*, 3.

13. Jonathan Culler offers this distinction in his "Foreword" to Todorov's *Poetics of Prose*, 10.

14. *Introduction to Poetics*, 6. Todorov enters a disclaimer to the effect that a "scientific" poetics does not aspire to the exactitude of the mathematical sciences.

sidered more fundamental. Among more fundamental branches of knowledge are psychology, epistemology, sociology, anthropology, history of ideas, and the like. The literary text is taken to be an expression of "something" and that "something" is to be reached through the poetic code in the text. Psychoanalytic, sociological, and anthropological studies of texts, for example, fall generally into this category.

14. Todorov claims that poetics bridges the gap between these two attitudes: it spans the cleavage between the particular and the general, between attention to the individual text and the attempt to establish laws governing the production and interpretation of all literary texts. Poetics, he writes, "does not seek to name meaning, but aims at a knowledge of the general laws that preside over the birth of each work. But in contradistinction to such sciences as psychology, sociology, etc., it seeks these laws within literature itself. Poetics is therefore an approach to literature at once 'abstract' and 'internal.'"[15] In contrast, the social sciences are abstract and external, while literary criticism is concrete and internal. Thus, while poetics does create abstractions, while it does generate a discourse that differs from the text itself, its categories presumably derive from, or are constantly referred to, the text itself, rather than to some other realm of knowledge and hence discourse. This dialectic is what marks it as a bridging discipline.

15. Concrete and abstract. The mediating character of poetics is the key to locating this study: poetics mediates between the concrete and the abstract. In the first instance, poetics will refer to "real" works, as Todorov insists: "the best stepping-stone toward theory is that of precise, empirical knowledge."[16] Of course, poetics will also attempt to discover what particular works have in common with other works, beginning with those of the same type (e.g., prose narrative). Identifying and isolating common features may take place at lower and higher levels of abstraction. On the high side, the category might embrace all forms of prose discourse; on the low side, the body of data might be limited to a period, to a genre, or to one or several subgroups, such as short prose folk narratives like those found in the Bible. In all cases, poetics consists in going back and forth between the particular, the specific, and the more general. As Todorov sums it up,

> Poetics, like literature, consists of an uninterrupted movement back and forth between the two poles: the first is auto-reference, preoccupation with itself; the second is what we usually call its object.[17]

This dialectic is what makes poetics both an abstract and an internal approach to literary texts.

15. Todorov, *Introduction to Poetics*, 6.

16. "Structural Analysis of Narrative," 71. Cf. *Introduction to Poetics*, 7, 11–12.

17. "Structural Analysis of Narrative," 76. Cf. 71: "poetics and description are in fact two complementary activities."

16. The bridging position of poetics does not mean that prose narrative has no relation to the external, e.g., the social world or history, nor does it mean that poetics is unable to contribute to disciplines such as sociology and anthropology that have as their proper objects external constructs. However, it is crucial that poetics establish the specificity of narrative, for example, before seeking to clarify the relation of narrative to those externalities. Only by so doing will it be possible to distinguish what in narrative owes to the constraints of the the specific discourse, and what owes to the pressures of mind set or social world or some other externality.

17. Similarly, the bridging position of poetics requires that it not be collapsed into interpretation, into hermeneutic. Poetics is scientific insofar as it seeks to establish the grammar of modes of discourse as such. It therefore must be kept independent of hermeneutic. However, poetics may well provide interpretation with critical instruments, which of course need not be employed in a wooden fashion; indeed, criticism has the obligation, for its part, to correct these instruments as it applies them to an ever expanding body of texts.[18]

18. One further remark is called for in this connection. In his introduction to Todorov's *Introduction to Poetics,* Peter Brooks identifies two requirements of poetics, the first of which we have already discussed, the second of which is germane at this point:

> Poetics must offer a systematic understanding of literary discourse as that which comprehends its individual manifestations, and it must understand in systematic fashion its own discourse on literature.[19]

The second requirement arises from the fact that the abstract qualities of literature at which poetics aims exist not in literature itself, but only in the language of poetics. Poetics employs literature as the occasion for developing a secondary mode of discourse, which, in the last analysis, is auto-referential. It is therefore incumbent upon poetics to establish and then sustain a rigorously critical relation to its own language. To be sure, part of the rigor of that self-criticism will depend on its constant reference to its object, viz., literature, or, in the present instance, the prose narrative text. That brings us back to the fundamental bridging position of poetics and to the dialectic that connects the object of poetics, the literary text, with its own systematizing discourse as it attempts to isolate and formulate the properties that mark the narrative text off from all other kinds of discourse.

A poetics of biblical narrative will of necessity coin new terms, if it is foundational work, and will attempt to organize those terms into a new

18. Cf. Todorov, "The Structural Analysis of Literature," 73, for a statement of this point.

19. "Introduction" to *Todorov, Introduction to Poetics,* ix.

secondary discourse. This is particularly the case, if, as this study intends, the investigation proceeds on the basis of a rigorous dialectic between a fresh body of textual data and a revised set of perspectives on that data.

19. Linguistics and interpretation. Poetics is a bridging activity in another important respect: it mediates linguistics and interpretation, although it is neither one nor the other. Brooks states the matter succintly: "The misuses of structuralist thought in literary criticism most often appear as a failure to understand the importance of poetics as the necessary intermediate ground between linguistics and interpretation."[20] This is also the view of Jonathan Culler, which presumably is consonant with the work of Todorov:

> Poetics, at least as it has developed in France, is based on linguistics but is not simply an application of linguistic categories to the language of literature . . . in literature perfectly ordinary linguistic constructions combine, according to conventions which are not linguistic but literary, to produce literary meanings.[21]

While poetics is a descendant of linguistics, it entails a shift in levels: poetics shifts away from smaller linguistic units at the level of the sentence and below, to larger linguistic units at levels above the sentence. Thus, Culler continues:

> The move from linguistics to poetics involves a shift of level. Linguistics defines the units of a language and the way they combine to form meaningful sentences; poetics moves up to a second level and studies how phrases and sentences form literary units which combine to produce characters, plots, thematic structures.[22]

Poetics is concerned, on Culler's view, to identify and systematize those combinations of "ordinary linguistic constructions" that result in literary meanings, or, put differently, poetics "studies how phrases and sentences form literary units which combine to produce characters, plots, thematic structures." Ordinary linguistic structures are phrases and sentences, and literary meanings refer to constructs like character, plot, theme.

20. The "literary meanings" to which Culler refers sound strangely like some or most of the traditional categories of literary criticism. Indeed, his own sketch in *Structuralist Poetics* makes that abundantly clear, as does the work of Todorov in his various publications, as Brooks asserts: "Todorov's effort at a synthetic poetics must make use of what he has inherited from the traditions of poetic reflection—particularly studies in genre, also work in metrics, in stylistic 'registers,' in narrative 'point of view,' and so forth—which, of diverse provenance, sometimes appear a rather heteroclite assem-

20. In the "Introduction" to *Introduction to Poetics*, xviii.
21. In his "Foreword" to *Poetics of Prose*, 9f.
22. "Foreword" to *Poetics of Prose*, 10.

blage. And he must, while organizing this material, do some invention of his own."[23] It is thus clear that the categories of poetics, until recently, were derived from the traditional rubrics of literary criticism, as augmented by more recent studies of formalist and structuralist inspiration.[24] But it is precisely in this connection that ambiguity sets in. Brooks refers to these categories as "a rather heteroclite assemblage," and suggests, in the same passage, that:

> The significant elements from which literary discourse is constructed are far from being clear even to professional literary critics, and in particular there is very little agreement as to what might be called "minimal units," elementary paradigms.[25]

21. These confessions suggest that the traditional categories of literary criticism are not commensurate with the aims of poetics, that the structures which presently serve to bridge linguistics and interpretation are in fact derived from one abutment. It is therefore quite possible that poetics needs to generate new categories, ones that are correlative with its base, which is linked primarily to the opposite abutment, viz., linguistics.

It is a yawning chasm that separates the textual surface from the traditional rubrics of literary criticism. In the transition from the lower to the higher levels, from linguistics, which focuses on the sentence and below, to criticism, which addresses comprehensive and abstract categories, such as plot, it is quite possible that one or more intermediate steps or levels have been omitted. It is an unduly long step from the single sentence to plot. It seems entirely commensurate with the aims of poetics to seek to build outward and upward from combinations of sentences, from what we shall term *segments* and sequences of segments, in the direction of more global categories. In that case, poetics would treat units larger than the sentence—supersentential units—but units that are nevertheless, in the first instance, observable on the surface of the text, before proceeding to units and relations that are not explicit in the text.

If linguistics and interpretation are the two abutments of a single span, poetics takes as its goal the creation of as many supporting piers and trusses as possible, in order to get safely and effectively from the text to its interpretation. Yet poeticians need not suffer from delusions of grand bridge building: we shall never complete the span with steel and concrete; critics and interpreters will still be required to make the final leap over the abyss of meaninglessness and complete the link by intuition. Nevertheless, poetics need not be deterred by the prospect of penultimate defeat. There is always one more small section of the roadbed to be laid over some new pier. And

23. "Introduction" to *Introduction to Poetics*, xii.
24. The work of Genette is an exception.
25. "Introduction" to *Introduction to Poetics*, xii.

sightings on the other side through the fog of mixed and inadequate signals are becoming more frequent and promising.

THE TEXT CONTINUUM

22. Benjamin Hrushovski has developed a theory of the text continuum that is especially germane to the question of the relation of the text to the traditional categories of literary criticism, and represents an advance over previous discussions. The literary text, Hrushovski observes, is organized on two levels: the surface level and the reconstructed level. The surface level of the text does not present the reader with a plot or characters as such. Rather, the reader builds such constructs up from discontinuous and heterogeneous elements in the continuous text. And it is this reconstructed level that is customarily addressed in literary criticism of both traditional and structuralist persuasions. Poetics in most of its recent forms has done little to show how the critic gets from the surface level of the text to the reconstructed level.

23. The continuous text presents the reader (and critic) with a sequence of sentences that unfolds step by step. The first question to be posed of the text is, What are those steps and how are they organized? For, as Hrushovski rightly claims, "any close observation of a text will show a high degree of organization of the text continuum which is distinct from the organization of the reconstructed level."[26] Hrushovski then distinguishes the formal organization of the text, by which he means items like the division into chapters and paragraphs, and semantic groupings, which appear to bear no necessary relation to the formal organization. In any case, the primary organization of the text is by segment, however we define such units. He puts the matter this way:

> A long text cannot possibly be of one piece. It is usually divided into many small segments with a whole network of motivations for the introduction of such segments and for their closure, shifters from one segment to another, transitions from one semantic focus to another, etc.[27]

In the illustration he provides from *War and Peace*,[28] it seems that the semantic unit coincides with the formal organization of a different sort, viz., the scene in a traditional sense. And elsewhere Hrushovski refers to "external" markers of segmentation, "such as the dramatic technique of dividing a chapter into scenes by introducing a new character or making a character exit."[29] "External" was perhaps a poor choice of qualifier in this instance; markers of segmentation such as entrances and exits are perhaps surface markers, but they are certainly not external to the text. If anything, they are more internal

26. *Segmentation and Motivation*, 7.
27. *Segmentation and Motivation*, 7.
28. *Segmentation and Motivation*, 9–11.
29. *Segmentation and Motivation*, 36.

to the text than the semantic markers to which he refers. At all events, it is precisely these surface markers, indicating the segmentation of the continuous narrative text, that are the object of the present investigation, as a first but crucial step in building a bridge from the surface to the reconstructed levels of the text. The pursuit of these markers will result in additional controls for the critical reading of the text.

24. Hrushovski's theory of the organization of the text continuum is too complex to be recapitulated here in full. It is sufficent to say that his scheme calls for the recognition of "a highly complex network of patterns of all kinds."[30] Patterns may be made up of any of the elements of language itself or of elements of anything that can be presented in language. A pattern, to put the matter broadly, is the linking of two or more elements in text; the elements may be continuous or discontinuous and constructed by any means whatsoever. Patterns generally are of two kinds: patterns based on principles of equivalence (rhyme would be an example from poetry), and patterns that are derived from structures perceived in the real world. The great variety of patterns in literature corresponds in large measure to the endless variety of phenomena in the real world and all possible worlds. His point is well worth emphasizing: "we not only use literature to understand the world, but we use the world, as well as all possible worlds, to understand and construct literary texts."[31] Later in his discussion he connects this observation with remarks on frames of reference at various levels and the issue of verisimilitude. Finally, there are patterns that represent a mixture of equivalence and the order of reality, e.g., literary genres, such as the pattern of a tragedy.

25. Hrushovski's analysis is highly provocative. Nevertheless, he does not pursue the question of the surface organization of texts, but proceeds to a level involving a network of patterns of all kinds, none of which depends on, or is directly related to, the surface organization of the text. In spite of his blinking of surface markers—Hrushovski's use of the words "formal" and "external" to describe them suggest that he has not considered them worth pursuing—he has addressed the tangible text at a more concrete level and in ways that are more fruitful than any other poetician on the contemporary scene, with the possible exception of Gérard Genette.

26. Like other theorists of narrative, Hrushovski notes that not all elements in the literary text belong to the literary organization, which stands in contrast to language, where all elements at the lower levels are taken up into the higher levels (phonemes and morphemes into sentences, for example).[32] There are elements extraneous to given patterns in almost every narrative segment. These elements may contribute to other patterns, or they may simply be literary "debris."

30. *Segmentation and Motivation*, 4.
31. *Segmentation and Motivation*, 4.
32. *Segmentation and Motivation*, 11.

Textual segments, on Hrushovski's view, are junctions: a junction is a textual segment in which patterns at various levels and of different kinds converge. Junctions thus do not directly serve plot or any other kind of structure in the text, but rather, taken as units, have "their own continuous consistency." This, he notes, is a quite different view of the text continuum than the prevailing one. The arrangement of segments is not a reshuffling of elements in the deep structure, such as plot, "but the presentation of an unfolded continuum which has its own logic and its own organization and from which a reader is led to construct both 'form' and 'meaning,' plot," etc.[33] In other words, the narrative is not made up of plot, character, setting, etc., but of sentences joined in a hierarchy of segments and sequences. And it is this organization that we must first seek to understand in poetics.

A SKETCH OF A NARRATIVE POETICS

27. Constraints of discourse. Like the sentence, discourse in general exhibits recurrent features that can be grouped as regularities and then stated in the form of grammar. Narrative discourse is a subspecies of discourse and, as such, is subject to the same general constraints, although particularized in a form suitable to narrative. The result would be a limited number of "rules" for the structuring of narrative discourse. Such rules should be of use for both the analysis and the production of narratives.

B. W. Newman has provided an outline of the features of discourse as such (not just narrative discourse) that contribute to it as a structured event. It must have, he states, (1) markers for the beginning and the end of the discourse. (2) Markers for internal transitions are also required, since discourse cannot consist of an undifferentiated flow of words and sentences. Furthermore, (3) the temporal, spatial, and logical relation of the various parts must be indicated in some way, and the discourse will provide for variation in successive references to the same objects, events, or qualities in order to avoid excessive repetition. Finally, (4) there will be ways to indicate what in the narrative is in focus and what not, what is in the foreground and what belongs to the background.[34] Some of these constraints will be taken up in the sketch to follow; others will be reserved for subsequent treatment.

28. A preliminary sketch of a narrative poetics will give body to the preceding definitions. To provide the relevant body, that sketch should be based on an actual text, and for that purpose a simple narrative segment found in the Gospel of Mark will serve adequately. In this case we are dealing with a narrative that is one verse long, but which exhibits all the essential characteristics of the self-contained narrative. For convenience of reference and anal-

33. *Segmentation and Motivation,* 11.

34. *Interpreter's Dictionary of the Bible,* Supplementary Volume, 237–41.

ysis, the text will be presented as a series of narrative statements, utilizing the sentence structure of the text as the basis.

——— • *The Call of Levi* • ———

Mark 2:14

(1) [14] As Jesus was walking along,
(2) he saw Levi, the son of Alphaeus,
(2.1) sitting at the toll booth,
(3) and Jesus said to him,
(3.1) "Follow me."
(4) And Levi got up
(5) and followed him.

The narrative statements are numbered consecutively for easy reference. The number (2.1) indicates that this statement is embedded in statement (2): (2.1) is actually an independent statement in the substructure of statement (2).[35] The reference (3.1) indicates that this statement is subordinated to (3), in this case as an object clause.

29. Every narrative and narrative segment has a beginning and an end. Another way of saying the same thing is: every narrative is finite. As a consequence, narrators must have devices to begin and end stories, and these devices can be described and catalogued. Moreover, since no story of any length can consist of a single, unbroken stretch of narrative prose, these same devices can be used to begin and end segments within stories.

30. Sometimes there is an "introduction" in which time, place, participants and other features of the setting are presented. In other instances, the "introduction" is lacking and the story begins with action. In our model narrative, there is no introduction; the story begins with the arrival of Jesus. An arrival is one common device for launching a narrative or narrative segment.

31. The story ends with a departure: Levi gets up and the two of them depart the scene. The action takes place in a temporal stretch lying between arrival and departure and in a space defined in the same way. The preceding and the following segments in the larger narrative take place at different times and places. Many written narratives and films make use of the simple device of an arrival to launch a story and a departure to bring it to a close. The same devices can also be used to begin and end segments within stories or sequences of segments.

32. When Jesus arrives on the scene, he "sees" Levi. This is another formal marker: sensory contact between two or more participants is a way of bringing the scene into focus for the action to follow. This device will subsequently

35. The independent statement is: *Levi was sitting at the toll booth.* The term substructure seems preferable to *deep* structure, which carries with it numerous associations. Substructure refers to the two simple sentences underlying the complex sentence.

be termed the *focalizer:* the focalizer is the juxtaposition in time and space of two or more participants, in anticipation of some action: the reader's attention is drawn, in this way, to the locus of the discourse.

33. Since our sample is a minimal story, there is but one action in the body of the narrative: Jesus calls Levi to follow him as a disciple. Levi's response constitutes part of the defocalizing process that brings the narrative segment to a conclusion.

34. In formal terms, we might summarize this narrative section with the following list of components:

arrival
sensory contact
"call"
departure

If we were to raise these components from the particular to the categorical, we could rename them:

pre-focalizer
focalizer
action
defocalizer

We would then be able to make a list of other particular ways of pre-focalizing, focalizing, and defocalizing narratives and narrative segments. Subsequently, we shall do precisely this and develop categories that more or less exhaust the possibilities of such devices.

35. Jesus and Levi are the participants in this narrative segment. Since Jesus appears both earlier and later in the Gospel of Mark and is the dominant figure, he may be termed the *continuity participant:* he provides one form of cohesiveness for the narrative as a whole. Levi, on the other hand, is the theme of this particular segment and can therefore be termed the *theme participant.*

36. In addition to participants, there is setting, which includes time, place, and other features. We might surmise from the larger context that this scene takes place by the Sea of Galilee, although we would not know that from the knowledge gained from this particular segment. We do learn that Levi is seated at a toll booth and is thus probably a tax collector. That provides an important clue that links this segment paradigmatically to other parts of the narrative: tax collectors play a significant role elsewhere in the Gospel. Similarly, Levi becomes a follower, and that, too, provides a thematic link with other similar stories in Mark concerning discipleship.

37. To bring this elementary sketch to a close, we must also observe that longer narrative texts are composed of narrative segments, more or less like our model. These segments are arranged into sequences, each of which also has its own beginning and end. And sequences in turn are linked together in hierarchies, which form the narrative text as a whole.

Inasmuch as the text continuum of stories is made up of segments and sequences arranged in hierarchies, narrators will also have devices to connect one segment with another, one sequence with another, and to indicate the relationship of the one to the other at different levels.

38. This brief sketch of the poetics of narrative provides essential clues to both the syntagmatic arrangement of stories and to paradigmatic features. *Syntagmatic* refers to the sequential arrangement, the before/after movement of the narrative, while *paradigmatic* refers to thematic connections, such as those provided by recurring symbols, themes, motifs, that also contribute to the "meaning" and cohesiveness of narratives.

39. Types of narrative statements. This provisional sketch can be developed one step further by considering types of narrative statements. They are of two types:

(1) those that express an action or a happening,
(2) those that express status.[36]

The first type might be called "do" statements, the second "is" statements.

A "do" statement represents an action or a happening. An action is performed by an agent:

(1) *Peter healed the lame man.*
(2) *Jesus took her by the hand.*

A happening is a change of state affecting a patient:

(3) *The lame man was healed (by Peter).*
(4) *The fever left her.*

The lame man is the subject of the passive verb in (3), but he is nevertheless the patient (the one affected by the action). Compare these two further statements:

(5) *Burton raised the sails on his boat.*
(6) *Burton sailed out of the harbor.*

In (5), Burton is the agent, in (6), he is the patient: he is the agent in sail raising, but he is the patient with respect to the action of the wind. This is by way of reminder that narrative statements are not identical with the surface structure of actual sentences in the text.

40. The second type of narrative statement is the status or "is" statement. A status statement may identify a character:

36. The terminology used by Chatman, *Story and Discourse*, 31f., is process statement for the first type, and stasis statement for the second.

(1) *John is an apostle.*

It may qualify a participant or element of the setting:

(2) *Simon's mother-in-law was sick.*
(3) *The fig tree had nothing but leaves on it.*
(4) *It was evening.*

The distinction between "do" and "is" statements is not absolute; indeed, the two shade off into each other, particularly when it is recalled that the statements in question may be *restatements* of the surface text. For example, an action statement may index or imply a character or an element of the setting:

(5) *Jim loves Jane.*

The following are implications of (5):

(a) There is a character named Jim.
(b) There is a character named Jane.
(c) Jim is a lover.
(d) Jane is lovable.

One statement thus indexes two participants or characters with respect to both identity and quality: (a)–(d) are status statements implied by (5). Similarly, the status statement

(6) *Jim is a lover.*

projects or anticipates some event in which Jim's quality as a lover is expressed. Actual sentences in a narrative text may thus entail more than one type of narrative statement in the paraphrase or restatement.

Entailment is not restricted to the interchange of action and status statements. It may also involve the implication of one action for another action, or the implication of a status statement for another status statement. The statement

(7) *The Holy Spirit came upon the apostles.*

implies that certain events followed. One action statement may therefore index another action. In a comparable way, the statement

(8) *God is love.*

implies other status statements: there are other persons who may be the object of that love (unless, of course, divine love is entirely self-referential).

41. Peter's mother-in-law. These categories may be put partially to the test by considering another short text. There is a very brief, more or less self-contained narrative text in Mark 1:29–31 (the account of the healing of Peter's mother-in-law). We may set out the narrative statements and label each one.

In accordance with the empirical bent of this study, we shall make use of the actual sentences of the text in listing narrative statements.

——— • *Peter's Mother-in-law* • ———

Mark 1:29–31

INTRODUCTION
(a1) 29 And immediately he left the synagogue,
(a2) and entered the house of Simon and Andrew with James and John.
(s3) 30 Now Simon's mother-in-law lay sick with a fever

NUCLEUS
(a4) and immediately they told him of her.
(a5) 31 And he came
(a6) and took her by the hand
(a7) and lifted her up,

CONCLUSION
(h8) and the fever left her;
(a9) and she served them.

a = action; s = status; h = happening

The narrative statements are numbered consecutively from (1) to (9). The type of statement is designated by the letter preceding: (s3) is a status statement; (h8) is a happening; the remainder are actions.

42. In terms that were enunciated earlier, this short story could be summarized as a three-statement narrative:

(s1) Peter's mother-in-law lay sick with a fever.
(a2) Jesus healed her.
(a3)(s3) She rose and served them (=she was healed).

This summary indicates that the story involves a single event that mediates a change in status. The three-statement summary assumes that this short story stands alone. Viewed as a segment of the larger narrative, the Gospel of Mark, however, it could be reduced to one narrative statement: (a1) Jesus healed Peter's mother-in-law. This statement would constitute one of a whole series of events in which Jesus is the narrative subject. This difference in summaries suggests that sets of narrative statements belong to a hierarchy and that their place in the hierarchy prompts different summaries, depending on whether the segment is being viewed as an isolated account, as part of a larger sequence, or as an element in the whole narrative.

Quite aside from the question of whether these paraphrases are correct, in this study we shall attempt to avoid paraphrase or summary unless necessary. We shall work with the statements of the narrative text itself. That means, among other things, that we shall endeavor to retain any ambiguity presented by the series of statements provided by the text—ambiguity that is resolved (interpreted in one direction) by a summary. That will often require the consideration of greater detail. But since we are concerned here with the way in which surface structures are read as story, it is essential that we stay as close to the textual surface as possible.

43. Hierarchies of narrative statements. The representation of a stream of activity, whether fact or fiction, in narrative discourse, takes the form of a series of more or less discrete *actions* expressed by narrative statements, as sketched above. Since neither the chain of *actions* nor the series of statements can be represented in language as an undifferentiated flow, as uniformly continuous, certain actions and happenings are singled out and grouped together in cohesive units or clusters representing an *event*.[37] These clusters may be termed narrative *segments*. Narrative segments are arranged, in turn, in *sequences*, which customarily have a hierarchical structure. Segments, which may consist of many narrative statements (cf. Peter's mother-in-law with nine narrative statements = one segment), may be represented abstractly as an egg: 0. A sequence of segments would then be a series of eggs: 00000. Since a narrative is often made up of more than one sequence, some means is required of indicating the grouping of segments. Square brackets will serve that function in an elementary way. A narrative consisting of nine segments grouped into three sequences of equal length would look like this when represented abstractly: [000][000][000]. Narrative statements, to recapitulate, are grouped into segments, and segments are arranged in sequences. There are, of course, groupings of sequences, sometimes to several levels. This hierarchical arrangement could be represented in the hypothetical story by doubling or trebling the square brackets. The nine-segment story taken as the hypothetical example might be arranged with three levels: an introduction consisting of one segment; a story nucleus[38] consisting of seven segments grouped into two sequences; and a concluding segment. Graphically, the arrangement would look like this: [0[[000][0000]]0]. Since this way of representing the clustering of narrative segments becomes confusing in complex stories, it will be necessary, subsequently, to simplify the means of representing larger clusters of sequences and clusters of clusters of sequences, etc. Simple graphics, such as those proposed above, will serve, however, to represent the basic structure of narrative texts.

44. Linking devices. Narrative segments are hooked together by a variety of linguistic and other devices. The discrete events of which the narrative consists are circumscribed both temporally and spatially. As a consequence, one group of linking devices consists of temporal and spatial connectors. Further-

37. An event thus consists of a kernel action grouped with secondary or satellite actions in a narrative segment.

38. A story nucleus is to be distinguished from a segment nucleus or kernel action.

more, a narrative would not be recognized as a narrative unless there were some continuity in participants. The sequence of statements

(1) *John fell in love with Mary.*
(2) *Jane left home.*
(3) *Bill's parents objected to Sue.*
(4) *Tom and Sally married.*

does not constitute a story since the statements appear not to be related to each other. It is therefore requisite for the narrative statements to indicate continuity and discontinuity in the relation of participants to events and to each other. And, finally, the events that make up a story require some minimal linkage. This linkage may consist merely of temporal sequence (*x* happened, then *y* happened), or it may involve thematic interlocking, or the narrator may employ recapitulation, analepsis, or prolepsis to indicate the interconnection of events.[39]

CONSTRAINTS OF NARRATION

45. These preliminary observations on segment, sequence, and linkage may now be brought together and restated as a set of contraints on narrative discourse. A set of constraints is the answer to the question, What, in view of the requirements enunciated thus far, does a narrator do when he or she tells a story?[40]

46. The focusing process. In the first place, the narrator must bring a finite set of participants together in a specific time (or times) and a particular place (or places). This may be called the *focusing* process:[41] out of myriads of possibilities certain participants are selected and brought into focus in a particular time and place. To say that a story is circumscribed temporally and spatially is only to say that a narrative must have some focus; it does not tell all stories simultaneously, or even all aspects of the story it does tell. In fact, a good story prompts the reader to fill in the gaps, appropriately, in the imagination. A story may thus be said to be the coincidence of a provocative and an answering imagination. A rough analogy would be the process of focusing a camera

39. For definitions of these terms one may consult the glossary for brief sketches, or the index for reference to discussions in text.

40. For a general statement of the constraints of discourse, cf. §1.27.

41. The focusing process is to be distinguished from what Genette and Rimmon-Kenan call focalization. Put simply, by focalization the two authors mentioned refer to the answer to the question, Who sees? They are inquiring, in other words, after the eyes through which the story is perceived, or what is called point of view in more traditional parlance (*Narrative Discourse*, 189–94; *Narrative Fiction*, 71–85). By focusing process I mean the answer to the question, What is seen? I am inquiring, in other words, after the object of perception: what does the narrative put in focus, or to what does the narrative call sensate attention? To use a rough analogy, Genette and Rimmon-Kenan are asking after the camera, I am asking after the scene on which the camera focuses.

on one plane within a field of infinite possibilities stretched out between the camera and the vanishing point in a field of vision. In a fairy tale that begins, "Once upon a time, a troll lived under a bridge. . .," time, place, and one participant are specified in the opening sentence. Stories require focal specifications to make it possible for the reader to follow the narrator to the beginning of the story.

47. The defocusing process. At the conclusion of the story the narrator—we move now to the second requirement—must reverse the focusing process so that the narrative is not left up in the air but comes to rest. *Defocusing* a story is achieved by dispersing the participants, expanding the space, lengthening the time, or introducing what is felt to be a terminal note. Stories are usually defocused by a combination of these elements or their surrogates. Thus, in the classical conclusion to fairy tales, the prince marries the princess (in most plots felt to be a terminal function) and they live happily every after (time extended indefinitely). Defocusing rounds the story off, so to speak, much as a musical composition returns to its tonic and the work is felt to be complete. In narrative, tonic is the return to a new state of equilibrium or rest after passing from an initial state of equilibrium through a crisis or state of disequilibrium.

48. Nuclei and narrative segments. Finally, the narrator must allow something to happen. Between the processes of focusing and defocusing lie the narrative nuclei or segments. A narrative nucleus may be defined as a narrative segment consisting of a cluster of actions or happenings that constitute an event.[42] The action that is central to a nucleus or narrative segment is the theme of that segment. Other actions, happenings, descriptions, and the like in the segment should contribute to the depiction of the theme event, if that event is in sharp focus. In a narrative consisting of an introduction, conclusion, and one nucleus, the theme of the nucleus and the theme of the story will be identical.

If the narrative consists of more than one nucleus, the narrator has the task of making the themes of the individual segments serve the theme central to the body of the narrative as a whole. The more complex the narrative, the more skill is required to keep the theme and themes in proportion and in focus.

49. Narrative: a chain of events. The elements of the narrative, when joined together, have the formal shape of a chain of events (represented by eggs in figure 2) with opposing funnels at either end to indicate the focusing and defocusing processes. Participants, times, places, and descriptions are funneled into the narrative, grouped in action clusters or segments, and then dispersed again at the conclusion. Since the narrative segments are more or

42. The term nucleus is related to the term segment as the part to the whole. The nucleus is actually the central part or body of the narrative segment; the latter consists altogether of introduction, nucleus, and conclusion. The nucleus is thus the heart of the narrative segment. These terms will be developed more fully in chapters 3 and 4.

less discrete units linked together by a variety of linguistic (and other) devices, the body of the narrative should perhaps be represented as a chain.

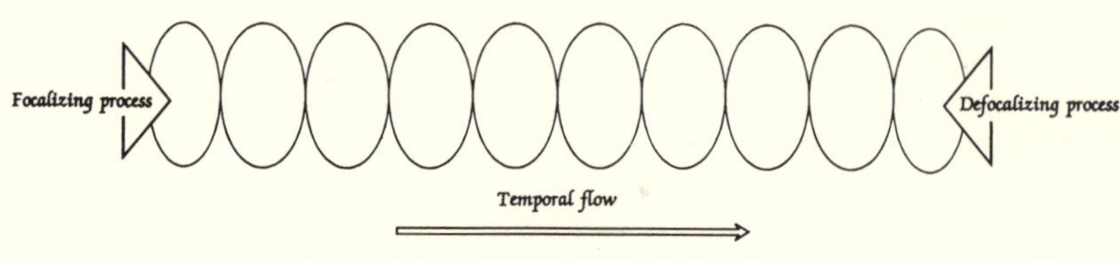

Figure 2

TEXTUAL ANALYSIS AND NARRATOLOGY

50. At the end of his work, Chatman proposes a list of open questions that need to be addressed by those wishing to advance narratology or poetics.[43] Like many recent theorists, he raises fewer questions that call for the investigation of specific bodies of narrative texts than more general questions that call for reflections on the margins of narrativity (extreme or marginal cases). Nevertheless, he poses questions like: How are events connected in narrative texts? What role does setting play, particularly in relation to the representation of character? What unspoken codes are transmitted by narrative texts, codes that may carry more powerful messages than the explicit text? Such questions prompt investigations that will produce fresh bodies of data, on the basis of which theory can correct itself and take new bearings on the issues.

Vladimir Propp compiled the first significant body of empirical data, which launched the modern study of narrative on its course. Propp's work has continued to play a central role in the discussion. His position in current narratology shows that more strongly empirical studies are required to provide theorists with fresh fodder for their musings. This study, as a consequence, is a foray into the surface features of narrative texts.

Poetics as practiced by those, particularly of the French school, who are in or border on the structuralist movement appears a highly abstract and impractical discipline. Discussions consisting of extremely high generalizations seem remote to particular texts; literary theory tends to push aside literary criticism; narratology does not seem to contribute to the analysis of

43. *Story and Discourse,* 263–66.

narrative texts. Yet poetics need not be entirely or even predominantly theoretical and abstract. Genette has taken the course that seems to me the most commendable: he has developed a theory of narrative or a narratology based on a close reading of *Remembrance of Things Past* by Proust. He has undertaken neither a critical analysis of Proust in the service of theory, nor has he subordinated poetics to criticism by making the former an incidental by-product of the latter. He has refused to choose between the two: criticism and theory. Rather, he proposes a method of analysis in which, by seeking the specific, he finds the universal, and by isolating and articulating the universal, he descries the resources of criticism.[44]

51. The focus of this study is on the surface of specific narrative texts, all or most of which fall into the category of folk or popular literature.[45] The choice was deliberate in this case as it was Propp's: large advances are possible only if analysis is focused on texts that are highly repetitive and consequently relatively simple. On the basis of such texts, we might hope to advance the problem of the surface analysis of narratives in relation to their underlying story or stories. That means, above all, that we intend to focus on the composition of the narrative statement, on the arrangement of sets of narrative statements in clusters or segments, and on the hierarchical structure of segments in sequences. By limiting the range of topics considered in detail, we have perhaps increased the chances of success: we hope not merely to repeat what has been said, but to advance poetics a firm step or two. At the same time, this more empirical approach may prove to be more congenial to those who are involved in the analysis of actual texts and who are not exclusively or primarily interested in the theory of narrative. In any case, I hope to provide data sufficient to satisfy the appetites of those who either want nourishment for growth or who want simply to devour.

44. Genette lays these policies out in *Narrative Discourse*, 22–23.
45. Cf. the elaboration of goal in §§8–12.

— · 2 · —

The Narrative Transaction

• 2 •

THE COMPONENTS OF NARRATIVE

1. There are four components of the narrative transaction:

(1) the initiator of the act: the author
(2) the receiver: the listener, reader, or critic
(3) the medium of communication: the text
(4) the referents of the narrative: the story

It would be helpful if there were a coherent set of terms for these components and if the set were used consistently. It would delight the philologian were that set built on the same root. Alas, it is highly improbable that one set will be widely adopted by critics, and even more improbable that such a set would be employed consistently. Nevertheless, it is worth venturing a few remarks on the subject, in spite of the fact that I will not adopt my own suggestions without considerable vacillation.

2. The first component (1) is often referred to as the narrator, in which case (3) could be termed the *narrative,* and the receiver (2) could be called the *narratee.*[1] Or, the author (1) could be referred to as the *teller,* while the text (3) would be the *tale,* and the receiver (2) might be called the *tellee.*[2] In the first set, one would require narration or *narrate* to refer to the act, and the phrase *the narrated* to indicate the referents (4), the subject of the narrative. In the second set, telling or *tell* would function for the act, while (4) could be termed the *told.* Neither set seems particularly satisfactory, especially when one considers the additional distinctions and nuances that must be made. Yet the terms commonly used—author, reader, discourse or text, and story—are frequently ambiguous and imprecise. In this study several distinctions are required: we shall attempt to develop consistent terminology for these distinctions. Other discriminations are secondary, and for these less precision is required.

In the first chapter we endeavored to delineate what was meant by the text (narrative, tale). In chapter 2, we shall investigate the terms narrator, narratee, and story (the narrated, the told) as representative of the second, third, and fourth components of the narrative transaction.

1. The term is employed by Chatman, *Story and Discourse,* 150, who gives credit (150 n. 7) to Gerald Prince, "Notes Toward a Categorization of Fictional 'Narratees,'" 100–105, for coining the expression.

2. According to Webster's Third Unabridged, the noun suffix *-ee* is used with words denoting the human undergoer, recipient, or beneficiary of an action, e.g., *appointee, draftee, grantee, trainee, trustee. Narratee* would thus be the indirect object of *narrate* as a verb, *tellee* the indirect object of the verb *tell,* as illustrated, for example, in the sentence *she told him a tale: him* in this sentence is the tellee.

3. Listing the four components of narrative as in §2.1 is deceptively simple. Each component can readily be subdivided into two or more aspects. These further subdivisions become extremely important because it is on them that theories of narrative are erected. Moreover, views of what narrative is and how it functions arise from relationships discerned between and among these aspects. In this investigation, the relationship between story and text and between story and narrator will provide numerous points of departure. It is therefore appropriate to sketch the additional distinctions that lie at the base of this study and indicate the particular relationships that are to be explored.

THE NARRATOR

4. Facets of the narrator. The narrator or teller, in current literary criticism, involves at least three distinguishable facets: the real author, the implied author, and the narrator who plays a role within the narrative itself.[3] The real author stands outside the narrative text, even when the author represents himself or herself as a narrator within the text. Within the narrative text, the real author is represented indirectly by the implied author (so identified by Wayne Booth[4]), who has to be reconstructed from the text itself; he or she has no voice.[5] Nevertheless, it is clear from actual texts that real authors assume various guises when creating texts, guises that are reflected indirectly in the text. Critics learn to distinguish these imagined selves from the way in which they design particular texts. And it is a convenient mask: real authors can thereby distance themselves from the creators of their stories, so to speak. On the other hand, the implied author is also distinguishable from the narrator who appears within the story. This distinction is particularly evident when the narrator is "unreliable."[6]

5. The three masks of the narrator just identified are usually named *author, implied author,* and *narrator.* The term narrator is reserved in contemporary literary criticism for the teller within the primary narrative, while the term author is used for the creator and performer of the narrative and his alter ego—the implied author. If one now subsumes all functions of the act of narration under the heading of narrator, there is potential for confusion.

The principal reason for selecting one term rather than three is that all the aspects of narration lie on a single spectrum, from narrators belonging to stories embedded within stories, to authors entirely external to the text. A single term for the entire spectrum thus seems appropriate. All aspects of

3. Rimmon-Kenan, *Narrative Fiction*, 94–103 and 74–76, has a good summary of these and related distinctions.

4. *The Rhetoric of Fiction*, 70–73.

5. Chatman, *Story and Discourse*, 148, refers to the reconstructed author as "it"; Rimmon-Kenan, *Narrative Fiction*, 88, warns against personifying this construction.

6. Also a coinage of Booth, *The Rhetoric of Fiction*, 158f.

narration are to be viewed, moreover, from the standpoint of the traces they leave in the narrative text. In that case, too, the whole spectrum of issues becomes immediately relevant. Finally, the substantive, narrator, is correlative with the verb, narrate, and for that reason also seems apropos. Narrator and narration, in other words, include all aspects of the narrating act, or what the French call the enunciation.[7] As a consequence, the tripartite terminology common in literary criticism will be abandoned in this study, for the most part, and the issues taken up from a different perspective.

Genette, Chatman, and Rimmon-Kenan agree on a general scheme for identifying and organizing the traces left in the text by the narrator and the act of narration. I have adopted their basic organization in this study. However, only a few of the facets will find a place in the issues to be addressed subsequently. In addition, a number of the distinctions common in current criticism seem more relevant to modern than ancient narrative with its much lower level of authorial consciousness.[8]

One further caveat is required. In the discussion of narrator we shall distinguish consistently between the questions, Who speaks? and Who sees? The second question has to do with point of view, while the first has to do with the narrating act.[9]

6. Temporal traces. The first group of traces has to do with the temporal relation of the narrating act to the events being narrated. The relationship dictated by common sense is that the narrator relates events that are already past (the past tense of the verb is therefore predominant). However, there are also predictive narratives (future tense), and narratives that are represented as being simultaneous with the actions narrated, like the enunciating that accompanies a baseball game or golf tournament (present tense, characteristic of some recent novels). Finally, a less common form is the interpolated relationship, in which the narrating instances are interspersed with actions, as in the epistolary novel involving several correspondents.[10]

7. Narrative layers. A second group of traces concerns what may be termed narrative layers. Narrative layers have to do with narrative embedding, and with the relation of narrators to the tales they tell. Every tale has at least one narrator, who makes his or her presence known directly or indirectly, even if that presence is reduced to mere quotation: somebody is quoting the direct speech being reported. But within the primary narrative, there may be addi-

7. I am indebted to Genette, *Narrative Discourse*, 213–15, for the putting the matter in this light.

8. For example, the concept of implied author does not seem to me to be particularly relevant to narrative before the rise of the printed text.

9. Rimmon-Kennan, *Narrative Fiction*, 71–74, sketches the distinction and its consequences.

10. Genette outlines and discusses these types, *Narrative Discourse*, 216–23; cf. Rimmon-Kenan, *Narrative Fiction*, 89–91.

tional narrators, who tell parts of the same or other stories. The depth of layering is in principle unlimited.[11]

According to Rimmon-Kenan, "the highest level is the one immediately superior to the first narrative and concerned with its narration."[12] Two things are affirmed by this formulation. First, the primary narrative is the reference point in analyzing layers, and it is to the primary or first narrative that other layers are said to be "up" or "down." The second point is that the narrator always belongs to the layer "above" the tale being narrated: the narrator is narrating a story that is, from the standpoint of traces in the text, outside or below or behind him or her.[13] The story of Jesus in the Gospel of Luke is, to take one example, the primary or first narrative. The narrator, Luke, is one layer above the first narrator, as the prologue to the Gospel indicates: Luke as the narrator looks back on or is outside of the events being narrated.[14]

The story of Jesus in the Gospel of Luke as the primary narrative is termed the *diegetic* level by Genette.[15] The term to be employed here is first or primary narrative. The highest layer, the layer to which Luke the narrator belongs, could then be termed the *hyperdiegetic* layer, meaning, simply, the layer above the first narrative.[16] If, instead of simply *diegetic*, we adopt the term *intradiegetic* to indicate that the narrator at the next level down belongs within the first narrative at the first level, then *hypodiegetic* would be a suitable term for the narrator who appears within a story that is within the first narrative. For levels below *hypodiegetic*, it would be necessary to double and triple the prefix, *hypo-*.

These distinctions are represented graphically as follows:

11. Genette, *Narrative Discourse*, 227f., provides the basic discussion; cf. Rimmon-Kenan, *Narrative Fiction*, 91f.

12. *Narrative Fiction*, 91f.

13. It is difficult to find metaphors for the phenomenon that are not misleading. "Outside" suggests that the narrator stands outside the story being told; "below" indicates that the narrator is "looking down" on events from a superior position; "behind" is derived from the past tense of the verbs ordinary used in narration after the fact.

14. Neither Genette nor Rimmon-Kenan takes adequate note of the difference between the levels to which the narrator belongs and the layers of narrative. In this analysis, an attempt is made to develop more precise designations for the two.

15. Genette uses the Greek term for narrative as a convenient way to talk of levels without the use of extended qualifiers. Diegetic will be used subsequently to refer to recounting as a mode of discourse (§§6.2, 25ff.), as distinguished from mimesis, and so will not be employed here in its simple form.

16. For this level Genette employs the term extradiegetic (*Narrative Discourse*, 228), also adopted by Rimmon-Kenan (*Narrative Fiction*, 91), which does not strike me as a happy choice. *Extra-* suggests that the narrator is external to the narrative and that leads to confusion with perspective or point of view. In addition, *extra-* does not correlate with the layers "down" from the first narrative. A correlative term would be "up" and that is best represented by the term hyperdiegetic.

The struggle with terminology betrays the relatively young character of narratology.

Narrators	*Narrative Layers*
1. Hyperdiegetic	
	1. First or Primary Narrative
2. Intradiegetic	
	2. Second Narrative (narrative within the first narrative)
3. Hypodiegetic	
	3. Third Narrative (narrative within second narrative)
4. Hypo-hypodiegetic	
	4. Fourth Narrative (narrative within third narrative)

It should be recalled that the narrator always belongs to the layer above the narrative being narrated. Thus, the hyperdiegetic narrator is "above" the first or primary narrative; the intradiegetic narrator belongs to the first narrative but narrates a second or embedded narrative, and so on.

8. As already suggested, Luke is the hyperdiegetic narrator of the Gospel of Luke. Jesus is an intradiegetic narrator; the stories he tells belong to the second narrative. In the second part of the parable of the Prodigal Son, the servant meets the older son coming in from the field and tells him what has happened. His recounting of the reception of the younger son by the father (Luke 15:27) amounts to a story within a story, which is also within the Gospel of Luke, another story. That makes the servant's recapitulation a third narrative, in relation to which he is the hypodiegetic narrator. This layering is summed up in the diagram on the next page.

Layering of a similar type is repeated by Luke at Acts 10:1–11:18, when Peter tells his own story and that of Cornelius to the group gathered in Jerusalem.[17]

9. Another set of distinctions cuts across the levels just outlined. If a narrator does not participate in the primary narrative, he or she is said to be *heterodiegetic*.[18] If the narrator does participate in the first narrative, the narrator is *homodiegetic*.[19] Thus Luke is a hyperdiegetic/heterodiegetic narrator in

17. A detailed analysis is found in §§6.36–38.

18. Literally "belonging to another story." Genette, *Narrative Discourse*, 228; Rimmon-Kenan, *Narrative Fiction*, 95.

19. I.e., belongs to the same story.

relation to the gospel story he narrates, while Jesus is an *intradiegetic/heterodiegetic* narrator in relation to the parables he narrates. On the other hand, in Acts 11:1–18, Peter is an *intradiegetic/homodiegetic* narrator.

Narrator	*Narrative Layers*
1. Luke (hyperdiegtic)	
	1. Gospel of Luke (first narrative)
2. Jesus (intradiegetic)	
	2. Prodigal Son (second narrative)
3. Servant (hypodiegetic)	
	3. Recap of reception (third narrative)

10. Other traces. Other aspects of narration leave traces in the narrative text. Among them are the degree to which the hyperdiegetic narrator is discernible in the text. Chatman refers to this aspect as covert, as distinguished from overt narration,[20] while Rimmon-Kenan calls it degree of perceptibility.[21] The two poles obviously lie on a spectrum that runs from minimal traces to maximum overtness.

Of interest here are the evidences left by the overt narrator. Chatman lists them from the weakest to the strongest marks of the narrator's presence.[22] The weakest evidence is (1) description of setting (occurs in stories only minimally narrated); (2) identification of characters comes next, followed by (3) temporal summary, which is an attempt to account for a lapse in time or the omission of certain events; the fourth (4) is definition of character, which implies the narrator's knowledge of characters in the narrative, and somewhat stronger yet as a mark of the narrator's presence is (5) reports of what characters did not say or think. Finally, the narrator intervenes directly in the

20. *Narrative Discourse*, 198–262.

21. *Narrative Fiction*, 96–100.

22. *Story and Discourse*, 219–51, nicely summarized by Rimmon-Kenan, *Narrative Fiction*, 96–100.

text in (6) commentary, which may take the form of an interpretation of the story, moral judgments on persons and acts, and generalizations of various sorts.

Another aspect of narration is the unreliability of the narrator. This usually becomes evident in discrepancies between the narrator and the implied author.[23] But the reader's suspicions of the veracity and reliability of the narrator are also aroused when the narrator has limited knowledge (intradiegetic/homodiegetic narrators are often of this type because they belong to the story world and hence are limited in knowledge),[24] when the narrator's own interests or emotions are involved, and when the narrator manifests a dubious moral perspective.[25]

These traces of the narrator and narration will be of concern only in passing in the chapters to follow.

NARRATEES, READERS, AND READING

11. Facets of the receiver. The receiving end of the narrative transaction is customarily divided into three aspects, as in the case of the narrator (§§2.4–5). The three aspects are called, respectively, the narratee, the implied reader, and the real reader.[26] The narratee appears within the narrative, while the implied reader is the one (or ones) to whom the narrator addresses the tale. The real reader, on the other hand, is anyone who actually listens or reads, whether or not addressed. "The agent adressed by the narrator," to use the definition of Rimmon-Kenan,[27] must either be the narratee or the implied reader, by definition, but it can also refer to the real reader when the implied reader and the actual reader are identified by the narrator.

12. Since the narratee and readers belong to the narrative transaction as one of its components—every tale is addressed to some tellee, even if that receiver is merely the narrator in a listening mode—what traces does that fact leave in the narrative text? A correlative question is, What signals does the narrator leave in the narrative text for the reader to pick up?

In general, the discriminations made among narrators will apply, *mutatis mutandis,* to the narratee. Once again, some distinctions appropriate to modern fiction seem less relevant to ancient folk narrative. In any case, the

23. Chatman, *Story and Discourse,* 148f.

24. Rimmon-Kenan, *Narrative Fiction,* 103.

25. Rimmon-Kenan, *Narrative Fiction,* 100–103, has provided the outline for these remarks.

26. Alan Culpepper, *Anatomy of the Fourth Gospel,* 205–27, has an excellent sketch of the issues and problems, with bibliography. Important discussions include Prince, "Introduction a l'étude du narrative," 178–96; Genette, *Narrative Discourse,* 259–62; Chatman, *Story and Discourse,* 149–52, 253–62; Rimmon-Kenan, *Narrative Fiction,* 103–5.

27. *Narrative Fiction,* 104.

narratee and readers will figure less prominently in a study oriented primarily to the narrative text than would be the case in reader response criticism, and preliminary remarks will accordingly be brief.

13. Narrative layers. The narratee, according to Genette, belongs to the same narrative layer as the correlative narrator.[28] Accordingly, a hyperdiegetic narrator addresses a hyperdiegetic narratee, while intradiegetic and hypodiegetic narrators correspond to intradiegetic and hypodiegetic narratees. Thus, the hyperdiegetic narrator, Luke, aims his narrative at the hyperdiegetic narratee, Theophilus (Luke 1:1–4), just as the author of John 19:35 and 20:31 addresses the "you" (plural) of his hyperdiegetic audience. The hyperdiegetic narratee, who here merges with the implied reader, is the receiver with whom the real reader can readily identify. In other words, the three levels are collapsed into each other.

An intradiegetic narrator, on the other hand, addresses the intradiegetic narratee, on the grounds that both narrator and narratee must belong to the layer above the tale the one is narrating to the other. That has interesting ramifications, as Genette points out.[29] The presence of an intradiegetic narratee has the effect of keeping real readers at a distince: the narratee within the narrative is always intruded between the story and the implied and real readers.

14. The effect of the intradiegetic narratee on the parables told by Jesus—parables are, after all, intradiegetic tales in the gospels—is to insulate the hyperdiegetic reader from the parable. The two groups, the tax collectors and sinners, together with the Pharisees and scribes, of Luke 15:2, preside over the hearing of the parable of the Prodigal told in Luke 15:11–32. The listeners are already divided into two groups, the contrasting responses of which to the parable are made explicit by Luke's narrative context. Luke insulates the reader from the parable by usurping real reader response in providing his own within the narrative. Luke thus prevents the parable from functioning as it might as a first narrative. As a first narrative, the terms of the response would not have been given with the story; the terms are metaphorical and the listeners would have had to figure out what those terms stood for and how they were going to respond, and would have done so without prompting. It can thus be said that a parable by definition has no implied readers, or, more precisely, that the parable permits all readers to elect their relationship to the tale.

15. The relation of narrators and narratees (readers) to layers of the narrative may be once again summarized diagrammatically (cf. the diagrams in §§2.7–9):

28. *Narrative Discourse,* 259.
29. *Narrative Discourse,* 260.

Narrator	*Narrative Level*	*Narratee*
hyperdiegetic: Luke		hyperdiegetic: Theophilus
	first narrative: Gospel of Luke	
intradiegetic: Jesus		intradiegetic: tax collectors, etc.
	second narrative: Parable of the Prodigal	
hypodiegetic: servant		hypodiegetic: older son
	third narrative: recap of events	

References are again to the Parable of the Prodigal (Luke 15:11–32) and at the third level to the recapitulation of the servant to the older son at Luke 15:27.

16. The reader and reading. A narrative text is not to be identified with the written text as a fixed object. Readers add to and subtract from what is printed on the page. In reading the text, the reader realizes the text: he or she responds to various markers and signals in the text, discovers patterns, supplies what is felt to be missing, constructs plot, character, and the like, and relates the world of the text to other known or imagined worlds.[30]

17. As Hrushovski warns, in recognizing the role of the reader, the critic does not deliver the text over to "a subjectivist anarchy."[31] On the contrary, the reader, even the naive reader, is responding to signals embedded in the text by the narrator. In this sense, the text is aimed at particular readers, termed implied readers, who are invited to respond as the text suggests, at times even dictates. This concept is summed up well by Wolfgang Iser:

> It is generally recognized that literary texts take on their reality by being read, and this in turn means that texts must already contain certain conditions of actualization that will allow their meaning to be assembled in the responsive mind of the recipient. . . . Thus the concept of the implied reader designates a network of response-inviting structures, which impel the reader to grasp the text.[32]

30. See chapter 12 for sketches of these worlds or fields of reference.
31. *Segmentation and Motivation*, 2.
32. *The Act of Reading*, 34.

The naive, unstudied, intuitive reading is thus not an arbitrary response, but one structured in part by the text itself. A narrative poetics might thus be defined as a compendium of the instructions incorporated into the text for the implied reader.

18. It is necessary to distinguish the naive, intuitive reading from the critical reading, which involves second and subsequent readings, and consequently the effort to account for and justify particular readings. Criticism is sometimes said to have to do with a "proper" reading of the text. A proper reading refers to a close analysis of the organization of the text itself, based on a reading of surface structures insofar as possible, of that organization in relation to the norms of the language and genre in force at the time the text was composed, and of all these factors in relation to the world and worlds of the story, narrator, and reader. The critical reading will aim at what Hrushovski calls a maximal or ideal reading, which is a reading based on the assumptions that all the markers in the text are cogent and fully functional and that all possible patterns and signals have been recognized.

The critical reading is also based on the assumption that all readings, whether correct or incorrect, are based on the same textual data and interpreted by comparable or shared techniques. In other words, proper readings do not arise out of an anarchy of criticism, but out of a community of the circumcised ear.[33] Put differently, naive readings are subject to review and testing at the hands of those whose experience of certain types of texts is large and disciplined, whose knowledge of interpretative ploys and theory is comprehensive, and whose critical acumen is acute. Reviews of this order amount to a kind of interference with ordinary reader response. By making explicit what transpires in the act of reading, however, criticism reviews and refines readings of all kinds, at many levels. To be eligible for this form of indoor sport, the critic belongs to a guild of the sort often formed by thieves, pickpockets, and merchants.[34] Membership in a guild means that interpreters of texts have agreed, in principle, to construct theories of how texts are organized and how they are to be read, and then, in practice, to adhere to those principles. Criticism is a language game, with rules, as Wittgenstein might have said. But compacts among critics do not guarantee specific readings; they merely make the process seem more orderly than it is.

In the end, all readers must advert to the text to discover, or rediscover, their bearings as readers of texts. They must do so, that is, if they wish to become implied readers and submit, for the time, to the directions of the text and read as it directs them to read. This is to subscribe neither to the autonomy of the text nor to the absolute liberty of the reader; it is to recognize that in the encounter of reader with text, both reader and text take their rise, are,

33. These remarks are indebted to Hrushovski, *Segmentation and Motivation*, 3, and Frank Kermode, *Genesis of Secrecy*, 1–21.

34. The felicitous suggestion is that of Kermode, *Genesis of Secrecy*, 2.

in fact, coconstitutive. Or, as Iser puts it, the reading is the place where the text and the reader meet, on ground located in neither party to the transaction, but in some space accessible to both.

STORY

19. Introduction. The third and final component of the narrative transaction to be considered in this chapter is story. We shall first of all examine multiple "summaries" of the story of Jesus in the Book of Acts as a concrete way of getting at the reasons for discriminating story from discourse. These multiple "summaries" or paraphrases suggest that every expression is, in an important sense, a selection from an underlying story that turns out to be ineffable because made up of an infinite string of actions or because highly abstract. The question must then be raised about levels: how many distinguishable levels are there between particular expressions and the highest story level imaginable?

It will then be helpful to develop a definition of story, which in turn is derived from and related to particular manifestations of stories in narrative texts. Essential clues for a narrative poetics or grammar emerge from this analysis.

THE STORY OF JESUS

20. Acts 3:12–16. In Acts 3:12–26, Peter preaches a sermon to a large group of people assembled in Solomon's Portico. In the course of that sermon he recounts the *story* of Jesus of Nazareth; we may label this narrative text D1 (for discourse 1) for easy reference. For our purposes here, we take note of only the first part (vss 12–16) of the long sermon (vss 12–26). We begin with the introduction:

> 12And when Peter saw it he addressed the people, "Men of Israel, why do you wonder at this, or why do you stare at us, as though by our own power or piety we had made him walk?"

Since we are not concerned here with the narrative frame, we may ignore the framing clauses. The balance of the discourse may be divided into individual statements and numbered for reference. A narrative statement consists, as a rule, of a sentence with a single main verb, on the grounds that a narrative is a chain of actions linked together into a story.[35] However, in order to facilitate the analysis, we shall often set out vocatives, temporal notices, and designations of place as separate statements, although, strictly speaking, they are not. Arranged, then, as narrative statements, the text reads:

35. Compare the definition of story as a chain of events below, §§2.44–51.

(1) [12] Men of Israel,
(2) why do you wonder at this,
(3) or why do you stare at us,
(4) as though by our own power or piety we made him walk?

The first four statements of the sermon are introductory: they address the audience directly regarding the healing of the lame man that had just taken place. Peter then turns to a series of earlier events (earlier in relation to the event that is the temporal point of reference: the healing of the lame man)[36] that comprise the *story* of Jesus.

(5) [13] The God of Abraham and of Isaac and of Jacob, the God of our fathers, glorified his servant Jesus,
(6) whom you delivered up
(7) and denied in the presence of Pilate,
(8) when he had decided to release him.
(9) [14] But you denied the Holy and Righteous One,
(10) and asked for a murderer to be granted to you,
(11) [15] and killed the Author of life,
(12) whom God raised from the dead.
(13) To this we are witnesses.

Then, in the statements that follow (vs 16), Peter again turns directly to his audience and to the healing event which is the immediate occasion for the sermon.

(14) [16] And his name, by faith in his name, has made this man strong
(15) whom you see and know;
(16) and the faith which is through Jesus has given the man perfect health in the presence of you all.

These statements are succeeded by an additional long paragraph in which Peter continues to address his audience directly by drawing out the implications of the story of Jesus for his listeners (3:17–26): "And now, brethren, I know you acted in ignorance . . . Repent, therefore, and turn again." In sum, Peter has embodied a brief narrative account of the story of Jesus in his sermon, which he then uses in appealing to his audience.

21. We may ignore the fact, for the moment, that Peter's sermon is embedded in a sequence of events that runs from Acts 3:1 to 4:31, which in turn is a part of the longer narrative of the Book of Acts.[37] It is sufficient to recognize that one version of the story of Jesus (D1) is nested in a sermon; that is, it is being told for its relevance to the audience before Peter, as its homi-

36. Technically called an analepsis: the narration of an event or events that took place earlier chronologically than the event or events being narrated presently. The term is derived from Genette, *Narrative Discourse,* 40. Analepses are discussed in §§8.5–6.

37. To be analyzed subsequently in detail in chapters 3 and 4.

letic context testifies. The tale of Jesus is embedded in a telling that is construed as significant for those listening: "Repent therefore, and turn again." It is narrative as narration: performance in this case entails consequences for the auditors. It should be noted, in passing, that Peter's narration is embedded in a further narration, viz., Luke's, which is addressed to Theophilus (Acts 1:1). Whereas Peter's narration is made explicit in the narrative, Luke's is not made explicit at this point (the reader has to recall that Luke is narrating for his own audience). To complicate matters still further, this passage in Acts 3 may be read from the lectern in some church: this is yet another performance with its own audience. The listener on that Sunday morning is at fourth remove from the original events:

(1) the original events: the told
(2) Peter's narration of those events
(3) Luke's narration of Peter's narration
(4) the minister's performance of Luke's narration of Peter's narration

Item (2) is the first telling, (3) is the second telling, and (4) constitutes the third telling. There thus may be several levels in the telling process, some of which are internal to the primary narrative, others of which may be external, that is, may not be a part of the primary text at all.[38]

22. Acts 5:30–32. The question of telling or narration may arbitrarily be set aside and the issue of the text or tale itself addressed. The first step in analyzing the discourse (D1) is to simplify the statements in order to reduce the bulk to manageable proportions.[39] Perhaps we could reduce the actual statements to the following kernels:

(5) God glorified Jesus
(6) You (Men of Israel, vs 12) delivered him up to Pilate
(7) You denied him to Pilate
(8) Pilate had decided to release him
(9) You denied him
(10) You asked for a murderer to be granted to you
(11) You killed him
(12) God raised him from the dead
(13) We (Peter and John) are witnesses to these things

This set of narrative statements is one version of the story of Jesus. How do we know that this version is one among several? We have come to that conclusion empirically by comparing D1 with other manifestations of what is

38. For a classification of these narration levels, see the discussion of narrator above, §§2.7–9.

39. The simplification of narrative statements is to be distinguished from the summary or paraphrase. In simplifying, one does not eliminate sentences from the text; one merely reduces the verbiage. In the paraphrase, an attempt is made to compress a much larger number of statements into what, in the interpreter's view, are the essential items.

taken to be the same story. For example, we might look at a neighboring version in Acts 5:30–32 (D2).

> [30]The God of our fathers raised Jesus whom you killed by hanging him on a tree. [31]God exalted him at his right hand as Leader and Savior, to give repentance to Israel and forgiveness of sins. [32]And we are witnesses to these things, and so is the Holy Spirit whom God has given to those who obey him.

Again reducing the discourse to simplified narrative statements, we get the following result:

(1) God raised Jesus
(2) You killed Jesus
(3) God exalted Jesus
(4) Jesus gives repentance and forgiveness to Israel
(5) We (Peter and the apostles, vs 29) are witnesses to these things
(6) The Holy Spirit is also a witness

It does not require close analysis to see that D2 in Acts 5 has fewer narrative statements than D1 in Acts 3, and that D2 has two narrative statements that differ from anything found in the first version. The earlier version, D1, on the other hand, is a bit longer and contains some items not found in D2. Both accounts appear to be limited to events connected with the passion and resurrection.

23. Acts 10:36–43. These two narrative accounts may be compared with yet another narrative version in Acts 10:36–43 (D3), which is not confined to events connected with the passion and resurrection and which thus contains additional narrative material. One may include verses 34b and 35 to provide the rhetorical context:

> [34] Truly I perceive that God shows no partiality,
> [35] but in every nation any one who fears him and does what is right is acceptable to him.

(1) [36] You know the word which he sent to Israel, preaching good news by Jesus Christ
(2) (he is Lord of all),
(3) [37] the word which was proclaimed throughout all Judea, which John preached:
(4) [38] how God anointed Jesus of Nazareth with the Holy Spirit and with power;
(5) how he went about doing good
(6) and healing all that were oppressed by the devil,
(7) for God was with him.
(8) [39] And we are witnesses to all that he did both in the country of the Jews and in Jerusalem.
(9) They put him to death by hanging him on a tree;
(10) [40] but God raised him on the third day

(11) and made him manifest,
(12) [41] not to all the people but to us who were chosen by God as witnesses,
(13) who ate and drank with him after he rose from the dead.
(14) [42] And he commanded us to preach to the people,
(15) and to testify that he is the one ordained by God to be judge of the living and the dead.
(16) [43] To him all the prophets bear witness that every one who believes in him receives forgiveness of sins through his name.

These statements may again be simplified to facilitate comparison and discussion:

(1) God sent Jesus to preach to Israel
(2) Jesus is Lord of all
(3) Jesus preached throughout Judea, after John preached
(4) God anointed Jesus
(5) Jesus went about doing good
(6) Jesus healed those who were oppressed by the devil
(7) God was with Jesus
(8) We are witnesses to what Jesus did
(9) Jesus was put to death
(10) God raised Jesus on the third day
(11) God made Jesus manifest
(12) God chose us as witnesses of his resurrection
(13) We ate and drank with him after his resurrection
(14) Jesus commanded us to preach to the people
(15) Jesus commanded us to testify: Jesus is judge
(16) All the prophets bear witness to Jesus

24. The sixteen narrative statements in Acts 10:36–43 begin with Jesus' preaching, which succeeds that of John, and end with his charge to the disciples to continue that preaching. The temporal limits of the discourse are those of the canonical gospels, especially of Luke and Matthew, excepting, of course, the birth and childhood stories and the prologue to the Gospel of John. The temporal limits just indicated do not, however, encompass the testimony of the prophets (16), who are presumably the Old Testament prophets, although the narrator may have have been alluding to early Christian charismatics. The canonical gospels also refer to the Old Testament prophets, which means that they, too, exceed the temporal boundaries of their discourse time. In any case, the beginning of the temporal sequence in Acts 10 antedates that of the versions in Acts 3 and 5, and the end of the sequence goes a bit beyond either as well. The chronological period covered by a narrative is referred to as narrative stretch. Another way of putting the matter is to say that the narrative stretch of Acts 10 exceeds that of both Acts 3 and Acts 5 in both directions.

25. The preponderance of narrative statements in Acts 10 are action statements. However, there are two statements that may be called status statements:

(2) Jesus is Lord of all
(3) God was with Jesus

These statements affirm the status of Jesus (they are "is" statements), while in the remainder Jesus does something or has something done to him (he is either agent or patient).[40] Neither of the versions in Acts 3 and 5 contains a status statement.[41]

It is evident that the version in Acts 10 contains narrative statements not found in the versions examined earlier. There are points, of course, at which the three versions overlap, but they do not overlap entirely. If we are now to refer all three to the same story, it would have to be said that the story of Jesus contains a range of possibilities that encompasses all three versions but is not identical with any one of them.

In anticipation of later discussion, it should be observed that we have just worked through specific texts in the direction of the story; later, we shall attempt to come back by the same route and make some observations about how the narrative text is related to hypothetical stories.

STORY AND ITS TEXT

In developing the distinction between story and discourse, or story and its text, on the basis of particular texts taken from the Book of Acts, the essential reasons for the discrimination were not systematically elaborated. It is now appropriate to remedy that deficiency.

26. Multiple sets of narrative statements. It was just remarked that D1, D2, and D3 are versions of the story of Jesus. This assertion implies that the one story of Jesus gave rise to more than one narrative expression. If there is more than one version of the *same* story, it can scarcely be contested that the *story* of Jesus is to be discriminated from its expression in particular sets of narrative statements. Furthermore, since no two sets of narrative statements appear to be identical (what would be the point of identical sets?), varying narrative statements of the same series of events are to be distinguished from each other. This opens up the possibility that an unlimited number of sets of narrative statements can be inspired by the same story, each set of which might differ slightly or greatly from all the other versions, either adding to or subtracting from the action and status statements of other sets.

40. A patient, for those unacquainted with current grammatical terminology, is the receiver of the action. In the sentence, "Jesus was put to death," Jesus is the receiver or patient of the action, although he is the subject of the sentence. The term patient was developed to cover just such cases where the "subject" undergoes the action.

41. The difference between action statements and status statements was developed earlier in §§1.39–40.

To reiterate, every version of the story is to be distinguished not only from all other versions of the same story, but also from the chain of events, real, legendary, or fictive, to which all versions presumably refer.

27. Media of expression. A story may find its expression in a linguistic medium, and it is this possibility that we have been discussing. Yet the same story may also find expression in other media. The story of Jesus, for example, has often been narrated in pictures. Grünewald's *Eisenheim Altarpiece* is only one of many in which the passion is given minimal story-form. At the other end of the spectrum, the story of Jesus is frequently portrayed in the "comic strip" format adapted for Sunday School use. The same story can be represented in films, such as in *Jesus Christ Superstar*, or in *The Gospel of St. Matthew*. Similarly, the story of Jesus is often portrayed on the stage, in the dramatic mode, as in the passion play at Ober-Ammergau in Germany or in the Black Hills, South Dakota. The story may also be "told" in dance. All of these media, picture, film, drama, dance, have been employed to convey a single story, or a story taken to be a single story, and each of the media has its own requirements of expression, its own grammar.

28. Order and repetition. There is yet another feature of narrative discourse that supports these distinctions and linkages.

The events presented in D1 (Acts 3:12–16) are not narrated in chronological order. God did not glorify Jesus (5) before he was killed (11). Furthermore, there is a certain amount of repetition: more than one narrative statement refers to the same event. The denial of Jesus (7) and the denial of the Holy and Righteous One (9) are evidently intended to refer to the same event; and the assertion that God glorified Jesus (5) and the statement that God raised him from the dead (12) may also refer to the same event. In narrative discourse, consequently, events may be related out of chronological order, or one event may find expression in more than one narrative statement. In story, on the other hand, events presumably take place in chronological order (events are time bound) and one event can happen only once. Narrative discourse thus takes liberties with chronological order and repetition.

These are the basic reasons given for discriminating story from discourse. These same observations also provide clues, to be followed up subsequently, on which a narrative poetics can be based.

STORY LEVELS

29. Narrative statements. Narrative texts are made up of sets of narrative statements. It has been assumed up to this point that a narrative statement corresponds to a sentence in the narrative text. This is not necessarily the case. A statement in a narrative text of any length is rarely taken by narratologists to be synonymous with actual sentences in a narrative text. The reasons for this are three. First, if narrative statements were the same as sentences in the text, the number of statements in most narrative discourses would be too great to use without discrimination. The sentences of *War and Peace* or *Moby-Dick* are too numerous to be the basis for critical analysis. The second reason is that narrative statements, unlike many sentences in the text, are taken to be primarily verbal: they either express a state of affairs or the transition from one state of affairs to another.[42] Actual sentences in the text are often not action statements, particularly in passages that are predominantly descriptive. There are thus many sentences in narrative discourse that do not contribute to the "story" line, by which is meant the chain of events constituting the story. A third reason is that narrative statements are not always expressed in words. Narrative "statements" may be made in dance, in cinema, and in the frames of a comic strip. This fact suggests that "statement" is not to be taken literally, but is to be understood as a construct based on actual sentences in the text.

30. The following three narrative statements might be taken to represent a summary or a paraphrase of the basic love story:

(1) Boy and girl meet.
(2) Boy and girl fall in love.
(3) They marry.

These statements are perhaps a poor expression of the love story, yet they may well represent the three essential events usually taken to make up such stories. They can be understood as an abstraction from or summary of specific narrative texts of much greater length. As such, they can be understood as one level of narrative discourse. The level of the paraphrase or summary is usually taken to be intermediate between the customary full text and the underlying (or overlying) story.

This distinction, when added to the discrimination of discourse from story, suggests a three-tiered phenomenon:

story
⇧
paraphrase
⇧
text

These levels, however, are ambiguous. It is not evident to what precisely they refer, even at the discourse end of the spectrum, nor is the relationship among them clear. Recent discussion has not resolved the issues. It lies beyond the scope of this study to attempt to untangle the very complex issues

42. Todorov, *Poetics of Prose*, 110ff. Cf. the discussion in §§1.39–40.

involved. The primary aim is to locate the present project on the spectrum these levels represent and to attempt to clarify the nature of the text level.

31. Surface and deep structure. We shall first take up the story end of the spectrum. Rimmon-Kenan borrows the notions of surface and deep structure from narrative grammarians and defines them as follows:

> Whereas surface structure is the abstract formulation of the organization of the observable sentence, deep structure—with its simpler and more abstract form—lies beneath it and can only be retrieved through a backward retracing of the transformational process.[43]

The concepts of surface and deep structure come ultimately from sentence grammar and transformational grammar in particular. Indeed, Rimmon-Kenan illustrates the difference between surface and deep structure by reference to sentence grammar. For example, the two sentences

(1) Jim loves Jane.
(2) Jane is loved by Jim.

are said to be related to each other as transformations of a common deep structure. The relation of (2) to (1) can be stated as rules that can be applied with regular results to all comparable cases: the direct object in (1) becomes the subject in (2), and the subject in (1) becomes the agent in (2) introduced by the preposition. Or the relationships can be stated in the reverse. It is unclear whether the deep structure is a structure that is different from either (1) or (2) or whether the structure is "deep" because it can be expressed by rules that are not the same thing as the structures they represent. In either case, transformationalists and structuralists hold that both surface and deep structures are different from actual sentences.

32. Rimmon-Kenan adds a second qualification to the two terms: the surface structure of story is syntagmatic, while the deep structure is paradigmatic.[44] The latter is based on logical relations among the elements.[45] Deep structures are thus not themselves narrative, which is why the suggestion was made above that the deep structures of sentences may not themselves be sentences, but, for example, abstract formulas.

33. And, finally, Rimmon-Kenan states that "story (including its surface structure) is a construct and an abstraction from the set of observable signifiers which is the text, and is thus intangible in itself." This poses a problem for poetics, she continues, since it is not clear how the intangible can be presented. Chatman makes a similar point:

43. *Narrative Fiction,* 10.
44. *Narrative Fiction,* 10–11.
45. Rimmon-Kenan says these relations are static, but Culler, *Structuralist Poetics,* 92, with reference to Greimas, says they may be either static or dynamic.

> Though this chapter has treated story as an object, I do not mean to suggest that it is a hypostatized object, separate from the process by which it emerges in the consciousness of a "reader."[46]

The two agree that story is intangible and an abstraction; they also agree that the way from the text to the abstraction is not clear.[47]

34. Why is the story level considered intangible and abstract? The answer usually given is that the story level is no longer a succession of events, or syntagmatic, but is in fact a paradigm consisting of a set or sets of logical relations. One example of of such an abstract set has been proposed by A. J. Greimas. His conception of the set is represented in figure 3 by a lazy-H diagram with six points of reference representing what he calls "actants" (participants who perform a basic function).

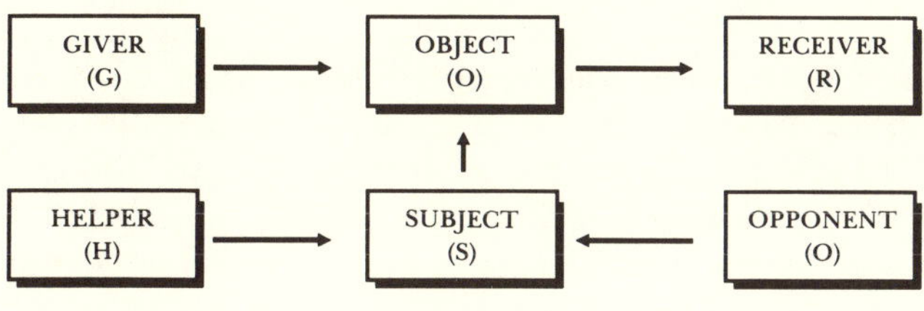

Figure 3

The relations among these six actants cover most, if not all, the possible relations in any particular plot. The explanatory power of such a diagram can be exemplified by the genre of the detective story, as Dominic Crossan sketches it: the subject is the detective, who has been hired by some agency, perhaps the insurance company or even the owner of the stolen property; the Object is the stolen property, while the Receiver is the owner of the goods in

46. *Story and Discourse,* 41.

47. How to get from the surface of a verbal narrative text to a summary or paraphrase is a thorny issue that has not yet been resolved. A number of scholars have addressed the issue, among whom are: W. O. Hendricks, "The Structural Study of Narration," "Methodology of Narrative Structural Analysis"; Seymour Chatman, "New Ways of Analyzing Narrative Structure." Rimmon-Kenan has a helpful summary of the possibilities, *Narrative Fiction,* 13–28. John Lipski, "From Text to Narrative," 202, concludes: "Despite the variety of models, there is as yet no clear method of traversing the path from the concrete text to the abstract narrative structure, without either quantitative or qualitative gaps intervening" (quoted by Rimmon-Kenan, *Narrative Fiction,* 28).

question. The Opponent is the thief and the Helper might be the police or a companion of the detective.[48] This chart of actants and possible relationships is certainly intangible and abstract in relation to the text, but is it appropriate to refer to this diagram as a story or as the story level? It would seem more appropriate to reserve the term story for a representation that is syntagmatic.

35. Story as continuum. Story may be understood in another, contrasting way. A sequence of activities in real life is taken to form a continuous stream. This temporal flow, as a consequence of one's experience of oneself, is assumed to be unbroken. And because memory, both individual and collective, trails off imperceptibly into the past and anticipates an uninterrupted future, the rise and demise of that flow lies beyond reflective consciousness. History is a ceaseless stream that rises in some primeval mountain and flows into a mythic sea.

Story in this sense is therefore not the string of actions reported by the discourse. On this point all parties agree. It is rather a continuum of events from which the discourse is a selection and thus an abstraction (the removal of some items from an unbroken chain in order to attend to the balance). The story, in other words, is the continuum of events consisting of the totality of all points on a trajectory, as in the metaphor of the arrow released from the bow on its way to some target: it presumably must pass through an infinite number of points before reaching its target. If story is an infinite number of points on a trajectory of activity, the narrator selects representative details—setting, participants, events, including where those details begin and end in the temporal chain—to stand for the whole, and the reader infers the continuum in accordance with common expectations. This view appears to be shared by Chatman, who emphasizes the process of selection.[49] It does not appear to matter whether the continuum of events is fictional or historical: the imagined chain would in any case be patterned on the "real" world, that is, the world as experienced. On this view, story is indeed a succession of events and it is intangible, as well as ineffable: there will always be some further detail to be told, some new selection of events to be made, some new angle of vision to be reflected, as a consequence of which the story is always outstanding: it cannot be expressed in words, for to tell the whole story would be to narrate every detail, of every moment, across an unlimited temporal and spatial horizon.

36. The three-tiered diagram that is commonly assumed thus requires emendation. If we reserve the term story for the unbroken continuum of events that can never be exhausted in the telling, we will need some new term for the abstract paradigm of the structuralists. Since that level is a paradigm, we might well call it the story paradigm. The result is the four-tiered diagram

48. Crossan, *Dark Interval*, 64f., slightly modified.
49. Cf. *Story and Discourse*, 27ff.

in §37. The line separating Story Paradigm from the lower group is meant to indicate that the first is categorically different from the bottom group. There is a qualitative distinction between the two, the first being paradigmatic, the second syntagmatic. We are restricting story and its related terms to manifestations and constructs that are syntagmatic in character.

37. There are difficulties with this arrangement. First of all, the Paraphrase is allegedly a selection from the Text, which in turn is a derivative of Story: the Paraphrase thus appears to be misplaced in its position between Story and Text. Moreover, the Story Paradigm seems to be based on the Paraphrase and is thus also separated from the level with which it is most intimately connected. Further, taking Story in the sense we have defined it, Story Paradigm, Paraphrase, and Text are all constructs, "made up," as it were, in relation to Story, which corresponds to the unbroken continuum of experience. Put differently, Text, Paraphrase, and Story Paradigm are interpretations of Story.

Story Paradigm

⇧

Story

⇧

Paraphrase

⇧

Text

These considerations suggest a new order of levels. The story as continuum is expressed by the text, which is a selection of items from the unbroken chain of events. It should be noted, parenthetically, that the narrative text is also a continuum, and that very palpable fact makes it easier for the reader to assume that the underlying story is continuous. The paraphrase is, in turn, a summary of the text; we can arbitrarily define paraphrase as dependent upon some text. Finally, the story paradigm is a logical, abstract, and non-syntagmatic representation of the relationships represented by the paraphrase, which is an interpretation of the text. Critics have possibly been misled by the metaphor "deep" (deep structure, etc.) to position story paradigm at the top of the diagram. If we mean by "deep" the ultimate source, we should perhaps restrict that sense to story as continuum. We could perhaps avoid the difficulties of the metaphor by placing the levels on a spectrum from right to left and thus avoiding the term deep. However, we can also represent the matter as a set of relationships on the vertical plane without prejudice to whether one end of the spectrum is "up" or "down," "deep" or "surface" as in the diagram in §38. This order seems justified by the observation that in the descending order one moves further and further from the story as continuum of events.

In other words, the movement is in the direction of ever higher levels of abstraction.

38. The story paraphrase. We have been looking at story levels from the story end of the spectrum. We should now turn to the textual level and inquire about the relation of the so-called paraphrase or summary to the text.

Story

⇩

Text

⇧

Paraphrase

⇧

Story Paradigm

The paraphrase, according to Rimmon-Kenan, may take either of two forms. Both forms rest on the assumption that the constituent element of any story consists of a chain of events.[50] The first form of paraphrase is the construction of a series of event labels. The labels need not necessarily be identical with words in the text. For example, in a murder mystery, phrases like "squeezed the trigger," "a shot echoed through the night," "drew his gun and fired," may be used to depict the murder, although the event-label itself does not appear in the text. New Testament translators regularly label Mark 2:14 "The Call of Levi" and Mark 1:29–31 "The Healing of Peter's Mother-in-law," although in neither case do the words "call" or "heal" appear in the text. Event-labelling is thus more or less arbitrary and will be carried out in different ways by different critics. Uniformity in the process is difficult to achieve.[51]

39. A second form of paraphrase consists of narrative propositions. The essential difference between this procedure and event-labelling is that the proposition consists of a simple sentence containing subject (agent or patient) and predicate expressing action.[52] Todorov claims that the subject will always be a proper noun (a common noun would imply a status statement in addition to an action).[53] Moreover, Todorov divides narrative predicates into two types, those that depict a state of equilibrium and those that describe the passage from one state to another. A narrative would then consist minimally of three propositions, the first and last of which are states of equilibrium and the middle one of which is the event representing the transition from one to

50. *Narrative Fiction*, 15 and 134, n. 10.

51. Rimmon-Kenan, *Narrative Fiction*, 13–14, discusses the issues.

52. Cf. Rimmon-Kenan, *Narrative Fiction*, 14.

53. For example, the statement "a tax collector followed Jesus" contains the statements "Levi is a tax collector" and "Levi followed Jesus."

the other.[54] On either of these forms a paraphrase consists of a series of events.

40. The view of story as essentially comprised of events has much to commend it. The organization of the text continuum appears to support it. Nevertheless, the palpable text contains other patterns that are not made up of events. Rimmon-Kenan's description of the text bears this out:

> Whereas 'story' is a succession of events, 'text' is a spoken or written discourse which undertakes their telling. Put more simply, the text is what we read. In it, the events do not necessarily appear in chronological order, the characteristics of the participants are dispersed throughout, and all the items of the narrative content are filtered through some prism or perspective.[55]

She includes event in her description of the tangible text, but she adds character and point-of-view as additional elements. The three together constitute the staple elements of literary (narrative) criticism. Hrushovski adds other elements. "A text," he writes, "is a highly complex network of patterns of all kinds."[56] A pattern consists of a link between two or more elements, continuous or discontinuous in the text and effected by any means whatsoever; the material out of which they are constructed may be homogeneous or heterogeneous.[57] In one segment from *War and Peace*, Hrushovski identifies five heterogeneous discontinuous patterns to which elements in the brief episode contributed: the characterization of Bagration; the characterization of Andrej; the relation between the two; Tolstoy's attention to the history of armament; the historic relation of the Russians to the French.[58] These elements contribute only indirectly to the plot.

41. Hrushovski's view of the textual unit (sketched in §§1.22–26) is that it is a junction of one or more patterns. One pattern may consist of events contributing to the plot, but there are other kinds of patterns that contribute to the richness and complexity of the narrative text. Patterns belong to a "network of hierarchies" involving character, social and moral norms regulating character, ideas and themes, among other elements, all of which offer a plethora of possibilities to the astute reader, who may wish to isolate now this and now that pattern and single it or them out for attention. The network of patterns, in other words, lies beyond the reach of the single reading and affords the basis for multiple readings.

42. The generalized point to be emphasized in this context is that the paraphrase consisting of events, however constructed and however basic, is only one form of the reconstructed text, albeit perhaps the basic form. Reconstructions of the palpable text are almost unlimited in scope, given the

54. To this discussion we shall return below, §§2.47–48.
55. *Narrative Fiction*, 3.
56. *Segmentation and Motivation*, 4.
57. *Segmentation and Motivation*, 5.
58. *Segmentation and Motivation*, 10.

great variety of possible patterning, although perhaps the interesting and cogent ones are limited in a given period of interpretation. The textual surface, the segments of the text continuum, permit the confluence of elements of patterns in a wide variety of ways. This process may be represented in an abstract fashion by allowing the letters *a–n* to represent points along the continuous chain of events on the story level, the numbers *1–9* to stand for aspects of the characterization of participants, and Greek letters *α–θ* to refer to themes taken up by the author. Recall that these aspects are only three among many possibilities. An author selects events *a, d, j, k* from the continuum and turns them into a plot. (A second story might well draw on some of the same events or others to form a second and quite different plot.) The author may elect to relate one event out of chronological order. This hypothetic story might be then be represented as:

[a],[d],[j],[k].

The text, however, contains more than references to events. It also portrays character, setting, theme, and does so from a certain perspective, to mention only some elements. We must thus add other items to the abstract representation. If each event stands for the nucleus of a narrative segment, our story would have four segments, each of which might contribute to patterns involving character and theme, to take two examples:

[a,1,γ,7],[6,d,2],[β,θ,j,4],[k,8,ζ,9]

This way of representing the features of narrative segments is close to Hrushovski's view of the narrative unit as a junction of elements contributing to various patterns.

43. As the provisional sketch of a narrative grammar in §§1.27–44 indicated, in this study we trace a number of standard elements in the surface organization of the text from segment to segment, elements that contribute to a variety of patterns. Those elements include but are not limited to participants and participant sets, temporal references and connectives, spatial references and connectives, and actions grouped according to whether they occur in the introduction, nucleus, or conclusion of segments and sequences. We shall thus create summaries of different types and erect the piers for building a bridge from the text to the reconstructed text. The bridge in this case is a metaphor for controls for getting from one to the other; the controls are designed to regulate the critical process as its leaps from the textual surface to any kind of reconstruction.

THE STORY AS SUCCESSION OF EVENTS

44. The story as syntagmatic. The narrative text does seem to be segmented primarily on the basis of events, which more or less represent the backbone of the narrative, in spite of the qualifications registered earlier. While other elements are certainly involved, it has proved productive to assume that the surface organization of the text, predominantly around events, points to the event-character of the story as continuum. At all events, we shall assume as much. We return to the story level and review the concept of story as a succession of events.

45. A story can be defined as a succession of events.[59] If the grammar of the sentence and the grammar of narrative discourse are homologous, this definition implies that story is grammatically a verb: verbs consist of actions and happenings.[60] Propp took this view in his work on the Russian fairy tale. Propp subordinated character to function and defined a fairy tale as a set of functions (actions) performed by a variety of characters. It also corresponds to the emphasis on the "actant" in recent structuralist thought: an actant is not congruent with a single participant in a narrative, but is defined by what he or she does; an actant may thus embrace the actions of more than one participant, or, conversely, one participant may perform the functions of more than one actant. The question then arises whether any series of happenings constitutes a story or whether further qualifications are necessary. Rimmon-Kenan poses this question in an arresting way by contrasting the following examples of discourse. She asks, Why is the following limerick considered a story?

> There was a young lady of Niger
> Who smiled as she rode on a tiger.
> They returned from the ride
> With the lady inside
> And the smile on the face of the tiger.

And why, by common consent, is the following ditty not taken to be a narrative?

> Roses are red
> Violets are blue
> Sugar is sweet
> And so are you.

The answer she gives is that if the narrative statements that make up the story betray some chronological order (as distinguished from logical order), then it is a story; but if the statements are not organized chronologically, then it is some other form of discourse. The lady on the tiger is presented as a sequence (took a ride, returned), while the ditty is not: all four statements are simul-

59. I am drawing here and in what immediately follows on the initial definitions of Rimmon-Kenan, *Narrative Fiction,* 2.

60. That the two forms of language are homologous is disputed by some scholars. The view that story consists basically of events does not rest, however, on the similarity of the two.

taneously true; there is no before/after sequence.[61] Moreover, the second—and this may be the more important feature—contains no action statements at all. A set of status statements (affirming only the status of things) could not constitute a narrative, except by inference.[62]

46. Two biblical passages may be set alongside the two examples given above to illustrate the difference between story and non-story. Both are from Paul's letter to the Corinthians.

> [4]Love is patient and kind; love is not jealous or boastful; [5]it is not arrogant or rude. Love does not insist on its own way; it is not irritable or resentful.

This set of statements derived from 1 Cor 13:4–5 is not a story. All statements are simultaneously true; there is no before/after sequence. Moreover, no actions are portrayed in the set. As a consequence, this string constitutes some other form of discourse than story.

A second set is taken from 1 Cor 15:3–5.

(1) [3] Christ died;
(2) [4] he was buried;
(3) he was raised on the third day;
(4) [5] he appeared to Cephas;
(5) he appeared to the twelve.

This list is a string of five events from which both causality and closure appear to be missing, yet it is readily recognized as a story. Of course, death usually entails burial, so it could be said that (2) is caused by (1). But causal relationships are not made explicit in the text. Nor is closure expressed in the set as represented. However, the text continues:

(6) [6] then he appeared to more than five hundred . . .
(7) [7] then he appeared to James;
(8) then to all the apostles.
(9) [8] Last of all, as to one untimely born, he appeared also to me.

Closure is provided by (9): the string of appearances comes to an end with Paul himself. This set appears, moreover, to form a segment: Jesus departs and then returns (this is the structural equivalent of an arrival, action, departure).[63]

47. Event: change in status. Gerald Prince has argued that a minimal story

61. Rimmon-Kenan, *Narrative Fiction,* 14f., in partial dependence on Prince, "Aspects of a Grammar of Narrative," 49; Cf. Prince, *A Grammar of Stories*, 23f.

62. Confirmed by Chatman, *Narrative Discourse,* 32. Status statements are akin to paradigmatic elements in a story, while action statements are said to be syntagmatic in character. Stories in fact are made up of both kinds of statements. The relation of the two is complex: cf. §§1.39–40. Meanwhile, the issue here is whether syntagmatic statements constitute the backbone of narrative.

63. The notion of narrative segment is discussed in §1.43.

consists of three conjoined statements, the first and third of which are stative, the second of which is active.[64] The three are conjoined by features that are both temporal and causative: the three events succeed one another in time in fixed order and the second is taken to be the cause of the third. An example would be:

(1) X was rich;
(2) X lost his fortune;
(3) X was poor, as a result.

Statement one is stative, as is statement (3), while (2), an action, is the cause of the status represented by (3). Such as story might be represented abstractly like this:

X is F at t^1
H happens to X at t^2
X is G at t^3 (t stands for time)

That would presumably represent one type of story, although not the only kind. It is an interesting case because, as a story, it consists of only one action.[65]

Actually Prince's minimal story is the definition of an event, where event is defined as a change in status. A narrative, according to Arthur Danto, is the explanation of a change. It is an explanation in the sense that it accounts for the change from one status to another. Formally speaking, the initial status or situation is followed by an action that produces or causes the second status, as, for example, in the following three-line story:

(1) The automobile was undented.
(2) Stephanie backed into a parked car.
(3) The automobile was now dented.

This is quite comparable to the story of the lame man in Acts 3:1–11:

(1) A lame man was sitting at the gate of the temple.
(2) Peter healed the lame man.
(3) The lame man was cured.

These mini-narratives contain a single action surrounded by two status statements. The action accounts for the change in status. The group of statements constitutes an action.

48. It is now possible to sharpen the definitions of terms used thus far. A story consists of a succession of actions or happenings that portray changes in the status of various characters and other elements in the setting of the story.

64. *A Grammar of Stories*, 16–31.

65. Prince's analysis corresponds to that given by Todorov and summarized above, §2.39, in which a story consists of two states of equilibrium with a middle segment representing the passage from one state to another.

A group of actions or happenings comprising a change may be called an event. A story may consist of one event, as in the case of Prince's minimal story, but it usually consists of a series of events (changes). An event may consist of one or several actions or happenings, which, in the narrative, are customarily grouped so as to indicate that they constitute a complex event.

Is simple succession enough to define a story?

Rimmon-Kenan objects to Prince's definition on the grounds that mere sequence of events may be enough to warrant the designation story. She notes that the definition given by Prince involves three principles of organization: (1) temporal succession; (2) causality; (3) inversion, which is a form of closure or terminal function. She believes that only the first is required to form a story. Her reasoning is that causality can virtually always be projected onto temporality, and, further, there are many strings of events that we recognize, intuitively, as stories that do not exhibit either causality or closure. She cites Chekhov's "Lady with Lapdog" as an example. Quite apart from her persuasive arguments, Chatman cites the sequence (borrowed from E. M. Forster):

(1) the king died
(2) the queen died

which, he says, is a story because the reader supplies the causal link implied by the juxtaposition of the two events. It is unnecessary, consequently, for the link to be made explicit, as in this sequence:

(1) the king died
(2) and then the queen died of grief[66]

Nevertheless, the human mind is so constructed that it is inclined to connect events set down in a list, even without explicit connectives. It takes a very deliberate and concentrated effort on the part of the reader to avoid connecting the two statements in the first version. This is essentially Rimmon-Kenan's argument. The connection, however, is not expressed in the text. We could therefore have a story, presumably, consisting of three actions or happenings:

F happens to X at t^1
X does H at t^2
X does G at t^3

Such a string might lack any expression of causality or closure. In spite of the argument about what constitutes a minimal story, it is obvious that most stories involve both causality and closure as well as temporal succession.[67] It is

66. Chatman, *Story and Discourse*, 45f.

67. The exception would be the modern anti-story where temporal succession, causality, and closure are avoided. The "plot" of such stories is termed a plot of revelation rather than a plot of resolution; the latter is the traditional form of plot. Chatman discusses this matter in *Story and Discourse*, 56–59.

also obvious that it is virtually impossible to have a story without some continuity in participants.[68]

49. Continuity. A succession of events constitutes a story, then, only if some continuity in events is expressed or implied. That continuity need not be causal. It may simply be sequential. Be that as it may, it has to be said that a story customarily consists of narrative statements representing actions and states, and that these statements have to be linked in some way. There are several possibilities for such linkages. Chatman considers them under the heading of "existents," which includes space, character, and setting. I prefer to label them:

succession of events (sequentiality)
continuity of participants
temporal linkages
spatial connectives

Succession and temporality may overlap. For the moment, however, it is best to consider them as separate items.

50. Rimmon-Kenan stipulates that succession is a loose narrative link. It implies that events occur in the same narrative world, viz., in a world in which the events occur in connection with agents or patients that sustain some relationship to each other and some continuity from event to event. That implies, further, that there are some temporal links, however remote, and that the spaces in which the action takes place are related to each other. The two statements, *the king died / the queen died*, is not a story if the king and the queen are unrelated, if their lives do not touch spatially or temporally in any way. Of course, one could imagine the narrative means by which the death of Alexander could be linked to the death of Cleopatra three centuries later. Yet the point is that such linkages would have to be found in order for the two to be combined in the same story.

51. If there is a continuity of participants, such as

(1) Peter and John went up to the temple.
(2) Peter and John healed the lame man.
(3) Peter made a speech to the assembled crowd.

the linkage is tighter than if a mere succession of events were involved, with the agents unstated or differing from action to action. For example, if the statements above were rewritten as

(1) Paul went up to the temple.
(2) Peter and John healed the lame man.
(3) Stephen made a speech to the assembled crowd.

the reader would not know they were embedded in a story apart from the

68. Cf. §1.44, on linking devices.

narrative context of the Book of Acts. Continuity of participants is what sentence grammar and narrative grammar have in common: both consist of subject (agent or patient) and verb (action or happening).

Narrative discourse consists, of course, of a string of narrative sentences, rather than just one narrative statement. As a consequence, narrative grammar has to do with the succession of such sentences, so not only is the continuity of participants an issue, but also the temporal and spatial relations between and among the statements. If these features are a constraint on narrative discourse, they are presumably also constraints on anything called story. Story thus consists of a succession of events involving participants that are related to each other in some way; the events must also occur in times and places that are linked to each other. These constraints, when defined and systematized, will constitute a basic step in a poetics of narrative discourse.

3

The Shape of the Narrative Unit

• 3 •

INTRODUCTION

1. The surface organization of narratives. In order to tell a story, a narrator must bring a limited number of participants together in a particular time or place. This may be termed the focusing process. The narrator must then allow something to happen: between the focusing introduction and the defocusing conclusion lies at least one narrative nucleus. A nucleus consists of a cluster of actions or happenings that constitute an event. At the conclusion of the story, the narrator must reverse the focusing process and defocus the story. Defocusing is achieved by dispersing the participants, expanding or relocating the space, lengthening or blurring the temporal focus, or by introducing a terminal note.

The warrant for these generalizations lies, of course, in the myriads of stories told and recorded in the history of the human race. Since we cannot examine even a small portion of those stories, we shall have to be satisfied with a sample. But, like Propp, we shall discover that even a small sample will soon exhaust the possibilities of the surface organization of narratives.

2. The self-contained mini-narrative. It will be more efficient and less confusing if the analysis begins with the self-contained mini-narrative. A self-contained mini-narrative is nothing other than a short, short story with an introduction (focusing process), a single nucleus, and a conclusion (defocusing process). The mini-narratives in the New Testament are all embedded in longer narratives, yet many of them show traces of their oral pre-history and thus of their earlier independent status. This double character means that the analyst must beware of possible influences stemming from oral discourse, on the one side, and of modifications occasioned by the written context into which they are introduced, on the other. Nevertheless, there are ample more-or-less self-contained short stories that can provide the basis for preliminary observations.

The mini-narrative offers a second advantage to the elementary analysis: a self-contained short story does not pose the problems of continuity, coherence, and hierarchy of narrative segments immediately encountered in longer stretches of narrative. The simplicity of the free-standing mini-narrative will be exchanged subsequently for the complexities of the larger narrative context.

3. Analysis of the Lame Man

——— • *The Lame Man at the Gate Beautiful* • ———

Acts 3:1–10

INTRODUCTION

(1) [1] Now Peter and John were going up to the
temple at the hour of prayer, the ninth hour.
(2) [2] And a man lame from birth was being carried,
(3) whom they laid daily at the gate of the temple
(4) which is called Beautiful
(3) to ask alms of those who entered the temple.

NUCLEUS

(5) [3] Seeing Peter and John about to go into the temple,
(6) he asked for alms.
(7) [4] And Peter directed his gaze at him, with John,
(8) and said,
(8.1) "Look at us."
(9) [5] And he fixed his attention upon them,
(10) expecting to receive something from them.
(11) [6] But Peter said,
(11.1) "I have no silver and gold,
(11.2) but I give you what I have;
(11.3) in the name of Jesus Christ of Nazareth, walk."
(12) [7] And he took him by the right hand
(13) and raised him up;
(14) and immediately his feet and ankles were made strong.

CONCLUSION

(15) [8] And leaping up
(16) he stood
(17) and walked
(18) and entered the temple with them,
(19) walking
(20) and leaping
(21) and praising God.
(22) [9] All the people saw him walking and praising God,
(23) [10] and recognized him as the one who sat for alms at the Beautiful Gate of
the temple;
(24) and they were filled with wonder and amazement at what had happened
to him.

4. Narrative statements. The text of this story is divided into narrative statements and numbered for ready reference. A narrative statement may be defined generally as a sentence with a single main verb (the verb is the essential item since a narrative consists of a series of actions and status statements). In breaking the surface of the text into narrative statements, we have retained the surface sentence structure. This occasionally leads to difficulties and ambiguities. Statements (2)–(4) in the articulation provided above represent one sentence in the text (in both Greek and English). Nevertheless, there are at least three statements in this single sentence. Were we to break the sentence up into its constituent parts, the result would look something like this:

(2) A lame man was being carried
(3) He was laid daily at the gate of the temple to beg alms
(4) The gate in question is called Beautiful

Statement (2) contains a verb chain consisting of finite verb and infinitive (used to express purpose). We could have broken (3) into two further statements:

(3.1) He was laid daily at the gate of the temple
(3.2) He used to beg alms

However, we have elected to number (3) as a single statement in order to retain the relationship between placement (gate of the temple) and activity (begging alms). In addition, statement (4) occurs in the middle of statement (3). This necessitated repeating (3) in the enumeration.

It should also be observed that directly quoted speech (direct discourse) is subordinated to the introductory verb ("Peter said, . . ."). Its embedded status is indicated by the system of enumeration [e.g., (11.1), (11.2), (11.3)] and by indentation.

These devices are primarily for the convenience of reference to the surface features of the text.

5. Acts 3:1–10 as a short story. It is quite possible to divorce 3:1–10 from its narrative context in Acts and read and understand it as an independent, self-contained short story. Certain information is supplied by the narrative environment in Acts, to be sure. The reader would not know that Peter and John were apostles, for example, if the reader had only this single segment. Yet one could infer that Peter and John were followers of Jesus from 3:6: "in the name of Jesus Christ of Nazareth, walk." And the narrator does not tell us in this segment that the temple in question is in Jerusalem; but we do learn that it had a gate called Beautiful. Nevertheless, the information provided is quite adequate to a *narrative* understanding of the story on its own; it is unnecessary to have the larger narrative context in Acts in order to "read" the grammar or structure of this story segment.

6. The surface organization of the Lame Man. The story of the lame man is organized in a simple fashion. In an *introduction* (reference code: INTRO), the narrator presents Peter and John, who function as a single participant, and the lame man. The setting includes the time (the hour of prayer, the ninth hour) and the place (the gate of the temple called Beautiful). The INTRO occupies the first four narrative statements (Acts 3:1–2).

A well-shaped *nucleus* (code: NUC) encompasses 3:3–7, narrative statements (5)–(14). The cluster of actions of which the nucleus is composed consists of a verbal exchange between the apostles and the lame man (statements (5)–(11c)), Peter's healing act (statements (12)–(13)), and the effect of the cure (statement (14)).

The *conclusion* (code: CON) follows in 3:8–10. The lame man demonstrates that he is cured by standing, walking, and leaping (statements (15)–(21)). Bystanders testify (silently) that this man jumping about is indeed the lame beggar who customarily sits at the gate and begs for alms (statements (22)–(23)). And they are amazed at what has transpired (statements (23)–(24)).

The division into INTRO, NUC, CON rests on formal and not on subjective grounds. The analysis will endeavor to establish those grounds. That will be a first step in the development of a narrative poetics.

THE INTRODUCTION: THE FOCALIZING PROCESS

7. *Participants, time, locale.* In order to have a narrative, two or more participants must be brought together in a common time and place.[1] The first questions to be asked are thus those concerning participants (P), time (*t*), and locale (*l*).[2]

8. *Principal participants.* In the INTRO to the healing of the lame man, Peter and John are presented as a participant with a single function, that of healer.[3] Since they are continuity participants (CP), they are not identified beyond their names; they are adequately identified in the larger narrative.

1. For the moment we may ignore obvious exceptions to this generalization. For elementary purposes it is necessary only to note that the rule of two participants may be satisfied in a number of ways: in addition to the ordinary way, one person may be divided and thus be represented as in the state of self-communion (common in modern psychological novels); a group normally functioning as a single participant may be divided (common in the gospels and Acts; note Acts 4:15ff.); or something other than a person may function as a participant (usually termed personification).

2. It will be necessary to develop a kind of shorthand for use in textual analysis and notation. These codes will be made as perspicuous as possible so that the user will not have to refer constantly to tables or glossaries. In the present case, capital (P) will stand for participant(s), small (*t*) for time, and small (*l*) for locale. These codes are enclosed in parentheses in the text of the discussion (but not in tables and graphs) in order to make their status evident.

3. (CP) stands for continuity participant: a participant appearing earlier and/or later in the narrative, as well as in the current scene, and who thus provides the narrative with a degree of continuity or coherence. In this instance, Peter and John belong to the group "apostles" and consequently represent a major participant in the book of Acts. In addition, Peter dominates the first part of Acts, just as Paul dominates the second part. The (CP) "apostles" is therefore focused in a variety of ways during the course of the narrative.

The second participant is a certain lame man, who is identified as being lame from birth. In miracle stories this form of identification (*id*) underscores the gravity of the malady and enhances the powers of the healer. Because the lame man is introduced into the narrative for the first time, he is identified in respect of those items relevant to the ensuing narrative. In folk narrative of the type under consideration, identification is extremely economical; in modern prose fiction of the nineteenth century, by contrast, identification may be very extended.

The lame man is the "subject" of this mini-narrative. This does not mean that he is the agent of the principal action, but that the narrative is "about" him. In a sense, the subject is the "object" of the narrative discourse, what it is about, its theme. Peter and John, and the apostles generally, are the theme of the larger narrative, the book of Acts; the lame man is the theme of this particular segment, just as Ananias and Sapphira are the theme of 5:1–11. The lame man may therefore be termed the theme participant (TP) for this segment. To designate the "subject" of a narrative segment is also to stipulate what is in focus: the lame man is in focus in this segment.

A third participant, "all the people," is introduced subsequently in 3:9. Since this segment forms part of the conclusion, we may defer consideration of the third participant.

The theme participant or (TP) will of course change from segment to segment. In analyzing longer narrative stretches, it will therefore be necessary to employ some other form of notation than (TP) and (CP). The mode of notation adopted in this poetics is the use of capital letters (A, B, C) to designate participants, usually in the order of their appearance. In the narrative segment under consideration, Peter and John will be designated (A), the lame man (B), and, as we shall see, the crowd (C).

9. The principal participants are often, though by no means always, presented in a discrete introduction. A formal introduction usually means that the discourse will be less taxing on the reader: participants, time, and place are presented prior to the commencement of action so the reader may have time to become oriented. If introductions take place during the course of the action, the setting is visualized only with closer attention and greater effort (cf. the story of the good Samaritan (Luke 10:29–37), for example, where introductions are given laconically and only in course). Identification and description interlaced with action commonly means that the information rate of the discourse is high. In folk narrative of the type found in the New Testament, the information rate is normally not high. But there are exceptions: the parables of Jesus and sermon on the mount; the latter, of course, is not narrative discourse.

10. Focalizers. It was stipulated earlier that a narrator must bring the participants together in a specific place and time. In this story, Peter and John

(A) are on their way to the temple. This provides the reader with the *local setting* (*ls*). The temple is of course in Jerusalem, which is the general locale of the larger narrative segment (1:12, 2:5, 14, etc.). At the same time, the lame man (B) is being carried in the direction of the gate of the temple called Beautiful. The two participants are on a collision course, so to speak; the narrator has set them in motion along trajectories that will make contact at some point. That point of contact will function as the initial focus of the narrative. The trajectories and focal point may be represented as in figure 4.

The Focalizing Process

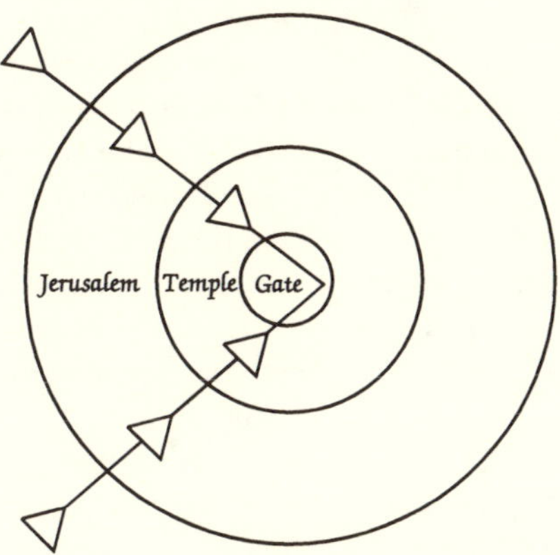

Figure 4

Since the movement of Peter and John will result in narrative contact with the lame man, their movement may be called a *pre-focalizer:* "were going up to the temple" directs the attention of the reader in a preliminary way to the place where contact will be made. And because their movement anticipates contact in the form of an *arrival,* this aspect of the INTRO may be specified as *pre-focalizer: arrival* (code: *pre-f:arr*). Correspondingly, the movement of the lame man, "was being carried [to the gate of the temple]," is a reciprocal pre-focalizer: a second participant "reciprocates" the focalizing process. Pre-focalizers serve to bring the scene into preliminary focus; they point the reader or listener to the narrative space where the action is about to begin.

11. Space. The wedge or funnel represents the focalizing process: narrowing the space, time, and possible participants down so that the reader comes to fix on a particular time, place, and participants. It is as though the reader were seated on a mobile camera crane which starts at some distance away from the scene and then draws gradually closer ("zeroes in on"): from the wider to the more defined space (time, participants) as the scene comes into focus. It comes as no surprise, then, that in general the narrator gives the more inclusive space and then narrows that space to a more specific, delimited space. In the account of the lame man, the more inclusive space is Jerusalem (not indicated in the passage itself, but known from the larger context), which is narrowed in 3:1 to the temple, in reference to the (CP) and which is then further narrowed to that gate of the temple called Beautiful, in 3:2, with reference to the lame man.

Figure 4 demonstrates in diagrammatic form how spatial focus is achieved in Acts 3:1–10.

12. Spatial focus in Acts 3:1–10 may be even more closely specified. In fact, the lame man arrives at the gate of the temple *prior* to Peter and John, where he is in position when Peter and John approach: he is there prepared to ask for alms from his customary position. From his point of view, the focalizing process *positions* him so that Peter and John make contact as they enter. The movement of Peter and John was labeled *pre-f: arr* because an arrival was anticipated. In the case of the lame man, the movement anticipates a position from which contact will be made; his movement is therefore labeled *pre-f: pos.*

This combination (arrival, position) is only one among several narrative devices which may be employed to bring participants together.

13. Time. The time of the events depicted in Acts 3:1–10 is "the hour of prayer, the ninth hour" (11). That time is of course approximate. Peter and John are on their way, presumably intending to arrive at the temple just prior to the hour. First contact is accordingly made just before 3:00 P.M. The ensuing events must have occupied several minutes; just how long is not specified. However, it is still prayer time since "all the people" are there and Peter has a good audience for his speech (given immediately following prayers, or does it interrupt prayers?). For the purpose of this narrative, the *temporal setting* (*ts*) "the hour of prayer," is more than adequate.

14. Background. Narrators often report information about participants, setting, action that does not belong to the chain of events that constitutes the story line or the narrative thread. Such information is often described as "background." It may appear in the introduction where the narrator is setting the stage; it may come as a narrative pause where the narrator interrupts the flow of events to provide additional information; it may be inserted into the depiction of events themselves. Grammatically, background information takes the form of nominals (nouns or their equivalents) which identify, or adjectivals (adjectives or their equivalents) which characterize.[4] Such descrip-

4. Types of narrative statements are discussed in §§1.39–40.

tive actions are either customary (habitual) or take place in story time, i.e., a time before or outside the time represented by the actual narrative, yet a time belonging to the story.[5]

15. In the account of the lame man, the reader learns in the INTRO that the lame man was habitually brought to the gate of the temple each day, there to beg alms ("whom they used to position daily at the gate of the temple called Beautiful to beg alms from those who were on their way into the temple" [3:2]). Since this description refers to repeated actions prior to discourse time (i.e., in time beyond the temporal units of the book of Acts; cf. story time above), the imperfect tense in Greek (*ἐτίθουν*) or a participial construction (*εἰσπορευομένων*) is the appropriate verbal form. This imperfect and its participial counterpart may be termed the *descriptive imperfect* (*impf: desc*). This descriptive imperfect recurs in periphrastic form in 3:10: ". . . him as the one who used to sit . . ." (*αὐτὸς ἦν ὁ . . . καθήμενος*).[6]

16. Pre-focalizing imperfects. From the descriptive imperfect discussed in 3.15 is to be distinguished the *pre-focalizing imperfect:* "Peter and John were on their way . . ." (*ἀνέβαινον*) (3:1); "the lame man was being carried . . ." (*ἐβαστάζετο*) (3:2). Movements denoting trajectories that lead to narrative contact and a resulting action are signaled by the imperfect or a corresponding participial construction in Greek. With respect to Peter and John, an arrival is anticipated (3.10), so the action may be labeled *pre-f:impf/arr*; in the case of the lame man, position is anticipated, with the resulting notation *pre-f:impf/pos.* It is unnecessary to be this precise in labelling, as a rule. However, the imperfect will often be a clue (in Greek) to the limits of the focalizing INTRO.

17. Action anticipators. The lame man habitually begged alms from persons on their way to the temple (3:2). This customary action telegraphs the first action of the sequence: he begs from Peter and John (3:3). When an introductory remark telegraphs the initiating action, the statement may be termed an *action-anticipator* (*aa*).

18. Textual notations. The analysis of Acts 3:1–2, the INTRO, may be represented as a series of notations on the text itself. At the left margin appears the enumeration of the narrative statements of the text, insofar as these can be isolated on the surface of the text (a complete sequence would involve reducing surface structures to kernel statements). At the extreme right appear the grammatical notations given in the shorthand form indicated above (*passim*) and recapitulated in the glossary provided below (§3.19).

5. The distinction between discourse time and story time is discussed below, §8.2.

6. The descriptive imperfect overlaps, of course, with the habitual or customary imperfect known from sentence grammar. Funk, *Grammar II:* §§790–92.

——— • *The Lame Man* • ———

Acts 3:1–2[7]

INTRODUCTION

(1)	[1] Peter and John	A (CP)
	were on their way	*pre-f:arr*
	to the temple	*ls*[1]
	at the hour of prayer, the ninth hour.	*ts*
(2)	[2] And a certain man	B (TP)
	who had been lame from birth	*id*
(3)	and who was habitually placed each day	*impf:desc*
(4)	at the gate of the temple called Beautiful	*ls*[2]
(3)	to beg alms from those entering the temple	*aa*
(2)	was in the process of being carried (there)	*pre-f:pos*

19. Codes.

A, B, etc	participants
CP	continuity participant
TP	theme participant
ls	local setting
ts	temporal setting
pre-f	pre-focalizer
aa	action-anticipator
arr	arrival
pos	position
desc	description
id	identification

THE NUCLEUS

20. Action initiation. The nucleus of this story (3:3–7) consists of a series of actions clustering around a focal event: the healing of the lame man. The actions are all related to the two participants; in several instances actions relate the two participants to each other. Actions may be sorted out, listed, and categorized for analytic purposes. The progression of actions leading up to and away from the focal event may be noted. Actions leading away from the focal event continue in the conclusion (3:8–10).

The action(s) of the nucleus are initiated by a focalizing process that leads up to the first contact between or among participants. Initial contact may be made explicit or it may be assumed. In the story of the lame man it is explicit:

7. The text has been retranslated to accommodate the grammatical notations and to clarify the structure of the second, long sentence. As a consequence, the arrangement but not the enumeration of narrative statements varies slightly from the version given earlier (3.10).

"seeing Peter and John about to go into the temple, . . ." The first contact is thus visual: the lame man sees Peter and John. The point of contact on which the narrator focuses is eye contact from the perspective of the lame man. "Seeing," consequently, may be labeled a *focalizer*, and because it has to do with perception, it may be labeled (*f:perc*).

Peter reciprocates the contact in 3:4: "And Peter directed his gaze at him, . . ." This may be called a *reciprocating focalizer* (*f:recip*). The two participants have now come into view for each other. The action will follow from this initial contact.

21. Actions. The first action in the series is a request for alms on the part of the lame man. It has already been noted that the initial action is forecast in 3:2 by the *action-anticipator* (§3.17; *aa*).

The actions in 3:3–8 may be listed as follows:

INTRODUCTION		
3:3	(5)	B sees A
	(6)	B asks A for alms
3:4	(7)	A looks at B
	(8)	A says to B "you look at us"
3:5	(9)	B looks at A
	(10)	B expects to receive something
3:6	(11)	A says to B "I have no silver or gold, but I give you what I have: in the name of Jesus Christ of Nazareth get up and walk."
3:7	(12)	A takes B by the right hand
	(13)	A raises B up
	(14)	The ankles and feet of B are made strong
CONCLUSION		
3:8	(15)	B jumps up
	(16)	B stands
	(17)	B walks around
	(18)	B goes with A into the temple
	(19)	B walks around
	(20)	B jumps around
	(21)	B praises God

22. Role or *agent* shifts back and forth four times: (B) is the agent of actions (5) and (6); (A) is the agent of actions (7) and (8); (B) is the agent of (9) and (10); with (11)–(13) the agency shifts back again to (A). Action (14) interrupts the chain of process statements: "the ankles and feet of (B) were made strong" is a *happening*. A happening is a change of state in which a participant is *patient* (the one to whom something happens). However, with action (15), (B) once again becomes the agent of an action; he continues as agent through (21).

It is striking that a happening occurs in the midst of a long string of actions with agents. The grammatical form points to the *theme event.* Just as the lame man is the theme participant, so the event in which his lameness is cured is the theme event. That this is so is confirmed by the conclusion in 3:8–10.

THE CONCLUSION

23. Marks of segmentation. With 3:9, statement (22), the narrator introduces the reader to a new participant, "all his people," whom we may designate (C) for convenience. The introduction of a new participant often signals the beginning of a new narrative segment. In addition, there is a new focalizing verb:

3:9 (20) all the people *see* B walking around and praising God.

The new participant (C) focuses on (B); this confirms the presence of a new subsegment, in this case the *conclusion* (CON).

A third mark of segmentation is evident in 3:10 (24): the healing of the lame man is referred to as though it were a past event ("at what *had* happened to him"), marked by the pluperfect in Greek (τῷ συμβεβηκότι αὐτῷ) and by the past perfect in English. Reference to an event in the same narrative as past puts temporal distance between the current action and that event.

24. These three marks of segmentation point to a narrative seam between statements (21) and (22) (3:8 and 3:9). In that case, the CON begins with (22) and (15)–(21) belong to the NUC. However, there is one decisive marker that prompts a division between (14) and (15): in (18) (B) leaves his position at the gate of the temple and enters the temple with Peter and John. This move constitutes a departure, followed by a relocation of the scene, now presumably inside the temple. "All the people" are evidently inside the temple as well, so they were not immediately party to the events that had transpired at the gate. A change in locale coupled with a new participant set signals a new subsegment: (15)–(21) are to be taken as part of the CON. The seam therefore comes between (14) and (15).

It should also be observed that (18) prepares for the scene to follow in 3:11ff.: the locale shifts from the gate to the "temple" and then to Solomon's Portico. How the participants get from the "temple" to Solomon's Portico, the narrator does not say. In any case, the move inside (18) is preparation for that shift and should therefore be labelled *departure/locale change* and *pre-f:arr.*

In spite of the marks of segmentation that set off the NUC from the CON, the time is continuous from the hour of prayer and the locale of the NUC is closely linked to the locale of the CON (cf. 3:8 with 3:2). Place and time bind 3:1–10 together in spite of the seam at 3:7/8. We are therefore justified in calling 3:8–10 a *subscene.*

25. Narrative segmentation is hierarchical, as might be expected. The break between the INTRO (3:1–2) and the NUC (3:3–7) is less marked than the break between the NUC and the CON (3:8–10). Yet the break at the end of 3:10 is even more clearly marked (there is a change in locale, which creates a new scene beginning in 3:11). Accordingly, 3:1–10 is a narrative unit, a scene, with two subordinate seams at different levels. These relationships may be represented graphically in figure 5.

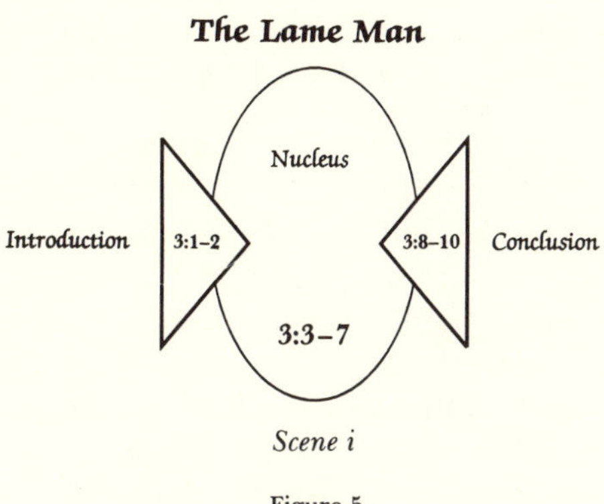

Scene i

Figure 5

26. Recapitulation and terminal functions. The actions of the lame man himself as narrated in (15)–(21) are a demonstration of his cure. His demonstration and therefore his cure are remarked by the crowd (C) which observes his actions. Statement (22) is a selective recapitulation of the actions of (B) just narrated (code: *recap*), which is another marker of a concluding segment. This form of repetition also confirms the observation that the healing of the lame man is the theme of the story.

A second form of recapitulation follows:

3:10 (23) C recognizes B *id*

The narrator now has the crowd assure the reader that the man jumping around and praising God is the same man who used to sit at the gate of the temple and beg. This *id* matches the one given in the INTRO and is therefore another form of recapitulation.

27. These two forms of recapitulation have the function of rounding off the narrative, of bringing it to narrative rest. A story may be defined as the passage from equilibrium to a state of disequilibrium or tension, which in turn is resolved or relieved, producing narrative rest, much as a musical composition returns to its tonic at the end. In this case, a certain man is depicted as lame and a beggar. He encounters two other men who have been represented as having certain powers. Expectations run high. Although the lame man expects money (3:5), he receives restored limbs, which surprises him. The people see what has happened and confirm it. The tension is released.

28. Terminal functions. Narrative rest is marked by *terminal functions* (*termf*). In fairy tales, when the prince marries the princess and we are told that they lived happily ever after, we may be sure the story is over. Of course, not all terminal functions are as evident as marriage and the indefinite extension of time ("ever after"), but many are clearly discernible, particularly if taken in the context in which they are familiar.

For the New Testament, being struck with awe or filled with fear are often terminal functions. After all, awe and fear tend to paralyze, thus arresting the chain of actions. Thus

3:10 (24) C filled with awe and amazement

is a *tf*, bringing this narrative segment to a close. Prior to the response of the people, the cured lame man praises God (3:8, 9). Praising God and prayer function frequently as terminal activities in the New Testament.

29. Defocalization. The CON is to be viewed from yet another perspective.

The INTRO brings the narrative into focus by gathering participants into a common space and time and causing them to interact. A narrative is brought to a close by reversing the focalizing process: the action ceases and narrative rest is produced; the locale is defocalized and the time expanded or shifted. A narrator need not be fully explicit about all elements, of course, in either the INTRO or the CON.

The spatial setting of the lame man is the gate of the temple. In 3:8 the lame man exits that space and enters the temple, in anticipation of a change of locale in the next narrative segment, Acts 3:11ff. One way of defocalizing a narrative is thus to have a *departure* (*dep*) or *locale change* (*lchg*).

The focalization of participants means to bring clearly defined units into view, persons or clusters that function as a single participant. A way of defocalizing a narrative is to expand the participants into an indefinite number. The reader cannot easily focus on a group without clear limits. This device may be called *participant expansion* (*pe*). In the lame man, the third participant is "all the people": while they function as something of a chorus, and thus as a unit, nevertheless, the focus of the story is becoming blurred. Defocalization is like having the camera pull away from the scene so that its distinctive features become hazy.

30. Textual notations. The analysis of the NUC and CON may again be represented as a series of notations on the text itself. The arabic numbers to the left refer to narrative statement; the grammatical notations are to be found at the right margin.

• *The Lame Man* •

Acts 3:1–10 *(continued from §3.18)*

NUCLEUS

(5)	[3] Seeing Peter and John about to go into the temple,	B/*f:perc*
(6)	he asked for alms.	
(7)	[4] And Peter directed his gaze at him, with John,	A/*f:perc-recip*
(8)	and said,	
(8.1)	"Look at us."	
(9)	[5] And he fixed his attention upon them,	B
(10)	expecting to receive something from them.	
(11)	[6] But Peter said,	A
(11.1)	"I have no silver and gold,	
(11.2)	but I give you what I have;	
(11.3)	in the name of Jesus Christ of Nazareth, walk."	
(12)	[7] And he took him by the right hand	A
(13)	and raised him up;	
(14)	and immediately his feet and ankles were made strong	B/*h*
(15)	[8] and leaping up	
(16)	he stood	
(17)	and walked	
(18)	and entered the temple with them,	*dep* / *lchg* / *pre-f*
(19)	walking	
(20)	and leaping	
(21)	and praising God.	*tf* CON
(22)	[9] And all the people saw him walking and praising God,	C/*f:perc* / *recap*
(23)	[10] and recognized him as the one who used to sit for alms at the Beautiful gate of the temple;	*recap:id*
(24)	and they were filled with wonder and amazement at what had happened to him.	*tf*

31. Additional codes

a	action
f	focalizer
h	happening
dep	departure
perc	perception
recip	reciprocal
termf	terminal function
recap	recapitulation

THE SHAPE OF THE NARRATIVE UNIT

32. The focalizing process (INTRO) was visualized as a funnel which narrows space, time, and participants until they present focused particulars. The defocalizing process is that same funnel in reverse, as it were. The chain of events connecting INTRO with CON is just that: a chain. The narrative unit may thus be represented as two wedges (or funnels) facing opposite directions linked by a chain of events (figure 6).

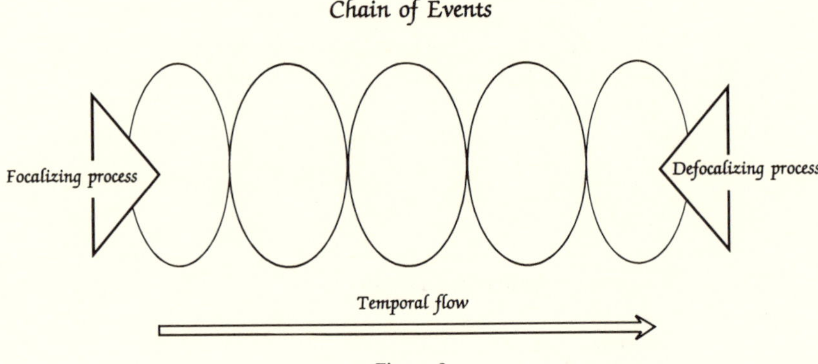

Figure 6

—· 4 ·—

The Sequence of Narrative Units

The Lame Man at the Gate Beautiful

Acts 3:1–4:31

INTRODUCTION

scene ia

(1)	3 1 Now Peter and John were going up to the temple	A	*ls*	*pre-f:arr*
	the hour of prayer, the ninth hour.		*ts*	
(2)	2 And a man lame from birth was being carried,	B	*id*	*pre-f:arr*
(3)	whom they laid daily at that gate of the temple		*ls*	
(4)	which is called Beautiful		*id*	
(3)	to ask alms of those who entered the temple.			*aa*

NUCLEUS

(5)	3 Seeing Peter and John about to go into the temple,	B(A)		*f:perc*
(6)	He asked for alms.			*a1*
(7)	4 And Peter directed his gaze at him, with John,	A(B)		*f:recip*
(8)	and said,			
(8.1)	"Look at us."			
(9)	5 And he fixed his attention upon them,	B(A)		
(10)	expecting to receive something from them.			
(11)	6 But Peter said,	A(B)		
(11.1)	"I have no silver and gold,			
(11.2)	but I give you what I have;			
(11.3)	in the name of Jesus Christ of Nazareth, walk."			
(12)	7 And he took him by the right hand			
(13)	and raised him up;			
(14)	and immediately his feet and ankles were made strong.	B(patient)		

CONCLUSION

scene ib

(15)	8 And leaping up	B	
(16)	he stood		
(17)	and walked		
(18)	and entered the temple with them,	(A)	*lchg / lc / pre-f:arr*

(19)	walking			
(20)	and leaping			
(21)	and praising God.			*termf*
(22)	9 And all the people saw him walking and praising God,	C(B)		*f:perc*
(23)	10 and recognized him as the one who sat for alms		*id*	
	at the Beautiful Gate of the temple;		*id*	
(24)	and they were filled with wonder and amazement	C patient		*termf*
	at what had happened to him.	(B)patient		

INTRODUCTION

scene iia

(25)	11 While he clung to Peter and John,	(B)A		
(26)	all the people ran together to them in the Portico called Solomon's, astounded.	C(A)	*lc*	*f:arr*

NUCLEUS

(27)	12 And when Peter saw it,	A		*f:perc-recip*
(28)	he addressed the people,	A(C)		*a1*
(28.1)	"Men of Israel,	(C)	C*id*	
	why do you wonder at this,	(C)		
(28.2)	or why do you stare at us,	(C)		
(28.3)	as though by our own power and piety we made him walk?	(B)		
(28.4)	13 The God of Abraham and of Isaac and of Jacob, the God of our fathers, glorified his servant Jesus,			
(28.5)	whom you delivered up	(C)		
(28.6)	and denied in the presence of Pilate,			
(28.7)	when he had decided to release him.			
(28.8)	14 But you denied the Holy and Righteous One,	(C)		
(28.9)	and asked for a murderer to be granted to you,	C		
(28.10)	15 and killed the Author of Life,			
(28.11)	whom God raised from the dead.			
(28.12)	To this we are witnesses.			
(28.13)	16 And his name, by faith in his name, has made this man strong	(B)		
(28.14)	whom you see and know;	(B)	*id*	
(28.15)	and the faith which is through Jesus			

	has given the man this perfect health in the presence of you all.	(B)	*id*
(28.16)	17 And now, brethren, I know that you acted in ignorance,	(C)	
(28.17)	as did your rulers.	(C)	
(28.18)	18 But what God foretold by the mouth of all the prophets,		
(28.19)	that his Christ should suffer,		
(28.20)	he thus fulfilled.		
(28.21)	19 Repent therefore,	(C)	
(28.22)	and turn again,	(C)	
(28.23)	that your sins may be blotted out,	(C)	
(28.24)	that time of refreshing many come from the presence of the Lord		
(28.25)	20 and that he may send the Christ appointed for you, Jesus	(C)	
(28.26)	21 whom heaven must receive		
(28.27)	until the time for establishing all that God spoke by the mouth of his holy prophets from of old.		
(28.28)	22 Moses said,		
(28.28.1)	'The Lord God will raise up for you a prophet from your brethren		
(28.28.2)	as he raised me up.		
(28.28.3)	You shall listen to him in whatever he tells you.		
(28.28.4)	23 And it shall be		
(28.28.5)	that every soul that does not listen to that prophet shall be destroyed from the people.'		
(28.29)	24 And all the prophets who have spoken, from Samuel and those who came afterwards, also proclaimed these days.		
(28.30)	25 You are the sons of the prophets and of the covenant	(C)	
(28.31)	which God gave to your fathers	(C)	
(28.32)	saying to Abraham,		
(28.33)	'And in your posterity shall all the families of the earth be blessed.'		
(28.34)	26 God, having raised up his servant, sent him to you	(C)	
(28.35)	to bless you in turning every one of you from your wickedness."	(C)	

CONCLUSION

scene iib

(29)	4 1 And as they were speaking to the people,	A(C)	*tc*	
(30)	the priests and the captain of the temple and the Sadducees came upon them, 2 annoyed	D(A)	P*id*	*f:arr*
(31)	because they were teaching the people		*recap*	
(32)	and proclaiming in Jesus the resurrection from the dead.			
(33)	3 And they arrested them			*a1*
(34)	and put them in custody until the morrow,		*tc* (cf.4:5)/*def:termf*	
(35)	for it was already evening.			def: *tc=termf*
(36)	4 But many of those who heard the word believed;	C		*def:termf*
(37)	and the number of the men came to about five thousand.			*def:pe*

INTRODUCTION

scene iii

(38)	5 On the morrow		*tc* (cf. 4:3)	
	their rulers and elders and scribes	E	*id*	
	were gathered together in Jerusalem,		*ls*	*pre-f:arr*
	6 with Annas the high priest and Caiaphas and John and Alexander,	E	*id*	
	and all who were of the high priestly family.			

scene iiia

(39)	7 And when they had set them in the midst,	E(A)		*f:arr*

NUCLEUS

(40)	they inquired,	E		*a1*
(40.1)	"By what power or by what name did you do this?"			
(41)	8 Then Peter, filled with the Holy Spirit, said to them,	A(E)		
(41.1)	"Rulers of the people and elders,			*recap*
(41.2)	9 if we are being examined today concerning a good deed done to a cripple, by what means this man has been healed,			
(41.3)	10 be it known to you all, and to all the people of Israel,			

(41.4)	that by the name of Jesus Christ of Nazareth, whom you crucified, whom God raised from the dead, by him this man is standing before you well.		
(41.5)	11 This is the stone which was rejected by you builders,		
(41.6)	but which has become the head of the corner.		
(41.7)	12 And there is salvation in no one else,		
(41.8)	for there is no other name under heaven given among men by which we must be saved."		
(42)	13 Now when they saw the boldness of Peter and John,	E	
(43)	and perceived that they were uneducated, common men,		
(44)	they wondered;		
(45)	and they recognized that they had been with Jesus.		
(46)	14 But seeing the man that had been healed standing beside them,	E(B)	
(47)	they had nothing to say in opposition.		
scene iiib			
(48)	15 But when they had commanded them to go aside out of the council,	E(A)	*def:dis*
(49)	they conferred with one another,	E^1/E^2	*f-recip:dia*
(50)	16 saying,		*a1:dia*
(50.1)	"What shall we do with these men?		
(50.2)	For that a notable sign has been performed through them is manifest to all the inhabitants of Jerusalem,		
(50.3)	and we cannot deny it.		
(50.4)	17 But in order that it may spread no further among the people,		
(50.5)	let us warn them to speak no more to any one in this name."		
scene iiic			
(51)	18 So they called them	E(A)	*f:arr*
(52)	and charged them not to speak or teach at all in the name of Jesus.		*a1:dia*
(53)	19 But Peter and John answered them,	A(E)	
(53.1)	"Whether it is right in the sight of		

	God to listen to you rather than to God,			
(53.2)	you must judge;			
(53.3)	[20] For we cannot but speak of what we have seen and hear."			
(54)	[21] And when they had further threatened them,	E(A)		*def:termf*
CONCLUSION				
(55)	they let them go,			*def:dis*
(56)	finding no way to punish them, because of the people;	(C)		*def:termf*
(57)	for all men praised God for what had happened.	C		*def:termf*
(58)	[22] For the man on whom this sign of healing was performed was more than forty years old.	B	*id*	
INTRODUCTION				
scene iv				
(59)	[23] When they were released	A		*pre-f:dep*
(60)	they went to their friends	F		*f:arr / lchg*
(61)	and reported what the chief priests and elders had said to them.	A(F)	*recap*	*f:perc*
NUCLEUS				
(62)	[24] And when they heard it,			*f:perc-recip*
(63)	they lifted their voices together to God			*a1*
(64)	and said,			*a1*
(64.1)	"Sovereign Lord, who didst make the heaven and the earth and the sea and everything in them,			
(64.2)	[25] who by the mouth of our father David, thy servant, didst say by the Holy Spirit,			
(64.3)	'Why did the Gentiles rage,			
(64.4)	and the peoples imagine vain things?			
(64.5)	[26] The kings of the earth set themselves in array,			
(64.6)	and the rulers were gathered together, against the Lord and against his Anointed'			
(64.7)	[27] for truly in this city there were gathered together against thy holy			

servant Jesus, whom thou didst anoint, both Herod and Pontius Pilate, with the Gentiles and the people of Israel, [28]to do whatever thy hand and thy plan had predestined to take place.

(64.8) [29] And now, Lord, look upon their threats,

(64.9) and grant to thy servants to speak thy word with all boldness,

(64.10) [30] while thou stretchest out thy hand to heal,

(64.11) and signs and wonders are performed through the name of thy holy servant Jesus."

CONCLUSION

(65) [31] And when they had prayed, *a:term*

(66) the place in which they were gathered together was shaken;

(67) and they were all filled with the Holy Spirit A+F=*pe*

(68) and spoke the word of God with boldness. *def:ae*

Healing of Lame Man

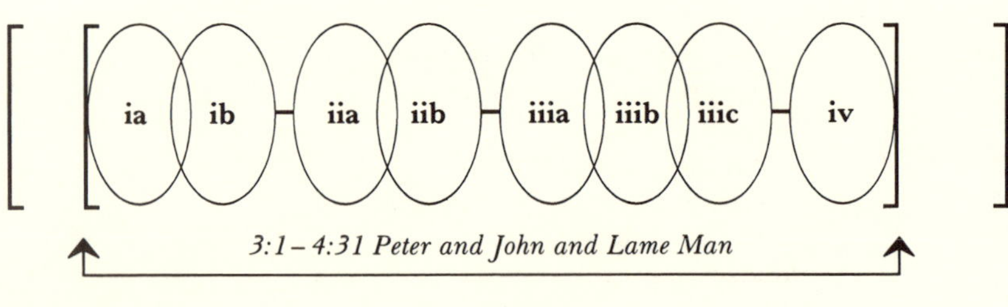

Narrative Structure

Figure 7

• 4 •

The isolated mini-narrative was analyzed in chapter 3 in an effort to determine its formal shape. In this chapter the mini-narrative will be set in an intermediate narrative context in order to analyze how narrative units are joined together.

ISOLATING THE NARRATIVE SEQUENCE

1. Hierarchy of segments and sequences. As the basis of the analysis of the sequence of narrative units, the intermediate segment, Acts 3:1–4:31, will be utilized.

The choice of Acts 3:1–4:31 is not arbitrary. This narrative stretch may be readily isolated from what precedes and what follows. A first step in the study of narrative stretches involving two or more narrative units is thus to isolate those stretches from their contexts. Put differently, it is necessary first to observe the continuities and discontinuities, or the hierarchy of relationships between and among units. Expressed diagrammatically, 3:1–4:31 is a narrative unit within the whole of Acts (so far as our present analysis has gone), and 3:1–10 is a unit within 3:1–4:31 (figure 7). The discontinuities and continuities will now be examined with reference to participants, time, and space.

2. Continuity participants. It was observed in the study of Acts 3:1–10 that Peter and John were the *continuity participant* (the two function as one participant in this narrative segment; code: CP). Peter and John remain the continuity participant in the stretch 3:1–4:31. In the preceding narrative segment, Acts 2:1–42, the continuity participant is Peter and the eleven (2:14) or Peter and the rest of the apostles (2:37), whereas in the narrative stretch that follows, 5:1–11, Peter functions virtually alone, although reference is made to the apostles as a group in 5:2. In any case, Peter and John are distinguished in 3:1–4:31 from Peter and the eleven (2:1–42), on the one side, and from Peter alone (5:1–11), on the other. This has the effect of marking the limits of the intervening narrative sequence.

This observation may be generalized: the limits of a narrative sequence may be marked by a shift or by shifts in participant sets.

3. The continuity participant in the Book of Acts as a whole is, of course, the apostles. The observations made in the preceding paragraph permit this further generalization: changes in participant scope do not affect participant continuity through and beyond narrative segments, but changes in scope may mark the limits of particular narrative segments.[1]

1. Participant scope has to do with the scale on which participants are viewed. The scale may contract, for example, from the group as a whole ("the apostles") to a few

The apostles represent the broadest scope of the participant group conceived as the acting subject of Acts. Yet Acts is also divided into shorter narrative sequences focused on one or more of the apostles, in different combinations. These changes in focus on the participant subject may be termed *changes in scope*. One participant group gives definition to the entire narrative; changes in scope give definition to shorter narrative sequences or segments within the whole.

4. Temporal duration. The limits of the narrative stretch 3:1–4:31 are further determined by *temporal duration*. In this stretch, temporal duration is internally marked as continuous, while the temporal relation to the stretches that preceded and follow is unmarked.

The scene in Solomon's Portico (3:1–4:4) follows immediately upon the scene at Beautiful Gate (3:1–10). Peter and John are arrested at the end of the day and put in prison to await events on the morrow (4:4). The next day a hearing takes place, they are released, report to their friends, and pray before the day is out (4:5–31). There is thus clear temporal continuity within this narrative stretch.

Temporal continuity is broken at either end of this narrative stretch by the indefinite times of the narrative summaries in 2:43–47 and 4:32–37. The temporal continuity of 3:1–4:31 is thereby made to contrast with the temporal discontinuities at beginning and end.

As in the case of participant continuity (§§4.1–3), temporal continuity is often marked both negatively and positively: breaks at beginning and end; internal continuity.

5. Spatial definitions. The *space* of 3:1–4:31 is also clearly set off from the indefinite space of 2:43–47 (one place where they could all be together, place of distribution, temple, private homes; all indicators are generalized) and the unmarked space of 4:32–37.

The account of the lame man begins at Beautiful Gate, moves momentarily into the temple (3:8), thence to Solomon's Portico where the crowd gathers (3:11). The officials blunder into the portico at the day's end and haul the apostles off to prison. This is all well-defined and appropriately linked space. The next day, other officials gather at an unspecified place in Jerusalem (4:5), which makes its connection with the temple and jail plausible. When released, the exonerated apostles find their friends somewhere in the city (4:27), at a place subsequently shaken by the Holy Spirit (4:31).

The linking of proximate stages upon which the sequences of events is played out gives the narrative a cohesiveness that makes it easy to separate

members of the group ("Peter and John"), to one member of the group ("Peter"), or the scale may expand. Changes in scope do not increase the number of participants, although changes often mark the limits of narrative segments.

from the surrounding narrative terrain, which, in this case, is unfocused in the brief segments immediately preceding and following.

THE COHERENCE OF THE NARRATIVE SEQUENCE

6. Internal coherence. Evidence has been adduced for isolating Acts 3:1–4:31 from its larger narrative context as a narrative sequence manifesting its own internal coherence (§§4.1–5). Thus far the discontinuities with what precedes and follows have been emphasized. However, those discontinuities gain their force by contrasting internal continuities, as already suggested. As a consequence, it may be said that narrative continuity/discontinuity depends upon a series of contrasting features, neither of which can function adequately without the other. As Saussure would put it, the system is a series of contrasting features without positive terms.[2] Nevertheless, the narrative stretch under analysis may now be viewed from the perspective of its internal continuities—in contrast, of course, to the discontinuities that border it.

7. In the analysis to follow, reference will be made to four internal segments or scenes, as follows:

Scene	i	Acts	3:1–10
	ii		3:11–4:4
	iii		4:5–22
	iv		4:23–31

It will be the next order of business to justify this outline and, in so doing, to develop some tentative rules for narrative segmentation. Segmentation refers not only to breaking the narrative into its constituent parts, but also to arranging the parts in sequences (hierarchies). It will be shown, for example, that scenes i and ii are more closely related to each other than ii is to iii; scenes i and ii constitute a sequence, in other words. Scenes iii and iv also constitute a subsequence over against scenes i and ii. Another way of stating these relationships is to say that there is a more significant break at Acts 4:4/5 than at any other point within the narrative stretch 3:1–4:31. Segmentation is a fundamental exercise in narrative analysis: on it depends the proper understanding of the surface structure of narrative texts.

8. Temporal and spatial segmentation. The temporal duration of the narrative sequence is two days. The first day begins at 3:00 P.M., the hour of prayer, and ends with the incarceration of Peter and John, "for it was already late" (Acts 4:4). Additional events take place on "the next day" (Acts 4:5). The temporal period represented by the narrative is accordingly divided into two

2. The work of Saussure is sketched briefly in §§12.9–11.

major parts by a nocturnal pause between 4:4 and 4:5. On either side of that pause the time reflected in the narrative is continuous (figure 8).

Healing of Lame Man

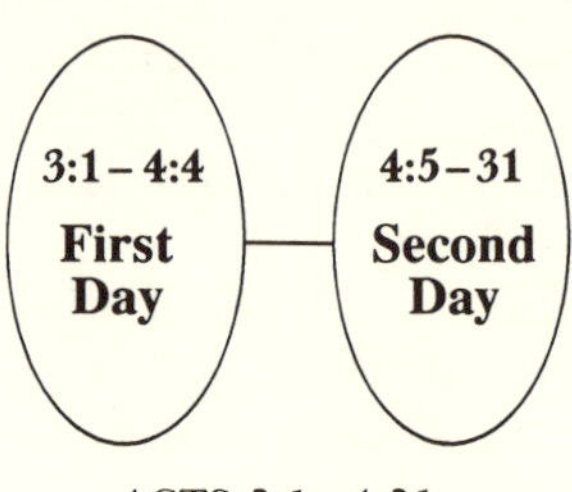

ACTS 3:1 – 4:31

Temporal Segmentation

Figure 8

The events of 3:1–4:4, the first day, take place in and around the temple: the gate of the temple (3:2, 3), inside the temple (3:8), and Solomon's Portico (3:11). On the second day, events are located by the narrator merely "in Jerusalem" (4:5, 23), but obviously not in the temple area. The spatial division between temple and Jerusalem reinforces the temporal break at 4:4/5, but the proximity of temple and Jerusalem also reinforces the cohesiveness of this narrative sequence.

9. Locale changes provide clues for the further segmentation of the narrative.

In the first half of the sequence (first day, in and around the temple), the healing of the lame man takes place at the gate of the temple (3:1–10), while Peter's sermon and the arrest occur in Solomon's Portico (3:11–26). There is thus a spatial break at 3:10/11.

In the second half of the narrative sequence (second day, somewhere in Jerusalem), the first series of events (4:5–22) is set in Jerusalem where the council is gathered (4:5f.), the second series (4:23–31) also in Jerusalem but elsewhere, at a place where the friends of Peter and John are collected (4:23).

Based on considerations of locale, the narrative stretch may be divided into four parts of differing ranks (figure 9).

10. Participant sets and focus. Participant sets and focus are also instructive for the structure of the narrative.

In the entire narrative segment, the participants are as follows:

A. Peter and John
B. lame man

C. crowd
D. priests, captain of the temple, Sadducees
E. rulers, elders, scribes
(changes in focus:)
Annas the high priest
Caiaphas
John
Alexander
high priestly family
E^1/E^2 (council in dialogue with itself)
F. friends of A

It should be recalled that two or more persons having a single function are grouped together as single participants. In the list above, every participant, except for the lame man, involves more than one person.

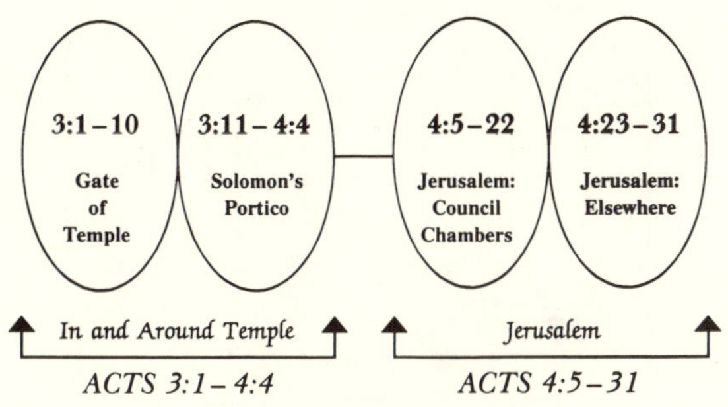

Figure 9

11. The participant sets occurring in this narrative stretch may be represented graphically for convenience (figure 10). The groupings not only reinforce scene breaks, but also prompt the recognition of subscenes.

The participant set of the first day, or first subsequence (3:1–4:4), consists of (A), (B), (C), and (D). (C) and (D) do not appear in the second part of the story, and (B) appears in the second part only as a silent bystander. The participant set of the second day, or second subsequence, consists of (A), (E), (F), with ([B]). The two distinctive sets are thus correlative with the major narrative break at 4:4/5 already observed in connection with temporal and spatial segmentation.

12. Participant analysis may be used to develop segmentation further.

In scene i the active participants are (A), (B), (C); in scene ii they are (A),

(C), (D). In the first scene, (B) is in the foreground or is in focus, and thus may be termed the *theme participant* (TP). But in scene iia, the crowd comes into the foreground: Peter's sermon is directed to them (3:12, 13, 14, etc.). The events of the first day are brought to a close with scene iib (4:1–4), in which (A) shares the stage with (C): (D) arrests (A) and puts them in prison, but the general response of (C) to the sermon of Peter is also indicated.

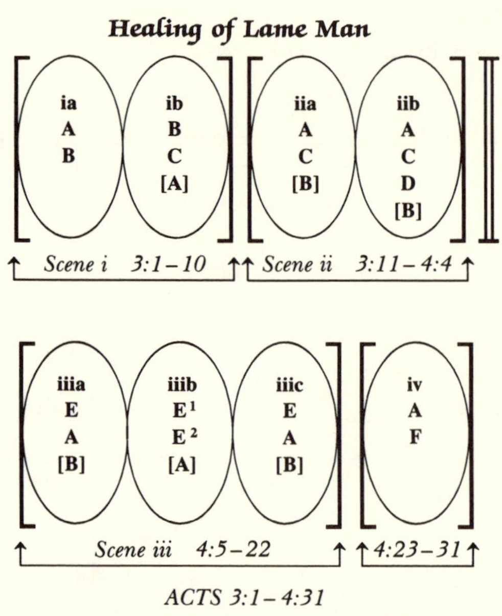

ACTS 3:1–4:31

Segmentation by Participant Sets

Figure 10

[ ] **Brackets indicate a silent, passive bystander or an absent participant under discussion.**

These observations may be summarized in graphic form (figure 11). Participants placed at the top in each segment are in the foreground. The combination of participant set and foregrounding constitutes (partial) justification for segmentation. In addition, the hierarchy of scenes and subscenes is indicated by the relationship of the spheres to each other.

In scenes iii and iv, (A) is in the foreground throughout, even during the brief period when (A) is absent from the scene (iiib, 4:15–17): (A) is the subject or theme of the dialogue internal to (E). In scene iv (4:23–31), (A) and (F) gradually merge, so that when the scene closes (4:29–31), (A) and (F) are no longer distinguished: this narrative segment (3:1–4:31) has returned to its theme baseline, the acts of the apostles.

13. Thematic continuity. The theme participant of Acts 3:1–4:31 is the lame man and the theme is his healing. This participant and this subject are in the dramatic foreground in 3:1–10, as indicated in chapter 3 and §§4.10–12 above. It will be illuminating to observe how the narrator employs these thematics as adhesive in the longer discourse, while introducing a second,

Healing of Lame Man

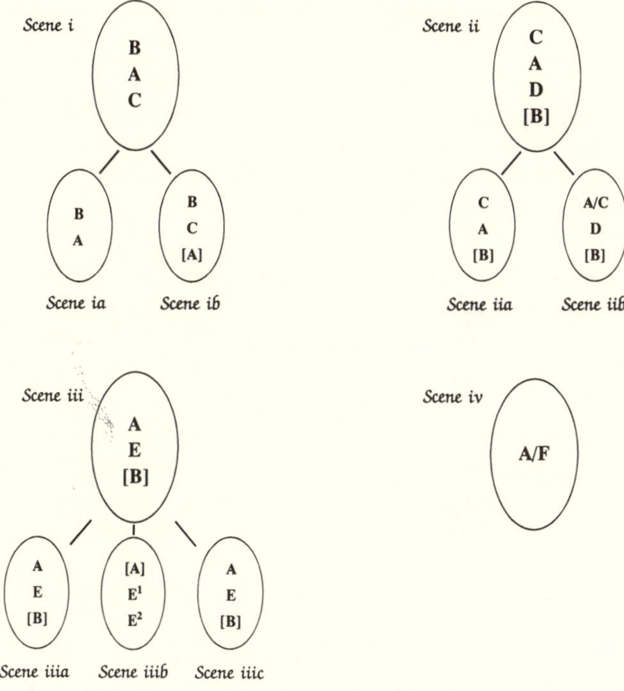

Participant Sets & Foregrounding

Figure 11

competitive theme, so to speak. In other words, the analysis will now shift from simple participant-set analysis to the analysis of actions viewed as themes, i.e., as threads linking two or more scenes or subscenes.

14. The second narrative segment (3:11–4:4) within the larger story is connected very tightly to the preceding unit, 3:1–10.

scene i

CONCLUSION

(22) [9] And all the people saw him . . .

(23) [10] and recognized him . . .

(24) and they were filled with wonder and amazement at what had happened to him.

scene ii

INTRODUCTION

(25) [11] While he still clung to Peter and John,

(26) all the people ran together to them in the Portico called Solomon's astounded.

NUCLEUS

(27) [12] And when Peter saw it,

(28) he addressed the people,

(28.1) Men of Israel, why do you wonder at this,

(28.2) or why do you stare at us,

(28.3) as though by our power or piety we made him walk?

At the opening of the second scene, the lame man is seen clinging to Peter and John, although he is no longer to be an active participant in the narrative. His mention links the second scene closely to the first: "While [the lame man] still clung to Peter and John. . . ." Moreover, at the CON of scene i, "all the people" are filled with wonder and amazement at what had happened to the lame man (24), a theme which is renewed in (26) by the word "astounded," and then picked up again in (28.1) and (28.2): "wonder" and "stare." Thus, the close of scene i and the opening of scene ii are tightly linked by the lame man, his healing, and the response of the crowd to what had happened. The linking extends as far as line (28.3); at this point Peter turns to other matters in his sermon. These linkages indicate a high level of narrative cohesion.

After a section recapitulating the destiny of Jesus (3:13–15), Peter renews the healing theme in vs 16. He reiterates: you know this man (cf. 3:10) and he was healed in your presence. Both features recall the drama of the opening scene. These are again evidences of a tightly conceived narrative.

In the second part of his sermon (3:17–26), Peter remonstrates with his audience, urging them to respond positively to his call to repentance. While in the midst of his altar call, as it were, "The priests and captain of the temple and the Sadducees"—quite a crowd—come upon them (4:1). The reader is told, at no little surprise, that the authorities were "annoyed" because (a) "they were teaching the people" and (b) "proclaiming in Jesus the resurrection from the dead" (4:2). No mention is made of the lame man. The narrator has evidently elected to pick up themes introduced in or by Peter's sermon: (a) the sermon itself is presumably "teaching," and (b) the resurrection is mentioned directly in 3:15 and indirectly in 3:26. For these offenses, the speakers are confined for the night (4:3), while many in the audience have responded positively to Peter's preaching (4:4). The second part of Peter's sermon links this particular incident with the broader theme of Acts: the proclamation of the apostles and the responses of the people and the authorities to that proclamation. Again, there is strong evidence of a high level of narrative coherence.

15. The next day, another group of authorities assemble, send for Peter and John, with this question:

4:7 "By what power or by what name did you do this?" In view of the CON to scene ii (4:1–4), the reader expects the question to refer to (a) teaching and (b) proclaiming the resurrection. But it does not. Instead, it reverts to the healing of the lame man, as Peter's response makes evident (4:8–10). However, Peter goes on to repeat the alleged offences of the day before (4:10–12). In the debate which follows (4:13–17), the presence of the lame man (4:14) and the widespread testimony to his new condition (4:16, 21) make it impossible for the authorities to contravene the healing miracle. Accordingly, they fall back on the second theme, introduced with the appearance of the authorities at the close of scene ii: they charge Peter and John not to speak or teach in the name of Jesus (4:18).

The type of thematic linkage being employed by the narrator in this context may be schematically represented as a series of links in a narrative chain (figure 12). By alternating themes the narrator is able to provide a series of

Healing of Lame Man

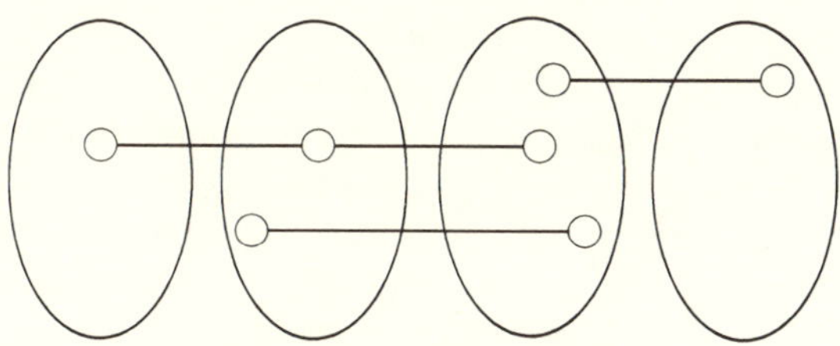

Thematic Narrative Linkages

Figure 12

links that gives the narrative a high level of cohesiveness, even though the themes in question are not necessarily integral to each other (or they are not so represented).

16. In scene iii (4:5–22), competition between the two themes is worked out: the sign of the lame man is allowed to stand; the apostles are to cease teaching and preaching. It is not surprising, consequently, that the lame man is formally dismissed from the narrative at the close of scene iii, with a further identification, viz., his age (4:22). Meanwhile, Peter and John advise the authorities that they will not be able to remain silent (4:19–20).

The narrator does not abandon the healing theme in scene iv (4:23–31), although he abandons the lame man. In 4:30 the story returns to the healing theme briefly but in a general way:

(64.10) [30] While thou stretchest out thy hand to heal,
(64.11) and signs and wonders are performed through the name of thy holy servant Jesus.

Meanwhile, the narrator reverts to the speaking and teaching theme (4:29, 31), which is the central theme of the larger narrative, and that is the note on which this narrative sequence ends.

17. The internal cohesion of this narrative stretch is provided by the theme of the lame man and his healing as a sign, together with the theme of the apostles teaching and the contrasting responses to that teaching (the people and the authorities). The first theme is certainly predominant. Nevertheless, the initial theme diminishes steadily as the story progresses; in the end it is present only in a generalized way. The apostles' sermon to the people, on the other hand, is introduced midway in the discourse and is then developed in conflict with the authorities. This second theme brings the reader back to the baseline of the larger story, which has already been established in Acts 2: the proclamation of the apostles and the beginnings of the Christian movement. In this way the narrator not only provides internal cohesion for the story, but he also embeds the story firmly in the book as a whole.

18. The segmentation of Acts 3:1–4:31. The study of segmentation sketched in the preceding paragraphs (§§4.1–17) reveals the relatively complex structure of Acts 3:1–4:31. There are four principal scenes, which may be represented graphically as in figure 10 (above, §4.11). The double line at the end of scene ii indicates that scenes i and ii form a sequence, just as do scenes iii and iv. The subscenes are depicted as individual eggs; segmentation below the subscene level is not represented.

It remains to define the formal limits of the various narrative units: INTRO, NUC, CON; scene, subscene, sequences of scenes.

MICROFEATURES SIGNALING SEGMENTATION

19. Introduction. The features analyzed in §§4.1–18 may be termed macrofeatures: temporal and spatial markers, participant sets and focus, and the hierarchy of scenes and subscenes. These features combine with other textual markers that may be called microfeatures. Indeed, it is impossible, finally, to segregate macro- and microfeatures into discrete categories. Yet it is helpful to think of microfeatures as markers that will be discerned by reading the text even more closely than was done in §§4.1–18. The initial analysis of 3:1–10 in chapter 3 was an analysis of microfeatures. We shall therefore begin in this section with the close analysis of scene ii (3:11ff.), which will produce finer degrees of segmentation; we shall call the end-product *micro-segmentation* (figure 13).[3]

Healing of Lame Man

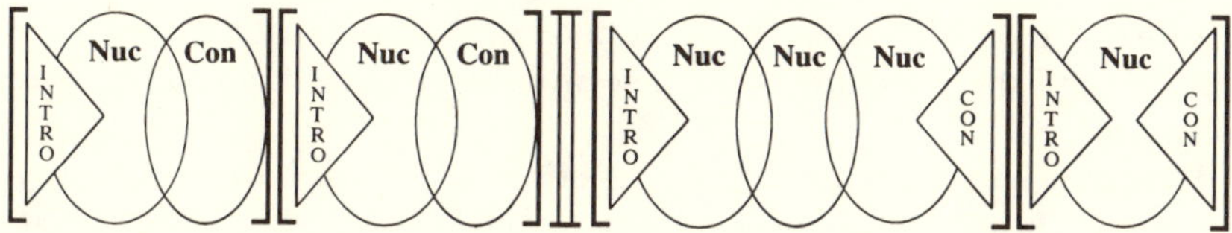

Micro-Segmentation

Figure 13

20. Scene ii: focalization. A new scene (ii) is brought into focus in 3:11f.: all the people run together (*f:arr*) to Peter and John (with the lame man still clinging to them) in Solomon's Portico (a new place = *lchg*). When Peter sees them gathered (*f:perc*), the action begins. The gathering of all the people constitutes the principal focalizing activity (an arrival of many individuals more or less simultaneously), which Peter sees, a perception that motivates him to address the assembled throng. Lines (25)–(26) thus represent the INTRO to scene ii, (3:11).

21. Scene ii: participant identification. The reader has been introduced to participants (A), (B), and (C) in scene i, so they do not require further introduction. However, participant (A), Peter and John, following their introduction in 3:1 and mention at the beginning of the NUC (3:3–4), have been referred to by pronoun (3:5 [2x], 3:7, 3:8), except where Peter is distinguished from John (3:6). These observations permit the following generalization: participants are introduced (with identification: *id*, if for the first time) at the outset of a scene and then tracked through the balance of the scene by pronoun, except where ambiguity would result. Correlatively, if participants

3. The analysis of 3:1–10 is presupposed here. The reader may wish to refer to chapter 3 for the details.

are continued into a second scene in an active role, they are normally marked by the repetition of some form of proper identification (e.g., the use of proper name, original identifying word or phrase, or by the introduction of new nomenclature). In this case, "Peter and John" and "all the people" (the introductory *id* in 3:9), rather than the use of pronouns, signals the beginning of a new segment in which (A) and (C) are to have active roles. By contrast, the lame man is continued in scene ii only in pronominal form (3:11, 3:12, 3:16 [2x]) because his figure recedes into the background.

22. A change in nomenclature serves the same function. In the parable of the laborers in the vineyard (Matt 20:1–16), participant (A) is introduced as a "householder" at the beginning of scene i (20:1). At the outset of scene ii (20:8), he is labelled "owner of the vineyard." Between the two references he is referred to only by pronoun. He is thus *renamed* to signal the beginning of scene ii, and the introduction of new and synonymous nomenclature reinforces that signal.

P*nom* may be used to indicate the repetition of nominals to identify participants at the head of a narrative segment, while P*nomchg* will indicate the same function with change in nomenclature.

23. Scene ii: participant (C). Pursuant to the role of participant (C) (crowd) in scene ii, it should be noted that (C) is brought into ever sharper focus. "All the people" of 3:9 (scene ib) are an amorphous mass; indeed, their introduction at the close of scene i contributes to the defocalizing process (§3.29). In a second stage, they are made to run together, i.e., to come into focus as a single, cohesive group, at the beginning of scene ii (3:11). They can then be addressed as "Men of Israel" and given a unified function in Peter's speech (3:12–26). (C*id*), line (28.1), thus contributes to the shaping of scene ii and the focal role now played by the "Men of Israel."

24. Scene ii: temporal distance. In 3:12 the healing of the lame man is referred to as an event that took place in the past:

(28.3) as though by our own power or piety we made (πεποιηκόσιν) him walk.

Scene ii thus puts temporal distance between itself and scene i by relegating the healing of the lame man to past time. This reference is reinforced by 3:16:

(28.13) And his name, by faith in his name, has made this man strong (ἐστερέωσιν)
(28.14) whom you see and know;
(28.15) and the faith which is through Jesus has given (ἔδωκεν) him this perfect health in the presence of you all.

Scene ii obviously looks back on scene i as an event that took place in an earlier narrative segment.

In addition to these formal features, the beginning of scene ii is marked by a locale change and by a shift in participant set (in relation specifically to scene ib) and in participant foregrounding or focus (§§4.9, 12). There is thus a constellation of macro- and microfeatures that point to the narrative break between 3:10/11.

25. Conclusion to scene ii. Peter's speech is interrupted by the priests, captain of the temple, and Sadducees (D): the interruption provides an immediate temporal link (*temporal connective: tc*) with the preceding event, and the arrival of the officials constitutes a fresh focalizer (*f:arr*). (D) is of course a new participant and is introduced with explicit nominals (P*id*).

Lines (32) and (33) *recap* the speech of Peter and characterize it as "teaching the people," which annoys the authorities. This emotive characterization prompts them to arrest the two apostles, which initiates the unfocused action of scene iib, and to put them in prison, which is also, obviously, a terminal function (*termf*): their current activity is temporarily suspended.

Their incarceration is to last until the morrow, which is a temporal link pointing forward to scene iii (*tc*; cf. 4:5), and incarceration is more appropriate than a hearing, because it is already evening, i.e., the authorities will not be available at so late an hour; this temporal connection points backward to the scene just closing and serves as a terminal notice (*tc* = *termf*).

Finally, the response of (C) to the sermon is given notice in lines (37) and (38): many believe, which is often a *termf* in the New Testament. In addition, the size of (C) is now shown to be greatly expanded: the number of believers now comes to about five thousand, which is a form of participant expansion (*pe*) and a defocalizer. With this notice (C) is dismissed from the narrative.

26. Acts 4:1–4 (scene iib) has been designated the CON to scene iia (3:11–26). This function is clear from the following features. The arrival of (D) and the arrest of (A) interrupts an event (scene iia; *a:term*) in progress; it therefore concludes that scene. In addition, 4:1–4 is replete with terminal functions and defocalizers. There are at least four of them. Participant (C) was introduced into scene ib (3:9–10) and now disappears from the narrative after being in focus in scene ii (iia and iib). The departure of (C) clearly brings a narrative segment to an end. Finally, a major temporal break occurs at 4:4/5 (§4.8), as does a spatial break (§4.9), and with scene iii (4:5ff.) a new participant set is introduced. On the other hand, locale, time, and focal participant are continuous with what precedes. Scene iib thus has strong ties to scene iia and serves as its conclusion.[4]

27. Scene iii: focalization and segmentation. The rulers, elders, scribes, and the high priest with his relatives (E) gather together somewhere in Jerusalem (*ls*) and thus position themselves (*pre-f:pos*) to interrogate Peter and John. This takes place following the nocturnal pause (*tc*; cf. 4:3). Peter and John are

4. This scene is also cast in a contrasting narrative mode, recounting, as we shall observe in §6.6.

ushered into the assembly (*f:arr*) and the interrogation begins. The stage has been set for scene iii (INTRO).

The hearing and interrogation is divided into three subscenes:

iiia	4:7–14
iiib	4:15–17
iiic	4:18–20
CON	4:21–22

The segmentation of scene iii is represented graphically in figure 13 (above, §4.19).

28. Scene iiia. In scene iiia, the authorities question Peter and John regarding the lame man now healed. Peter then responds by summarizing the speech he had given earlier to "all the people" (*recap*). The authorities are prompted by the character of the response and by the presence of the lame man to reflect on the situation. Subscene iiia is brought to a close and iiib opened by dismissing participant (A); in addition, the reflections begun silently in lines (43)–(48) are now brought to the surface and continued as a separate subscene (iiib). In other words, the series of silent observations at the close of iiia (*saw, perceived, wondered, recognized, seeing*) lays the basis for the separation of E into E^1 and E^2 and the brief conference which follows.

29. Scene iiib. With (A) absent, (E^1) and (E^2) confer with one another and arrive at a plan of action (iiib).

30. Scene iiic. Subscene iiic is refocused by bringing (A) back into the hearing (*f:arr*). The charge is delivered by (E) (4:18b), to which (A) gives a further threatening response (4:19–20). This leads to a rather elaborate CON.

31. Conclusion of scene iii. The authorities threaten Peter and John, which is often a terminal function (compare) the officer about to let the speeder go with a warning) and dismisses them (*def:tf*), having determined they dare not punish them (a negative juridical sentence and thus also a terminal function). Line (58) recalls the response of (C) to the earlier sermon: the praise of God for the healing puts the authorities in an awkward position, but it also serves as a terminal function in its own right. Finally, the lame man is identified as a responsible witness himself (*more than forty years old*) and dismissed from the narrative with this observation. This form of *id* may be labelled *terminal identification* (*id:term*). The preeminent example of *id:term* is the obituary.

There are no fewer than five defocalizers in the CON to scene iii:

(1) threaten (*termf*)
(2) dismissal (*dep*)
(3) negative sentence (*termf*)
(4) praise of God (*termf*)
(5) terminal identification of B (*id:term*)

32. Scene iv. Scene iv has a discrete INTRO and CON, with a single NUC. Its parts are given in graphic form in figure 13 (§4.19).

The notice of (56), "they let them go," is renewed in (60), "when they were released." The execution of the release (*pre-f:dep*) permits them to go to their friends, which constitutes a new arrival (*f:arr*), for which the release was the preparation. The new arrival involves a new participant (F) and a new location (*lchg*). The time is, of course, continuous.

The reader knows what the chief priest and elders said to Peter and John since that scene has just been enacted (scene iii). But the friends (F) were not present, so (A) must tell (F) what happened. That report constitutes a new focalizer of perception (*f:perc*). The friends listen to the report, of course, which provides the story with a reciprocating focalizer of perception (*f:perc-recip*): (A) talks, (F) listens.

As the analysis indicates, scene iv is focalized by a series of clearly marked steps:

(1) A is released (anticipated departure from previous locale)
(2) A arrives at the place of friends
(3) A recapitulates the previous scene (A calls the attention of F to what had happened)
(4) F hears the report (reciprocal focalizer)

In addition to the marks of focalization just enumerated, the *recap* of the previous scene, or rather the notice that it was recapitulated, puts temporal distance between scenes iv and iii (*a:retro*).

The NUC of iv consists of the single action of prayer ("they lifted their voices together to God"; *dia*) (4:24–30). Since the prayer is jointly of (A) and (F), the distinction between the two participants is blurred; that prepares for the CON.

The CON is clearly marked. The activity forming the NUC of scene iv, prayer, is terminated in (66) (*a:term*), (A) and (F) are merged into one generalized participant (*pe*), and the previous action of Peter and John is now generalized (*ae*): they speak the word of God with boldness (didn't they tell the authorities they would do so?). The specific scenes just concluded are merged back into the larger story implied by the Acts of the Apostles, so to speak, by expanding the participants (A and F combined = an indefinite number) and expanding the action (speaking with boldness = an indefinite number of times and places). A story depicted in four scenes is brought to a conclusion in such a way as to anticipate further events involving apostles and their friends, the Holy Spirit, and perhaps healing (cf. lines 65.10–11), yet the series of scenes just in focus are brought in their specificity entirely to rest: the narrative has returned to its tonic.

— · 5 · —

Focalizers, Actions, Defocalizers

• 5 •

In this chapter, we shall renew the discussion of the shape of the narrative unit (chapter 3) by extending the range of narrative material being considered and by concentrating on formal aspects of the INTRO (focalizers), the NUC (actions), and the CON (defocalizers). The development of these microfeatures of narrative, as we termed them in §4.10 and §4.19, provides the database of which the Table of Codes is a summary.

FOCALIZERS AND PRE-FOCALIZERS

1. Narrative linkages. In his ground-breaking study, *Morphology of the Folktale,* Propp demonstrated that "functions" or acts of a participant constituted the basic elements of the Russian fairy tale.[1] He further held that these "functions" or actions were connected into a series or narrative by virtue of certain narrative devices. For example, if the hero is to pursue the heroine, the hero must learn that the heroine has been abducted. The notification of the hero is the link between abduction and pursuit. Such linkages or connectors may be thought of as causes or motivations, or at least occasions.

Propp identified several of these narrative devices, although he did not treat them systematically. For the story to move, for one action to lead to another, participants must (1) *find out* something (by announcement, overhearing a conversation, complaint, or the like), or (2) *see* something. Another means of connecting actions is (3) to *have something brought.* Finally, events may be linked by (4) an *arrival* or by (5) a celebration to which participants are invited (another form of arrival).

These suggestions of Propp lead to the observation that narrative devices of just this type are generally employed to connect narrative segments and are not limited to the expression of causal links and motivations. As in many other instances, Propp has once again been extraordinarily provocative in foreshadowing new ways of perceiving and analyzing narrative.

2. The hints provided by Propp may be generalized and turned into a systematic treatment of the narrative devices by means of which narrative segments are initiated or focalized (and, subsequently, of the narrative devices by means of which segments are concluded or defocalized). These devices fall into three principal categories, as the labels given them in the

1. Functions are acts of a participant "defined from the point of view of [their] significance for the course of the action." *Morphology,* 21.

Table of Codes indicate. It should be recalled that the focalizing process involves three elements, the codes for which are:

1. Participants
   P = participant
   CP = continuity participant
   TP = theme participant
   A,B = specific participants
   id = identification (and qualification)
2. Locale
   ls = local setting
   lc = local connective
   (with link to preceding segment)
3. Time
   ts = temporal setting
   tc = temporal connective
   (with link to preceding segment)

When two or more participants are brought together in a common time and place, the narrative may be said to be brought into focus, or focalized. By that is meant: the reader (or listener) is transported, by means of certain narrative devices, to a particular time and place, with certain participants present, to perceive specific non-verbal actions or listen in on specific verbal acts. In other words, a narrative makes a reader a spectator, an onlooker, of what is transpiring on the narrative stage. The narrative devices by means of which this relationship of reader to events is effected include what may be called *pre-focalizers* and *focalizers*. In the Table of Codes, the following abbreviations are employed:

arr = arrival
f = focalizer
perc = perception
prec = precipitator
pre-f = pre-focalizer
recip = reciprocal

Pre-focalizers and focalizers fall into the following categories:

4. Pre-focalizers and focalizers
   arr = arrivals
   someone arrives or comes forward
   someone is brought, sent, or called
   persons meet (mutual arrival)
   someone finds someone
   perc = perceptions
   someone sees something
   someone hears something

someone finds something (perceives it)
someone tastes something[2]
perc-prec = perception precipitator
a sound signal (a cry, rush of wind, earthquake)
a visual signal (vision, flash of light, cloud, eclipse)
dia = dialogue
someone attracts another's attention by speaking
attention-getters ("hello," "hey, you," "pardon me")

These categories require further explanation and illustration. In providing the requisite commentary, we shall again be keeping close to the surface features of the narrative.

3. Focalizers and pre-focalizers. (1) In the story of the lame man in Acts 3:1–10, the lame man is positioned at the gate of the temple (3:2) and Peter and John are on their way to the temple (3:1). As Peter and John are about to go into the temple, the lame man "sees" them (3:3). This act of seeing on the part of the lame man is a narrative device that focalizes the scene for the reader also. A focalizer is thus any narrative device that instructs the reader where to focus the senses, where to look for the action that is about to take place. In this instance, the text prompts the reader to look up to see Peter and John approaching and to surmise (from 3:2) that a request for alms is impending.

A narrative is a set of linguistic devices designed to make the reader an observer of a particular event or sequence of events. A focalizer simply instructs the reader where to look (or listen, or touch, etc.). The function of the focalizer may be expressed in still another way: it is the means by which the first narrative contact between two participants is established.

A focalizer need not be an invocation of the senses internal to the discourse. The narrator might have had Peter and John simply arrive at the gate where the beggar was seated and then have the lame man request alms. Stipulating the focus of the lame man on Peter and John was not really required. Indeed, the common form of the focalizer is simply the arrival or meeting of two or more participants.

4. A pre-focalizer is any narrative device that prepares the way for or anticipates a focalizer.

Again, in the story of the lame man, Peter and John are in motion, on their way to the temple. This movement anticipates their *arrival* at the gate of the temple, and thus functions as a *pre-focalizer*; at the gate, the lame man will make visual contact with them. Correlatively, the lame man is being carried to the gate of the temple. This motion anticipates his *position* there when Peter and John *arrive* and is thus also a *pre-focalizer*.

Expressed diagrammatically (figure 14), the lame man is in position when

2. Less commonly, touch and smell may be employed.

Peter and John arrive. The point of contact is the moment the lame man spies them (visual contact = focalizer).

Healing of Lame Man

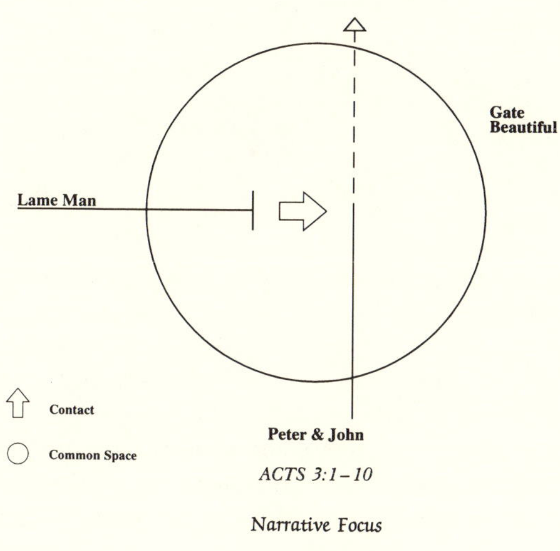

ACTS 3:1–10

Narrative Focus

Figure 14

ARRIVALS

5. Sensory contact between two participants is merely a subspecies, in more explicit form, of contact between or among two or more persons being brought together in a common time and place. A generalized form of such contact may be termed *arrival*: someone arrives on the scene and the story begins, or both (or all) parties arrive on the scene and the action begins (mutual arrival). Occasionally the participants are already in position when the scene opens, in which case some other focalizing device is required.

The categories of arrivals include the following:

someone arrives or comes forward
someone is brought, sent, or called
persons meet (mutual arrival)
someone finds someone

Each of these categories may be readily illustrated from narrative materials drawn from the New Testament.

6. Simple arrivals. A leper arrives:

Mark 1:40

(1) And a leper came to him *f:arr*
(2) beseeching him,
(3) and kneeling
(4) said to him, . . .

Nicodemus arrives:

John 3:1–2

(1) [1] Now there was a man of the Pharisees, named Nicodemus, a ruler of the Jews.
(2) [2] This man came to Jesus by night *f:arr*
(3) and said to him, . . .

Jesus is in position at Jacob's well in Samaria. Then comes a woman:

John 4:7

(1) There came a woman of Samaria to draw water. *f:arr*
(2) And Jesus said to her, . . .

In each case, participant contact is effected by means of an arrival. Arrivals are often employed in cinema to initiate the narrative.

An arrival may be preceded by the receipt of a report, as in Acts 11:1ff., which functions as a pre-focalizer.

Acts 11:1–2

(1) [1] Now the apostles and the brethren who were in Judea heard that the Gentiles also had received the word of God. *pre-f:perc*
(2) [2] So when Peter went up to Jerusalem, *f:arr*
(3) the circumcision party criticized him, . . .

7. Someone is brought, sent, or called. In the account of the healing of the deaf mute, someone arrives by being brought:

Mark 7:31–32

(1) [31] Soon after this he returned from the region of Tyre, *pre-f:arr*
(2) and went through Sidon to the Sea of Galilee, through the region of Decapolis. *pre-f:arr*
(3) [32] And they brought to him a man *f:arr*
(4) who was deaf and had an impediment in his speech; *id*
(5) and they besought him . . .

Jesus returns from Tyre and goes to the Sea of Galilee, a movement that anticipates further events. In this case, a deaf man is brought to him. The first two narrative statements are pre-focalizers anticipating an arrival. The arrival consists of the deaf man and his friends.

A very similar example occurs in Mark 8:22:

(1)	And they came to Bethsaida.	*pre-f:arr*
(2)	And some people brought to him a blind man,	*f:arr*
(3)	and begged him . . .	

In these examples, as in previous ones, the focalizer is the label given to the first narrative contact; the pre-focalizers lead up to that contact and anticipate it.

Instead of being brought, one may be sent as a form of arrival.

Luke 20:10

(1)	When the time came,	*ts*
(2)	he sent a servant to the tenants, that they should give him some of the fruit of the vineyard;	*f:arr*
(3)	but the tenants beat him, . . .	

8. Persons meet: mutual arrivals. When persons meet, that is also a form of arrival: a mutual or simultaneous arrival.

Acts 16:16

(1)	As we were going to a place of prayer,	*pre-f:arr*
(2)	we were met by a slave girl . . .	*f:arr*

Acts 10:25

(1)	When Peter entered,	*pre-f:arr*
(2)	Cornelius met him . . .	*f:arr*

In these illustrations, someone is on his or her way somewhere or arrives someplace, and a second party meets the first party to establish initial narrative contact. The first statement in each case functions as a pre-focalizer in that it anticipates participant contact.

9. Someone finds someone. The verb "find" in both Greek and English may refer either to an act of perception ("he found that his billfold was empty") or to an encounter or meeting, as in the following examples.

John 1:43

(1)	The next day Jesus decided to go to Galilee.	
(2)	And he found Philip	*f:arr*
(3)	and said to him, . . .	

John 9:35

(1)	Jesus heard that they had cast him out,	*pre:f:perc*
(2)	and having found him	*f:arr*
(3)	he said, . . .	

John 5:14

(1)	Afterward,	*tc*
	Jesus found him in the temple,	*f:arr*
(2)	and said to him, . . .	

It is difficult in these instances to decide whether the verb denotes an arrival or whether it depicts an act of perception. In either case, however, initial narrative contact is involved.

10. The doubling of focalizers. More than one focalizer may, of course, be used to open a particular scene. In the story of the ten lepers (Luke 17:11–19), Jesus enters a village (an arrival). He is met by ten lepers (another arrival), who stand at a distance and call to him. The initial point of contact comes when the lepers meet him (= the focalizer). Jesus entering the village is a pre-focalizer because it anticipates but does not fulfill that contact. There is no discrete pre-focalizer for the lepers; their movement is expressed, so to speak, in the "meeting" itself. But in this story there is a second focalizing device: a perception precipitator expressed in this instance as an attention-getter. The lepers stand afar off as protocol requires and call to Jesus: they get his attention (and the reader's) not by standing in his way in the road, but by calling to him. The second, sensory focalizer reinforces the first.

These observations may once again be stated as a series of notations on the text itself:

Luke 17:12–13

(1)	12 And as he entered a village,	*pre-f:arr / ls*
(2)	he was met by ten lepers,	*f:arr*
(3)	who stood at a distance	
(4)	13 and lifted up their voices	*f:perc-prec*
(5)	and said, . . .	

The spatial relationships expressed in this set of focalizing devices may be represented graphically, as in figure 15.

Ten Lepers

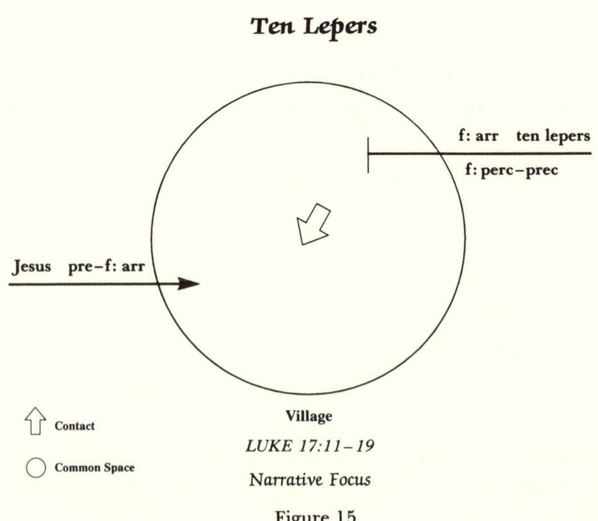

Village

LUKE 17:11–19

Narrative Focus

Figure 15

We shall encounter even more complex sets of focalizing devices eventually. Meanwhile, it is in order to turn to sensory devices.

SENSORY FOCALIZERS

11. In the story of the lame man in Acts 3, the lame man "sees" Peter and John as they pass through the gate. This act of perception focalizes the scene for the reader: one now knows where to look for the first action. This device is internal to the narrative discourse: a participant in the story is made to focus his or her senses on a particular person or object as a means of bringing the senses of the reader to a pinpoint. The senses of the participant internal to the discourse are analogous to those of the reader: the one draws the other after it.

In film, the shot/reverse shot is one means of simulating eye or visual contact: the scene is viewed from the perspectives of each of two participants as they make sensory contact.

Visual contact is only one form of sensory contact that may serve to initiate a narrative segment. As indicated in the Table of Codes, there are at least four types of sensory contact:

someone sees something
someone hears something
someone finds something (i.e., perceives it)
someone tastes something

These are focalizers of perception. Each of the types may be illustrated by reference to specific texts.

12. Someone sees or notices something. Two elementary examples of the visual focalizer are found in the double call story in Mark:

Mark 1:16

(1)	And passing along by the Sea of Galilee,	
(2)	he saw Simon and Andrew . . .	*f:perc*
(3)	And Jesus said to them, . . .	

Mark 2:14

(1)	And as he passed on,	
(2)	he saw Levi the son of Alphaeus . . .	*f:perc*
(3)	and he said to him, . . .	

The story of the leper, cited earlier in its Markan version, opens in the Lukan account with an arrival followed by a visual focalizer:

Luke 5:12

(1)	While he was in one of the cities,	
(2)	there came a man full of leprosy;	*pre-f:arr*
(3)	and when he saw Jesus,	*f:perc*

(4) he fell on his face,
(5) and besought him, . . .

Statement (2) functioned as the focalizer in Mark 1:40, but here it functions as the pre-focalizer simply because Luke focalizes the account through the perception of the leper.

The same simple focalizer may follow a more elaborate introduction:

John 5:2ff.

(1) [2] Now there is in Jerusalem by the sheep gate a pool,
(2) in Hebrew called Bethzatha,
(3) which has five porticoes.
(4) [3] In these lay a multitude of invalids, blind, lame, paralyzed.
(5) [5] One man was there,
(6) who had been ill for thirty-eight years.
(7) [6] When Jesus saw him . . . *f:perc*
(8) he said to him, . . .

In this instance, the lame man is in position in one of the porticoes when Jesus comes upon him (the reader surmises Jesus' arrival) and "sees" or focuses on him. The reader is not told how Jesus arrived, other than that, in John 5:1, Jesus "goes up" to Jerusalem.[3]

13. Someone hears something. Hearing as a focalizer often refers to overhearing something, receiving a report, or learning of news relevant to the action to follow.

Jesus makes some remarks about blindness and sight to the man born blind (John 9:35–39), and then

John 9:40

(1) Some of the Pharisees near him heard this, *f:perc*
(2) and they said to him, . . .

Similarly, in another passage in the Gospel of John, the crowds in Jerusalem are talking about Jesus when

John 7:32

(1) The Pharisees heard the crowd thus muttering about him, *f:perc*
(2) and the chief priests and Pharisees sent officers to arrest him.

Hearing as a sensory perception is much more common as a pre-focalizer than a focalizer. In the account of the paralytic borne by four, for example, a report is heard:

3. Other examples of visual focalizers may be found in Acts 3:9, 3:12; John 6:5, 9:1; Luke 5:12; John 1:29; Mark 10:14; Acts 10:35.

Mark 2:1–3

(1)	[1] And when he returned to Capernaum,	*pre-f:arr*
	after some days,	*tc*
(2)	it was reported that he was at home.	*pre-f:perc*
(3)	[2] And many were gathered together,	*pre-f:arr*
(4)	so that there was no longer room for them, not even about the door;	
(5)	and he was preaching the word to them.	*pre-f:perc*
(6)	[3] And they came, . . .	*f:arr*

Here we have a scene in which Jesus arrives, his arrival is reported so that people begin to gather at his home, he preaches to them, and then four men come bearing a paralytic. The action proper begins with their arrival. Everything up to that point is introduction and thus serves to bring the scene gradually into focus.

14. Someone perceives something. In §5.9 we treated finding in the sense of encountering, coming upon, meeting. Here finding has the sense of perceiving and so is properly a subcategory of focalizers of perception. Of course, finding in either of these senses always borders on the other ("he found his sister in the huge crowd" may mean that he ran into her or it may indicate that he espied her from a distance), so that it is not always easy to make a firm distinction.

In the story of Sapphira (Acts 5:7–11), following an encounter with Peter the woman falls down dead.

Acts 5:10

(1)	When the young men came in	
(2)	they found her dead, . . .	*f:perc*

Finding in this instance means that they perceived that she was dead. That would also appear to be the meaning of this focalizer:

John 11:17

(1)	Now when Jesus came,	
(2)	he found that Lazarus had already been in the tomb four days . . .	*f:perc*

Jesus perceived or learned that Lazarus had died four days previously.

In the account of the cleansing of the temple in John 2, finding may mean perceiving, although it could also be interpreted as encountering, meeting:

John 2:13–14

(1)	[13] The Passover of the Jews was at hand,	
(2)	and Jesus went up to Jerusalem.	*pre-f:arr*
(3)	[14] In the temple he found those who were selling oxen and sheep and pigeons, . . .	*f:perc*

Finding in the sense of perceiving does not appear to be common as a focalizer.

15. Perception precipitators. The perceptions of participants in the narrative discourse may be triggered by a variety of devices. These same devices may function by analogy to focus the senses of the reader or listener. Among the most common of such stratagems is the attention-getter employed in everyday life. One person meets another on the street and one says, "Hello." This is a signal of meeting and perhaps the opening of a conversation. Or, after an inordinate delay, a diner wants service and so addresses a passing aproned official: "Waiter!" Vocatives and interjections of this order may also function similarly in narrative discourse to attract the attention of participants and observers.

The perceptions of participants may be precipitated in more powerful ways by the forces of nature or by unusual visual and aural occurrences. A car crash on the street prompts people up and down the avenue to pause and gawk. The lightning flash or a peel of thunder has a comparable effect. All of these are means by which attention may be focused and the reader's senses brought to bear on the scene being depicted.

16. Unusual visual or aural signals. Perception may be focused by an unusual visual or aural signal. In Acts 2:1ff., it is the day of Pentecost; the apostles are gathered in one place when a sound comes from heaven like the rush of a mighty wind. Tongues of fire come to rest on the heads of the Twelve. They begin to speak in strange tongues. Understandably, these strange phenomena attract the attention of the devout Jews gathered in Jerusalem for the feast.

Acts 2:1–6

(1)	[1] When the day of Pentecost had come,	
(2)	they were all together in one place.	
(3)	[2] And suddenly a sound came from heaven like the rush of a mighty wind,	*f:perc-prec*
(4)	and it filled all the house where they were sitting.	
(5)	[3] And there appeared to them tongues of fire, distributed and resting on each one of them.	*f:perc-prec*
(6)	[4] And they were all filled with the Holy Spirit	
(7)	and began to speak in other tongues, as the Spirit gave them utterance.	*f:perc-prec*
(8)	[5] Now there were dwelling in Jerusalem Jews,	
(9)	devout men from every nation under heaven.	
(9)	[6] And at this sound the multitude came together,	*f:arr*
(10)	and they were bewildered,	
(11)	because each one heard them speaking in his own language.	*f:perc*

In this example, there are both visual and aural perception precipitators, which prompt the multitudes to gather in one place (i.e., become a participant): each one then hears the apostles speak in his or her own tongue. It may thus be said that the narrator makes both sides of the focalizing process explicit: the sights and sounds that prompt participants (and readers) to focus their attention, and the response of the participants ("at this sound the multitude came together," and they heard the apostles speak).

Sight and sound are again combined in the focalization of the account of Paul's conversion on the road to Damascus.

Acts 9:3–4

(1)	[3] Now as he journeyed	*pre-f:arr*
(2)	he approached Damascus,	*pre-f:arr*
(3)	and suddenly a light from heaven flashed about him.	*f:perc-prec*
(4)	[4] And he fell to the ground	
(5)	and heard a voice saying to him, . . .	*f:perc*

Paul responds to the blinding light by falling to the ground. This would have been sufficient as a focalizer for this segment. However, the narrator chooses to add the voice from heaven, which Paul "hears." The narrator employs both sight and sound as prompters; Paul's response to the visual signal is to be inferred from the fact that he fell to the ground, but his response to the voice is made explicit.[4]

17. Vocatives and attention-getters. Vocatives are a common focalizing device, although they are also used frequently in combination with other devices.

Acts 27:21

(1)	As they had been long without food,	
(2)	Paul then came forward among them	*f:arr*
(3)	and said, "Men, . . ."	*f:perc-prec*

This speech follows a severe storm at sea on the voyage from Palestine to Italy.[5]

In the parable of the Ten Maidens, the maidens fall asleep when the bridegroom is delayed.

Matt 25:6

(1)	But at midnight there was a cry,	*f:perc-prec*
(1a)	"Behold, the bridegroom!	
(1b)	Come out to meet him."	

In this instance both the notice of the cry and the cry itself are expressed.

4. For other focalizers of this order the reader may consult Acts 12:7, 16:26, and 10:3 (a vision of an angel).

5. For a similar use of the vocative cf. Acts 17:22 and 3:12 (used in conjunction with another focalizer).

They serve to focus the sleepy attention of the maidens, who now struggle to trim their lamps.

Occasionally, the narrator elects to focalize a segment merely by the use of dialogue. This, of course, is a simple form of the perception precipitator. An example occurs in the story of the stilling of the storm (Mark 4:35–41).

(1) On that day, when evening had come,
(2) he said to them,
"Let us go across to the other side." *f:dia*

Mark 4:35 Jesus then departs, with his disciples, in a boat to cross the sea. Segments focalized merely with dialogue appear to be rare in the New Testament, but are much more common in modern literature.

ACTIONS

18. Types of action statements. A narrative consists of a series of "statements."[6] Narrative statements are of three basic types: those depicting

(1) actions, in which a participant is agent;
(2) happenings, in which a participant is patient;
(3) status statements, in which something or someone is said to exist or is characterized.

The first two types could be grouped under the heading of "do" statements: something is done or happens, as distinguished from "is" statements, in which the identity of someone or something is affirmed or a quality is attributed to that person or object.[7]

19. Action statements are exemplified by the following:

(1) They came to Capernaum
(2) Jesus said, "Let us go hence"
(3) They thought they would receive more
(4) He had compassion on her
(5) They perceived they were uneducated, common men

Statement (1) is a non-verbal physical act performed by an agent; (2) is a verbal physical act which has been given a narrative frame ("Jesus said"). The third statement (3) is a mental act that has not been verbalized (or is so represented), while (4) indicates a feeling or emotion, and (5) belongs to the type that includes perceptions and sensations.

20. From action statements like these are to be distinguished *happenings*:

6. Cf. the sketch in §§1.39–40 and the discussion of definition in §§2.29–30, 39–40.
7. Types of narrative statements were discussed in a preliminary way in §§1.39–40.

(6) The boat sailed out of the harbor
(7) The fever left her
(8) It rained on Tuesday
(9) The window broke

The boat in (6) is not the agent of sailing, strictly speaking; the movement of the boat is not attributable in common parlance to an agent, any more than raining in (8) is attributable to an agent. Both are said to be happenings or agentless events. The lad who reports to his mother, with ball bat in hand, the window broke (9), is giving grammatical expression to a devout wish. Statement (7), the fever left her, also belongs to the category of happenings. Chatman defines a happening as "a predication of which the character or other focused existent is narrative object."[8] The character or object is the affected (patient) rather than the effector (agent).

21. In contrast, status statements assert the existence or identity of something, or they describe.

(10) The man was deaf
(11) It was Tuesday
(12) John the Baptist was a prophet
(13) This is a lonely place

Statement (12) identifies John the Baptist as a prophet, while (10) describes a participant as deaf. In (11) the status of the day of the week is asserted, and the character of a place is depicted in (13).

In analyzing particular texts, narrative statements may be numbered consecutively throughout a narrative or narrative segment for easy reference, e.g. *1a, 2s, 3h, 4s, 5a,* etc., where *a, h, s* refer to the type of narrative statement. Where such distinctions are not essential, the designations *a, h, s* may be omitted (often the case in graphic analyses in this book).

22. The Widow's Son at Nain. The narrative account of the Widow's Son at Nain affords examples of most types of narrative statements. In addition, this narrative segment presents the further opportunity of elaborating the focusing process sketched above in §§5.1–17.

——— • *The Widow's Son at Nain* • ———

Luke 7:11–17

INTRODUCTION

[11] Soon afterward
(1*a*) he went to a city called Nain, *pre-f:arr*[1]
(2*a*) and his disciples and a great crowd went with him.
(3*a*) [12] As he drew near to the gate of the city, behold *pre-f:arr*[2]

8. *Story and Discourse,* 45. Chatman also has an outline of the type of action statements from which the discussion derives.

(4*s*) a man who had died
(5*h*) was being carried out, *pre-f:arr*[1]
(6*s*) the only son of his mother,
(7*s*) and she was a widow;
(8*a*) and a large crowd from the city was with her. *pre-f:arr*[1]

NUCLEUS

(9*a*) [13] And when the Lord saw her, *f:perc*[1]
(10*a*) he had compassion on her
(11*a*) and said to her,
"Do not weep."
(12*a*)[14] And he came
(13*a*) and touched the bier, *f:perc*[2]
(14*a*) and the bearers stood still.
(15*a*) and he said,
"You man, I say to you, arise."
(16*a*)[15] And the dead man sat up,
(17*a*) and began to speak.
(18*a*) And he gave him to his mother.

CONCLUSION

(19*h*)[16] Fear seized them all;
(20*a*) and they glorified God,
(21*a*) saying,
"A great prophet has arisen among us!"
and
"God has visited his people!"
(22*h*)[17] And this report concerning him spread through the whole of Judea and all the surrounding country.

23. Non-verbal physical actions are amply represented in this narrative: (1*a*), (2*a*), (12*a*), etc. Quoted speech is also found in this story: (15*a*). Statement (10*a*) is an expression of emotion, while (9*a*) indicates a perception. The dead man is the patient in (5*h*) as is the crowd in (19*h*). Statements (4*s*), (6*s*), and (7*s*) describe the status of the young man and identify him and his mother. As in folk literature generally, action statements tend to dominate the narrative; folk stories are often weak in description.

24. In this account, Jesus is on his way to a city called Nain (1*a*); he draws near the city (3*a*). As he does so, a dead man is being carried out (4*h*). These three statements are pre-focalizers because they anticipate, lead up to the contact between Jesus and the coffin. It is thus possible to have more than one pre-focalizer arranged in a series.

The first narrative contact occurs, not between Jesus and the dead son, but between Jesus and the mother of the boy (9*a*). The mother had been introduced in (6)–(8). Since the son is dead, he cannot make contact with the miracle worker on his own; his mother does so, as it were, on his behalf, as his representative. Nevertheless, the introductory statements prepare the reader only indirectly for contact between Jesus and the mother. The reader is led to believe that Jesus will immediately encounter the son. The mother is introduced and identified backhandedly: she moves along with the crowd in the funeral procession (8*a*). In statement (9*a*), Jesus "sees" her: the focalizer in (9) goes together with the pre-focalizer in (8): she is moving along with the procession and will come into contact with Jesus.

In narrative statement (12*a*, 13*a*), Jesus finally makes contact with the bier containing the dead man. This constitutes a second focalizer: an arrival. We are probably to interpret (13*a*), "he touched the bier," not as a focalizer, but as the first action in this subscene. The focalizer in (12) follows on the pre-focalizers in (1*a*), (3*a*), and (4*h*). Statements (1*a*) and (3*a*) can be interpreted, in retrospect, as pre-focalizers for contact with the mother in (9*a*). We thus have a complex of focalizers and pre-focalizers involving Jesus, the dead son, and his mother. The relationship of the statements to the three participants may be represented graphically in figure 16. The sequence of contacts is as

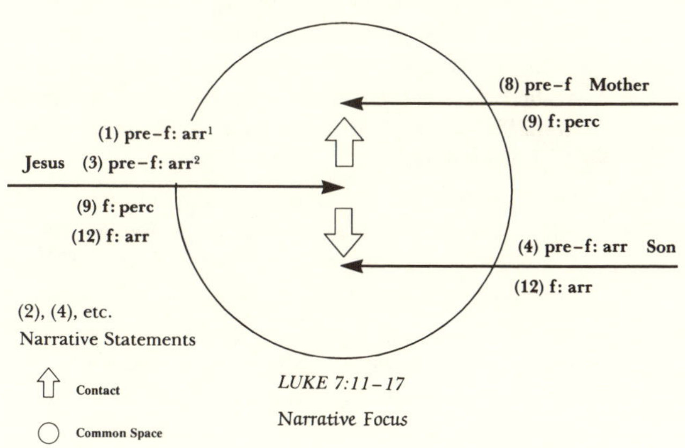

Figure 16

follows: (a) pre-focalizers in statements (1) and (3) anticipate contact with the son, which is delayed; (b) statements (6)–(8) indirectly anticipate contact with the mother; (c) contact is made with the mother in (9); (d) contact is made with the son in (12)–(13).

DEFOCALIZERS

25. Introduction. The defocalizing process was sketched in §1.47 and then treated in some detail in §3.29 in connection with the analysis of the narrative in Acts 3:1–10. It is now our purpose to elaborate the defocalizing process in greater detail.

It is worth noting that defocalizing a narrative or narrative segment involves the same elements as focalizing: participants, locale, time, actions. These elements will, of course, be differently organized, but the ingredients remain the same. The defocalizing process is, in fact, the reverse of the focalizing of a narrative segment: when focalizing, one brings together a specific number of participants in a particular time and place in order to perform a series of actions; when defocalizing, one disperses these same elements, so to speak, so that the focused scene is now defocused. This point will bear expansion subsequently.

26. The outline of the impending discussion is once again provided by the Table of Codes, the relevant portion of which may be reproduced here. The codes are followed by brief commentary.

——— • *The Defocalizing Process* • ———

1. Participants
   - *pe* = participant expansion: the participant set is significantly expanded so that the focus is blurred
   - *pc* = participant contraction: the participant set is contracted or a new participant set is formed, i.e., the narrative is refocused
   - *id:term* = terminal *id*: the identification of a participant is provided at the end of a segment
2. Locale
   - *lchg* = locale change: the scene shifts to a new locale
   - *le* = locale expansion: the locale is expanded so that the spatial focus is blurred
3. Time
   - *tchg* = temporal shift: the scene shifts to a new time
   - *te* = temporal expansion: the time is expanded so that the temporal focus is blurred
   - *termt* = terminal time: the time when things come to an end
4. Actions
   - *dep* = departure: one or more participants exit
   - *dis* = dismissal: one or more persons are dismissed from the scene
   - *termf* = terminal function: a terminal function occurs producing narrative rest
5. Other Devices
   - *pre-def* = pre-defocalizer (e.g., *dis*, followed by *dep*)

ae = action expansion: the action is expanded so that the focus is blurred
afore = action forecast: a future action is anticipated
a:term = the action is terminated
termf = terminal function: a terminal function produces narrative rest
rep = report: a report of what has transpired is dispatched
recap = the scene or scenes are recapped
constop = conversation stopper: the dialogue is brought to a close by a climaxing remark
pershift = perspective shift: there is a significant shift in perspective
com = commentary: the narrator intrudes upon the narrative with commentary

These elements may be illustrated singly and in combination.

27. *A cluster of defocalizers.* The short narrative of Mark 1:35–39, which sums up and defocalizes the first sequences in the Gospel of Mark (1:14–39), offers a variety of defocalizers and will serve to introduce the major categories.

——— • *Jesus Departs* • ———

Mark 1:35–39

INTRODUCTION

(1)	35 And in the morning,	*tc*[1]
	a great while before day,	*ts*[2]
	he rose	*pre-f:dep*
(2)	and went out to a lonely place,	*pre-f:pos*
(3)	and there he began to pray.	*impf:desc*
(4)	36 And Simon and those who were with him followed him,	*pre-f:arr*

NUCLEUS

(5)	37 and they found him	*f:arr*
(6)	and said to him	
(6.1)	"Every one is searching for you."	
(7)	38 And he said to them,	
(7.1)	"Let us go in to the next towns,	*def:dis / le*
(7.2)	that I may preach there also;	*def:ae / afore*
(7.3)	for that is why I came out."	

CONCLUSION

(8)	39 And he went throughout all Galilee,	*lchg / le*
(9)	preaching in their synagogues	*def:ae*
(10)	and casting out demons.	*def:ae*

In this concluding segment, Jesus has withdrawn to pray, (2)–(3); the disciples find him and report that everyone is looking for him, (5)–(6). To this report Jesus responds:

(7.1)	Let us go on to the next towns,	*def:dis / le*
(7.2)	that I may preach there also;	*def:ae / afore*
(7.3)	for that is why I came out.	

In saying "let us go on," Jesus is "dismissing" himself and the disciples from the scene. A dismissal (*dis*) often precedes an actual departure (*dep*), although upon occasion it functions alone as a defocalizer. More frequently, a departure stands alone as a defocalizer. Dismissal/departure are logically linked, the first being the verbal anticipation of the act itself. In any case, the dismissal or departure of principal characters shatters the focus that has just obtained.

Statement (7.1) also contains a locale expander: reference is made to the next towns (plural), in contrast to the setting of the present scene in a lonely place, and in contrast to the towns enumerated in 1:14–34. A locale expander of course blurs the focus on a particular place. We thus have two defocalizing devices in the same narrative statement.

Narrative statement (7.2) contains an action expander (*ae*) and an action forecast (*af*). Jesus has been (preaching and) praying; he will continue his preaching activities in the next towns. This is a statement of repeated activity and is non-specific; it is also a forecast of future activity, which is another way of dissipating the focus of the current scene.

The verbal defocalizers in 1:38 are followed with action statements in 1:39. Jesus goes throughout Galilee (8), which enlarges upon "the next towns" in (7.1). He thus changes locale (*lchg*) and the area is too large to focalize (except, perhaps, from a high-flying aircraft or space vehicle); it is consequently also a locale expander (*le*). Furthermore, as he goes through the towns of Galilee (combining (7.1) and (8)), he preaches (9) and casts out demons (10). His activity is again represented as repetitive (*ae*, doubled). Reference to repeated or customary actions is, of course, a defocalizing technique.

This narrative segment is strong in defocalizers because it serves to defocalize the first Markan sequence, as remarked earlier. Nevertheless, vss 38–39, especially vs 39, also defocalizes the brief scene of which it is a part. That leads to the observation that a set of defocalizers may defocalize both a segment and a sequence (of segments).

This brief examination of defocalizers in Mark 1:35–39 will serve as an introduction to the categories listed in the Table of Codes. Each category is now to be presented and illustrated. Subsequently, additional texts with clusters of defocalizers will be analyzed.

28. Participants. One technique for blurring a scene is to expand the number of participants significantly (code: *pe* = participant expansion). Jesus has just cleansed the leper in Mark 1:40–45// Matt 8:1–4//Luke 5:12–16).

Jesus then dismisses him; the leper spreads the word of what has happened. The segment concludes:

Mark 1:45
(1) and people came to him from every quarter *pe*

Matthew does not make use of this particular defocalizing device in the parallel segment, but Luke does:

Luke 5:15
(1) and great multitudes gathered to hear *pe*
(2) and be healed of their infirmities *ae*

When the Greeks in Antioch began to receive the word, Barnabas was sent to Antioch. He went to Tarsus and brought Paul back to Antioch with him. The short narrative segment Acts 11:19–26 is then defocalized as follows:

(1) 26 For a whole year they met with the church, *te*
(2) and taught a large company of people; *pe*
(3) and in Antioch the disciples were for the first time called Christians. *id:term*

In the first statement (1) the time is extended to a year: it is impossible to focus on a series of meetings taking place over twelve months, hence the defocalizing of the scene. Then, in (2), they teach a large company of people: the participant set is significantly expanded so that focus is lost. And finally, (3) provides a terminal *id* (*id:term*) for the disciples at Antioch. All of these are devices employed to round off a narrative and bring it to a state of rest.

29. Narrative segments may also be defocalized by contracting the participant set (*pc*), by making it smaller rather than larger. While not as common a technique in the New Testament as expansion, this device nevertheless functions well for this simple reason: any change in participant set marks the end (or beginning) of a narrative segment. In the account of the healing of the epileptic boy (Matt 17:14–20//Mark 9:14–29), the nucleus of the segment is brought to a close by the departure of the demon and the cure of the boy (Mark 9:16–27), both defocalizers. There follows a further defocalizing conclusion:

Matt 17:19
(1) Then the disciples came to Jesus privately *pc*
(2) and said,
(2.1) "Why could we not cast it out?"

The Markan version is quite similar:

Mark 9:28
(1) And when he had entered the house, *lchg*
(2) his disciples asked him privately, *pc*
(2.1) "Why could we not cast it out?"

In both instances, the father of the boy, the boy, and the crowd disappear from the scene and the disciples are alone with Jesus. This is a clear case of participant contraction. Of course, most departures are also instances of participant contraction, since one or more participants quit the scene. In the story of the epileptic boy, the conclusion (Matt 17:19–20//Mark 9:28–29), while forming a subscene, is tightly connected to the nucleus of the narrative segment, and serves as its CON.

30. Scene iii of the account of the lame man (Acts 4:7–22 of 3:1–4:31) is defocalized by a series of devices, listed and discussed in §4.31. Among them is a terminal identification (*id:term*):

(1) For the man on whom this healing was performed was more than forty years old *id:term*

This notice identifies the lame man as a reliable witness; he is dismissed from the narrative with this statement. It functions as the clincher to the argument Peter and John have been making: all men, including the lame man now healed, are praising God (not men) for what had happened. In a similar fashion, the account of Barnabas and Paul at Antioch (Acts 11:19–26) closes with an *id:term* (see §5.28 above). In this case, however, the *id* is not provided to substantiate the credentials of a witness, but to establish a newly emerging participant in the narrative—a group called Christians (apparently identical with disciples and the church).

31. A still different form of terminal *id* is found in John 21:24:

(1) this is the disciple who is bearing witness to these things,
(2) and who has written these things;
(3) and we know that his testimony is true. *id:term*

This statement is close to Acts 4:22 (a reliable witness), but it also identifies the author of the book just concluded, much as a testator signs a will at its conclusion. A will normally opens with an *id* of the person making the will, just as *ids* are customarily located in the introductions to narratives and narrative segments. But a signature to a document is a *id:term*, just as an epitaph or obituary is an *id:term*.

32. Locales. The treatment of locales in the defocalizing process is a relatively simple matter. A locale change (*lchg*) is either stated or implied with every departure (*dep*) and is a clear signal of segment end. For example,

Acts 12:17
(1) Then he departed and went to another place *dep / lchg*

concludes a subscene in the story of Peter's release from prison (Acts 12:1–19), just as

Acts 12:19

(1)	Then he went down from Judea to Caesarea,	*dep / lchg*
(2)	and remained there	*te*

concludes the larger narrative sequence.

33. The extension of the space in which a scene is set is another device for defocalizing a narrative. At Iconium (Acts 14:1–7), Paul and Barnabas are threatened by both Gentile and Jews, with the result that:

Acts 14:6–7

(1)	[6] they learned of it	*rep*
(2)	and fled to Lystra and Derbe,	*lchg*
	cities of Lycaonia,	*le*
	and to the surrounding country;	*le*
(3)	[7] and there they preached the gospel.	*ae*

They receive a report, first of all, of the impending threat,[9] and then they fled to Lystra and Derbe (*lchg*), and to the surrounding country (*le*). In other words, the single locale Iconium is exchanged for multiple places and the segment loses focus.

With this may be compared the example in Mark 1:39,

(1)	And he went throughout all Galilee,	*le*
(2)	preaching in their synagogues	*ae*
(3)	and casting out demons	*ae*

where the lonely place in which Jesus was praying (Mark 1:35) is expanded to include all of Galilee.

34. Times. Temporal changes are normally indicated in the introduction to a narrative segment in folk literature. However, there is a temporal notice typical of narrative conclusion. It may be called the terminal time (*termt*). A good example is found in Matt 26:45–46 (//Mark 14:41–42). At the conclusion of Jesus' prayers in Gethsemane, he says to the drowsy disciples:

(1)	[45] Behold, the hour is at hand,	*termt*
(2)	and the Son of man is betrayed into the hands of sinners.	*termf*
(3)	[46] Rise, let us be going;	*dis*
(4)	see, my betrayer is at hand.	*arr*

The hour in this context announces an end in the larger sense, but it also announces the end of a narrative segment. It is reinforced by a terminal

9. A report may be used both to focalize and to defocalize a narrative segment. Cf. the report as focalizer in §5.13.

function,[10] by a dismissal, and by the rare use of an arrival as a defocalizer.[11]

Other examples of a terminal time as defocalizer may be noted. John 13:30 is also connected with Judas:

(1)	So, after receiving the morsel,	
(2)	he immediately went out;	*dep*
(3)	and it was night.	*termt*

The terminal time is probably night in both its literal and its figurative senses.

An example with fewer ominous overtones is found in Acts 4:3. Peter and John have been preaching in the temple; the authorities come upon them while they are doing so and are considerably annoyed.

Acts 4:3

(1)	And they arrested them	*termf*
(2)	and put them in custody until the morrow,	*termf*
(3)	for it was already evening.	*termt*

Nothing could be done with them at the time, since it was already evening and courts and offices were closed for the day. A terminal time of this order often announces a nocturnal pause.

35. As in the case of space or locale, the extension of the temporal frame customarily has a defocalizing effect. At the conclusion of the account of Peter raising Tabitha (Acts 9:36–43), the narrator announces:

Acts 9:43

(1)	And he stayed in Joppa for many days with Simon, a tanner	*te*

The prolongation of the temporal duration defocalizes the scene with Tabitha. Other examples are quite comparable:

Acts 10:48

(1)	Then they asked him to remain for some days	*te*

Acts 12:19

(1)	Then he went down to Caesarea	*lchg*
(2)	and remained there	*te*

And the Book of Acts as a whole is defocalized by temporal expansion, in concert with other devices:

Acts 28:30–31

(1)	30 And he lived there two whole years at his own expense,	*te*

10. See §§5.40–48 for the development of this category.

11. The arrival of the betrayer betokens the end of the garden scene as well as the death of Jesus.

(2)	and welcomed all who came to him,	*pe*
(3)	[31] preaching the kingdom of God	*ae*
(4)	and teaching about the Lord Jesus Christ	*ae*
	quite openly and unhindered.	*ae*

The time is expanded to two more years and the participants are increased indefinitely, as are the activities of Paul. And so the story of Acts comes to narrative rest.

36. Actions. Many scenes are defocalized by the departure of one or more participants. It is a natural reversal of the focalizing process: a narrative segment opens by assembling participants, it closes by dispersing them. In the very brief scene, Mark 8:11–13,

(1)	[11] The Pharisees came	*f:arr*
(2)	and began to argue with him.	

Following a brief exchange,

(3)	[13] And he left them,	*dep*
(4)	and getting into a boat again	
(5)	he departed to the other side.	*dep*

After Jesus spies Peter and Andrew by the lake, he calls them.

Matt 4:20

(1)	Immediately they left their nets	
(2)	and followed him.	*dep*

When Jesus heals the man with leprosy, great crowds gather around him.

Luke 5:16

(1)	But he withdrew to the wilderness	*dep*
(2)	and prayed.	*termf*

Examples of simple departures used to defocalize a segment could readily be multiplied many times over.

Occasionally the departure is of a special sort:

Mark 1:31

(1)	and the fever left her;	*dep*

Or is very dramatic:

Acts 9:25

(1)	but his disciples took him by night	*termt*
(2)	and let him down over the wall,	*dep*
(3)	lowering him in a basket.	

37. A dismissal is a verbal departure. The teacher says, "Class dismissed." The students then effect the departure by leaving the room. This illustration suggests that a dismissal is often followed by an actual departure (the statement of an actual departure), but it may also stand alone as the defocalizer of a segment. The parable of the Laborers in the Vineyard (Matt 20:1–16) offers examples of both. At the conclusion of the first subscene, the narrator tells us:

(1)	he sent them into his vineyard.	*dis*

without mention of their actual departure. But the narrator treats the second subscene as follows:

Matt 20:4

(2)	and to them he said,	
(2.1)	"You go into the vineyard too,	*dis*
(2.2)	and whatever is right I will give you."	
(2.3)	So they went.	*dep*

Here a dismissal is followed by a departure.

A dismissal may take the form of sending:

Acts 10:8

(1)	and having related everything to them,	*recap*
(2)	he sent them to Joppa	*dis*

The dismissal may also include the speaker:

Mark 1:38

(1)	Let us go on to the next towns, . . .	*dis*

Finally, an invitation to come in as guests may function as a defocalizing function (a dismissal in reverse, so to speak):

Acts 10:23

(1)	So he called them in to be his guests	*dis*

38. Departures and dismissals are actions that defocalize a narrative segment. Thus, in a narrative framework, they are special kinds of actions, actions with a formal function, viz., to mark the end of a scene or subscene, although such actions may also contribute materially to the plot. Another kind of action belonging to this formal category is the action expander (*ae*). The affinity of this defocalizer to *te* (temporal expansion), *pe* (participant expansion), and *le* (locale extender) is evident: they all blur the focus by enlarging or multiplying elements in the setting; they have the effect of defocusing the lens while viewing a scene through a single-lens reflex camera.

At the conclusion of the sequence analyzed in chapter 4 (Acts 3:1–4:31), the text reads:

Acts 4:31

(1)	And when they had prayed,	*a:term*
(2)	the place in which they were gathered was shaken;	*termf*

(3) and they were all filled with the Holy Spirit *pe*
(4) and spoke the word of God with boldness. *ae*

Narrative statement (4) represents a generalized action: they spoke the word with boldness on several or many occasions after that, in accordance with the tenor of the narrative (see especially Acts 4:13, 19–20). The action of Peter and John in this sequence is singulative (they are represented as speaking boldly on a single occasion); the action of the company, on the other hand, is iterative (occuring an indefinite number of times).[12] The iterative action is one form of the defocalizer *ae*.

Other examples of iterative *ae* are:

Acts 5:42
(1) And every day in the temple and at home *te / le*
they did not cease teaching and preaching *ae*
Jesus as the Christ.

In this example, *te* and *le* reenforce the iterative character of the action. At the conclusion of the Book of Acts, Paul is represented as carrying on certain activities for two years:

Acts 28:30–31
(1) [30] and welcomed all who came to him, *ae*
(2) [31] preaching the kingdom of God *ae*
(3) and teaching about the Lord Jesus Christ quite openly and unhindered. *ae*

And, as a defocalizer to the first sequence in Mark, Jesus' activity is depicted as repetitive:

Mark 1:39
(1) And he went throughout all Galilee, *dep / ae / le*
(2) preaching in their synagogues *ae / le*
(3) and casting out demons. *ae*

Once again, a departure (*dep*) and locale expanders (*le*) are joined to *ae*.

39. The continuous action, as distinct from the repeated or iterative action, may also serve as a defocalizer. In the parable of the Good Samaritan (Luke 10:29–37), the Samaritan performs a series of singulative actions (or actions viewed as singulative) and then, to conclude the subscene the narrator says, he "took care of him," which can be construed as an extended, unbroken process.

Luke 10:34
(1) [he] went to him 1*a*

12. See chapter 6 *passim* for a discussion of singulative and iterative action in relation to showing and telling.

(2)	and bound up his wounds,	2*a*
(3)	pouring on oil and wine;	3*a*
(4)	then he set him on his own beast	4*a*
(5)	and brought him to an inn,	5*a*
(6)	and took care of him.	*ae*

The code *a* stands, of course, for action. The last action in the series extends the first five indefinitely: he did other things that night in looking after the victim. It thus defocalizes the scene.

Like the action of the Samaritan, prayer may be understood as an *ae* of the continuous type.

Luke 5:16

(1)	But he withdrew to the wilderness	*dep*
(2)	and prayed.	*ae*

Prayer is here conceived as a continuous activity in which Jesus was engaged following his withdrawal from the crowds.

TERMINAL FUNCTIONS AS DEFOCALIZERS

40. *Definition.* "Morphologically," Propp writes, "a tale may be termed any development proceeding from villainy or a lack, through intermediate functions to marriage, or to other functions employed as a dénouement."[13] It is with "other functions employed as a dénouement" that we are now concerned. Such functions may be designated *terminal.*

Thus far consideration has been given the several formal techniques for closing narrative segments, such as dismissal/departure, participant expansion, action expansion, and the like. These techniques are limited in number and can be described in abstract terms. There is another large category of actions that function to end a narrative or narrative segment; this category may be called terminal functions. The classical example is the fairy story that ends:

(1)	The prince married the princess	*termf*
(2)	and they lived happily ever after.	*ae / te*

In the context of the fairy tale, marriage is a terminal function.[14] In the Russian fairy tale, the overcoming of a lack or deficiency is a terminal function, corresponding to the occasion of a lack in the initial situation. In other words, the terminal function brings the narrative full circle or back to a state of equilibrium. A dénouement will often involve a restoration, accompanied by rejoicing or celebration, or a return of the hero (heroine). It

13. *Morphology*, 92.
14. Note Propp's function XXXI: marriage (*Morphology*, 63f.).

is easy to imagine a story which ends, "father returned home and we all rejoiced." Accordingly, terminal functions are actions that climax a story or serve to round it off: their function is determined by their position in the sequence of events. However, there are actions that serve generally as the termination of stories. It is possible, accordingly, to develop a general list of terminal functions; it is also quite possible to draw up a list on the basis of a specific corpus of narrative texts as Propp did for the Russian fairy tale. In this analysis we will employ Propp's technique but substitute New Testament narratives for Propp's collection of fairy tales. However, the list to follow is illustrative rather than exhaustive.

41. Death. Death is a universal terminal function. When the protagonist dies, the narrative ends absolutely. But death may also serve to defocalize intermediate scenes.[15]

In the account of Ananias and Sapphira (Acts 5:1–11), Ananias is confronted with his deception and shortage. The scene is brought to a close as follows:

Acts 5:5–6

(1)	5 When Ananias heard these words,	
(2)	he fell down and died.	*termf*
(3)	And fear came upon all who heard of it.	*termf*
(4)	6 The young men rose	*pre-def*
(5)	and wrapped him up	*pre-def*
(6)	and carried him out	*dep*
(7)	and buried him.	*termf*

Six narrative statements are utilized in closing this brief narrative; those statements are also, of course, part of the thematic action of the segment, which is the reason they are so extensive. Their magnitude alone indicates the gravity of the conclusion in relation to the nucleus of the scene. The death of Ananias is clearly a terminal function (statements (2) and (7)). The fear that comes upon all who hear of the event is also a terminal emotion (like rejoicing or living happily; one could also say that fear paralyzes), presumably with some durative effect. These terminal functions are reinforced by the departure and preparations for it in statements (4)–(6). The same set of defocalizers is employed in the account of Sapphira which follows (Acts 5:7–11).

42. Fear, awe, and praise of God. The list of terminal functions may be readily extended by referring to other narrative segments. Jesus heals the paralytic, and

15. Naturally, it is easy to imagine narrative situations in which death (or departure) also initiates a narrative. The taxonomy in this instance and in others to be introduced subsequently should not be taken absolutely. The function as terminal depends on the position of the action in relation to the sequence of events.

Matt 9:8

(1)	When the crowds saw it	
(2)	they were afraid	*termf*
(3)	and they glorified God, . . .	*termf*

In the Markan version,

Mark 2:12

(1)	. . . they were all amazed	*termf*
(2)	and glorified God, . . .	*termf*

In Luke (5:26), they also glorify God, but they are filled with awe instead of amazement or fear. In Acts 3:10, the people are filled with wonder and amazement at the cure of the lame man. Accordingly, there is a constellation of terms employed in healing miracle stories to express the reaction of the witnesses to the event; these terms are all *terminal functions.*

43. Conversion and faith. As may be expected, conversion in the New Testament is a terminal function. In response to the cure of Aeneas (Acts 9:32–35),

Acts 9:35

(1)	And all the residents of Lydda and Sharon saw him,	
(2)	and they turned to the Lord.	*termf*

Likewise, in the story of Tabitha which follows (Acts 9:36–43),

Acts 9:42

(1)	. . . Many believed in the Lord	*termf*

in response to her resurrection. Sometimes faith is correlative with another *termf*, as in the account of the proconsul at Paphos (Acts 13:4–12):

Acts 13:12

(1)	Then the proconsul believed,	*termf*
(2)	when he saw what had occurred,	
(3)	for he was astonished at the teaching of the Lord.	*termf*

44. Prayer and fasting. Another group of terminal functions is found in Acts 13:3:

(1)	Then after fasting and praying	*termf* / *termf*
(2)	they laid their hands on them	*termf*
(3)	and sent them off.	*dis*

Fasting, praying, and the laying on of hands have lasting effects (i.e., they are *ae* in many contexts), but they also bring one phase of the story to a close and thus begin a second phase. In a narrative, all defocalizers, save the last, serve to end one narrative segment so that another may begin.

The terminal functions gathered thus far from a limited corpus of texts include:

death
burial
fear
glorifying God
astonishment
amazement
awe
belief or faith
fasting
praying
laying on of hands

This list could be extended considerably, owing to the wide variety of action sequences possible. With respect to quantity, terminal functions are comparable to major vocabulary in sentence grammar: the list of subjects, verbs, and objects in a sentence with a transitive verb is extremely large. The list of terminal functions could also reach considerable proportions. Terminal functions of this order may also appear in other narrative grammar slots, e.g., as focalizers. The defocalizers examined earlier, on the other hand, are more akin to function words like "a, the, this, that, some, many, etc." in sentence grammar: the number is very limited and the list of them can readily be exhausted.

45. Reports. Particular defocalizers may be associated with specific types of stories. A special kind of terminal function—the report or dissemination of news (*rep*)—appears to occur predominantly in miracle stories. Jesus performs a healing miracle, for example, and the news of the cure is spread throughout the region. The cure of the leper (Mark 1:40–45) ends with these statements:

Mark 1:45

(1)	But he went out	*dep*
(2)	and began to talk freely about it,	*rep*
(3)	and to spread the news,	*rep*
(4)	so that Jesus could no longer openly enter a town,	
(5)	but was out in the country;	*lchg*
(6)	and people came to him from every quarter.	*pe*

In the following examples, a locale expansion is joined in each instance to a report:

Mark 1:28

(1)	And at once his fame spread everywhere	*rep*
	throughout all the surrounding region of Galilee	*le*

Luke 4:37

(1)	And reports of him went out into every place	*rep*
	in the surrounding region	*le*

Luke 5:15
(1) But so much more the report went abroad concerning him *rep / le*

Acts 9:42
(1) And it became known throughout all Joppa *rep / le* Acts 9:42

46. Conversation stoppers. Another example of a defocalizer linked to a particular kind of story is what may be termed a conversation stopper (*constop*). Frequently in dialogues the last word is assigned to the hero—Jesus or apostle or sage. The final word is designed to climax and close the exchange. In some narratives this function is made explicit. Jesus asks which of his dialogue partners will not pull an ox out of a well into which it has stumbled even though it is the sabbath. The narrator concludes:

Luke 14:6
(1) And they could not reply to this *constop*

Peter's explanation to the apostles and brethren in Judea of the conversion of Cornelius is defocalized with this statement:

Acts 11:18
(1) When they heard this they were silenced *constop*

The *constop* in this instance is followed by another terminal function (they glorified God). But the function need not be made explicit. In the dialogue found in Matt 12:1–8//Mark 2:23–28//Luke 6:1–5, the *constop* is the climactic aphorism:

Mark 2:27–28
(1) [27] The sabbath was made for man,
(2) not man for the sabbath;
(3) [28] so the Son of man is lord even of the sabbath. *constop*

This saying presumably puts an end to the conversation.

47. Commentary and recapitulation. A final group of defocalizers concerns the narrator. Occasionally, a narrator will take a backward look and in so doing breaks out of the narrative mode as such. At the conclusion of Hansel and Gretel, for example, the narrator addresses the reader directly:

(1) My tale's done.
(2) There runs a mouse;
(3) whoever catches it
(4) may make a big cap out of its fur. *com*

The spell of the fiction is broken and the reader is returned to the everyday world. The conclusion to the Gospel of John is quite comparable:

John 20:30–31

(1) [30] Now Jesus did many other signs in the presence of the disciples,
(2) which are not written in this book;
(3) [31] but these are written that you may believe . . . *com*

The narrator again drops the pretense of the fiction and addresses his readers directly in commenting on his book and its purpose. This description suggests the term *commentary* (*com*).

Commentary is also found along the way in narratives. When it occurs, it often has a defocalizing function, as in

John 5:18

(1) This is why the Jews sought all the more to kill him,
(2) because he not only broke the sabbath
(3) but also called God his Father,
(4) making himself equal to God. *com*

This comment of the narrator concludes the story of the lame man at the pool of Bethzatha. It is designed to make sure the reader does not miss a point already made obvious.

Other comments serve as aids to the reader. For example, the remark

John 4:54

(1) This was now the second sign that Jesus did
(2) when he had come from Judea to Galilee *com*

helps the reader keep count of the signs and recalls the first sign. And again, the narrator breaks out of the discourse mode by making the reader conscious that a story is being told.

48. Closely related to the commentary is the recapitulation. Although the *recap* may remain within the discourse mode, it nevertheless often functions to defocalize a narrative segment. One example is found at Acts 10:8. Acts 10:1–6 is an account of Cornelius' vision of an angel. Then, in 10:7, he summons two of his servants and a devout soldier,

Acts 10:8

(1) and having related everything to them, *recap*
(2) he sent them to Joppa. *dis*

The defocalizing function of the *recap* is supported here by a dismissal.

That a *recap* was given is simply stated in the text of Acts; the recapitulation itself is not provided. To recapitulate too much or too frequently would make a narrative boring. Nevertheless, there are occasions when an actual recapitulation makes good narrative sense. In these cases it may also have a defocalizing function. An excellent example is found in the parable of the Prodigal Son.

At the conclusion of the first section of the parable, the father gives instructions for the celebration. He concludes his remarks by saying,

Luke 10:23–24

(1)	[23] ". . . and let us eat	
(2)	and be merry;	*termf*
(3)	[24] for this my son was dead,	
(4)	and is alive again,	
(5)	was lost,	
(6)	and is found."	*recap*
(7)	And they began to make merry.	*termf*

That conclusion is repeated at the close of the second scene:

Luke 15:32

(1)	It was fitting to make merry	
(2)	and be glad,	*termf*
(3)	for this your brother was dead,	
(4)	and is alive;	
(5)	he was lost,	
(6)	and is found.	*recap*

The "my son" of scene i has become "your brother" in scene ii. The *recap* with subtle changes provides unmistakable emphasis; it also brings the parable to a ringing conclusion.

6

Showing and Telling

•6•

SHOWING AND TELLING

1. It has been assumed, up to this point, that there is only one type of narrative segment, the type that has been termed the focused "scene." It is now necessary to make allowances for a second major type of segment, the unfocused segment, in which the narrator "reports" what has transpired without permitting the reader to witness events directly or immediately. Eventually it will be necessary to consider a third type of segment, one which consists primarily of description. Meanwhile, the distinction between the focused and the unfocused segment must be given careful scrutiny.

The unfocused segment takes two forms: in one form, the events reported are singular (they happen once); in a second form, the events reported are iterative (they happen more than once or repeatedly). The first form may be termed *recounting in the singulative mode*;[1] the second we shall call *recounting in the iterative mode*. The latter often takes the form of a narrative summary.[2] In both cases, the narrator intervenes overtly between events reported and the reader, and thus openly "mediates" the story.

2. The focused scene described heretofore may be characterized as a scene in which events are *enacted*, much as they are in the performance of a stage drama. In contrast to the enacted scene, events in the unfocused or mediated narrative segment are said to be *recounted*. Enactment and recounting, consequently, are the terms used to indicate the two contrasting types of narrative discourse. In the tradition of Henry James and his disciple, Percy Lubbock, these two types of narrative representation were dubbed *showing* and *telling*, respectively. The classical terms for the two types are *mimesis* and *diegesis*. Because the unfocused segment was often a summary of events in the iterative mode, it was often referred to as a summary, in contrast to the focused scene. In tabular form, the pairs of contrasting terms are:

focused scene	unfocused segment
showing	telling
mimesis	diegesis
scene	summary
enactment	recounting

1. I am adopting the term singulative from Genette, who proposes it as a neologism simply because this ordinary, normative type of narration—what happens once is narrated once—has not been given a name. He occasionally uses the adjective "singular" in the same technical sense. He discusses the matter in *Narrative Discourse*, 113f.

2. The unfocused mode is discussed at length below, §§6.6–10.

We shall return subsequently to the theoretical issues involved in this distinction. Meanwhile, it is necessary to define the focused scene more precisely in order to be able to distinguish the recounted segment from it.

SHOWING: THE FOCUSED SCENE

3. In the focused scene, the narrator transports the listener or reader, by means of words, to a specific time and place, with participants present, and allows her or him to look on and listen in. Actions and things are presented with sufficient "objectivity" to allow the reader to witness them directly; there is a minimum of narrator intervention. The narrator achieves this effect by bringing the scene into focus and by invoking the reader's senses directly. The words of the text re-present the actions in such a way as to give the illusion that they are recurring before the reader's eyes and ears. Of course, the other senses are also involved. However, narrators less frequently invoke the senses of touch, taste, and smell, and so it is merely parsimonious to refer predominantly to the two senses that are customarily invoked, viz., sight and hearing. Because the senses are directly involved, particularly sight and hearing, it is appropriate, rather than scientifically accurate, to say that things and actions are shown rather than told, that they are enacted rather than recounted.

4. The healing of the lame man in Acts 3:1–10 is shown or enacted: the reader is permitted to see and hear what transpires.[3] The reader is made to observe the positioning of the lame man at the gate of the temple and the approach of Peter and John, and to listen in on the verbal exchange between the two. Peter then takes the lame man by the right hand and lifts him up. The lame man, now cured, leaps up, walks around, enters the temple, and praises God, all visual confirmations of his cure: his healing is shown or enacted.

It is to be noted, however, that in the midst of a scene otherwise enacted, the narrator inserts a statement in the recounting mode: (14) "and immediately his feet and ankles were made strong." This narrative statement reports an interior state, not visible to the human eye: the state is therefore not shown but told. The telling would have been unnecessary, since the crowd, which is intended to represent the perspective of the reader, is perfectly capable of inferring from the man's actions that he has been healed. A statement in the recounting mode is inserted to indicate, perhaps, that the healing is the theme of this segment.[4] Nevertheless, in this segment, as in most segments, there is a mixture of showing and telling, of mimesis and diegesis.

3. The detailed analysis of this scene was summarized in §3.30.
4. This point was discussed earlier, §3.22.

Narrative segments in folk literature of the type we find in the New Testament are often of a mixed type. They may be predominantly one type or the other, but they are rarely purely mimetic: it is easier for the narrator to betray his or her presence than it is to disguise that presence entirely.[5]

5. Some generalizations are now in order regarding the characteristic features of showing or enactment of the focused scene.

The first feature is that enacted scenes must be focused: the time, place, and participants must be definite and particular. Actions must also be particular and thus singulative. For a scene to be focused means that the reader's senses are being invoked directly: he or she is permitted to see, hear, and upon occasion taste, touch, feel, what transpires, as nearly as words will create that illusion. As a consequence, enacted scenes are more dramatic and vivid than recounted segments; they are the verbal approximation of the scene in the stage drama. Furthermore, like the stage play, enacted scenes will be marked by direct discourse, that is, by directly quoted speech, as though the reader were listening in on the conversation, rather than by indirect discourse or indirectly reported speech.

The narrator's role in mimetic scenes is reduced to that of the camera.[6] Where the narrator sustains what appears to be a purely passive role in conveying the content of the scene, the narrative text seems to be "unnarrated," to use Chatman's term.[7] For a narrative to be "unnarrated," the narrator's presence to the narrating process must be reduced as close to zero as possible. For this reason, Rimmon-Kenan's figure is a good one: the narrator functions merely as a recording camera. As a consequence, in narrative statements, the narrator cannot provide information that is not accessible to the impartial eye of the camera. Statements concerning states of mind, indeed concerning interior states of any kind, are not permitted; such states must be shown rather than told. For the narrator to say, "and immediately his feet and ankles were made strong," is to report a state of affairs for which the evidence is known to the narrator but not sensibly presented to the reader. At this point in the Acts narrative, the reader is still dependent on the narrator for this bit of information. When, however, the lame man is depicted as walking about and jumping up and down, his cure is being shown. The reader is given the evidence upon which to base the conclusion that he has been cured; a statement to that effect is not required.

These, then, are the earmarks of narrative in the showing or mimetic mode.

5. The presence of the narrator to the narrative is discussed further below, §§6.5, 12.

6. For this characterization and the preceding remarks, cf. Rimmon-Kenan, *Narrative Fiction*, 108.

7. *Story and Discourse*, 33f.

TELLING: THE UNFOCUSED SCENE

6. Within the narrative sequence Acts 3:1–4:31, scene iib, Acts 4:1–4 functions as the CON to scene iib, although it constitutes a separate scene in its own right.[8] The text is reproduced here for convenience of reference.

(29) [1] And as they were speaking to the people,
(30) the priests and the captain of the temple and the Sadducees came upon them, [2]annoyed
(31) because they were teaching the people
(32) and proclaiming in Jesus the resurrection from the dead.
(33) [3] And they arrested them
(34) and put them in custody until the morrow,
(35) for it was already evening.
(36) [4] But many of those who heard the word believed;
(37) and the number of the men came to about five thousand.

The scene is recounted. The narrator reports that "the priests and the captain of the temple and the Sadducees came upon them" (Acts 4:1)—as though the segment were about to be focused by means of an arrival—but did so because they were "annoyed" (an interior state, obviously) because Peter and John were teaching the people and proclaiming the resurrection (Acts 4:2). Their "annoyance" is told, not shown, and we have to take the narrator's word for it that their objections are as stated. That Peter and John were teaching the people is evident from the preceding scene, although the reader would not necessarily know that this would annoy the authorities. But the speech just reported gives virtually no warrant for the conclusion that the apostles were proclaiming the resurrection of the dead: for that the reader is entirely dependent on the narrator.

7. The reader is next told that the authorities "arrested them and put them in custody until the morrow." These events are told, not shown: presumably the authorities had to move Peter and John to another location to put them in custody, so that the preceding scene loses its spatial focus; and they are detained overnight, with the result that the temporal focus is also dissipating. And, suddenly, it is "already evening" (Acts 4:3): the narrator announces a terminus of the preceding temporal stretch. Nothing in this segment is shown. However, the events that are reported are singulative up to this point. With Acts 4:4, however, the narrator passes to the iterative:[9]

(36) [4] But many of those who heard the word believed;
(37) and the number of the men came to about five thousand.

8. The evidence for these claims in presented in detail in §§4.25–26.

9. Genette also employs iterative as a technical term meaning the narration in a single statement of events occurring more than once. Events so narrated are taken together, synthetically; for example: "Many of those who heard the word believed." See above §6.1 and Genette, *Narrative Discourse*, 116 and n. 6.

"Many believed" is iterative: it happened more than once; and the number of participants has been expanded beyond specificity (5,000). Both of these are marks of the defocalizing process. Accordingly, Acts 4:1–3 is a recounted segment, part of which is in the singulative mode, and part of which is in the iterative mode. Expressed as a hierarchy of narrative segments and subsegments, the first part of the segment in the singulative is the CON to the previous scene, while the narrative summary in the iterative is the CON to the CON.

It is to be expected, of course, that recounting will be characteristic of narrative conclusions, where defocusing is underway, and of introductions to narrative segments, where focusing is in process, since recounting is by definition unfocused. To generalize: the INTRO and the CON of narrative segments will regularly be in the recounting mode; only the NUC is open to the possibility of enactment. But recounting is also to be found in the nuclei of narrative segments.

TELLING: THE NARRATIVE SUMMARY

8. The scenes with Ananias and Sapphira in Acts 5:1–6, 7–11 are enacted. First Ananias meets his fate, and then his wife follows three hours later. And then, in Acts 5:12ff., the narrator shifts into the recounting mode and produces a narrative summary:

(1) 12 Now many signs and wonders were done among the people by the hands of the apostles.
(2) And they were all together in Solomon's Portico.
(3) 13 None of the rest dared join them,
(4) but the people held them in high honor.
(5) 14 And more than ever believers were added to the Lord, multitudes of both men and women,
(6) 15 so that they even carried the sick into the streets,
(7) and laid them on beds and pallets,
(8) that as Peter came by at least his shadow might fall on some of them.
(9) 16 The people also gathered from the towns around Jerusalem,
(10) bringing the sick and those afflicted with unclean spirits,
(11) and they were all healed.

This passage is highly iterative: many signs were done; believers were added; sick are carried out into the streets; people gathered from towns around. What appears to be a whole series of events like the healing of the lame man are compressed or telescoped into one scene, with repetition indicated. The participants are pluralized: apostles, as opposed to Peter or Peter and John; multitudes of both men and women; the sick; people. Similarly, the places indicated are plural, for the most part (exception to be noted momentarily): the streets, beds and pallets, towns around Jerusalem. Since the narrator treats numerous events, participants, and places, the temporal stretch covered by the narrative is indefinite; put another way, various temporal moments are conflated. The events narrated cover times, the relation of which to the preceding scenes and the scenes to follow is not indicated.

9. At one point in the segment, statement (2), the narrator states that the participants are still in Solomon's Portico. That singular location is belied by the events of (6)–(8): streets do not run through Solomon's Portico and people coming from surrounding towns must have taken place over a period of days (or weeks?). This discrepancy between singular and plural locations has led many commentators to speculate that the segment 5:12–16 is composite.[10] From a narrative point of view, it could be assumed that the location remains constant from the setting of Peter's speech in 3:11ff. in Solomon's Portico, through the incidents with Ananias and Sapphira in 5:1–11, to this narrative summary. In that case, the contradiction may be limited to 5:15, (6)–(8). Statements (1)–(5) and (9)–(11) could all be set in Solomon's Portico. On the other hand, it is possible also to divide the summary at 5:14/15: Statements (1)–(5) would then be located in Solomon's Portico, while the events reported thereafter would have an indefinite setting: in the streets and elsewhere, place unspecified. The first solution requires us to understand that the narrator lapsed or that the summary is composite; the second solution goes together with a general tendency for time, place, participants, and action to become increasingly less definite the deeper we get into the narrative summary.

In any case, the narrator is recounting in the iterative mode in which time, participants, actions, and even space are heaped up, pluralized, conflated.

10. The narrative summary in Acts 5:12–16 may be compared with one in Acts 2:43–47, where the mode is strictly iterative: times, places, participants, and actions are all pluralized and generalized. It may also be compared with the summary in Acts 4:32–37, which begins in the iterative mode, but modulates into the singulative in 4:36f., as a way of making the transition back to the focused scenes of 5:1–11.

It is worth repeating: segments that are pure enactment, or pure recounting in the singulative mode, or pure recounting in the iterative mode, are rare. There is often a mixture of modes. Mixed modes may mean that the narrator has suffered a narrative lapse, that the text is corrupt or composite, or that the narrator is attempting to achieve some particular effect by deliberately conflating the modes. The choice among these possibilities will be determined by the care with which the narrator is assumed to craft his or her text, with explanatory possibilities offered by the context, or with the chances of a corrupt or defective text.

10. Haenchen, *Acts*, 243–46, discusses the various options.

DESCRIPTION

11. A third type of narrative segment consists of description. In description, the narrator focuses either on participants or setting, or both, in the absence of action.[11] Pure description involves a narrative pause, consequently, if by narrative pause is meant that the course of the action is interrupted or arrested during the duration of the description. However, description is often mingled with recounting in the iterative mode. For example, in the statements,

(1) John was trim and tanned, a perfect specimen of that type of man who is perpetually ready for action.
(2) John used to swim twenty laps at the club pool every morning.

(1) is a descriptive statement, while (2) is a series of habitual actions recounted in the iterative mode. These two types of statements are often intertwined in what are predominantly descriptive segments.

12. Having now identified the third major type of narrative segment, we are in a position to summarize the types of segments as they have been defined in this study:

1. the mimetic segment: the focused scene
2. the diegetic segment: the unfocused scene
   a. the action is singulative
   b. the action is iterative
3. the descriptive segment: actionless; focus on participants and setting

It should be emphasized that these types rarely occur in pure form. More often than not, mimesis is mixed with diegesis, and description may occur at virtually any point in the narrative.

13. Biblical narrative is relatively poor in descriptive material. The reader learns very little about the physical appearance of characters, for example, and even the descriptions of setting are frustratingly brief for the historian. The Gospels betray nothing of the appearance of Jesus or the named disciples. And the geography of Palestine is only generally represented or is ambiguous. The classical novel, on the other hand, is marked by an alternation of scene and narrative summary interlaced with description. In contrast to the classical form, the modern novelists have tended to create a series of scenes joined by ellipses left to be filled in by the reader.[12] The modern novel and the cinema are comparable in this respect. Nevertheless, there are

11. Treatments of description in recent narratology tend to be embryonic. Chatman does the most with the subject: *Story and Discourse*, 74–78 and 96–145. Genette, *Narrative Discourse*, 99–106, and Rimmon-Kenan, *Narrative Fiction*, 52f., take the subject up under the heading of duration. On duration, see below, §§6.18–24.

12. On this point, see Chatman, *Story and Discourse*, 75.

some forms of description in biblical narrative, and these may be readily noted.

14. Descriptive statements may be segregated into two broad categories: those that treat setting and those that focus on participants. Setting includes geography, architecture, and other objects belonging to setting.

Brief descriptions of space, both geographical and architectural, are common.

Acts 1:12

(3) . . . the mount called Olivet,
which is near Jerusalem, a sabbath day's journey away

John 5:2

(4) Now there is in Jerusalem by the sheep gate a pool,
in Hebrew called Bethzatha,
which has five porticoes.

We also find descriptive material directed to objects in the narrative setting, such as the following:

John 2:6

(5) Now six stone jars were standing there,
for the Jewish rites of purification,
each holding two or three measures.

Descriptive statements like these are rarely expanded beyond a sentence or two.

In the works of the Jewish historian, Josephus, on the other hand, geographical and architectural descriptions are much more frequent and of greater length. In the *Jewish War*, 4.451ff., there is an extensive description of the region around Jericho, much too long to be quoted here; in 5.148ff., he gives a detailed account of the temple in Jerusalem and its immediate environs. These descriptions are inserted into historical narrative material; narrative of this type would not be required, of course, to meet the more restrictive requirements of modern fiction, where description is usually permitted only to the extent that it contributes to the development of plot or character. In the Book of Revelation, however, the narrator pauses frequently to describe what he sees in his heavenly vision. Late in the story, for example, he sees the new Jerusalem descending from heaven and he "pauses" to describe it:

Rev 21:11–14

(6) [11] Its radiance [was] like a most rare jewel, a jasper, clear as crystal. [12]It
had a great, high wall, with twelve gates, and at the gates twelve angels,
and on the gates the names of the twelve tribes of the sons of Israel were
inscribed; on the east three gates, [13]on the north three gates, on the
south three gates, and on the west three gates. [14]And the wall of the city

> had twelve foundations, and on them the twelve names of the twelve apostles of the Lamb.

But descriptions of this length are infrequent in biblical narrative.

15. Descriptive material focused on participants is even less common than description with setting in view. There is a succinct description of John the Baptist in Mark:

Mark 1:6

(7) Now John was clothed with camel's hair,
and had a leather girdle around his waist,
and ate locusts and wild honey.

The final clause in this statement illustrates how difficult it is to segregate pure description from diegesis. Eating locusts and wild honey is a habitual activity, of course, and therefore belongs to the category of recounting in the iterative mode. Even the two preceding clauses imply a kind of customary activity: John dressed regularly in a garment of camel's hair and habitually wore a leather belt. But even these descriptive statements are included in Mark's account because of their connection with Elijah, the prophet.[13] The normal descriptive statement focused on participants is even leaner. The following are typical:

John 3:1

(8) Now there was a man of the Pharisees,
named Nicodemus,
a ruler of the Jews.

Acts 2:5

(9) Now there were dwelling in Jerusalem Jews,
devout men from every nation under heaven.

16. Alongside these we may set two descriptions derived from modern fiction. In Owen Wister's novel, *The Virginian*, which is the precursor of the American Western, and which is regarded by many critics as the classic Western, the narrator, an easterner, has just arrived at Medicine Bow, Wyoming, without his baggage but full of hope to recover his health. From the train window he has observed a cowboy perform a skillful roping demonstration on an obstreperous pony. He does not yet know that this man is the Virginian, the one who has been sent to take him to his ultimate destination at Sunk Creek. He steps onto the platform and sees the Virginian close up for the first time. This is what he sees:

(10) Lounging there at ease against the wall was a slim young giant, more beautiful than pictures. His broad, soft hat was pushed back: a loose-knotted, dull-scarlet handkerchief sagged from his throat, and one cas-

13. Cf. 2 Kings 1:8.

ual thumb was hooked in the cartridge-belt that slanted across his hips. He had plainly come many miles from somewhere across the vast horizon, as the dust upon him showed. His boots were white with it. His overalls were gray with it. The weather-beaten bloom on his face shone through it duskily, as the ripe peaches look upon their trees in a dry season. But no dinginess of travel or shabbiness of attire could tarnish the splendor that radiated from his youth and strength.[14]

There is nothing like this in biblical narrative, so far as I am aware. It is pure description, and the character of it is mimetic: the narrator takes the reader to that station platform and lets him or her take a lingering look at the cowboy.

17. The second example is from the fiction of William Faulkner. It illustrates how description, particularly in introductory material, is often joined with recounting in the iterative mode.

(11) Nancy would set her bundle on the top of her head, then upon the bundle in turn she would set the black straw sailor hat which she wore Winter and Summer. She was tall, with a high, sad face sunken a little where her teeth were missing. Sometimes we would go part of the way down the lane and across the pasture with her, to watch the balanced bundle and the hat that never bobbed nor wavered, even when she walked down into the ditch and climbed out again and stooped through the fence.[15]

The activity of Nancy as she went to fetch or deliver laundry is described as habitual—not her actions on one particular occasion, but on many occasions, run together, conflated, typified. In the midst of these typical actions, the narrator inserts descriptive phrases or statements, such as, "the black straw sailor hat," or "She was tall, with a high, sad face sunken a little where her teeth were missing." Again, there is nothing comparable in biblical narrative; insofar as character is developed and setting is depicted in the biblical material, character is displayed predominantly by singular actions, and setting is described minimally and only for the immediate occasion.[16]

DURATION

18. The various types of narration are directly related to the tempo of the narrative. Some retard the speed of the account, others accelerate the telling.

14. Wister, *The Virginian*, 3.

15. Faulkner, "That Evening Sun Go Down," 205f.

16. One is reminded of Erich Auerbach's comparison of the Homeric style in the *Odyssey* with that of the biblical writer in Genesis, *Mimesis*, 1–20. According to Auerback, Homer is more descriptive of the surface aspects of participant and setting; the biblical narrator is extremely parsimonious of description by comparison.

The tempo of types is referred to as *duration*. We shall now explore duration as another means of characterizing the types.

Duration concerns the relation of discourse time to story time, viz., the relation of the time it takes to narrate or read a narrative text to the time it took the events to transpire to which that text refers.[17] Discourse time (DT) may approximate story time (ST), as it tends to do in directly reported speech, in the script of a stage drama, for example. In that case, the two times would be isochronous or equal.[18] But in the ellipsis, where the narrator skips a segment of time in the story, DT is 0, while ST is n (n stands for a temporal span of unspecified duration). On the other hand, in a descriptive pause, ST stands still and is thus 0, while DT = n. These three possibilities appear to define the spectrum, from DT = 0, on the one end, to ST = 0 on the other. In the middle, DT and ST would be isochronous. However, other relative gradations are equally possible: DT could be less than ST (expressed as DT < ST), or DT could be greater than ST (expressed as DT > ST), but in neither case would DT or ST be 0. These possibilities may be set out as points on a continuum:

DT = 0, ST = n
DT < ST
DT = ST
DT > ST
DT = n, ST = 0

These points will be illustrated subsequently.

19. The difficulty inherent in the conception of duration is that there is no objective way of measuring discourse time (story time could presumably be measured by the clock). Authors will differ greatly in how long it takes them to narrate the same series of events, and even readers or reciters will vary considerably among themselves in reading or performing a narrative text. Nevertheless, in the single case of directly reported speech, it appears that DT would regularly approximate ST, more or less, if allowances were made for stage directions in the text and for notices of the change of speaker. Since duration has to do with the *relation* between the two times, it may be wiser to speak of narrative tempo.[19] The question then becomes: what is the tempo of the narrator in relation to the events being narrated? Of course, a narrator who was constant in narrative pace would produce a boring text. Variation in pace lends spice to the telling. An interesting narrative, as Genette astutely

17. The primary discussions of duration are to be found in Genette, *Narrative Discourse*, 86–112; Rimmon-Kenan, *Narrative Fiction*, 51–56; Chatman, *Story and Discourse*, 67–78; Culpepper, *Anatomy of the Fourth Gospel*, 70–73.

18. Isochronous is Genette's term: *Narrative Discourse*, 87; it is a Greek word meaning, simply, equal time(s).

19. Genette uses the term movement; Rimmon-Kenan substitutes tempo, which strikes me a good choice.

observes,[20] cannot do without rhythm or anisochronies. One of the tasks of an analytic poetics, consequently, is to map out narrative tempo. It is proposed to chart tempo in relation to the types of narrative segments as identified above.

20. We may begin with the ellipsis. At the conclusion of scene ii (Acts 4:1–4), in the sequence, Acts 3:1–4:31 (§§4.25–26), Peter and John are put in prison at evening (4:3). The next scene (4:5ff.) opens on the following morning. The temporal break at Acts 4:4/5 covers the period of one night: the noctural pause is not narrated.

Similarly, in the twin stories of Ananias and Sapphira (Act 5:1–11), there is an ellipsis of three hours between the death of Ananias and the incident featuring Sapphira:

Acts 5:7
(1) After an interval of about three hours his wife came in, . . .

In these two instances ST is *n*, while DT is 0.

It may be imagined that ellipses have little to do with narrative tempo, since what is not narrated does not directly affect the pace of the story. On the other hand, a narrative that moves directly from one focal event to another gives the impression of being more "clipped" and fast paced, compared to the narrative that inserts transitions, for example, or that is laced with retarding descriptions. In any case, ellipses are one means of accelerating the tempo of the discourse.

21. In a summary statement, a narrator may depict the passage of a considerable span of ST in a single narrative statement.

Acts 9:43
(2) And he stayed in Joppa for many days with one Simon, a tanner.

Luke 2:52
(3) And Jesus increased in wisdom and stature, and in favor with God and man.

(2) covers a few days, while (3) probably covers several years. In these cases, DT is shorter than ST, but not zero: DT < ST.

22. The time it takes to narrate Peter's speech in Acts 3:12–26 approximates the time it took Peter to deliver the speech in story time: DT = ST. Of course, the one only approximates the other, since the written text makes no provision, in this instance, for pauses, or gestures, or interruptions. Yet the duration of the one cannot be greatly different from the duration of the other.

Even when the narrator is depicting non-speech events, the text may be made to approximate or mimic the temporal duration of the events them-

20. *Narrative Discourse*, 88.

selves. For example, when the lame man is healed, the narrator tells the reader:

Acts 3:8
(4) And leaping up
(5) he stood
(6) and walked
(7) and entered the temple with them
(8) walking
(9) and leaping
(10) and praising God.

The narrative text is here stretched out in order to give some textual expression to the duration of the reported events. We may again say, for convenience if not for scientific accuracy, that DT = ST.

23. In biblical narrative, examples are rare of discourse time that exceeds story time. That is because biblical narrative tends to be action narrative, which is to say, poor in description, reflective interlude, commentary, and the like. One can read for long stretches in the Gospels or in Acts before coming to anything like extended DT. Even then, the deceleration tends to be extremely brief.

In Acts 9:10ff., there is a story of another Ananias, the one who visits Paul in Damascus and assists with his conversion. The story has a single narrative statement as INTRO:

Acts 9:10
(11) Now there was a disciple at Damascus named Ananias.

Then the narrative plunges into events. There is not much by way of description or setting in the INTRO, yet it is typical of biblical narrative. Further examples of brief descriptive statements are given in §§6.14–15.

There are, of course, genealogies, such as we find in Luke 3:23–38 and frequently in the book of Genesis. And we have some instances of narrator commentary, which also has a decelerating effect:

John 4:2
(12) (although Jesus himself did not baptize, but only his disciples)

John 20:30–31
(13) [30] Now Jesus did many other signs in the presence of the disciples, which are not written in this book; [31]but these are written that you may believe that Jesus is the Christ, the Son of God, and that believing you may have life in his name.

In these instances the narrator breaks out of the narrative mode and addresses the reader directly. Statement (13) has a counterpart in John 21:25, and the two are paralleled by Luke's introductory dedication in the Gospel of Luke, 1:1–4, and the address to Theophilus in Acts 1:1. The descriptions in the Book of Revelation were mentioned in §6.14 as further illustrations of decelerating facets of biblical narrative. Nevertheless, such facets occur in minuscule amounts compared to modern fiction.

24. The relation of these points of reference on the spectrum of tempo to the types of narrative segments we have been discussing is more or less obvious. The focused scene, as it has been defined and described, most often consists in large part of directly reported speech: it is therefore the kind of segment in which DT more or less = ST. The unfocused scene customarily represents a faster tempo than the focused scene, even when the unfocused scene depicts singulative events, but especially when it is iterative and summarizes: DT < ST. The ellipsis is the case in which DT is reduced to 0, while ST = *n*. Examples of minor and major ellipses abound in biblical narrative as in other kinds of narrative. It is much more difficult to find examples of the opposite tempo, the one in which DT is greater than ST, or where the tempo is slower. As suggested above, the not uncommon genealogies in biblical texts are one example where ST stops but DT continues. There are other examples in the Pentateuch, particularly when legal material is introduced into the narrative. By and large, however, biblical narrative is poor in description and other decelerating phenomena, such as reflection and commentary.

MIMESIS AND DIEGESIS

25. The distinction between mimesis and diegesis opens up a bundle of questions for both theorist and critic.[21] The questions begin with three observations made by Genette. (1) Every narrative is narrated by a narrator—to put the matter as plainly as one knows how—and is therefore mediated. As Genette states: "No narrative can 'show' or 'imitate' the story it tells" without mediation.[22] Booth has also formulated the restriction: ". . . we must never forget that though the author can to some extent choose his disguises, he can never choose to disappear."[23] (2) Language cannot imitate non-verbal actions. Stated differently, language signifies without imitating. (3) Language does not "imitate" verbal actions. Insofar as speech acts are reproduced as directly quoted speech, Genette claims that the reproduction is language itself and not an imitation.[24] As a consequence, the crucial distinction is not between showing and telling, but among different degrees of telling.[25]

21. Recent theorists give full treatment to the issue: Genette, *Narrative Discourse*, 161–211; *Figures*, 127–33; Chatman, *Story and Discourse*, 32–34, plus chapters 4 and 5; Rimmon-Kenan, *Narrative Fiction*, 71–85, 106–16.

22. *Narrative Discourse*, 164. His discussion of the three observations is to be found on pages 164–69.

23. *The Rhetoric of Fiction*, 20.

24. Genette makes this point at length in *Figures*, 127–33.

25. Rimmon-Kenan, *Narrative Fiction*, 108, summarizes Genette and then comes to this conclusion.

We may grant the theoretical point of Genette's first observation without qualification. If diegesis is defined as mediated narrative, then all narrative is diegetic in some minimal sense. Even directly reported speech customarily has a narrative frame of reference consisting, minimally, of the identification of speakers and the like, which of course requires a mediating presence. Further, in a modern narrative made up of what is called *immediate speech*—unspoken and without auditor—someone has to *record* that speech, and so, to that extent, immediate speech also involves the intervention of a recorder between thought and perception, on the one hand, and reader, on the other.[26] It is impossible, accordingly, that any form of narrative can be entirely free of narrative patronage.

26. By granting the theoretical point of Genette's first observation, we have not, however, resolved the issue: is a distinction between mimesis and diegesis, between enactment and recounting, warranted, even if the one is an illusion, a literary sleight-of-hand? And if so, on what empirical evidence is the distinction based? It remains a fact that narrative texts do create the illusion of mimesis or showing. The question is how they do, and how this illusion is to be distinguished from other types of narrative in which the narrator overtly intervenes between events and reader.

There are at least two reasons modern theorists have resisted discriminating mimesis and diegesis. In the first place, there has been a strong reaction against the Jamesian school in American criticism, a school which held that showing was the only proper mode of fiction. This reaction has been fueled by works like that of Booth, *The Rhetoric of Fiction*, which is a defense of telling. This reaction has appeared to invest the work of theorists like Genette and Rimmon-Kenan. The second, more complex reason follows from the first. Since theorists have been inclined to discredit the distinction on theoretical grounds, they have not been inspired to conduct an examination of the empirical evidence. Theory has developed largely out of the remarks by Plato and Aristotle on the subject, but without serious reference to the data. Indeed, Genette points out that Proust is a paradox or a contradiction of the norms he lays down on theoretical grounds,[27] and Rimmon-Kenan proceeds with a brief discussion of the illusion of mimesis after denying the validity of the distinction.[28]

27. Narrative is a literary device for making a listener or reader an observer of an event or series of events, as suggested earlier. Genette proposes to define that device according to two factors: (1) quantity and rate of narrative information, and (2) perspective or point of view. As he puts it, "one can tell *more* or *less* what one tells, and can tell it *according to one point of view or*

26. Genette discusses this phenomenon, *Narrative Discourse*, 173f.
27. *Narrative Discourse*, 166f.
28. *Narrative Fiction*, 108.

another."[29] The narrator can furnish the reader with more or fewer details and the narrator can regulate the quantity and quality[30] of information by adopting one or more perspectives. Genette illustrates these factors by analyzing a viewer's relation to a painting. The detail one is able to discern in a painting is proportional to the distance separating one from the object. As a consequence, he characterizes his first factor as *distance*: the farther away, the fewer the details. *Perspective*, on the other hand, refers to the eyes through which the narrator permits the reader to view the action. Using the same illustration, Genette suggests that information is regulated by where this pair of eyes (or pairs of eyes, if the narrator changes perspectives during the course of the narrative) is located. For example, does the perspective indicate some particular angle of vision? Is there an impediment partially blocking or restricting what these eyes can see? And so on. On this conception of the matter, it would appear that distance and perspective are intimately related.

28. In developing the first of his factors, distance, Genette goes on to state that recounting or diegesis is more distant from the objects and events it reports than is mimesis. We know that, he claims, because diegesis *tells less and tells it in a more mediated way*. In mimesis, by contrast, the quantity and rate of information rises because the narrative text is "closer" to the events being narrated.

The generalizations are based, it seems, on a false reading of Plato and on a confusion of categories. These sound like serious charges, but in fact they are minor criticisms, perhaps, in view of the large number of illuminating new distinctions and categories Genette introduces to the benefit of every literary critic. Nevertheless, it has to be said, first of all, that correlating mediation with reduction in detail, or recounting with brevity, involves the confusion of two categories and does not necessarily help us to a firm distinction between diegesis and mimesis. Genette makes this correlation on the basis of Plato's rewriting of the introductory scene to the *Iliad*. Homer conceives the scene in a mimetic mode, the preeminent mark of which is direct discourse. Plato rewrites the scene in a diegetic mode by turning direct discourse into indirect, which in this case shortens the speeches and prayer, and by eliminating "useless and contingent detail." It is these two observations on the part of Genette that led him to conclude that recounting and reduction in detail (and therefore in length) are correlative. In my judgment, this is an unfortunate, although often empirically valid, conclusion.

29. What Plato in fact eliminates in his diegetic rewriting are the "picturesque" details that contribute to the "realistic effect." In other words, Plato eliminates the features of Homer's text that function as direct stimuli to the reader's senses, the features that *show* rather than tell the story. In so doing,

29. *Narrative Discourse*, 161f.

30. Quality refers to the reliability of the narrator, a facet of the concept of narrator that we need not explore in this context.

he turns the mimetic into the diegetic. The reduction in detail is incidental. The difference, according to Plato, is that in diegesis the poet does not pretend that anyone other than himself is speaking, while in mimesis the poet delivers a speech as though it were someone else talking.[31] Plato's distinction rests on whether the narrator attempts to create the illusion of mimesis or whether the narrator does not seek to conceal his or her presence at all. Never mind the length. When Genette adds a second and, for him, decisive factor, viz., that diegesis entails a reduction in detail and length, he departs from Plato's argument and erects a theory on the basis of a single example.

It is the case, of course, that diegesis often does involve a reduction in detail and length. We have amply observed the phenomenon above. But diegesis does not necessarily require an erosion of close specification. To take the matter of the representation of speech in narrative: Thucydides constructs long periods for his speakers and does so in indirect discourse. One could argue that such indirectly reported speeches are as long or longer than would be their directly reported counterparts. The verbal representation of non-verbal events is also ambiguous: biblical narrative is highly mimetic, yet it is very poor in descriptive detail. Description, generally speaking, is rich in detail and yet description, because it often belongs to the introductory part of narrative segments, is often diegetic. Of course, it is also possible to create description in the mimetic mode. In any case, there is good reason to segregate factors that Genette lumps together: the mediated or diegetic narrative mode is to be kept separate from the quantity of information. We shall explore this point in connection with some biblical texts anon.

30. To summarize: The presence or absence of a narrator does not necessarily bear on the distinction between mimesis and diegesis. A heavily mediated narrative segment may, of course, be unfocused, but there are also mediated narratives that are focused, as we shall observe. But we shall have to learn to distinguish narrators.

Nor is the amount of narrative information discriminating. Focused narratives are rich in sensible information because focused: the reader's senses are being enlisted directly in the narrative experience, but focused narrative may also be poor in descriptive material. Recounting, on the other hand, may be rich in descriptive material and thus more detailed than focused narrative.

The two criteria are simply not discriminating.

THE INTRADIEGETIC NARRATOR AND MIMESIS

31. The distinction between mimesis and diegesis, between showing and telling, can be observed in the segment Acts 10:23b–33.

31. *Republic*, 393.

In the introductory material, which leads up to focused nuclei, we have several narrative statements, all reporting events in an unfocused way:

Acts 10:23b–24

(1) 23 The next day he [Peter] rose
(2) and went off with them,
(3) and some of the brethren from Joppa accompanied him.
(4) 24 On the following day they entered Caesarea.
(5) Cornelius was expecting them
(6) and they had called together his kinsmen and close friends.

Narrative statements (1)–(3) reflect an indefinite space ("he rose and went off") and an unspecified group of participants ("some of the brethren from Joppa"). Above all, the departure scene does not invoke the reader's senses directly. With (4) it becomes clear that a journey has taken place, only the start and finish of which are noted. These introductory statements thus cover a long stretch of time (one day at least, from arising one morning to arriving the next day), the center of which is left blank. As is often the case in recounting, two times are conflated.

The actions in (1)–(4) are not iterative, although action statements in introductory material often are. But (6) is iterative: Cornelius *had called together his kinsmen and close friends*, i.e., he took actions to assemble this group of people, the number and particularity of which are unspecified. His activities are also spread over an unspecified period of time in the past. And the number of participants involved is indefinite. These are all earmarks of recounting.

32. Statements (1)–(4) and (5)–(6) are used to assemble two different groups of participants in proximity to each other. Peter and the three emissaries of Cornelius, together with an unspecified number from Joppa, have arrived in Caesarea. Cornelius, who lives there, anticipates their arrival and assembles his kinsmen and close friends. The two sets of introductory statements—both unfocused—lead up to a focused scene: we can anticipate that the items constituting a scene will become particular enough for the reader to envision a "real" scene.

Acts 10:25–26

(7) 25 When Peter entered,
(8) Cornelius met him
(9) and fell down at his feet
(10) 26 and worshipped him.
(11) But Peter lifted him up,
(12) saying,
"Stand up;
I too am a man."

Peter enters Cornelius' house, presumably, and Cornelius meets him (a reciprocal arrival, so to speak, although Cornelius is already in positon; yet he moves to meet Peter, a notice that is essential to the deference expressed in the next actions). Cornelius then falls down at Peter's feet and worships him. These actions are portrayed as they would be in a stage drama or cinema: they are enacted and the reader is able to "see" them in his or her imagination. The narrator next introduces direct discourse, and thus reinforces the focused character of the scene: the reader overhears the conversation.

33. This scene is followed by another, closely linked scene:

Acts 10:27–29
(13) [27] And as he talked with him,
(14) he went in
(15) and found many persons gathered;
(16) [28] and he said to them,
"You yourselves know how unlawful it is for a Jew to associate with or to visit any one of another nation; but God has shown me that I should not call any man common or unclean. [29]So when I was sent for, I came without objection. I ask then why you sent for me."

Peter now moves further into the house (= a change of locale) and finds the relatives and friends of Cornelius assembled (= new participant set). These statements indicate a modification of the first scene (a fresh arrival on the part of Peter; the guests are in position), yet the scene does not lose its focus.

34. Cornelius now replies to Peter's query about why Cornelius had sent for him (10:30–33). The character of this response bears directly on the criteria for distinguishing mimesis and diegesis advanced by Genette and Rimmon-Kenan.

The response of Cornelius runs as follows:

Acts 10:30–33
(17) [30] And Cornelius said,
(17.1) "Four days ago, about this hour, I was keeping the ninth hour of prayer in my house;
(17.2) and behold, a man stood before me in bright apparel,
(17.3) [31] saying,
(17.31) 'Cornelius, your prayer has been heard
(17.32) and your alms have been remembered before God.
(17.33) [32] Send therefore to Joppa
(17.34) and ask for Simon who is called Peter;
(17.35) he is lodging in the house of Simon, a tanner, by the seaside.'
(17.4) [33] So I sent to you at once,
(17.5) and you have been kind enough to come.
(17.6) Now therefore we are all here present in the sight of God, to hear all that you have been commanded by the Lord."

It is to be observed that the earlier scene Cornelius is rehearsing is in fact focused, although it is entirely mediated. The entire response, save for the introductory phrase ("And Cornelius said") is direct discourse and first person. Inside the reported speech we have a focused scene:

Time: four days ago, about this hour
Place: in my house
f:pos: Cornelius was keeping the hour of prayer
(ἤμην . . . προσευχόμενος)
f:arr: a man in bright apparel arrives

The speech of the man in bright apparel is given in direct discourse, although in the recapitulated version it is abbreviated (cf. 10:31–32 with 10:3–6). Nevertheless, the shortened RECAP is focused up to this point. Cornelius now repeats the defocalizer of the earlier scene: "So I sent to you at once" is a shortened version of 10:7–8. Cornelius now brings the story up to date: You have come and we are all assembled here to hear what you have to say. Put differently, Cornelius retells the earlier event in a focused way, however minimally, but then recounts the intervening events, so far as he knows them (i.e, the recounting is restricted to his perspective) as a way of breaking back into the current story line. Just as he breaks out of the prevailing temporal line at the beginning of his response (10:30), he now returns to that temporal line, viz., the current moment.[32]

35. To sum up, in Acts 10:30–33, we have a focused scene within a focused scene, the former fully mediated by an intradiegetic narrator: a narrator that appears within the narrative. Yet in the text both scenes are focused and thus mimetic. Accordingly, mediation is not a criterion for discriminating diegesis from mimesis. The most we can say is that the discernible presence of an *extradiegetic narrator* betokens diegesis; an *intradiegetic narrator* has the choice of either diegesis or mimesis.

Graphically, we need to represent the entire scene, Acts 10:23b–48, as a scene within a scene (figure 17).

36. The repetitions in the Book of Acts are well known. They will repay close analysis for their bearing on the poetics of narrative. In this context we may pursue the repetitions found in Acts 10:1–11:18, the story of Peter and Cornelius.

The recapitulation of Cornelius, examined above, is matched by Peter's rehearsal of his story in Acts 11:1–18. However, since Cornelius' story is now a part of Peter's story, when Peter recaps his own experiences, he will include the criticial experience of Cornelius in his story as a part of it. An examination of how he does that will be revealing.

37. In Acts 11:1–10, Peter repeats the event narrated in 10:9–16; both are focused scenes. Then he recounts how the three men arrived from Cornelius

32. In the terms of Genette, this is a homodiegetic analepsis: the relating of an earlier event that belongs to the same primary story line. This phenomenon is treated in §8.5. Genette's discussion is found in *Narrative Discourse*, 51–54.

and how he accompanied them back to Caesarea (11:11–12). They have now entered Cornelius' house. The narrative continues:

Acts 11:13–15

(25) [13] And he told us how he had seen the angel
(25.1) standing in his house
(25.2) and saying,
(25.21) "Send to Joppa
(25.22) and bring Simon Peter;
(25.23) [14] he will declare to you a message by which you will be saved, you and your household."
(26) [15] As I began to speak,
(27) the Holy Spirit fell on them just as on us at the beginning.

Peter & Cornelius

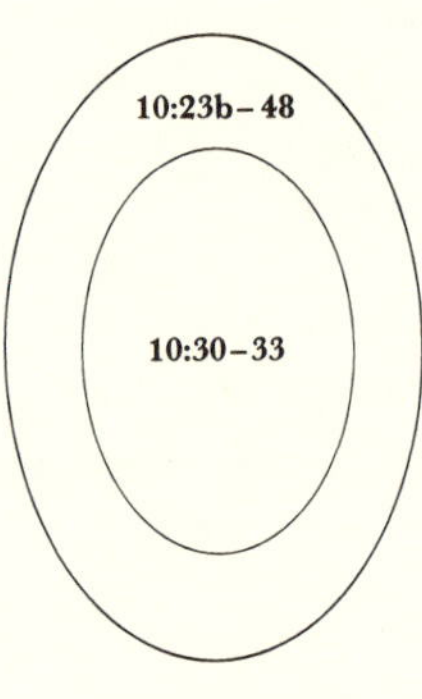

ACTS 10:23b–48

Scene Within a Scene

Figure 17

Peter is now recapitulating his own story to the circumcision party in Jerusalem, and within his account he gives Cornelius' account of an earlier event in his life. We thus have several narrative levels: the author of Acts narrates the original event (Acts 10:1–8); Cornelius rehearses that event (Acts 10:30–33); Peter repeats Cornelius' account (Acts 11:13–15). The first may be termed the hyperdiegetic level, the second the intradiegetic level, and the third the hypodiegetic level.[33] The frame of reference in which Peter reports

33. These terms are those of Rimmon-Kenan, borrowed from Genette and Bal: *Narrative Fiction*, 91f. and 140, n. 7. Hyperdiegetic, when used with reference to a narrator, means the narrator at the first level above the primary narrative; intradiegetic means the narrator within the story at the first level; hypodiegetic indicates a narrator at a second level within the story. This terminology was discussed in §§2.7–9.

Cornelius' account is recounted or diegetic: "And he told us how he had seen the angel standing in his house and saying, . . ." is indirectly reported in relation to the focused form in 10:30: "Behold, a man stood before me in bright apparel, saying. . . ." But even at this remove, with two narrators intervening, what the angel said is reported in directly quoted speech. There is thus the semblance of mimesis. The words of the angel are slightly altered, to be sure, in one respect, and both shortened and extended in other respects. Enough is repeated to enable the reader to identify the previously rehearsed speech, but that speech is now extended to include new material, as though the narrator had saved some critical words for the second rehearsal.[34] In any case, a focused scene is repeated a second time in the mimetic mode, and even

Peter & Cornelius

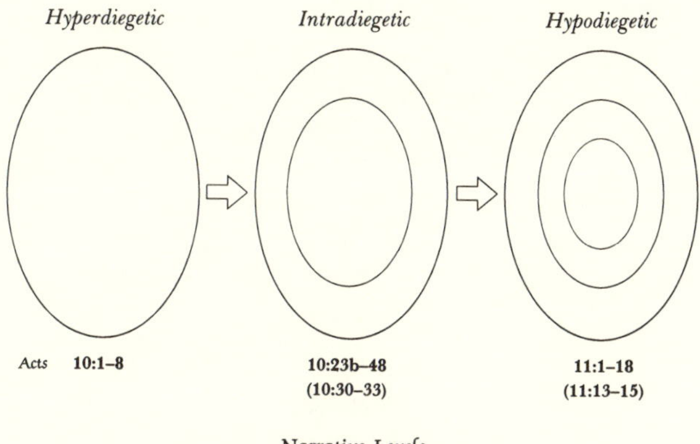

Narrative Levels

Figure 18

at its third repetition there remain some traces of the mimetic mode. It would thus appear that the presence of an intradiegetic or even a hypodiegetic narrator does not rob the narrative of its mimetic possibilities. And since the narrator in Proust's work is intradiegetic, Proust appears to confirm the phenomenon observed in Acts, rather than constituting an exception, as Genette is wont to think on the basis of his theory.

38. The levels of Cornelius' vision as narrated in Acts 10:1–8, 30–33, and 11:13–15 may be represented graphically as in figure 18.

34. Robert Alter treats the phenomenon of repetition in Hebrew narrative, with differences, in his work *The Art of Biblical Narrative*, 88–113.

In a similar fashion, though with only two levels, the author of Acts narrates Peter's vision on the housetop in 10:9–16, and then has Peter rehearse that scene before his colleagues in Jerusalem in 11:5–10. The second scene is also focused, and therefore mimetic, like the first—another instance of mimesis in the presence of an overt narrator.

ALTERNATION OF SHOWING AND TELLING

39. Unfocused narration or recounting can usually be distinguished from focused narration or enactment whenever either occurs in blocks. As we observed earlier, recounting is characteristic of introductions and conclusions, which tend to be iterative or generalized, and also of transitions, where a series of intervening events is compressed into a summary in order to come swiftly to the next focused event. Yet unfocused narration can occur anywhere, mixed with a more focused variety. It seems that there is a tendency in biblical narrative to insert elements of enactment, often in the form of direct discourse, into recounted narration, perhaps in accordance with the canons of folk literature generally.[35] In any case, most narratives consist of alternating blocks of showing and telling.[36]

40. The alternation of showing and telling, enactment and recounting, may be observed in the sequence Acts 9:1–30. The sequence is usually taken to concern the conversion of Paul. The sequence may be divided into narrative segments and subsegments in accordance with criteria established above.

The first scene embraces 9:1–9. The INTRO is made up of statements in the recounting mode:

Acts 9:1–2
(1) [1] But Saul,
(2) still breathing threats and murder against the disciples of the Lord,
(1) went to the high priest
(3) [2] and asked him for letters to the synagogues at Damascus,
(4) so that if he found any belonging to the Way, men or women,
(5) he might bring them bound to Jerusalem.

Statement (2) is iterative, as are (4) and (5). Statements (1) and (3) are singulative, but (3) is clearly mediated by the narrator. The scene has not yet achieved focus, hence the recounting mode is appropriate.

The NUC is brought into focus in 9:3:

Acts 9:3–4
(6) [3] Now as he journeyed
(7) he approached Damascus,

35. Cf. the remarks of Alter, *The Art of Biblical Narrative*, 65 and 63–87 *passim*.
36. Chatman, *Story and Discourse*, 75.

(8) and suddenly a light from heaven flashed about him.
(9) [4] And he fell to the ground
(10) and heard a voice saying to him, . . .

The blinding light is the focalizer, a perception-precipitator (*f:perc-prec*), in this case producing blindness. A second focalizer occurs in (10) in the form of *f:perc* (hearing), and direct discourse follows. The NUC, Acts 9:3–8a, is a focused scene.

The CON begins in the midst of vs 8, when a *lchg* takes place:

(11) [8b] so they led him by the hand
(12) and brought him into Damascus.
(13) [9] And for three days he was without sight,
(14) and neither ate
(15) nor drank.

The scene set on the Damascus road is defocalized when Paul's companions lead him on into the city. The narrator then reports that Paul remained blind for three days and neither ate nor drank, statements that cover states or activities over a period of time and which are therefore unfocused.

The INTRO to the next segment (9:10–17a) is extremely brief:

(16) [10] Now there was a disciple at Damascus named Ananias.

The introduction of a new participant with *id* forecasts a new scene.

The NUC is focalized simply by voice:

(17) The Lord said to him in a vision, . . .

and a long exchange in direct discourse follows (9:10b–16).

The CON is as brief as the INTRO:

(18) [17] So Ananias departed

which involves a *dep* and a *lchg*. An enacted NUC is sandwiched between introductory and concluding statements that are in the recounting mode.

41. Thus far we have considered scenes i and ii. Scene iii is found in Acts 9:17b–19. The INTRO, which begins mid-sentence, is again very brief:

(19) [17b] and entered the house.

The CON to scene ii and the INTRO to scene iii consist of a single compound sentence.

In (19), Ananias arrives at Paul's house. The NUC, which begins in 9:17c, is focalized by touch—a rare example of a focalizer utilizing the sense of touch:

(20) [17c] And laying his hands on him
(21) he said,
(21.1) "Brother Saul, the Lord Jesus
(21.2) who appeared to you on the road

(21.3) by which you came
(21.1) has sent me that you may regain your sight
(21.4) and be filled with the Holy Spirit."
(22) [18a] And immediately something like scales fell from his eyes
(23) and he regained his sight.

Statement (22) is mimetic: scales falling from the eyes is a graphic means of suggesting that Paul's blindness is ending; (23) confirms that inference in a recounted statement. Recounting thus appears in (23) in the transition to the CON:

(24) [18b] Then he rose
(25) and was baptized
(26) [19] and took food
(27) and was strengthened.

The combination of (24)–(25) suggests a *lchg*, while (26) and (27) refer to conditions occurring over a period of time. The scene is defocalized once again by recounting.

42. The next three narrative segments (segments iv–vi) are predominantly in the recounting mode. Since they offer a relatively long stretch of narrative in that mode and because they present some new phenomena, they are best considered together.

Acts 9:19b–30

segment iv

(28) [19b] For several days he was with the disciples at Damascus.
(29) [20] And in the synagogues immediately he proclaimed Jesus,
(30) saying,
(30.1) "He is the Son of God."
(31) [21] And all who heard him were amazed,
(32) and said,
(32.1) "Is not this the man who made havoc in Jerusalem of those who called on this name?
(32.2) And he has come here for this purpose, to bring them bound before the chief priests."
(33) [22] But Saul increased all the more in strength,
(34) and confounded the Jews who lived in Damascus by proving that Jesus was the Christ.

segment v

(35) [23] When many days had passed,
(36) the Jews plotted to kill him,
(37) [24] but their plot became known to Saul.
(38) They were watching the gates day and night, to kill him;
(39) [25] but his disciples took him by night
(40) and let him down over the wall,
(41) lowering him in a basket.

segment vi

(42) [26] And when he had come to Jerusalem
(43) he attempted to join the disciples;
(44) and they were all afraid of him,
(45) for they did not believe he was a disciple.
(46) [27] But Barnabas took him,
(47) and brought him to the apostles,
(48) and declared to them
(48.1) how on the road he had seen the Lord,
(48.2) who spoke to him,
(48.3) and how at Damascus he had preached boldly in the name of Jesus.
(49) [28] So he went in and out among them in Jerusalem,
(50) [29] preaching boldly in the name of the Lord.
(51) And he spoke
(52) and disputed against the Hellenists;
(53) but they were seeking to kill him.
(54) [30] And when the brethren knew it,
(55) they brought him down to Caesarea,
(56) and sent him off to Tarsus.

43. Statement (29) is iterative: Paul proclaimed Jesus in the synagogues (plural). Another form of the iterative appears in (28): "For several days he was with the disciples." This statement does not, strictly speaking, signify repeated action, but what we might call durative action, an action that might be represented as a solid line (______) rather than as a series of dots (. . . . . .).[37] A third type of iterative statement is found in (43): "he attempted to join the disciples." Once again, the action represented by this statement is not, strictly speaking, repeated; the word used to described it is "attempted," for which the technical grammatical term, "conative," is employed.[38] The iterative, as defined earlier, is a single narrative statement in which repeated events, taken synthetically, are represented.[39] We must broaden that definition to include the durative and the conative, but we will continue to utilize the term iterative to refer to all types of repeated or durative or conative action combined in one narrative statement.

44. With these qualifications in mind, it can now be said that narrative segments iv–vi, sketched above, are made up of iterative statements in the recounting mode, with the exception of singulative statements in the recounting mode, to be noted. Stated differently, all statements are diegetic in character; some are iterative, some singulative.

Statements (39)–(40) are singulative: they refer to a single, unrepeated event. With these we may compare (30)–(30.1) and (31)–(31.2). During the

37. In the parlance of Greek grammar, the durative is also termed linear *aktionsart*, or kind of action.

38. From the Latin word *conari, conatus*, to attempt.

39. See above, §6.1, 6–7.

days Paul was in Damascus, he used to speak in the synagogues (more than once: iterative). Then, in direct discourse, we are told that he said, "He is the Son of God." Did he always say exactly the same thing on those several occasions? Or did he vary his sermon, saying now this and now that? It was more likely the latter. For that reason, Genette dubs the type of narrative statement found in (30.1) the "pseudo-iterative" and he defines it in this way: "The narrative affirms literally 'this happened everyday,' to be understood figuratively as 'everyday something of this kind happened, of which this is one realization among others.'"[40] The second example is comparable. All who heard Paul on those various occasions were amazed and used to say, "Is not this the man who made havoc in Jerusalem of those who called on his name?" This is another example of the pseudo-iterative: they said something like this each time, of which this is one realization.

It is perhaps unnecessary to examine the narrative statements in these segments one by one in order to demonstrate that each is in the recounting mode. It is more illuminating to observe the various elements that go to make up focus in mimetic scenes. We may begin with time. The temporal span of the three segments as a whole and of the segments individually is indefinite: "several days" (28) is followed by "after many days" (35); a journey to Jerusalem indicates a time lapse of indefinite span (42), and the events of (49)–(56) take place over an unspecified period of time. The times of the three segments are telescoped, so to speak: longer temporal stretches are compressed into iterative statements.

The locales indicated in these segments are relatively large and therefore constitute unfocused space. Damascus, synagogues, over the wall (which runs all the way around Damascus), Jerusalem, Caesarea, and Tarsus are as close to defined space as the narrator gets in this passage.

The sets of participants are quite indefinite. In the first segment, the participants are disciples, all those who heard him, and the Jews in Damascus. These are scarcely focused groups. The second segment has the Jews and disciples, while disciples, Barnabas, apostles, Hellenists, and the brethren are found in the third segment. Among these, only Barnabas is sufficiently defined to function in a focused scene; indeed, the events reported in (46)–(48) are singulative, but the statements are nevertheless diegetic, as the indirectly reported statements in (48.1–3) reveal.

45. Why has the narrator inserted three rather substantial segments in the recounting mode at this point in his narrative, when he appears, by and large, to narrate in the mimetic mode? We can attempt at least a partial answer to this question.

As a general rule, it may be imagined that more important events are

40. *Narrative Discourse*, 121–22.

narrated in the mimetic mode and thus in a more decelerated fashion,[41] while events of lesser importance are summarized or narrated in accelerated fashion. Rimmon-Kenan states the matter in this way: "Acceleration and deceleration are often evaluated by the reader as indicators of importance and centrality. Ordinarily, the more important events or conversations are given in detail (i.e., decelerated), whereas the less important ones are compressed (i.e., accelerated)."[42] Then she warns us: "This is not always the case." The narrator may wish to effect shock or irony and thus reverse the relationship: important events may be narrated briefly or elided, while trivial happenings may be given full treatment. In folk literature, it is to be expected that the norm is: length betokens importance. If Acts falls into that category, the narrator at this juncture in his narrative is inserting connective events, which, although of less importance to the story, are nevertheless necessary to link the conversion of Paul just narrated with subsequent stories about Peter and Paul to follow. Yet this observation warrants further investigation before being adopted as firm.

That the narrator places less emphasis on the events of these segments is supported by two further observations. First, segment iv, Acts 9:19b–22, appears to function as a CON to scenes i–iii, Acts 9:1–19a, all of which are mimetic in nature. Conclusions, as stated earlier, are regularly transitional in character and diegetic. It is also possible, secondly, that segments iv–vi serve as the CON to the statements and stories about Paul that begin in 7:58. And, finally, the general narrative summary that appears in 9:31 is probably the CON to the sequence that begins in 6:8. In other words, we have three conclusions, in ascending order of generality:

Segment iv:	CON to 9:1–19a
Segments iv–vi:	CON to references to Paul, which begin in 7:58
9:31:	general CON to sequence beginning in 6:8

This would account, at least in part, for the decision by the narrator to switch to the diegetic mode at 9:19b.

41. See above on duration, §§6.18–24.
42. *Narrative Fiction*, 56.

7

Segmentation

• 7 •

INTRODUCTION

1. Some tentative rules for narrative segmentation were developed in §§4.7–32 on the basis of Acts 3:1–4:31. Those rules were derived from the analysis of participant sets and focus, temporal and spatial markers, and thematic considerations in the sequence as a whole; rules at this level were based on what may be termed *macrofeatures*. A closer reading provided additional clues to segmentation; such clues were based on what may be termed *microfeatures*. They included focalizers and defocalizers, participant identification, temporal distance between segments, and locale changes. On the basis of both macro- and microfeatures, a hierarchy of segments and sequences was developed, consisting of introductions, nuclei, and conclusions, at various narrative levels.

As remarked earlier, segmentation is a fundamental exercise in narrative analysis. Upon it depends the critic's ability to read the surface structures of a text and to proceed from them to interpretative questions. The greater the control of surface markers, the more enhanced the possibility of nuanced interpretation. Of course, the mastery of the grammar of the narrative no more assures the correct interpretation of narrative texts than skill in sentence grammar assures the final interpretation of periods.

2. The rules for segmentation are summed up in the Table of Codes. The section on Marks of Segmentation is reproduced here for convenience of reference.

• *Marks of Segmentation* •

1. With reference to participants:
   - P*set* = introduction of a new set of participants
   - P*id* = the formal introduction of a new participant
   - P*nomchg* = change in nomenclature of a participant
   - P*noun* = reuse of noun (rather than pronoun) to identify a participant
   - P*reid* = reidentification of a continuing participant
2. With reference to time:
   - *ts* = a temporal setting (notice)
   - *tchg* = a temporal change
   - *a:retro* = reference to a preceding action as past
3. With reference to place:
   - *ls* = a locale setting (notice)
   - *lchg* = locale change
   - *dep* = a departure

4. With reference to focalizers and defocalizers: any new focalizer following a defocalizer

These codes will be further explicated as rules for segmentation. The explication will utilize texts in the form of healing miracle stories and parables.

THE HEALING OF THE INFIRM WOMAN

3. Many healing miracle stories reported in the Gospels are of the single-scene variety. However, we occasionally find more complex healing narratives consisting of two or more scenes. The story of the woman who had a spirit of infirmity represents an intermediate stage in the development of more complex narratives. In this instance, we have what form critics call a pronouncement story joined to a healing story to form a two-scene narrative. The text may be divided into narrative statements and analyzed as follows:

——— • *The Healing of the Infirm Woman* • ———

Luke 13:10–17

scene i

(1) [10] Now he was teaching in one of the synagogues on the sabbath.
(2) [11] And there was a woman
(3) who had a spirit of infirmity for eighteen years;
(4) she was bent over
(5) and could not fully straighten herself.
(6) [12] And when Jesus saw her,
(7) he called her
(8) and said to her,
(8.1) "Woman,
you are freed from your infirmity."
(9) [13] And he laid his hands upon her,
(10) and immediately she was made straight,
(11) and she praised God.

scene ii

(12) [14] But the ruler of the synagogue, indignant
(13) because Jesus had healed on the sabbath,
(14) said to the people,
(14.1) "There are six days on which work ought to be done;
(14.2) Come on those days
(14.3) and be healed,
(14.4) and not on the sabbath day."
(15) [15] Then the Lord answered him,
(15.1) "You hypocrites!
Does not each of you on the sabbath untie his ox or his ass from the manger,

(15.2) and lead it away to water it?
(15.3) [16] And ought not this woman,
(15.4) a daughter of Abraham whom Satan bound for eighteen years,
(15.3) be loosed from this bond on the sabbath day?"
(16) [17] As he said this,
(17) all his adversaries were put to shame;
(18) and all the people rejoiced at all the glorious things that were done by him.

A close reading of this narrative will yield several clues for a grammar of segmentation.

MARKS OF SEGMENTATION

4. Participant sets. The first observation concerns participant sets (P*set*). The participants in this story are Jesus, whom we will designate (A), the infirm woman (B), the ruler of the synagogue (C), and the people (D). The P*set* of the first scene consists of (A)/(B); that of the second set, (C)/(D)/(A). There are four different participants. The axiom of folk literature is that only three animate participants may be permitted on the narrative stage at one time. That suggests that there must be more than one scene since there are four characters. And, indeed, the shift in P*sets* at (12) confirms the fact that there are two scenes. In this story, the first scene takes place between Jesus and the woman; the woman drops out of the second scene and is replaced by the ruler of the synagogue and the people. On the basis of a shift in P*sets* alone it is certain that the story consists of two scenes.

5. New participants. This mark of segmentation is reinforced by a second, related mark. A new P*set* may not involve the introduction of a new participant into the narrative. However, when a new participant is formally introduced in connection with a shift in the set, it is doubly certain that a new segment has begun. The ruler in the synagogue is presented as a new participant, i.e., with P*id*, in this case, (C)*id*: he is called "the ruler of the synagogue," rather than being designated "he," or "the man," which would make it difficult to identify him. P*id* means, in other words, that the new participant is identified by nomenclature that sets him or her off from all other participants.

6. Naming participants. A third mark of segmentation is also related to the naming of participants. In the parable of the Laborers in the Vineyard (Matt 20:1–16), the leading figure is called "a householder" at the outset of the story. At the beginning of the second scene, he is referred to as "the master of the vineyard." A third rule therefore is: it is a mark of segmentation if a participant is given a new name or title. This mark may be given the code P*nomchg*, which stands for participant: nomenclature change.

In the first scene of the account of the infirm woman, Jesus is referred to by the common name, Jesus (6), as frequently in the gospel narratives. In the second scene, at the point where he becomes the initiator of the action (15), he is called "lord." This P*nomchg* marks the second scene off from the first.

7. A variation of the third rule concerns the full identification of a continuing participant who might, in a non-segmented narrative, be referred to by pronoun or some other reduced form of identification. For example, in the parable of the Prodigal Son, one son is identified in the introduction as "the younger of them." At the beginning of the first scene, he is called "the younger son," and is tracked throughout that scene thereafter by pronoun. At the beginning of the second scene, he is once again referred to as "the son" when he becomes the initiator of the action. P*reid* means that a continuing participant is reidentified at the opening of subsequent segments, whether or not there would be confusion in roles were that participant not so identified.

8. Temporal shifts. An explicit shift in time also attests a change in scene or a new segment of the narrative. In the parable of the Laborers in the Vineyard (Matt 20:1–16), referred to above, the story opens "early in the morning" (Matt 20:1). The householder repeats his visits to the marketplace to hire workers until the eleventh hour. Then, "when evening came" (vs 8) he calls his steward to pay wages. The shift to evening clearly marks a new segment in the story. A temporal shift of this order has been coded *tchg* (for temporal change).

9. Correspondingly, when a subsequent segment of the narrative looks back on previous events as past, the reader also knows that a new narrative segment has been created. Also in the Laborers in the Vineyard, agreements made and work done earlier in the day are referred to in the second scene as though they were past. This temporal distancing by means of the pluperfect (in English, the past perfect: past from the standpoint of a narrative told in past time) also marks temporal segmentation. The code for this retrospective view of previous events is coded *a:retro* (standing for action: retrospective).

An explicit temporal change is not provided in the story of the infirm woman. However, the reader is told that the ruler of the synagogue was indignant "because Jesus *had healed* on the sabbath." In the second segment, the activity of the first scene is cast into the past, indicating by the tense of the verb that the second scene is set in a new and subsequent time.

10. Locale changes. A shift in locale is often employed as a token of segmentation. Both scenes of the healing of the infirm woman take place in the synagogue; there is thus no change of locale to mark the beginning of the second segment. The healing of the lame man in Acts, on the other hand, takes place at the gate of the temple (Acts 3:2). In the next scene, Peter addresses the multitude in Solomon's Portico (3:11): the change in locale (*lchg*) sets off the new narrative segment.

The three scenes of the Prodigal Son are likewise marked by locale changes. The first scene is set "in a far country" (Luke 15:13). In the second, the son is returning home, but is still some distance away when his father comes out to meet him (15:20), while the third scene, featuring the older son, takes place outside the house, as the older son is returning from the field (15:25). There are thus three distinct *lchgs* marking the three divisions of the narrative.

11. A shift in locale is often preceded by a departure at the conclusion of the previous segment. Occasionally a departure is the only clue to a change in place. A departure and a new spatial setting tend, of course, to reinforce each other, although one or the other may stand alone as a signal.

In the account of the healing of the ten lepers (Luke 17:11–19), which is also made up of two segments, the ten lepers depart at the end of scene i (17:14). The grateful leper returns to open the second scene (vs 15). We do not know whether the locale in the two scenes is identical. For the purposes of the narrative that knowledge is unnecessary. For purposes of segmentation, departure and arrival are clear enough indicators.

12. Focalizers and defocalizers. Narrative segments of the mimetic variety are customarily opened with what has been termed a focalizer (§§5.3–17). Focalizers will often stand in contrast to a preceding defocalizer, the contrast between the two indicating where the narrative seam is.

In the Prodigal Son, the younger son, after squandering his patrimony in a far country, departs for home at the end of scene i (Luke 15:20). Then scene ii opens with these statements: "But while he was yet at a distance,/ his father saw him" (15:20). Seeing is a focalizer in this instance, marking the beginning of the second scene; it contrasts with the departure that closes the previous scene.

Similarly, at the end of scene ii, "they began to make merry" (vs 24), which is a terminal function (*termf*), another form of defocalizer. That is followed, at the opening of scene iii, by the statements:

(1) [25] Now his older son was in the field;
(2) and as he came
(3) and drew near the house,
(4) he heard music and dancing.

Statement (4) is a sensory focalizer: the attention of the older son is focused on the merriment that is taking place indoors. Once again, a focalizer is preceded by a defocalizer, marking the transition between narrative segments.

THE MIRACLE AT THE POOL

The marks of segmentation have been defined and illustrated in §§7.2–12. As the further illustration of those rules, we shall turn next to longer connected sequences, involving miracle stories, as in the case of the account of the Infirm Woman considered above. At the same time, however, the analysis and commentary on these texts will permit a more synoptic view of the rudiments of a narrative poetics. The first to be examined is the account of the healing of the lame man at the pool Bethzatha (John 5:1–18), to be followed by a close analysis of the changing of the water into wine (John 1:1–11).

13. The Miracle at the Pool, as we shall term the story, is a complex narrative consisting of four segments. The first step is to set out the text in the form of narrative statements and to annotate those statements with narrative codes.

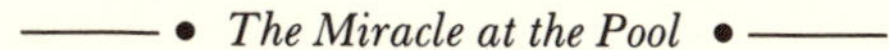

The Miracle at the Pool

John 5:1–18

scene i

P*set*:	A = Jesus/B = patient
Place:	Pool by the Sheep Gate
Time:	Feast of the Jews; a sabbath

INTRODUCTION

(1)	1 After this	*tc*
	there was a feast of the Jews,	*ts* (cf. 5:9b)
(2)	and Jesus went up to Jerusalem.	A:*lchg* / *pref:arr*
(3)	2 Now there is in Jerusalem	ls^{1}
	by the sheep gate a pool,	ls^{2}
(4)	in Hebrew called Bethzatha,	ls^{3}
(5)	which had five porticoes.	ls^{4}
(6)	3 In these there used to lie	Bid^{1}
	a multitude of invalids, blind, lame, paralyzed.	*impf:desc*
(7)	5 One man was there,	*pref:pos*
(8)	who had been ill for thirty-eight years.	Bid^{2}

NUCLEUS

(9)	6 When Jesus saw him	*f:perc*
(10)	and knew that he had been lying there a long time,	
(11)	he said to him,	
(11.1)	"Do you want to be healed?"	
(12)	7 The sick man answered him,	
(12.1)	"Sir, I have no man to put me into the water	
(12.2)	when the water is troubled,	
(12.3)	and while I am going	
(12.4)	another steps down before me."	
(13)	8 Jesus said to him,	
(13.1)	"Rise,	
(13.2)	take up your pallet,	
(13.3)	and walk."	

CONCLUSION

(14)	9 And at once	*tc*
(15)	the man was healed,	B:*tf*
(16)	and he began to walk.	B:*dep / le*
		[A:*dep:*cf. 5:13]

scene ii

P*set*: B = patient
C = “the Jews”
Time: a sabbath
Place: same (a crowded place)

INTRODUCTION

(17)	Now that day was the sabbath.	*ts*³*:retro* (cf. 5:1)

NUCLEUS

(18)	10 So the Jews said to the man who was cured,	C*id / f:perc /* B*id:retro*
(18.1)	“It is the sabbath,	*ts*³(cf. v. 9b)
(18.2)	it is not lawful for you to carry your pallet.”	
(19)	11 But he answered them,	
(19.1)	“The man who healed me said to me,	*a:retro* A*id:retro*
(19.1a)	‘Take up your pallet,	
(19.1b)	and walk.’”	
(20)	12 They asked him,	
(20.1)	“Who is the man who said to you,	*a:retro*
(20.1a)	‘Take up your pallet,	
(20.1b)	and walk’?”	

CONCLUSION

(21)	13 Now the man who had been healed did not know who it was,	B*id:retro / constop*
(22)	for Jesus had withdrawn,	A*:dep:retro*
(23)	as there was a crowd in the place.	*def:pe:retro*

scene iii

P*set*: A/B
Time: later
Place: temple

INTRODUCTION

(24)	14 Afterward,	*tc*

NUCLEUS

(24)	Jesus found him in the temple,	A*:f:arr*
(25)	and said to him,	
(25.1)	“See, you are well!	

(25.2)	Sin no more,	
(25.3)	that nothing worse befall you."	*def:dis*
(26)	15 The man went away	B:*dep*

segment iv

P*set*:	B/C/A
Time:	indefinite
Place:	indefinite

(26)	15 The man went away	B:*dep=arr*
(27)	and told the Jews that it was Jesus who had healed him.	*a:retro*
(28)	16 And this is why the Jews kept persecuting Jesus,	*com / iter*
(29)	because he used to do this on the sabbath.	*iter*
(30)	17 But Jesus answered them,	*direct discourse*
(30.1)	"My Father is working still,	
(30.2)	and I am working."	
(31)	18 This is why the Jews kept seeking all the more to kill him,	*com / iter*
(32)	because he not only used to break the sabbath	*iter*
(33)	but also kept calling God his Father,	*iter*
(34)	making himself equal with God.[1]	*iter*

14. Participant markers. The four segments as outlined in §13 coincide with shifts in P*sets*. The participants in the first scene are A/B; in the second scene, B/C; in the third scene, A/B; all three are mentioned in the final, unfocused segment.

The sick man is identified in scene ii as "the man who was cured" (18); Jesus is identified as "the man who healed me" (19.1). Both of these represent changes in nomenclature for continuing participants (P*nomchg*). In this connection, it is interesting to note that the authorities refer to Jesus as "the man who said to you" (20.1), also P*nomchg*, but with a subtle difference: the one who was cured had said that Jesus was "the man who cured me."

Jesus is reidentified (*reid*) at the beginning of scene iii, although the lame man is referred to by pronoun. The aberration of the identification rule (pronoun rather than *reid*) appears to have been occasioned by the *reid* of the man in (26), which functions as the CON to scene iii as well as the INTRO to segment iv. Thus, in the final segment, segment iv, all three participants are *reid*. Segment iv serves, of course, as the CON to the sequence (scenes i–iii).

15. Temporal and spatial markers. The temporal setting and changes also clearly mark off the four segments as indicated, although the narrator has added some rather subtle touches. The first scene is set during a "feast of the Jews"; we are not told immediately that it was also a sabbath. At the beginning

1. The translation is RSV, except for modifications of my own to clarify points of narrative grammar.

of the second scene it is now flatly stated that the day on which the preceding and following actions occurred was also a sabbath. That fact prompts the reader to pause, to reread the preceding segment reflexively, in order to calculate whether this new piece of information makes any difference. It does. The controversy that follows consequently takes on new meaning. By placing the temporal notice at the beginning of scene ii, rather than at the beginning of scene i, the narrator triggers a reflective pause on the part of the reader. For that reason, (17) is labelled *ts:retro*, which means that this temporal reference has retrospective significance as well as prospective meaning.[2] We shall note other examples of retrospective notices below, although not necessarily of the kind that produce reflexive rereading.[3]

Scene iii takes place "later." When the reader comes to segment iv, the focus of the narrative has dissipated: the time is indefinite since most of the events are in the iterative mode. Nevertheless, the four segments are clearly delineated by temporal changes.

The narrator also makes ample use of *a:retro*: he refers to events in preceding scenes as past. There are none, of course, in scene i, but in scene ii, in addition to the retrospective temporal reference already mentioned, (18) refers to the cure of the lame man as something past; in (19.1), the cured man refers to Jesus as someone who healed him in the past; and in (20.1), the authorities allude to Jesus as someone who told the lame man to take up his pallet and walk in the past. The lame man is again identified as someone who was healed in the past in (21). Finally, the reader learns, again belatedly, that Jesus had withdrawn unnoticed following the cure in scene i and that this was possible because there was a crowd in the place. In sum, scene ii is almost entirely retrospective in character: it goes back over the first scene in some detail and modifies what the reader has already learned. In doing so, of course, the reader now learns that there is a controversy and what the controversy is about.

Scenes i and ii take place at the pool by the Sheep Gate. We learn, again belatedly, that the place where they were was "crowded" (23). The space of the two scenes is thus continuous. The next scene, however, is set in the temple (24). The final segment, again, is not specifically localized. This indefiniteness goes together with recounting in the iterative mode.

16. *Focalizers and defocalizers.* Scene i is focalized in (9), and defocalized in (15) and (16). The latter are weak defocalizers, however, because the narra-

2. Norman Petersen develops this device in connection with his reading of Mark: *Literary Criticism for New Testament Critics*, 56–59. He takes references to past events in general to have this effect. I doubt that all such references do so, but I can imagine that the device about which we are speaking, and for which there is no technical name, so far as I know, can be used to great effect by the subtle author.

3. Termed analepses, which are discussed in §§8.3–7. Also cf. §11.10, where John 5:9 is identified as a special kind of analepsis, viz., a paralepsis.

tor has chosen to delay the announcement of Jesus' departure until later (22). Nevertheless, when the lame man begins to walk, the reader will assume a departure is imminent; in fact, however, the lame man remains in the same general space, which is also the setting of scene ii. The weak defocalizers go together with weak introductory material at the head of scene ii. We have already suggested that scene ii is a retrospective rereading of scene i, so the narrator evidently chose to join the two scenes together with a minimum of formal markers.

The defocalizers in (22) and (23) function for both scenes i and ii. Jesus actually departs at the end of scene i, and is able to do so because of the crowd (*pe*). Since the narrator has delayed these statements, he omits mentioning that the lame man also finally departs (he is next seen in the temple). By these various devices, the narrator has joined the two scenes closely together and yet they are also readily segregated. By observing the employment of narrative markers closely, the reader can learn to interpret the nuances of the narrative with greater finesse.

Scenes iii and iv, interestingly enough, are also closely linked. Scene iii is focalized in the normal way in (24), but the defocalizer in (26), which is a departure, also functions as an arrival in segment iv.[4] Since the final segment is unfocused, it does not have the customary focalizers and defocalizers.

17. Types of narrative discourse. Scenes i–iii are enacted. Segment iv, however, is recounted. The events are never brought into focus. Indeed, most of the statements are in the iterative mode: (28), (29), (31), (32), (33), (34). Statements (26) and (27) alone are in the singulative mode, and this serves as the immediate link to the preceding scenes: the final act of the lame man is to go and tell the Jews who cured him. The reader does not learn whether this was a hostile act toward Jesus or not. The account immediately modulates into some general observations regarding Jesus and "the Jews." It is curious that into the midst of statements that are part recounting and part commentary, the narrator has inserted one final piece of direct discourse: (30) is a fragment of enactment lodged between iterative recounting and commentary. The contrast is stark. The direct discourse in (30) is another example of the pseudo-iterative:[5] the Jews used to persecute Jesus, and he answered them, "My Father," etc. This happened many times and Jesus gave responses each time, of which this is one realization.

Finally, notice should be taken of the character of (28)f. and (31)ff. The narrator breaks out of the recounting mode and comments on the situation: the Jews persecuted Jesus because he used to heal on the sabbath; and the Jews sought to kill Jesus because, in addition to breaking the sabbath, he also kept identifying himself with God. We thus have a fourth type of narrative

4. For this reason, the statement is repeated in the analysis but given the same number.
5. Other examples and a definition are found in 6.44.

discourse, the commentary, to be distinguished from both enactment and recounting, as well as from description.

The narrator has thus combined, in a brief narrative segment, four types of narrative discourse: enactment, recounting in both the singulative and iterative modes, and commentary. Segment iv is a sampler segment.

THE MIRACLE AT CANA

18. One significant question of interpretation is whether the miracle stories in the Fourth Gospel serve the same purpose as they do in the Synoptics and Acts. The miracle accounts in the latter are told primarily to underscore the wonder-working powers of Jesus. In John, on the other hand, it has been argued that the miracles are told for the sake of the symbolic possibilities latent in them. The miracle itself is unimportant; it is the symbolic meaning that counts with John.[6] Narrative analysis will throw light on this question.

19. The first step is again to establish the segments and formal structure of the narrative.

• *The Miracle at Cana* •

John 2:1–11

scene i

P*set*:	A = the mother of Jesus	
	B = Jesus	
	C = the disciples	
	D = the servants	
Time:	On the third day	
Place:	Cana	
INTRODUCTION		
(1)	1 On third day	*ts*
	there was a marriage feast at Cana	*ls*
	in Galilee,	*ls*
(2)	and the mother of Jesus was there;	A*id*
(3)	2 Jesus was also invited to the	B*id*
	marriage, with his disciples.	C*id*
NUCLEUS		
(4)	3 When the wine failed,	*f:perc*
(5)	the mother of Jesus said to him,	
(5.1)	"They have no wine."	
(6)	4 And Jesus said to her,	
(6.1)	"O woman,	
	what have you to do with me?	

6. B. Olsson, *Structure and Meaning in the Fourth Gospel*, 19.

(6.2) My hour has not yet come."
(7) [5] His mother said to the servants,
(7.1) "Do whatever he tells you."
(8) [6] Now six stone jars were standing there, for the Jewish rites of purification,
(9) each holding two or three measures.
(10) [7] Jesus said to them,
(10.1) "Fill the jars with water."
(11) And they filled them up to the brim.
(12) [8] He said to them,
(12.1) "Now draw some out,
(12.2) and take it to the steward of the feast." *def:dis*

CONCLUSION
(13) So they took it [to him.] *def:dep*

scene ii
P*set*: E = steward of the feast
F = bridegroom
[D] = servants
Time: same
Place: same

NUCLEUS
(14) [9] When the steward of the feast tasted the water now become wine, *f:perc*
(15) and did not know where it came from
(16) (though the servants who had drawn the water knew),
(17) the steward of the feast called the bridegroom
(18) [10] and said to him,
(18.1) "Every man serves the good wine first;
(18.2) and when men have drunk freely,
(18.3) then the poor wine;
(18.4) but you have kept the good wine until now." *def:constop*

CONCLUSION
(19) [11] This, the first of his signs, Jesus did at Cana in Galilee,
(20) and manifested his glory;
(21) and his disciples believed in him.

20. The INTRO is comprised of (1)–(3). Jesus' mother, Jesus, and his disciples are introduced. The occasion is specified (a marriage); the time (on the third day) and the place (Cana) are indicated.

The P*set* in scene i consists of Jesus' mother, Jesus, and some servants. It is curious that the disciples, who were introduced in (3), do not appear in the NUC of the narrative.

In scene i, a lack is established (no wine) and the lack is overcome (six stone jars are filled with water). The scene closes with the departure of the servants bearing water, now presumably turned to wine, to the steward of the feast.

We have assumed that segmentation occurs at (13)/(14). On what evidence is that assumption based?

First of all, the servants depart at the end of (13) (*def:dep*). A new set of participants appears in the next stretch of narrative: the steward, the bridegroom, and the servants (new P*set*). Furthermore, the steward, who was proleptically introduced in (12.2), is now reintroduced with full identification (E*reid*) (14). Were there no segmentation at this point, we would expect (14) to read: "When *he* tasted the water now become wine," i.e. pronominal reference. Additionally, there is a pluperfect reference in (16) back to events in scene i (*a:retro*). And finally, the *dep* in (13) is followed, in (14), with a new focalizer: the steward "tastes" something (a rare example of the sense of taste being used to focalize a segment).

It is thus clear that (14)–(18.4) constitute a second scene in this brief narrative. This fact is not often noted. The P*set* consists of the steward, the bridegroom, and the servants. The disciples again do not appear.

Statements (19)–(21) function as the CON to the whole. The disciples now reappear. They appear in the INTRO and in the CON, but not in either NUC. They therefore belong to the frame of the story, rather than to the story proper. They do not participate except as silent witnesses. Nevertheless, they are important to the author's larger purpose: the disciples are those who witness the event and believe; it is to the disciples' point of view that the author invites the reader. But what do the disciples witness that leads them to believe?

21. The plot structure of the conventional miracle story is misfortune or lack/an overcoming of that misfortune or lack/and the witness to the powers of the miracle worker. We may enlarge on that plot summary.

The healing miracle is developed out of a lack or misfortune: a sufferer is introduced, usually with some indication of the gravity of the malady (e.g., the woman who had been infirm for eighteen years). This misfortune is overcome in the act of healing. Sometimes, as in Acts 3:1–10, the account of the healing is rather more developed than in the simpler forms of the healing narrative (e.g., the healing of Peter's mother-in-law, Mark 1:29–31). The witness of the observers serves as the conclusion, and this type of conclusion connects the narrative to its larger context, the witness to Jesus of Nazareth as the wonder worker.

For a proper understanding of the Miracle at Cana, it is important to notice how the CON to the more conventional miracle story is handled. In the account of the infirm woman (§7.3), the woman herself praises God at the end of scene i, presumably in gratitude for his goodness to her. But the conclusion to the narrative as a whole indicates that all the people rejoiced at the glorious things done by Jesus.

Similarly, in the story of the Lame Man in Acts 3, the lame man praises God, in addition to jumping up and down in demonstration of his miraculous cure. But the people recognize this man as the one who used to lie at the gate and so are filled with wonder and amazement.

This motif is extremely common in the healing stories, but it is not lacking in the nature wonders. At the conclusion of the story of the stilling of the storm (Mark 4:35–41), the disciples are filled with awe, because they are impressed with the powers of Jesus. When Jesus comes walking to them on the water (Mark 6:45–52), they are terrified, and when the wind ceases, they are astounded.

It is thus characteristic of the miracle stories that either the ones affected by the miracle or those observing testify to the impression made on them. In some cases, both forms of testimony appear. The purpose of this motif, of course, is to call attention to the marvelous powers of the miracle worker.

22. In the Miracle at Cana, the lack (failure of the supply of wine) is established and presumably overcome in scene i, although testimony to that fact does not occur until scene ii, and when it does, it is oblique testimony, in contrast to the conventional tale. On the conventional pattern, one would expect the testimony of independent witnesses, as in the story of the Lame Man (Acts 3). But the steward strangely ignores the miracle and reprimands the bridegroom for holding back the good wine until the inferior has been consumed. The steward's pronouncement is, in fact, unrelated to the miracle as such; it has to do rather with the significance of the new and better wine.

The theme of scene ii is thus patently a non-literal treatment of the changing of the water into wine. The structure of the narrative bears this out: testimony to the powers of the miracle worker is suppressed in favor of a dark saying about the order of wine service. And the disciples believe in him; they do not marvel, are neither astounded nor thunderstruck. The comparative structure of the miracle narrative demonstrates that in the story in John it is the symbolic meaning that counts.

THE PRODIGAL SON

Several of the parables found in the Gospels are unusually well crafted narratives. In any case, they offer material well suited to the practice of segment analysis. In this section, we shall consider two better-known examples, the Prodigal Son and the Good Samaritan.

23. The Prodigal may be parsed into narrative statements and segments as follows:

• *The Prodigal Son* •

Luke 15:11b–32

segment i
P*set*: A = father
B = two sons
B^1 = younger son
B^2 = older son
Time: [Once upon a time]
Place: [home]

(1) 11 There was a man who had two sons — A*id*
(2) 12 and the younger of them said — B^1*id / f:dia*
to his father,
(2.1) "Father,
give me the share of property that falls to me."
(3) And he divided his living between them. — *def:termf*

segment ii
P*set*: B^1
C = a citizen of that country
Time: not many days later
Place: a far country

(4) 13 Not many days later, — *tc*
(5) the younger son gathered all he had — *dep / lchg*
(6) and took his journey into a far country,
(7) and there he squandered his property in loose living.
(8) 14 And when he had spent everything,
(9) a great famine arose in that country,
(10) and he began to be in want.
(11) 15 So he went
(12) and joined himself to one of the citizens of that country,
(13) who sent him into his fields to feed swine.
(14) 16 And he would gladly have fed on the pods that the swine ate;
(15) and no one gave him anything.
(16) 17 But when he came to himself
(17) he said,
(17.1) "How many of my father's servants have bread enough and to spare,
(17.2) but I perish here with hunger!
(17.3) 18 I will arise
(17.4) and go to my father,
(17.5) and I will say to him,

(17.5a)	'Father,	
	I have sinned against heaven and before you;	
(17.5b)	19 I am no longer worthy to be called your son;	
(17.5c)	treat me as one of your hired servants.'"	
(18)	20 And he arose	*pre-def:dep*
(19)	and went to his father.	*def:dep*

scene iii

P*set*:	B^1/A
Time:	[later]
Place:	near home (20)

(20)	But while he was yet at a distance,	*pre-f:pos*
(21)	his father saw him	*f:perc*
(22)	and had compassion,	
(23)	and ran	
(24)	and embraced him	
(25)	and kissed him.	
(26)	21 And the son said to him,	
(26.1)	"Father,	
	I have sinned against heaven and before you;	
(26.2)	I am no longer worthy to be called your son."	
(27)	22 But his father said to the servants,	
(27.1)	"Bring quickly the best robe,	
(27.2)	and put it on him;	
(27.3)	and put a ring on his hand,	
(27.4)	and shoes on his feet;	
(27.5)	23 and bring the fatted calf	
(27.6)	and kill it	
(27.7)	and let us eat and be merry;	
(27.8)	24 for this my son was dead,	
(27.9)	and is alive again;	
(27.10)	he was lost,	
(27.11)	and is found."	
(28)	And they began to make merry.	*def:termf*

scene iva

P*set*:	B^2 = older son
	D = servant
Time:	simultaneous with party (28)
Place:	just outside the house (31)

(29)	25 Now his older son was in the field;	*B^2id*
(30)	and as he came	*pre-f:arr*^{1}
(31)	and drew near the house,	*pre-f:arr*^{2}
(32)	he heard music and dancing.	*f:perc*
(33)	26 And he called one of the servants	
(34)	and asked what this meant.	

(35)	27 And he said to him,	
(35.1)	"Your brother has come,	
(35.2)	and your father has killed the fatted calf,	
(35.3)	because he has received him safe and sound."	
(36)	28 But he was angry	*def:termf*
(37)	and refused to go in.	*def:non-arr*

scene ivb
P*set*: A/B^2
Time: [immediately following]
Place: [same]

(38)	His father came out	*f:arr*
(39)	and entreated him,	
(40)	29 but he answered his father,	
(40.1)	"Lo, these many years I have served you,	*a:retro*
(40.2)	and I never disobeyed your command;	
(40.3)	yet you never gave me a kid	
(40.4)	that I might make merry with my friends.	
(40.5)	30 But when this son of yours came,	*a:retro*
(40.6)	who has devoured your living with harlots,	
(40.7)	you killed for him the fatted calf!"	
(41)	31 And he said to him,	
(41.1)	"Son, you are always with me,	
(41.2)	and all that is mine is yours.	
(41.3)	32 It was fitting to make merry and be glad,	*a:retro*
(41.4)	for this your brother was dead,	*def:recap*
(41.5)	and is alive;	
(41.6)	he was lost	
(41.7)	and is found."	

24. The segmentation of the Prodigal Son seems quite evident on the basis of the criteria sketched earlier.

The P*set* in segment i consists of A/B^1: the father and the younger son.[7] In segment ii, the P*set* shifts to B^1 and C, a citizen of that far country (12). In the third scene, the P*set* consists of B^1/A. B^1 thus functions as the continuity participant binding i, ii, and iii together. With scene iva, the P*set* changes to B^2/D, who is one of the servants in the father's house. The final scene, ivb, has as its participants B^2/A. Just as B^1 provides continuity for i–iii, so B^2 links iva–ivb.

The divisions into four segments is evident on the basis of P*sets* alone.

25. There is no temporal notice given in segment i. The time has therefore been designated as "once upon a time" and put in brackets in the analysis to

7. I have elected to give the two sons a single designation, B, because they are introduced together in (1), and then divided into B^1 and B^2.

indicate that the designation lacks an explicit textual basis. The second segment opens, however, with an explicit temporal connective, "not many days later" (4). There are two temporal markers within segment ii, moreover, one at (8) and one at (16), simply indicating sequence: "when." In the first stage, the younger son squanders his fortune; "when" he has spent his money, he is on the point of starvation and winds up feeding swine; "when" he finally comes to himself, he reasons that he ought to return home. These internal markers indicate that segment ii covers an indefinite expanse of time. They also betray the fact that this segment is recounted. To this point we shall return momentarily.

Scene iii takes place later, how much later is not said, but enough later to permit the younger son to make the journey home. Scene iva is timed to coincide with the merrymaking going on in the father's house, and scene ivb takes place immediately following.

Although the temporal markers do not explicitly reinforce the four segments at every point, the temporal progression is sufficiently clear to warrant the sketch just offered.

26. The parable opens in the home of the father and the two sons. This is not stated, but it is clearly implied. The younger son changes locales to a far country in segment ii (6). He returns, of course, at the end of that segment, and is met by his father when he is still some distance away. Scene iii is set, therefore, near his home (20). When the older son returns from the fields, he pauses just outside the house (31); this is the setting of both scene iva and ivb.

27. With respect to types of narrative discourse, segments i and ii are basically recounted, in spite of the direct discourse found at (2.1) and (17.1ff). The later is interior monologue, in any case. But in neither case is the reader taken to a specific place and shown events; they are mediated, with the exception of the one piece of direct discourse in (2.1). Scenes iii–iv, on the other hand, are enacted. The father's actions in scene iii are graphically portrayed and his instructions to the servants are detailed; as a consequence, the latter function as a substitute for the actions themselves: "Bring quickly the best robe, and put it on him; and put a ring on his hand"; etc. Similarly, in scene iva, the older son hears music and dancing—which makes graphic the statement in (28): "They began to make merry." The servant recapitulates the events of scene iii, thus reinforcing the "shown" character of those events. Scene ivb is taken up almost entirely with an exchange between father and older son in direct discourse.

28. The use of focalizers and defocalizers undergirds the proposed segmentation. Segment i has a weak focalizer (*f:dia*), while segment ii lacks focalizers. Statement (3) functions as a defocalizer, but it is not as clear cut as a departure would have been. Segment ii ends with the younger son returning home (*def:dep*).

Scene ii is focalized in (21) in a graphic way and is rounded off with a terminal function (28): making merry. (A party is normally a function terminating work, or the day, or the year, etc.) In scene iva, the older son "hears" the music and dancing, which focuses the reader's attention on events from the older son's perspective. At the conclusion of the scene, the older son refuses to go in. That refusal has the value of a "departure" in the sense of a non-arrival where he ought to be. The final scene is marked by the arrival of the father and his entreaty. The scene closes with a recapitulation of the father's speech at the close of scene iii. That is a strong defocalizer.

29. Two further questions remain. The first is this: what is the overall organization of the narrative? The second concerns the elaborate use of retrospective statements in scenes iva and ivb. What is their function? The first question will be taken up here; the second will be reserved for the discussion of order (§§8.24–27 below).

The Prodigal Son

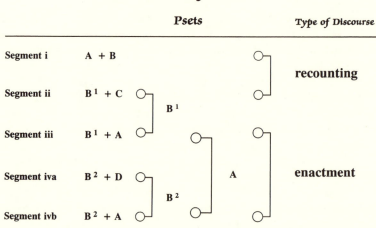

	Psets			Type of Discourse
Segment i	A + B			recounting
Segment ii	B^1 + C	B^1		
Segment iii	B^1 + A			
Segment iva	B^2 + D		A	enactment
Segment ivb	B^2 + A	B^2		

Luke 15:11b – 32

Figure 19

Segment i could be understood as an INTRO to the narrative as a whole. I have elected to designate it as a segment because there are a *tchg* at (4), a *lchg* at (6), and a new P*set* gathered at the beginning of segment ii. Nevertheless, segment i does provide the basic situation out of which the story develops, and is in that sense an "introduction."

There at least two ways to group the segments in this narrative. A grouping determined by the participant in focus will link segments i–iii (B^1), and segments iva and ivb (B^2). The younger son dominates the first group, the older son the second. However, the switch from recounting to enactment is also significant. Indeed, it was suggested earlier (§6.45) that enactment is one way of foregrounding events the narrator takes to be important. Showing also means a slower narrative pace in general (§6.45). A grouping by type of narrative discourse links segments i–ii, and then iii–iv. These two possible groupings are illustrated in figure 19. These two possible groupings go together with a structural ambiguity in the plot of the parable.

As I have argued in an earlier essay,[8] the Prodigal Son can be understood as a narrative in which the contrasting behavior of the two sons in relation to the father is at issue. Or, it can be understood as a narrative which contrasts the responses of the father and the older son to the behavior of the younger son. The former is the traditional way of reading the parable. However, the grouping based on the switch from recounting to enactment suggests the latter. In other words, the two ways of grouping the segments contribute to the structural ambiguity of the parable.

THE GOOD SAMARITAN

30. The parable of the Good Samaritan is readily resolved into narrative statements and segments.

——— • *The Good Samaritan* • ———

Luke 10:30–35

INTRODUCTION

(1)	[30] A man was going down	A*id*
	from Jerusalem to Jericho,	
(2)	and he fell among robbers,	
(3)	who stripped him	
(4)	and beat him,	
(5)	and departed,	
(6)	leaving him half dead.	*pre-f:pos*

NUCLEUS

scene i

(5)	[31] Now by chance a priest was	B^1*id*
	going down that road;	*pre-f:arr*
(6)	and when he saw him	*f:perc*
(7)	he passed by on the other side.	*def:dep*

scene ii

(8)	[32] So likewise a Levite,	B^2*id*
(9)	when he came to the place	*f:arr*

8. *Parables and Presence*, 55–65.

(10)	and saw him,	*f:perc*
(11)	he passed by on the other side.	*def:dep*
scene iii		
(12)	33 But a Samaritan,	C*id*
(13)	as he journeyed,	*pre-f:arr*
(14)	came to where he was;	*f:arr*
(15)	and when he saw him,	*f:perc*
(16)	he had compassion,	
(17)	34 and went to him	
(18)	and bound up his wounds,	
(19)	pouring on oil and wine;	
(20)	then he set him on his own beast	*pre-def:dep*
(21)	and brought him to an inn,	*def:dep*
(22)	and took care of him.	*def:ae*
CONCLUSION		
scene iv		
(23)	35 And the next day	*tchg*
(24)	he took out two denarii	
(25)	and gave them to the innkeeper,	
(26)	saying,	
(26.1)	"Take care of him;	*def:ae*
(26.2)	and whatever more you spend,	*def:ae*
(26.3)	I will repay you when I come back."	*def:dep / return*

31. This narrative is deceptively simple. In fact, it has several unusual features. We can best get at those features by observing the structure of the segments closely.

There are three main scenes, with a fourth functioning as a CON. The P*set* in the first three consists of (A), the man in the ditch, and one other participant, who arrives and departs before the next participant appears. The innkeeper in scene iv does not count as a separate character, since he is part of the setting. The scenes take place in rapid succession, except for the CON, which is separated from scene iii by a nocturnal pause. The place also remains constant, again except for the CON, where the scene shifts to the inn. All four scenes are enacted; even the INTRO borders on the mimetic. In short, the narrative is vivid, graphic in every detail, as brief as it is.

32. It is to be noted that scene i has a pre-focalizer, a focalizer, and a defocalizer. It lacks a NUC. Put differently, the priest arrives and departs without doing anything. Since that is the narrator's point, he abuts the departure on the arrival. Scene ii mirrors scene i: it has a double focalizer, followed by a departure. Again, there is no NUC. Scene iii, by contrast, has a pre-focalizer, two focalizers, and three defocalizers. In addition, it has a substantial NUC by comparison. The actions of the Samaritan are spelled out in detail. The tempo of the narrative has slowed markedly.

The retarded tempo is extended into the CON. The reader first of all has to endure a nocturnal pause, and then the narrator continues the detail of scene iii. The final scene is also defocalized leisurely, comparatively speaking. In each case, the structural feature of the narrative is made to serve the content; form and content are wedded.

The contrast between scenes i and ii, on the one hand, and scenes iii–iv, on the other, is emphasized by another feature. Scene ii is a duplicate of scene i, as the adverb "likewise" in (8) presages. While they are not verbally identical, they are structurally alike.[9] The repetition that is set in motion creates the expectation that scene iii will repeat the preceding scenes. That expectation is thwarted, however, by the mild contrasting statement that opens scene iii: "But a Samaritan . . . ." And then the retarding strategy takes hold.

9. For two other scenes, the second of which mirrors the first, compare Mark 2:16–18 with 2:19–20.

8

Order

• 8 •

INTRODUCTION

1. In folk literature generally, events are customarily narrated in the order in which they occur in story time. In story time, events are time bound and thus must occur in their natural order (e.g., birth before death). But narrative offers the possibility of relating events out of chronological order. A biography, for example, might begin with a person's death (the film *Citizen Kane* begins, for example, with the death of the protagonist) and then, in a series of "flashbacks" or analepses, trace the earlier events of that person's life (as in the film just mentioned).

We have already encountered the question of order in connection with the summary statement of Jesus' life in Act 3:12–16.[1] It was noted that the events presented in that summary were not narrated in chronological order. And this was cited as one reason for distinguishing narrative discourse from story. We must now examine the phenomenon of order more closely.

2. An analysis of the temporal order of a narrative involves the comparison of the order in which events are narrated in the text with the order in which they presumably occurred in story time. Of course, it is not always possible to reconstitute the story order, since the narrator may not provide sufficient clues and a "natural" order may not be inferable. Any discrepancy between the order in story time and the narrated order involves an *anachrony*.[2] An event narrated belatedly—at some point in the text order later than when it occurred in the story order—is an instance of *analepsis* (literally, a recovery, a resumption), while an event narrated prematurely—representing an incursion into the future of the story—is an example of *prolepsis* (literally, an anticipation, a taking beforehand). These are the two principal categories into which anachronies are divided, although it will subsequently be necessary to distinguish various types of analepses and prolepses.

In order to be able to discuss anachronies intelligibly, it is necessary to develop temporal points of reference. If we let 0 (zero) stand for the event currently being narrated, the now of the narrative text at any point along its course, then −1 would stand for the immediately previous event and −2 for the event twice earlier than the present moment, while +1 would stand for

1. §§3.20–21.

2. I am utilizing Genette's terminology for the phenomena connected with order: *Narrative Discourse*, 33–85. Alan Culpepper has discussed most of the phenomena and illustrated them from the Gospel of John in *Anatomy of the Fourth Gospel*, 54–73. Cf. Rimmon-Kenan, *Narrative Fiction*, 46–51; Chatman, *Story and Discourse*, 63–67.

the next future event, and so on. The use of these temporal points of reference can be illustrated by reference to an actual text.

ANALEPSIS

3. The events narrated in Mark 14:43–45 afford an example of simple analepsis:

(1) [43]And immediately, while he was still speaking, Judas came, one of the twelve, and with him a crowd with swords and clubs, from the chief priests and the scribes and the elders.
(2) [44]Now the betrayer had given them a sign, saying, "the one I shall kiss is the man; seize him and lead him away safely."
(3) [45]And when he came, he went up to him at once, and said, "Master!" And he kissed him.

It is evident that (2)—the agreement concerning the sign to be used at the arrest of Jesus—occurred prior to the arrival of Judas and the crowd in the garden (1). The order of events is therefore: (1) = 0/(2) = –1/(3) = 0.

Minus (and plus) numbers in this scheme represent relative temporal order. A –1 means that the event so labelled occurred at a point earlier in the story than the temporal point now being narrated. However, it is possible to be more precise in certain instances in which the earlier point to which the analepsis belongs can be determined. The events of Mark 14:1–45 may be enumerated as follows:

(1)	The authorities seek to kill Jesus	14:1–2
(2)	A woman anoints Jesus	14:3–9
(3)	Judas makes a deal	14:10–11
(4)	The Passover meal	14:12–16
(5)	The traitor	14:17–21
(6)	The Last Supper	14:22–25
(7)	Jesus predicts Peter's denial	14:26–31
(8)	The prayers in the garden	14:32–42
(9)	Judas arrives in the garden	14:43
(10)	Analepsis: the agreement to use a sign	14:44
(11)	Judas kisses Jesus	14:45

Judas' agreement with the chief priests regarding a sign to be used at the arrest must have taken place at (3): Judas makes a deal. The present temporal point of the narrative is (9), which is therefore = 0. If we count backward along this line, (10) hearkens back to what occurred at (3) and is thus = –6 in the chronological progression. To summarize, (9) = 0/(10) = –6/ (11) = 0. It would normally not be necessary, and often not possible, to determine the relative position of analepses in this elaborate fashion.

4. Singulative and iterative analepses. There are both singulative and iterative analepses. The analepsis narrated in Mark 14:44 is singulative: the event occurred only once. In the following example, the analepsis is iterative:

Mark 14:48–50
(1) [48]And Jesus said to them, "Have you come out as against a robber, with swords and clubs to capture me?
(2) [49]Day after day I was with you in the temple teaching, and you did not seize me. But let the scriptures be fulfilled."
(3) [50]And they all forsook him, and fled.

The events narrated in (1) and (3) also belong to the scene in the garden (14:42–52). Statement (2) refers to events earlier in the week when Jesus was frequently in the temple teaching (Mark 11:11–13:37). The reference, however, is not to a single event, but to something that occurred repeatedly: it is therefore an iterative analepsis. As a consequence, it can be located temporally only in a more general way. In relation to the enumeration given above in §3, this iterative analepsis goes back at least to –9, i.e., to a point at the conclusion of the events narrated in 11:11–13:37.

It is necessary to make two further distinctions. Statement (2) in the text just cited is not actually the narration of an event; it is an allusion to an event that is narrated only obliquely: Jesus' visits to the temple to teach are not depicted as such, but the fact that he did so is alluded to.

The second distinction is this: Statement (2) is a part of quoted speech; Jesus is speaking in the garden to those who have come to arrest him. As a speech act, (2) is also to be designated as = 0. The speech act takes place at the present moment of the narrative, although the events that speech refers to occurred earlier.

We must thus distinguish between the narration of events and allusions to events, and we should note that analepses (and prolepses) that are part of direct discourse belong, as speech acts, to the present moment of the narrative, and refer, at the same time, to events that transpired earlier (or subsequently).

5. Homodiegetic and heterodiegetic analepses. The analepses discussed in §§3 and 4, Mark 14:43–45 and 14:48–50, refer to events that belong to the same story line as the principal events in the Gospel of Mark. Because they do so, they are termed homodiegetic analepses (literally, analepses of the same [homo-] story line). Analepses that refer to events outside the first narrative (as the plotted events of the primary discourse may be called) are designated heterodiegetic analepses (literally, belonging to another story line). We also find examples of the latter in the passion narrative of Mark.

Mark 15:6–8
(1) [6]Now at the feast he used to release for them any one prisoner whom they asked.

(2) [7]And among the rebels in prison, who had committed murder in the insurrection, there was a man called Barabbas.

(3) [8]And the crowd came up and began to ask Pilate to do as he was wont to do for them.

Statement (1) refers to something Pilate regularly did during the feast, viz., release a prisoner of the crowd's choice. It is therefore an iterative analepsis; and, since it belongs to another story, it is also heterodiegetic. Statement (2) is an example of a singulative heterodiegetic analepsis: the story of Barabbas is of course another story; the event to which the narrator alludes here, however, happened on one occasion, just recently, which is what makes him a candidate for release at this moment in the first narrative.

6. Completing and repeating analepses. Completing analepses, or returns, as Genette also terms them,[3] go back to an earlier point in the narrative and fill in something that has been omitted. What is filled in may be an event or series of events, or it may be a detail of some importance. In Mark 14:43–45, the sign that Judas and the authorities had agreed to is not mentioned when Judas' deal is narrated (Mark 14:10–11). When the time comes for the betrayal, the narrator returns to the earlier point, and supplies the missing detail. Similarly, in John 5:1–9a, the account of the healing of the lame man at the pool of Bethzatha, the narrator fails to mention that it is the sabbath. But he opens the next scene (5:9b) with that detail. Naturally, that makes considerable difference in how the authorities react to the healing.

Mark 14:72 provides us with a good example of a repeating analepsis:

> [72]And immediately the cock crowed a second time. And Peter remembered how Jesus had said to him, "Before the cock crows twice, you will deny me three times." And he broke down and wept.

This notice repeats what had been narrated at Mark 14:29–31.

> [29]Peter said to him "Even though they all fall away, I will not." [30]And Jesus said to him, "Truly, I say to you, this very night, before the cock crows twice, you will deny me three times." [31]But he said vehemently, "If I must die with you, I will not deny you." And they all said the same.

The middle sentence in 14:72 repeats the prediction of 14:30. It is therefore a repeating analepsis. Completing and repeating analepses, by definition, are also homodiegetic.

7. Reach, extent; internal, external. It will be helpful to define two additional pairs of terms before turning to prolepses and more complex problems of order.

An anachronism may reach into the past or future to a greater or lesser degree from the present moment of the narrative. Its reach may encompass

3. *Narrative Discourse,* 51.

only the preceding moment in the narrative or it may go back as far as creation or forward to the eschaton. That temporal distance, great or small, may be called its *reach*. An analepsis or prolepsis may cover a period of time that is anything from a moment to an indefinite stretch. That period or duration may be referred to as its *extent*.

If an anachronism remains within the temporal boundaries of the narrative text, it is said to be *internal*. If its temporal reach is beyond the beginning of the discourse and its extent ends before the narrative opens, it is said to be *external*; similarly, if a prolepsis is located beyond the end of the first narrative temporally, it is said to be external.

PROLEPSIS

8. In the biblical world, a future that had been predicted was more impressive than one that had not been forecast. In its extreme form, "the plot of predestination," as Todorov terms it,[4] allows for the prediction of all important events, such as the return home of Odysseus and the birth of the messiah, so that the narration of the events themselves becomes anticlimactic. As Todorov puts it so succinctly, "Every nondiscursive event is merely the incarnation of a discourse, reality is only a realization."[5]

9. It is not surprising, in view of the general preference for plots of predestination in ancient narrative (as opposed to open plots of the modern variety) that prolepses abound in the Gospels. Alan Culpepper has catalogued a large number in the Gospel of John.[6] There are several in the passion narrative of Mark to go along with the analepses noted earlier. The following is a partial list:

(1a,1b)	The poor you always have with you; you will not always have me	14:7
(2)	She has anointed my body beforehand for burying	14:8
(3)	Whenever the gospel is preached, her story will be told	14:9
(4)	Jesus gives his disciples detailed instructions to prepare for the passover	14:13–15
(5)	Jesus predicts that one of the twelve will betray him	14:18
(6)	Jesus states that he will not drink with them again until he does so in the Kingdom of God	14:25
(7)	Jesus predicts the disciples will be scattered	14:27

4. *The Poetics of Prose*, 65.
5. The forecast is the primary datum, the fulfillment merely the inevitable realization.
6. *Anatomy of the Fourth Gospel*, 61–69.

(8)	Jesus predicts he will precede them to Galilee	14:28
(9)	Peter avers he will not deny Jesus	14:29
(10)	Jesus predicts Peter will deny him three times	14:30
(11)	Peter repeats his vow; others join in	14:31

The same distinctions apply to prolepses that were sketched in connection with analepses. External, heterodiegetic prolepses have little prospect of "interfering" with the first narrative. They are consequently of less immediate interest to the narratologist. Items (1a) and (3) above fall into this category. On the other hand, (6) is a homodiegetic, external prolepsis: it belongs to the primary story line, but presumably will not occur until some indefinite future. The event predicted in (8) is also external to Mark, whether or not the gospel is taken to end at 16:8.[7] That prediction is repeated in 16:7. Since the author of Mark assumes that everything forecast will occur, the reader will take it for granted that the prediction was realized.

10. Items (1b), (2), (4), (5), (7), (9)–(11) are all internal: they are fulfilled within the temporal framework of Mark. A repeating prolepsis is one in which a prediction is made and then its fulfillment (or nonfulfillment) is narrated. A completing prolepsis fills in, ahead of time, a blank that occurs later in the narrative.[8] All the examples cited above are of the first type: Jesus gives his disciples detailed instructions to prepare for the passover, and immediately events occur as predicted; Jesus predicts one of the twelve will betray him, and the betrayal scene in the garden is narrated shortly thereafter; Jesus predicts that the disciples will be scattered, and that is narrated in 14:50–52; and so on. In some cases the narration of the predicted event is only an allusion, as in the case of (4): "And the disciples set out and went to the city, and found it as he had told them; and they prepared the passover" (Mark 14:16). The event is narrated in detail as a prediction and the actual occurrence is an allusion. The reverse of this occurs in (5): Jesus predicts that one of those eating with him will betray him; the fulfilling event, however, is narrated in some detail in 14:43–50. In addition, this event had been prepared for in 14:10–11, prior to the prediction, where Judas is depicted as striking a deal with the chief priests. Analepses and prolepses of this order provide strong narrative linkages, producing a high level of narrative cohesiveness. Some of the prolepses are singulative (e.g., (2)), some are iterative (e.g., (3)).

In (9)–(11), two predictions are made, only one of which is fulfilled. The predictions, in fact, are contradictory, so that only one is capable of fulfillment; the fulfillment of one entails the nonfulfillment of the other. The vow of Peter that he will not deny Jesus is thus an exception to the rule that the

7. Alternative endings to Mark preserved in the tradition do not narrate a resurrection scene in Galilee.

8. Genette, *Narrative Discourse,* 71.

narrator expects predictions to be fulfilled. Expectations may be frustrated, however, only when one prediction takes precedence over another, contradictory, prediction.

11. The predictions of the passion of Jesus in Mark 8:31, 9:31, and 10:32–34 are internal, homodiegetic, singulative predictions that are subsequently given narrative fulfillment. The prediction of the destruction of the temple in Mark 13:2, by contrast, is external and heterodiegetic.

The account of the death of John the Baptist in Mark 6:14–29 is interpreted by some commentators as proleptic: it is a forecast, albeit indirectly, of the destiny of Jesus. But can we be sure it is a genuine prolepsis? Genette allows for the interesting possibility that some anachronic groupings are governed by principles other than plot.[9] He proposes the term *syllepsis* for this phenomenon (a taking together, literally). Geographical syllepses are well known from ancient travel narratives, in which place is often the occasion for clustering anecdotes. And thematic syllepses are also common: miracle stories or chreiai are gathered together in blocks. It is just possible that the pericope in the death of John is a thematic syllepsis: one passion narrative inserted into another.

12. The prolepses sketched thus far are all of a special kind: narrative predictions or prophecies. They are thus not the narration in advance of an event to occur later, but the forecast that a certain event will take place. However, we observed that in some instances the prediction was given in such detail that it amounts to a narrative account, although cast as a prophecy. Not unlike these predictions is the account of the new heaven and the new earth, and the new Jerusalem, given in Rev 21:1–22:5. The vehicle is a vision. The seer describes conditions and events of the future based on his vision. Again, we do not have events merely narrated out of order, but forecasts of things to come. Prolepses of the type Genette discovers in modern narrative are apparently rare in the New Testament.[10]

ANACHRONIES

13. *John 4:43–45.* This transitional passage in the Gospel of John affords the opportunity to analyze a series of anachronies.

(1) [43] After two days he left for Galilee.
(2) [44] For Jesus himself testified that a prophet has no honor in his own country.
(3) [45] So when he came to Galilee,
(4) the Galileans welcomed him,
(5) having seen

9. *Narrative Discourse,* 85, n. 119.
10. *Narrative Discourse,* 67–79.

(6) all that he had done in Jerusalem at the feast,
(7) for they too had gone to the feast.

The numbers in the lefthand column refer, in this case, not simply to narrative statements, but to events. Events (3) and (4) stand in immediate temporal proximity: Jesus arrives; he is welcomed. These twin events represent the temporal baseline of this segment (=0). What happened in Jerusalem took place prior to Jesus' arrival in Galilee. Immediately prior to the temporal base line of the narrative, (1) Jesus departs for Galilee. Before he departs, actions (2)–(7) take place. Grammatically speaking, action (6) is embedded in (5); (6) thus precedes (5) temporally: Jesus does something; the Galileans perceive him doing it. Action (7) of course precedes (6) and (5): they arrive before they see. It is difficult to be sure where (2) fits in. The logic and the grammar of the sequence require that Jesus leave for Galilee after having testified that a prophet has no honor in his own country.[11] That does not make much narrative sense. If "prophet" refers to Jesus and "his own country" is Galilee, why would Jesus depart for a place where he has no respect?[12] In any case, (2) in the present form of the text must precede (1).

The numbered events may now be coded in accordance with the scheme sketched above:

(1) = – 1
(2) = – 2
(3) = 0
(4) = 0
(5) = – 3
(6) = – 4
(7) = – 5

14. The numbered events could also be given in their absolute chronological order:

(7) (6) (5) (2) (1) (3) (4)

Since all the events narrated precede the present moment of the text, except, of course, for the events of that moment themselves, all are analepses. The analeptical items are narrated in retrograde order, from the most recent to the earliest. Items (1), (3), (7), and possibly (2) are singulative; items (4), (5), and (6) are iterative. All are homodiegetic. Questions of order in this passage are thus straightforward and readily resolved, with the possible exception of the position of (2).

11. As we shall have occasion to notice subsequently, in connection with the analysis of Mark 6:14–29, the Greek particle γάρ ("for") is a signal for an imminent analepsis.

12. "His own country" could be taken to refer to Judea, of course. Or the proverb may be a gloss on the text (Galilean faith is the kind that depends on signs and wonders; cf. 4.48).

15. Mark 6:14–29. The account of the death of John the Baptist presents a more complex set of problems than does the passage from the Gospel of John just analyzed. The passage itself is unique in the Gospel of Mark, as Howard Kee has observed:

> This interpolation embodies a marked departure for Mark on several counts. Nowhere else in the gospel is there such a story without any direct connection with Jesus. The language of the pericope is more cultivated than is usual for Mark; it lacks historical presents, and includes several Markan *ἅπαξ λεγόμενα* [words appearing only once in Mark], as Lohmeyer noted. Thus, the narrative seems to represent a somewhat higher cultural level than is normal for Mark, and may embody a report from a previously existing document.[13]

In addition to the features noted by Kee, this passage is unique also with respect to its order: nowhere else in Mark does the narrator transpose story order so radically over such a short stretch of narrative text.

The text reads as follows (events or groups of events are numbered for the sake of easy reference):

Mark 6:14–29
(1) 14King Herod heard of it; (2) for Jesus' name had become known. (3)
Some said, "John the baptizer has been raised from the dead; that is why
these powers are at work in him." (4) 15But others said, "It is Elijah." (5)And
others said, "It is a prophet, like one of the prophets of old." (6) 16But when
Herod heard of it he said, "John, whom I beheaded, has been raised." (7)
17For Herod had sent (8) and seized John, (9) and bound him in prison for
the sake of Herodias, his brother Philip's wife; (10) because he had married
her. (11) 18For John had said to Herod, "It is not lawful for you to have your
brother's wife." (12) 19And Herodias had a grudge against him, (13) and
wanted to kill him. (14) But she could not, (15) 20for Herod feared John,
knowing that he was a righteous and holy man, (16) and kept him safe. (17)
When he heard him, he was much perplexed, and yet he heard him gladly.
(18) 21But an opportunity came when Herod on his birthday gave a banquet
for his courtiers and officers and leading men of Galilee. (19) 22For when
Herodias' daughter came in and danced, she pleased Herod and his guests;
and the king said to the girl, "Ask me for whatever you wish and I will grant
it." 23And he vowed to her, "Whatever you ask, I will give you, even half of
my kingdom." 24And she went out, and said to her mother, "What shall I
ask?" And she said, "The head of John the baptizer." 25And she came in
immediately with haste to the king, and asked, saying, "I want you to give me
at once the head of John the Baptist on a platter." 26And the king was
exceedingly sorry; but because of his oaths and his guests, he did not want to
break his word to her. 27And immediately the king sent a soldier of the guard
and gave orders to bring his head. He went and beheaded him in prison,

13. *Community of the New Age*, 55.

[28]and brought his head on a platter, and gave it to the girl; and the girl gave it to her mother. (20) [29]When the disciples heard of it, they came and took the body, and laid it in a tomb.

16. This account of the death of John has been inserted, it appears, into the story of the sending out and return of the twelve (6:7–13, 30–32). It is an example, presumably, of one of Mark's literary techniques, viz., interrupting one narrative unit in order to insert another.[14] After the insertion, the original unit is resumed. The insertion, in this instance, is highly visible, since it interrupts an account to which it is only tangentially related. The reasons given for this literary technique include: (1) to heighten the tension; (2) to give the illusion of the passing of time; (3) to underscore Mark's theological interests.[15]

Our interest here is not in the literary technique as such, but in the nature of the inserted material. It should be observed, first of all, that most commentators divide the inserted passage into two parts: 6:14–16 and 17–29. The reasons for this division are obvious: (1) 6:14–16 belong to the present temporal sequence of the story; 17–29 take the reader back to an earlier time; (2) the P*sets* in the two segments are different; (3) the initial phrase of 6:14 is repeated in 16 ("[King] Herod heard of it . . ."), which has the effect of rounding off the first segment. This segmentation, however, may be ignored in analyzing the analepses that occur in the passage as a whole.

17. The first large step is to list the events or clusters of events in the order in which they are narrated and note their relative temporal order in relation to each other (numbers in parentheses refer to the numbers given in the text above).

(1)	Herod receives reports	0
(2)	Jesus' name becomes known	–2
(3)–(6)	Rumors circulate about Jesus	–1
(7)–(9)	John is imprisoned	–4
(10)	Herod marries Herodias	–8
(11)	John censors Herod	–7
(12)–(13)	Herodias wants to kill John	–6
(14)–(17)	Herod protects John	–5
(18)–(20)	John is put to death	–3

Everything from item (2) on is an analepsis. The sequence of the first three groups is as follows: (2) Jesus' name becomes known; as a consequence, rumors begin to circulate about him (3)–(6); (1) Herod receives reports (of

14. This technique is described by John R. Donahue, *Are You the Christ?*, 42f., 58–63. Cf. Kee, *Community of the New Age*, 54–56.

15. The first two reasons are suggested by E. von Dobschütz, "Zur Erzählungskunst des Markus," *ZNW* 27 (1928) 193–98. The third has been argued persuasively by Donahue, Kee, and others in the literature cited by them.

these rumors, of the activity of Jesus, of the activities of the disciples—the reference is not clear). This cluster hangs on item (1), which belongs to the present temporal moment of the narrative text.

Speculation about Jesus relative to John can arise only because John has disappeared from the scene: he was beheaded by Herod at the instigation of Herodias, using their daughter as agent. The death of John immediately precedes the appearance of rumors in the events narrated; it is therefore –3 in the list. John's death is preceded by his imprisonment: he was beheaded while in prison; Herod had put him there, presumably, because John had insulted Herodias and because Herod wanted to keep John safe from her (we may assume a double motivation from (10) and (16)). John's imprisonment is therefore –4. Herod's protection of John perhaps resulted in his imprisonment, so we list it as the next earliest item in the agenda: (14)–(17) = –5. The grudge of Herodias against John (12)–(13) is what prompts Herod to protect him; that grudge thus immediately precedes that protection. And that grudge follows from John's censure of the marriage of Herodias and Herod; the censure must, of course, follow upon that marriage. The grudge must therefore be –6, the censure –7, and the marriage –8.[16]

18. The course of events is easier to follow, perhaps, if they are put in absolute chronological order:

(10)	Herod and Herodias are married	–8
(11)	John censures the couple	–7
(12)–(13)	Herodias bears a grudge	–6
(14)–(17)	Herod "protects" John	–5
(7)–(9)	John is imprisoned	–4
(18)–(20)	John is beheaded in prison	–3
(2)	Jesus becomes popular	–2
(3)–(6)	Rumors circulate about Jesus	–1
(1)	Herod receives reports	–0

The immediate connection with the present narrative moment is (1), of course, and so the reception of reports is narrated first. Mark's interest in the death of John, possibly as a forecast of the ultimate fate of Jesus, prompts him to put that item last, in a position of emphasis. He rounds off the last item by having John's disciples place John's body in a tomb—a strong parallel to the conclusion of Mark's gospel.

16. It appears that the particle γάρ ("for") introducing the cause or reason for something also functions as marker of analeptic insertions. There are four examples in his narrative: (1) Herod receives reports, *for* Jesus' name had become known (6:14); (2) Herod believes that John has been raised from the dead, *for* Herod had put him in prison (6:17); John was in prison, *for* John had censored Herod (6:18); Herodias wanted to kill John but could not, *for* Herod feared John (6:20). Cf. Genette's remarks on subordination and coordination, *Narrative Discourse,* 40.

19. The events in this narrative segment can be related to the chronology of the gospel as a whole. John's imprisonment, (7)–(9), takes place prior to Mark 1:14: John is imprisoned before Jesus begins his ministry in Galilee. At the opening of Mark, however, John is still active (Mark 1:1–11). The events leading up to that imprisonment—John's censure of the royal pair, Herodias' grudge, Herod's protection of John—must take place between Mark 1:11 and 1:14. We have no way of knowing how much earlier Herod and Herodias were married. We thus cannot determine whether the reach of the marriage of the royal pair is external to Mark, or whether it is simultaneous with the activites of John described in Mark 1:1–11. We do not know whether that item is an external or internal analepsis. The remainder of the items, however, are clearly internal: they take place during the temporal period covered by the Gospel of Mark.

The events narrated in items numbered (18)–(20) occur between Mark 1:14 and 6:14: Herod gives his banquet and Herodias obtains the head of John by ruse during this period. Of course, we must assume that the death of John had taken place a bit earlier than 6:14, since time is required for Jesus' popularity to escalate and rumors to circulate following the death of John. But these events cannot be located more precisely.

It should be noted that item (18), the birthday banquet given by Herod, provides the temporal frame for the events grouped together under (19): everything from the daughter's award-winning dance to the presentation of John's head takes place during this banquet. This may well be a fiction, although commentators usually wrestle with historical questions arising out of geographical and other considerations. The burial of John, item (29), presumably takes place following the banquet. It might thus be accurate to represent this group of events as (18 [19]), (20).

20. The first group of events, (1)–(6), are homodiegetic: they belong to the primary story line of Mark. Events (7)–(20) are heterodiegetic: they belong to another story, the story of John, which touches the story of Jesus at certain points, but does not coincide with it. That is clear justification for the usual division at 6:16/17. In addition, (1)–(5) are iterative, while (6) could be either singulative or iterative (did Herod utter this conviction on one occasion, or did he come to it slowly, as a result of the rumors, like that reported in 6:14?). On the other hand, (7)–(11) are clearly singulative events; they are set off, as a consequence, from those reported in 6:14–16. With items (12)–(17) the narrator switches back into the iterative mode, as a means of covering a longer period of time and extended developments. And then, finally, the narrator returns to the singulative with the death of John, (18)–(20), which after all is the climax of this narrative segment.

21. James Joyce: "Eveline." The anachronies of narratives like the gospels of Mark and John stand in strong contrast to those of a modern "psychological" short story like "Eveline" by James Joyce. Long narrative sequences devoted to introspection (events taking place in reverie, in stream of consciousness, and the like) were not common, perhaps not even possible, at the time Mark was composed. The analepses and prolepses examined in Mark's passion narrative often occur in direct discourse, to be sure, but that is still a long step removed from the complete internalization of events past and future such as we find in "Eveline." I have inserted three markers in the text of "Eveline": 0 refers to the present moment of the narrative text; −1 refers to a time in the past; +1 refers to a time in the future. I have not endeavored to order past and future events in relation to each other (in some cases the narrator does not provide sufficient clues to make that possible). The paragraphs have been added to make the shifts readily identifiable. The text reads:

> [0] She sat at the window watching the evening invade the avenue. Her head was leaned against the window curtains and in her nostrils was the odour of dusty cretonne. She was tired. Few people passed. The man out of the last house passed on his way home; she heard his footsteps clacking along the concrete pavement and afterwards crunching on the cinder path before the new red houses.
>
> [−1] One time there used to be a field there in which they used to play every evening with other people's children. Then a man from Belfast bought the field and built houses in it—not like their little brown houses but bright brick houses with shining roofs. The children of the avenue used to play together in that field—the Devines, the Waters, the Dunns, little Keogh the cripple, she and her brothers and sisters. Ernest, however, never played: he was too grown up. Her father used often to hunt them in out of the field with his blackthorn stick; but usually little Keogh used to keep *nix* and call out when he saw her father coming. Still they seemed to have been rather happy then. Her father was not so bad then; and besides, her mother was alive. That was a long time ago.
>
> [0] She and her brother and sisters were all grown up; her mother was dead. Tizzie Dunn was dead, too, and the Waters had gone back to England. Everything changes.
>
> [+1] Now she was going to go away . . . to leave her home, like the others.
>
> [0] Home! She looked round the room, reviewing all its familiar objects which she had dusted once a week for so many years, wondering where on earth all the dust came from. Perhaps she would never see again those familar objects from which she had never dreamed of being divided.
>
> [−1] And yet during all those years she had never found out the name of the priest whose yellowing photograph hung on the wall above the broken harmonium beside the coloured print of the promises made to Blessed Margaret Mary Alacoque. He had been a school friend of her father. Whenever he showed the photograph to a visitor her father used to pass it with a casual word: "He is in Melbourne now."
>
> [−1] She had consented to go away, to leave her home.
>
> [0] Was that wise? She . . . weighed each side of the question . . . tried to. In her home anyway she had shelter and food; she had those whom she had

known all her life about her. Of course she had to work hard, both in the house and at business.

[+1] What would they say of her in the Stores when they found out that she had run away with a fellow? Say she was a fool, perhaps; and her place would be filled up by advertisement. Miss Gavan would be glad. She had always had an edge on her, especially whenever there were people listening. "Miss Hill, don't you see these ladies are waiting?" "Look lively, Miss Hill, please." She would not cry many tears at leaving the Stores.

[+1] But in her new home, in a distant unknown country . . .

22. This short story, of which only the first few lines are quoted above, consists of two scenes. One takes place while Eveline is sitting at the window at evening and falls into a reverie; the second is set at the pier, where she and her lover, Frank, are about to embark for Argentina and a new life together. The first scene is entirely introspective; the second is heavily so.

Since all of the events narrated in scene i take place in Eveline's reverie at evening, they all belong to the present moment of the narrative text as parts of her reverie. However, their content takes the reader both into Eveline's past and into her anticipated future. The narrator, in fact, takes the reader back and forth across the present moment [0] into the past [–1] and then into the future [+1]. The pattern is a perfect zigzag back and forth across the present: 0/–1/0/+1/0/–1/–1/0/+1/+1, provided we make allowance for the succession of –1's and +1's, which merely indicate two different temporal points or locales in the past or future. Joyce maintains this seesaw rhythm throughout scene i.

The content of segments marked –1 are of course analeptic, while that of segments marked +1 are proleptic. In every case the analepses are completing and homodiegetic. In every case, too, both analepses and prolepses are external, since they refer to events that lie beyond the very brief temporal limits of the narrative text.

23. The interiorizaton of the world was made possible by the emergence of writing and then print, according to Walter Ong.[17] Eveline sitting at her window bemusing the past and the present is a consequence of the privatization of reading and writing in the age of the printing press: prior to the print age, the predominant mode of storytelling was still oral and communal; stories were told before an audience and their telling was influenced strongly by audience response. It was thus not possible for the author of Mark to sit at a window at dusk and bemuse the events of the gospel; it was necessary for him to cast those events in an objective mode, to represent them as transpiring in a "real" past, not just in his head as thoughts. Nevertheless, it is worth observing that the analepses and prolepses of Mark's passion narrative

17. *Orality and Literacy,* 152. The whole of chapter 6, "Oral memory, the story line and characterization," 139–55, is relevant to this discussion.

(chapters 14 and 15), that occur in the nuclei of segments, are embedded predominantly in quoted speech, except where they appear in an INTRO or a CON. The appearance of references to the past or the future in transitional material is natural. The use of quoted speech as the vehicle for analepses and prolepses is perhaps the anticipation of the interiorization of the world in a subsequent age. Yet in Mark 6:14–29 quoted speech is not the primary vehicle; here the narrator elects the objectification of events, although narrated out of order.

24. The Prodigal Son. We analyzed the parable of the Prodigal Son in §7.23–29 in detail and called attention to the elaborate use of retrospective statements, especially in scenes iva and ivb. We return now to that issue and comment specifically on the use of analepsis and prolepsis in the parable.

In segment ii, after the younger son has squandered his patrimony and has come to himself, he engages in a soliloquy.[18] During that soliloquy, he says:

(17.3) [18] I will arise
(17.4) and go to my father.

These spoken lines anticipate the action narrated in subsequent lines:

(18) [20] And he arose
(19) and went to his father.

This is one vehicle for prolepsis: a participant anticipates a future action by speaking about it or anticipating it in thought.

Another example occurs in the same soliloquy:

(17.4) and I will say to him,
(17.4a) "Father, I have sinned against heaven and before you;
(17.4b) [19] I am no longer worthy to be called your son;
(17.4c) treat me as one of your hired servants."

Here the younger son is rehearsing a speech he is planning to make to his father when he returns home. That speech is actually given in truncated form later:

(26) [21] And the son said to him,
(26.1) "Father, I have sinned against heaven and before you;
(26.2) I am no longer worthy to be called your son."

At this point the father interrupts him with instructions to the servants to begin preparations for the feast of celebration. The narrator does not need to repeat the balance of the speech since he has already given it in full earlier and because the interruption serves to underscore the father's generous response

18. Statements 17.1–4. The narrative statement analysis is found in §7.23.

(the father can't wait to get the celebration underway: we don't need any talk of my son becoming a servant).

The second example is a verbal prolepsis of a verbal act: a rehearsal of a speech anticipates the actual performance of the speech. The first example is a verbal prolepsis of a non-verbal act: a participant says he is going to do something and then does it. To speak of a "verbal prolepsis" is of course to speak loosely: the narrative text itself is verbal, in relation to which direct and indirect discourse are verbal acts at a second level. To keep the terminology strict, we should perhaps speak of this phenomenon as "embedded verbal prolepsis" or "secondary verbal prolepsis" in order to distinguish this kind of prolepsis from the ordinary kind in which an event is simply narrated ahead of time.

25. In scene iva of the Prodigal Son, when the older son inquires of the servant the meaning of the sounds of merriment emanating from the house, the servant responds by recounting events from scene iii; this phenomenon was labelled *a:retro*, standing for a retrospective statement of an event or events that took place earlier. That, of course, is another label for analepsis. A second form of analepsis occurs in (40.1–4) in scene ivb: the older son refers to his life over many years, reaching back, presumably, beyond the point at which the younger son left home. And then, in (40.5–7), he alludes to the events of scene iii concerning the father's reception of the younger son upon his return. And, finally, the father recalls the final event of scene iii in (41.3), following which he RECAPS the speech he gave at the end of scene iii. All of these have been labelled *a:retro*.

In the first example, cited above, the servant tells the older son what had transpired at the welcome-back party for the younger son. The older son had missed that party, of course, and so the narrator is telling him what he missed. Since those events had been narrated in (27.1)–(28), the analepsis is repeating, with modifications, and the events are singulative. It is, of course, also an internal homodiegetic analepsis. In repeating those events, the narrator is telling the reader that they bear a special significance.

26. When the narrator comes to the analepses of scene ivb, he has the older son recall his own life in one important respect: "I have served you faithfully and never disobeyed one of your commands," the older son laments, "and yet you never gave me a kid for a banquet with friends" (40.1–4). This analepsis is a mixed, iterative, completing analepsis: it reaches back beyond the beginning of the parable but comes up to the time covered by the parable itself; it refers to repeated events or events that took place on no occasion (but should have); and it supplies information that is relative to the primary story line. The failure of the father to recognize the faithfulness of the older son is underscored as the older son continues: in contrast to my behavior over a long period of time, your younger son squandered his patrimony with harlots—a detail that is not narrated in segment ii—and yet you gave him the fatted calf when he returned (40.5–7). This analepsis is both repeating and completing: it repeats the slaughter of the fatted calf but adds the detail about how the younger son squandered his money. It is both iterative and singulative. Its reach is internal to the narrative text of the parable.

27. This retrospective rehearsal of events is intended to set the events of scene iii in a new light, viz., to show how unjustly the father has treated the older son, while pampering the younger son. Thereupon, the father also proceeds to reread the past, as it were, to get matters back in the right light, (that is, in his own light): It is true, the father allows, that you have always been faithful to me, as a consequence of which all that I have is yours; nevertheless, because your brother has come home, it was fitting to make merry. The father's reference to the behavior of the older son repeats what the older son had just said of himself, but it also confirms the history of the older son: its reference is thus double—both to the verbal claim of the older son and to his actual behavior. It is at once completing and repeating. The father's final remarks in (41.3–7) recapitulate the father's words at the close of scene iii. They are thus a repeating analepsis.

The battle of the rereadings is taking place in these analepses. The servant gives the facts in scene iva, and then the older son and the father contest their interpretation in scene ivb. This is one of the principal functions of the analepsis: to cast a part or the whole of the narrative in a new light. In the case of the Prodigal Son, the matter is not resolved within the text of the parable; resolution is left to the reader or listener.

28. The conversion of Paul in Acts 9, 22, and 26.[19] Among the many possibilities afforded by narratives in the New Testament to study analepses, the three accounts of Paul's conversion in Acts 9, 22, and 26 seem especially inviting. We shall not pretend to be exhaustive in examining the possibilities afforded by this threefold repetition, but shall limit ourselves to a few observations.

The initial account of Paul's conversion is narrated in Acts 9:1–22. Following Paul's arrest in Jerusalem toward the close of his career, he is permitted to address the crowd from the steps leading into the Roman barracks. In his address, 22:3–21, he reviews his life and especially his conversion, so that his speech repeats much of what had been narrated in 9:1–22. Then, in 26:2–23, he makes his defense before King Agrippa, although by this time he has already appealed to Caesar and so Agrippa is powerless to free him. In any case, he reiterates much of what he had said in 22:3–21, and thus recapitulates the account in 9:1–22 for a third time.

29. References to earlier events in 22:3–21 and 26:2–23 are both completing and repeating analepses. In his speeches, Paul recounts his experience on the Damascus road, but he also supplies missing information, such as the place of his birth (22:3), his upbringing in Jerusalem under Gamaliel (22:3, 26:4), and his strict life as a Pharisee (22:3, 26:5). These events reach back

19. Acts 9:1–30 was analyzed in detail in §§6:39–45.

beyond the beginning of the Acts narrative and so are external; the extent in the two speeches, however, is mixed: the events begin prior to the temporal beginning of Acts but they come forward into the temporal period of the Acts account. The events of the past are both iterative and singulative. All of them are, of course, homodiegetic: they belong to the primary story line of Acts.

30. In 26:2–23, Paul shifts back and forth from the present narrative moment to the past. In 26:2–3, Paul addresses King Agrippa and asks him to listen patiently (0). He then shifts to an account of his youth in Jerusalem (26:4–5 = –1). In 26:6–8, he returns to his present situation, where he stands on trial (0). Following this, he gives a rather lengthy account of events during the time of his persecution of Christian groups, his journey to Damascus, his conversion experience on the Damascus road, and the resulting charge given him by the heavenly voice (26:9–21 = –1). Finally, in 26:22–23, Paul shifts back to the present moment and his appeal to Agrippa (26:22–23 = 0).

During the charge given to Paul by the heavenly voice (26:16–18), the temporal perspective shifts to the future, but to the future from the standpoint of that moment in the past when Paul saw his vision on the Damascus road. That future concerned his commission as a missionary to the Gentiles, a commission he fulfilled, presumably, between his conversion and his defense before Agrippa. That future is thus still past from the standpoint of the present narrative moment. Furthermore, the succession of temporal moments involved are subordinate, one to the other, as follows: Paul's defense is the zero point (0), in relation to which we will designate his vision on the Damascus road as (–2), arbitrarily, in order to be able to label the forecast of his mission to the Gentiles as (–1) in the absolute chronology, although that (–1) is future in relation to (–2) and is thus a subordinated form of prolepsis.

31. This brief example of what Genette calls subordination and coordination[20] is exemplified in a more complex way in Acts 22. In order to keep matters as simple as possible, it will be helpful to make a list of events referred to in the speech in the order in which they appear but to give them chronological designations.

0	"And he said . . ." (the present narrative moment)
–6	Paul is born at Tarsus
–5	Paul is brought up in Jerusalem
–4	Paul is zealous for God
–3	Paul persecutes the Way; journeys to Damascus
–2	Events in Damascus
–1	Return to Jerusalem and trance
0	Return to the present narrative moment

It will be observed that the events are narrated here in straightforward retrograde order, from the earliest to the latest. However, in making up this

20. *Narrative Discourse,* 40.

list I have omitted four items that are narrated during Paul's trance after his return to Jerusalem. That is, four additional items are to be added to the list, but these items are subordinated to the trance in which Jesus says two things to Paul and Paul says two things to Jesus. These four things are:

(1) Jesus tells Paul to get out of Jerusalem (he does)
(2) Paul says that he imprisoned and beat believers
(3) Paul says that he approved the stoning of Stephen
(4) Jesus tells Paul to go to the Gentiles (he does)

Item (1) in this subordinate list takes place immediately after –1 in the master list; item (4) takes place immediately after that: Paul leaves Jerusalem in order to take up his work among the Gentiles, to speak broadly. But items (2) and (3) belong to the past from the standpoint of the trance in Jerusalem: (2), in fact, is the same as item –3 in the master list, while (3) does not appear in that list; (3) belongs in the interval between –3 and –2. In relation to the trance item, however, (1) and (4) are +1 and +2, while (3) and (4) are –2 and –1. The subordinate character of these four items could be indicated by including them in brackets as subordinate to item (–1), the trance:

–1 the trance
[–2 Paul imprisons and beats believers]
[–1 Paul approves of the stoning of Stephen]
[+1 Paul gets out of Jerusalem]
[+2 Paul goes to the Gentiles]

Once again, it should be observed that these events are not narrated; they are alluded to in quoted speech.

32. The environment of analepsis and prolepsis. Analepses and prolepses occur in particular narrative terrain, if the examples examined above provide reliable clues. As might be expected, references to past and future events, both homodiegetic and heterodiegetic, occur in INTROS and CONS to nuclei and in larger narrative transitions. The reason is that the narrator is inclined to reach backward and forward when attempting to connect a new NUC with preceding events and perhaps anticipate developments to come. Every *a:retro* (reference to some events as past) is an analepsis and a narrative linkage. These linkages belong logically to connective tissue, whether as part of an INTRO or CON or to an independent narrative transition or summary.

The vehicle for analepses and prolepses in the NUC of narrative segments is frequently quoted speech in the examples cited above. All the examples in Mark 14:7–31 are in quoted speech. However, examples also abound in indirect speech of various kinds, including remembering (e.g., Mark 14:72) and visions (e.g., Acts 16:9–10). Events narrated out of order, whether belatedly or prematurely, on the narrator's own authority, seem to be less common in ancient literature than in modern fiction.

9

Narrative Introductions

INTRODUCTION

(1)	He rode into our valley	S:*pre-f:arr*^{1}
	in the summer of '89.	*ls/ts*
(2)	I was a kid then,	B:*id*
(3)	barely topping the backboard of father's old chuck-wagon.	[F:*id*]
(4)	I was on the upper rail	B:*pre-f:pos*
	of our small corral,	*ls*
(5)	soaking in the late afternoon sun,	
(6)	when I saw him far down the road	B:*pre-f:perc*^{1}
(7)	where it swung into the valley from the	*ls*
	open plain beyond.	*ls*
(8)	In that clear Wyoming air	*ls*
	I could see him plainly,	B:*pre-f:perc*^{2}
(9)	though he was still several miles away.	*ls*
(10)	There seemed nothing remarkable about him,	S:*id*
(11)	just another stray horseman riding up the	S:*id*
	road toward the cluster of frame buildings	S:*pre-f:arr*^{2}
	that was our town.	*ls*
(12)	Then I saw a pair of cowhands,	
(13)	loping past him,	
(14)	stop and stare after him with a curious intentness.	B:P:*pre-f:perc*^{3}
(15)	He came steadily on, straight through the	*ls*
	town without slackening pace,	S:*pre-f:arr*^{3}
(16)	until he reached the fork a half-mile below our place.	*ls*
(17)	One branch turned left across the river	*ls*
	ford and on to Luke Fletcher's big spread.	LF:*id*
(18)	The other bore ahead along the right bank	*ls*
	where we homesteaders had pegged our claims	
	in a row up the valley.	HS:*id*
(19)	He hesitated briefly,	
(20)	studying the choice, and moved again steadily on our side.	S:*pre-f:arr*^{4}
(21)	As he came near,	S:*pre-f:arr*^{5}
(22)	what impressed me first was his clothes.	S:*id*
(23)	He wore dark trousers of some serge material tucked	
	into tall boots	[through (52)]
(24)	and held at the waist by a wide belt, both of a	
	soft black leather tooled in intricate design.	

(25) A coat of the same dark material as the trousers was neatly folded

(26) and strapped to his saddle-roll.

(27) His shirt was finespun linen, rich brown in color.

(28) The handkerchief knotted loosely around his throat was black silk.

(28) His hat was not the familiar Stetson, not the familiar gray or muddy tan.

(29) It was a plain black, soft in texture,

(30) unlike any hat I had ever seen,

(29) with a creased crown and wide curling brim swept down in front to shield the face.

(31) All trace of newness was long since gone from these things.

(32) The dust of distance was beaten into them.

(33) They were worn and stained

(34) and several neat patches showed on the shirt.

(35) Yet a kind of magnificence remained and with it a hint of men and manners alien to my limited boy's experience.

(36) Then I forgot the clothes in the impact of the man himself.

(37) He was not much above medium height, almost slight in build.

(38) He would have looked frail alongside father's square, solid bulk. [F:*id*]

(40) But even I could read the endurance in the lines of that dark figure and the quiet power in its effortless, unthinking adjustment to every movement of the tired horse.

(41) He was clean-shaven

(42) and his face was lean and hard and burned from high forehead to firm, tapering chin.

(43) His eyes seemed hooded in the shadow of the hat's brim.

(44) He came closer, S:*pre-f:arr*^{6}

(45) and I could see that this was because the brows were drawn in a frown of fixed and habitual alertness. B:*pre-f:perc*^{4}

(46) Beneath them the eyes were endlessly searching from side to side and forward, checking off every item in view, missing nothing. S:*pre-f:perc*^{1}

(47) As I noticed this, B:*pre-f:perc*^{5}

(48) a sudden chill,
(49) I could not have told why,
(48) struck through me there in the warm and open sun.
(50) He rode easily, relaxed in the saddle, leaning his weight lazily into the stirrups.
(51) Yet even in this easiness was a suggestion of tension.
(52) It was the easiness of a coiled spring, of a trap set.
(53) He drew rein not twenty feet from me. — S:*f:arr*
(54) His glance hit me, — S:*pre-f:perc*[2]
(55) dismissed me,
(56) flicked over our place. — S:*pre-f:perc*[3]
(57) This was not much,
(58) if you were thinking in terms of size and scope.
(59) But what there was was good.
(60) You could trust father for that. — [F:*id*]
(61) The corral, big enough for about thirty head if you crowded them in, was railed right to true sunk posts. — *ls*
(62) The pasture behind, taking in nearly half of our claim, was fenced tight. — ls
(63) The barn was small, — *ls*
(64) but it was solid,
(65) and we were raising a loft at one end for the alfalfa growing green in the north forty. — *ls*
(66) We had a fair-sized field in potatoes that year — *ls*
(67) and father was trying a new corn he had sent all the way to Washington for — [F:*id*]
(68) and they were showing properly in weedless rows. — *ls*
(69) Behind the house, mother's kitchen garden was a brave sight. — [M:*id*]/*ls*
(70) The house itself was three rooms—two really, the big kitchen where we spent most of our time indoors and the bedroom beside it. — *ls*
(71) My little lean-to room was added back of the kitchen.
(72) Father was planning, — [F:*id*]
(73) when he could get around to it,
(72) to build mother the parlor she wanted. — [M:*id*]
(74) We had wooden floors and a nice porch across the front.

(75)	The house was painted too, white with green trim, rare thing in all that region, to remind her,	
(76)	mother said when she made father do it,	[M:*id*]
	of her native New England.	[M:*id*]
(77)	Even rarer, the roof was shingled.	
(78)	I knew what that meant.	[B:*id*]
(79)	I had helped father split those shingles.	
(80)	Few places so spruce and well worked could be found so deep in the Territory in those days.	
(81)	The stranger took it all in,	S:*pre-f:perc*[4]
(82)	sitting there easily in the saddle.	
(83)	I saw his eyes slow on the flowers mother	B:*pre-f:perc*[6]
	had planted by the porch steps,	S:*pre-f:perc*[5]
(84)	then come to rest on our shiny new pump and the trough beside it.	S:*f:perc / aa*
(85)	They shifted back to me,	S:*f:perc*
(86)	and again, without knowing why, I felt that sudden chill.	
(87)	But his voice was gentle	
(88)	and he spoke like a man schooled in patience.	*a1*
(89)	"I'd appreciate a chance at the pump for myself and the horse."	
(90)	I was trying to frame a reply and choking on it,	
(91)	when I realized that he was not speaking to me but past me.	
(92)	Father had come up behind me	F:*pre-f:arr*
(93)	and was leaning against the gate to the corral.	F:*pre-f:pos*
(94)	"Use all the water you want, stranger."	

Note: Codes in [ ] indicate that one feature is embedded in another.

•9•

The techniques by which narratives are introduced deserve close study in themselves. In this chapter we shall analyze the INTRO to *Shane*, a Western written by Jack Shaefer, and the INTRO to the Gospel of Mark. The two examples will provide all the basic data needed to lay the groundwork for a poetics of INTROS.

THE INTRODUCTION TO SHANE

1. Summary. The INTRO to *Shane* consists of the arrival of the hero, Shane (S), as perceived by the young boy, Bob (B). The depiction of Shane's arrival is extended: into it the author works a lengthy description of Shane, an oblique presentation of Bob along with his father (F) and mother (M), and a sketch of the geography of the valley, including a detailed picure of the Starrett homestead. The narrator also introduces Luke Fletcher (LF), the antagonist, and the homesteaders (HS), although briefly. When Shane finally arrives at the handpump in front of the house, the reader has all the necessary data regarding locale, time, and participants. And the prolonged INTRO has dammed up a reservoir of expectation as Bob stares at Shane in awe during his ride of "several miles" into the valley.

2. Locale and setting. The strategies of the INTRO may be followed by attending, first, to statements bearing on locale and setting.

Statement (1) introduces the larger space, the valley in which the town and homesteaders and Luke Fletcher are located. Into that valley runs a road (6); it leads into the valley from the plain beyond (7). The clean Wyoming air (8) permits one to see things at a great distance. As a consequence, Bob can see Shane while he is still several miles away. The road passes through the town (15), which consists of a cluster of frame buildings (11). The road then forks (16), the left fork leading to Luke Fletcher's place (17), the right fork coming to the homesteaders' side of the river (18).

Shane eventually arrives at "our place" (56). Bob had, in fact, been sitting on the upper rail of the small corral (4), at the opening of the narrative. Now Shane looks the entire place over (56). The corral is depicted in (61), the pasture behind in (62), the barn in (63)–(64), the alfalfa in (65), the field of potatoes (66), the field of corn (67)–(68), mother's garden behind the house (69), and the house (70)–(80). Shane's eyes finally focus on the flowers Bob's mother had planted by the porch steps (83), and then come to rest on the shiny new pump (84). This odyssey of locales begins with the valley as a whole and in the end zeroes in on the pump in the front yard. The reader knows the stranger is about to ask for water. Meanwhile, the reader has had the grand tour of places while Shane rides into the valley, through the town, and up to the Starrett homestead. The geographical setting may be represented as in figure 20.

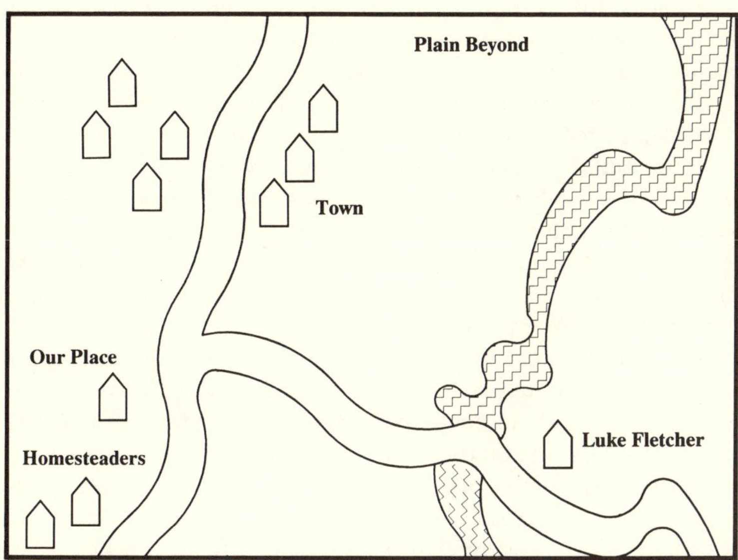

Figure 20

3. Perspective and focalization. The strategies of INTRO may be pursued by returning to the questions of narrator, point of view, and focalization, addressed initially in §6.25–30. In the earlier section, only the question of the distance of the narrator from the events being narrated was explored. Here it is appropriate to investigate perspective and focalization.

A story is presented in its narrative text through some angle of vision or perspective, commonly called point of view. This angle of vision is verbalized by the narrator, although it may not, in fact, be hers or his. For the first time in critical theory, Genette distinguishes the question of who speaks from the question of who sees. A narrative agent may both see and speak, but the two functions may also be distinguished, as they are, for example, in the INTRO to *Shane*. The narrator is an adult, but the perspective is that of the narrator years earlier when he was a young boy.

Perspective, as Genette and Rimmon-Kenan use the term, is limited to the visual orientation employed by the narrator.[1] That visual orientation is termed "focalization" by them. Focalization is a technical term in their parlance. It should be emphasized that what they mean by focalization is quite different from the use of the term "focalizer" in this study. The difference can be put simply: focalization for Genette is the perspective to which the narrative is oriented; focalization has to do with the perceiver. The focalizer, as defined in this study, refers to devices in the text that indicate what is in focus; the focalizer is a textual device or devices. Rimmon-Kenan suggests the difference in distinguishing the focalizer from the focalized. To borrow a metaphor from cinema, the focalizer is the camera, the focalized the scene on which the camera is focused. Focalization refers, in other words, to the agent of focus; focalizer (and the focalized) refers to the object that is in focus and the textual devices utilized in achieving focus. Owing to the potential for confusion, we have elected not to employ "focalization" in the sense proposed by Genette and Rimmon-Kenan; we shall adhere to the more conventional parlance, and call that point of view or perspective.

Perspective and point of view evoke visual associations, although they of course involve more than visual mediation. There is a cognitive component in perspective, along with an emotive element and an ideological aspect.[2] It is unnecessary to elaborate on these additional aspects in this context.

The agent of perspective may be located outside the narrative; in that case, the agent is external. If the agent is located inside the story, the agent is obviously internal. The agent in *Shane* is primarily the young boy, Bob, so the agent is internal. An external agent is felt to be close, as a rule, to the perspective of the narrator. By utilizing an internal agent, the narrator can put some distance between his or her voice and the perspective to which the narrator is oriented.

The focalized, or the object in focus, can be viewed either from within or from without. A view from the outside is one in which only the outer facets of things and events are perceived; a view from the inside permits the reader to know things and persons in ways not normally perceived by an observer. But internal and external are not to be correlated necessarily with the view from the outside or from the inside. There are actually four possible combinations.[3]

4. The focalizing agent in *Shane* is Bob as a youngster. The narrating voice is his as a mature adult. The narrative takes its peculiar cast, in this instance, from the fact that Shane, Bob's parents, Luke Fletcher, the homesteaders, and the events in which they are all embroiled, are perceived through the

1. Genette, *Narrative Discourse*, 185–211; Rimmon-Kenan, *Narrative Fiction*, 71–85; Culpepper, *Anatomy*, 20–34.

2. Rimmon-Kenan, *Narrative Fiction*, 77–82, gives a sketch of these additional aspects.

3. Genette and Rimmon-Kenan give examples of these types.

eyes of this young man. A. B. Guthrie was able to preserve and even enhance this perspective of Shaefer's novel in his screen version: the entire story is presented as it would appear to the young lad.[4]

Bob was a kid when the events to be narrated took place (2). He was only tall enough to look over the backboard of his father's old chuck-wagon; he was sitting on the corral rail, as boys are wont to do, soaking up the afternoon sun, when he espies Shane riding into the valley from the open plain beyond (the plain is not in view), (4)–(7). The stage is now set: Bob will watch Shane as he rides down the valley, through the town, and up to him sitting on the corral fence. Bob is in position (*pre-f:pos*); Shane is in motion toward him (*pre-f:arr*).

The eyes, as we said, are those of young Bob, but the words are those of adult Bob ("I was a kid then"): in the paragraphs to follow, it is not the child speaking but the adult; nevertheless, the eyes are juvenile, registering surprise and awe at the appearance and demeanor of Shane. The focalizing agent is thus internal to the narrative, while the distance is relatively great between those eyes and the voice that recalls earlier events. The eyes are contemporary with the events they see, but the narrator's voice is separated from those events by a span of years.

5. *Focalizers.* The focalizing process, it will be recalled, has the shape of a funnel: two participants are set on a contact course, and when they meet the action begins.[5] In the INTRO to *Shane,* the focalizing process is carried out primarily through the movement of Shane toward the shining new pump in the front yard of the Starrett place and young Bob's reciprocal gaze from his position on the upper rail of the corral fence. This reciprocal movement is carried out by an elaborate series of pre-focalizers, which function both to bring the narrative into focus and to create suspense. Guthrie has retained this strategy in mapping out the film version.

The string of pre-focalizers begins with Shane: (1) He rode into our valley in the summer of '89, which serves as S:*pre-f:arr*^{1}, i.e., as the first pre-focalizer anticipating Shane's arrival. Bob's is in position, on the other hand:

(4) I was on the upper rail of our small corral, . . .
(6) when I saw him far down the road

which is coded as B:*pre-f:pos* and B:*pre-f:perc*^{1}. The first positions Bob for the balance of the INTRO, while the second is the first of a series of pre-focalizers indicating Bob's perceptions of Shane as he approaches.

Shane continues his relentless progress down the valley road:

4. The film was released in 1953. Directed by George Stevens. Starring Alan Ladd, Jean Arthur, and Van Heflin. Screenplay by A. B. Guthrie, Jr.
5. Discussed in §3.10–12.

(11) just another stray horseman riding up the road toward the cluster of frame buildings that was our town.
(15) He came steadily on, straight through the town without slackening pace,
(20) studying the choice, and moved again steadily on our side.
(21) As he came near,
(44) He came closer,

There are thus no fewer than six explicit pre-focalizers anticipating Shane's arrival.

In a similar fashion, the narrator traces the movement of Bob's eyes:

(8) In that clear Wyoming air I could see him plainly,
(12) Then I saw a pair of cowhands, . . .
(14) stop and stare after him with a curious intentness.
(45) and I could see that this was . . .
(47) As I noticed this,
(83) I saw his eyes slow on the flowers mother had planted by the porch steps,
(84) then come to rest on our shiny new pump and the trough beside it.
(85) They shifted back to me,

There are no fewer than eight pre-focalizers of a visual nature, utilizing the gaze of young Bob. Statements (12) and (14) combine to make a pre-focalizer of an unusual character: Bob sees two cowhands who lope past Shane, then stop and stare at him. The narrator introduces another perceiver, at this point much closer to the hero, through whose eyes the primary focalizing agent, Bob, views Shane. Later, the narrator has Bob follow the eyes of Shane in (83)–(85) for a similar effect.

Beginning in (46), the narrator switches to Shane's perspective. The reader learns for the first time that Shane has been observing everything as he comes, and that his gaze reciprocates that of Bob. In addition to the initial notice in (46), the narrator plants five more markers:

(54) His glance hit me,
(56) flicked over our place
(81) The stranger took it all in,
(83) I saw his eyes slow on the flowers mother had planted by the porch steps,
(84) then come to rest on our shiny new pump and the trough beside it.

The final notice is, of course, the focalizer: espying the pump, Shane now asks for water, which is the first action of the body of the narrative.

It was said earlier that the narrative is focalized through the eyes of Bob. That claim obviously requires qualification. It is more accurate to say that in the section beginning with (53), Shane's gaze is utilized in a formal way, although it is still Bob who does the actual seeing; the comments are those of mature Bob, the narrator.

(53) His glance hit me,
(54) dismissed me,
(56) flicked over our place.

The narrator then adds another notice in (81) that encloses the long description of the Starrett place:

(81) The stranger took it all in.

In this passage, Shane does the looking, but Bob does the "seeing," and mature Bob does the telling. Consequently, the narrator can be said to employ the eyes of young Bob as his primary vehicle, but he also makes use of secondary perspectives: that of the two cowhands in (12)ff., and that of Shane in (54)ff. In both cases, however, the secondary perspective is made formally dependent on the primary perspective.

This elaborate preparation involving Shane and young Bob leads the reader to expect that the first narrative contact will be between these two. However, the narrator surpises the reader. Although Shane's eyes shift back to Bob (85), and Shane appears to address his request for water to Bob (89), Bob's father has meanwhile moved forward (92) and taken up a position behind Bob (93), with the result that Shane addresses Bob's father rather than Bob (cf. (91)). The reader is surprised by this abrupt turn in narrative strategy: the predominant line of development is aborted at the last minute and another line substituted. Nevertheless, this strategy forecasts the one the narrator will use throughout the story: persons and events are filtered predominantly, though not exclusively, through young Bob's perspective.

6. Participants and setting. There are two blocks of descriptive material in Shaefer's INTRO. One has Shane in focus: (22)–(52), the other concerns "our place": (57)–(80), (83)–(84). The movement of Shane is arrested during the first; it is therefore a narrative pause. At the outset of the second, Shane has arrived in front of Bob and the Starrett place. He now lets his eyes roam over the setting. This is also a pause, all the more suspenseful because the reader anticipates the first narrative contact momentarily.

Shane and "our place" are depicted in elaborate detail. Other participants are simply identified: Luke Fletcher (17) and the homesteaders (18). Bob's father and mother are introduced and identified, but only obliquely. Father is said to have possessed a chuck-wagon in those days (3), and Shane would look frail beside father's "square, solid bulk" (38). The balance of the descriptive statements concerning both father and mother are embedded in the description of "our place" (57)–(80), (83)–(84). Bob is given bare identification in (2) and in (78)–(79), again as a part of the survey of the farm and ranch.

Aside from the two descriptive blocks, the INTRO is mimetic in character, contrary to the general rule for INTROS. The arrival of Shane is focused from the outset: Bob's eyes are a camera sweeping the horizon and spotting Shane as he rides into the valley. Even during the first descriptive pause, the narrator does not resort to the iterative or the habitual; every statement in the depiction of Shane is specific and immediate. The perceiver's eyes continue to function as a camera recording simply what it sees. It is not until the narrator comes to the sketch of the farm, using the eyes of Shane as the focalizing agent, that he introduces the iterative. In (67), for example, "father was trying a new corn" is iterative: conative; (68) also implies the iterative, as does (75) and (78)–(79). But these statements all refer to Bob or his father or mother. There are no iterative statements pertaining to Shane; Shane apparently has no past.

It is, of course, the case that every statement in the INTRO is mediated. The mediator, however, is intradiegetic. As a consequence, the INTRO may be said to be in the mimetic mode, although INTROS are commonly recounted and iterative. The intradiegetic mediator is permitted to make narrative statements that are mediated and yet in focus.[6]

THE INTRODUCTION TO THE GOSPEL OF MARK

7. *Title.* We shall treat (1) as a title and translate it idiomatically: "This is how the gospel concerning Jesus Christ began."

8. *Structure of the Introduction.* In (2)–(2.3b) a prediction is made. It is attributed to Isaiah the prophet, who lived at a much earlier time. The act of Isaiah falls outside the events that belong to the narrative proper: the story of how the gospel concerning Jesus Christ took its rise begins, so far as narrated events are involved, with the appearance of John the Baptist in segment ib. Nevertheless, the prediction of Isaiah functions to introduce the first event of Mark's narrative, and it gives the narrative temporal depth by linking it to a memorable past.

The fulfillment of Isaiah's prediction is narrated in (3)–(11.4): John appears in the wilderness as predicted and he, in turn, predicts the coming of one mightier than he. He is thus preparing "the way of the Lord."

John's prediction consists of two parts:

(a) the one who comes after is mightier than John;
(b) the coming one will baptize with the Holy Spirit rather than with water.

The fulfillment of John's prediction is presumably narrated in what follows: Jesus of Nazareth is the mightier one, and he will baptize with the Holy Spirit. The might of Jesus is obstensibly exemplified in the mighty deeds

6. The significance of the intradiegetic narrator is explored in §6.31–38.

INTRODUCTION

title

(1) 1 This is how the gospel concerning Jesus Christ began

segment ia

(2) 2 It is written in Isaiah the prophet:
(2.1) "Behold, I send my messenger before thy face,
(2.2) who shall prepare thy way;
(2.3) 3 the voice of one crying in the wilderness: *ls*
(2.3a) Prepare the way of the Lord,
(2.3b) make his paths straight."

segment ib

(3) 4 And so John the baptizer JB*id*
made his appearance in the wilderness, *lc*
(4) preaching a baptism of repentance for the forgiveness of sins. *iter*
(5) 5 And everybody in Judea and Jerusalem used to go out to him; *iter*
(6) and they were regularly baptized by him in the river Jordan, *iter*
(7) confessing their sins. *iter*
(8) 6 And John was habitually clothed with camel's hair, *iter*
(9) and used to wear a leather girdle around his waist; *iter*
(10) he customarily ate locusts and wild honey. *iter*
(11) 7 And his preaching used to go like this: *iter*
(11.1) "After me comes he who is mightier than I,
(11.2) the thong of whose sandals I am not worthy to stoop down and untie.
(11.3) 8 I have baptized you with water;
(11.4) but he will baptize you with the Holy Spirit."

segment ii

(12) [9] In the time of John *tc*
Jesus came from Nazareth of Galilee *Jid / lc*
(13) and was baptized in the Jordan by John. *ls*
(14) [10] And just as he came up out of the water *f:arr*
(15) Jesus saw the heavens opening *f:perc*
(16) and the Spirit descending on him like a dove.
(17) [11] And there came a voice out of heaven,
(17.1) "You are my beloved son,
(17.2) in whom I am well pleased."

segment iii

(18) [12] The Spirit makes him go at once *dep*
out into the wilderness. *lc*
(19) [13] He spent forty days in the *arr*
wilderness *ts / iter*
(20) being tempted all the while by Satan. *iter*
(21) He kept company with wild beasts, *iter*
(22) and the angels took care of him. *iter*

BODY OF THE NARRATIVE

segment iv

(23) [14] Then when John was imprisoned, *tc*
(24) Jesus reappeared in Galilee *lc*
(25) and began preaching the Gospel of God. *iter*
(26) [15] He used to say, *iter*
(26.1) "The time is fulfilled,
(26.2) and the kingdom of God has drawn near.
(26.3) Repent all of you
(26.4) and believe in the gospel."

narrated in the gospel. Yet in the next narrative segment, (12)–(17.2), Jesus is himself baptized in water by John. However, he then sees the heavens open and the spirit descend. That same spirit drives him out into the wilderness, moreover, where he is tested for a symbolic period of forty days: (18)–(22). It would thus appear that Mark interprets John's prediction as an event in which Jesus is baptized by the Holy Spirit, rather than as one in which he baptizes with (or in) the Holy Spirit; grammatically expressed, the fulfillment is an event in which Jesus is patient, rather than one in which he is agent. The reader must eventually raise this question because nowhere in the Gospel of Mark does Jesus appear to baptize with the Holy Spirit.

It is possible, of course, that Mark is here referring to the general consensus of tradition, as expressed, for example, in Acts 19:1–7. There the gift of the spirit does accompany Christian baptism, as distinguished from the baptism of John. If this is the fulfillment of John's prediction, then Mark has made a minor error as a narrator: he does not complete the story he has promised. It is necessary to be constantly on guard against this problem in biblical narrative: is the narrative tightly constructed in that it is self-contained, or does the reader need to know things that are not made explicit by the narrative? In the latter case, the narrative is a loosely constructed work that presumes the presence of a much broader, living tradition, a story all the parts of which have not yet been reduced to an integrated narrative. Expressed grammatically, the question is whether the teller confuses story time with narrative time, and one or the other or both of those times with the time of narrating.

Finally, with the disappearance of John from the scene (23), Jesus reappears in Galilee and he, like John, begins to preach.

We may now review these scenes and ask what narrative markers support the reading just given.

9. Temporal markers. Norman Petersen has noted that the sequence, prediction/fulfillment, is twice repeated in this introductory section, as indicated below:[7]

Prophecy of Isaiah 1:2–3 one will appear in the wilderness and prepare the way	⇨	Fulfillment in John 1:4–6 appears in wilderness prepares the way
Prediction of John 1:7–8 mightier one comes baptizes with Holy Spirit	⇨	Fulfillment in Jesus 1:9–16:8 mightier one appears is baptized with the spirit

This double prediction/fulfillment sequence corresponds to the break between Mark 1:2–3/1:4–8 and between 1:4–8/1:9–16:8. The sequence does

7. *Literary Criticism for New Testament Critics,* 50f.

not, however, account for other breaks in the structure of the INTRO. To place and account for those, one must observe the "time": time of Isaiah, time of John, time of Jesus. The time of John, moreover, is divided into two periods: the time before Jesus comes on the scene, and the time John and Jesus overlap. We thus have three temporal phases, the second of which is divided into subphases:

(1) Time of Isaiah (story time)
(2) Time of John (narrative time)
  (2a) before Jesus
  (2b) with Jesus
(3) Time of Jesus (narrative time)

In the time of John (1:9), (12),[8] Jesus comes to the Jordan and is baptized by John. Immediately thereafter, the spirit drives Jesus out into the wilderness. The reader will assume that John's activities continue while Jesus is being tempted. The narrator reports in (23), (1:14) that John was imprisoned prior to Jesus' appearance in Galilee. Thus, the time of John both precedes and overlaps with Jesus. During the period when the two overlap, two events occur: the baptism of Jesus and the temptation of Jesus. At the conclusion of the period of temptation the time of John comes to an end.

The temporal phases in Mark 1:2–15 provide the frame of reference for five narrative segments, delineated and grouped as follows:

(ia)	(2)–(2.3b), 1:2–3	
	Isaiah's prediction	time: in past, in remote story time
		place: unspecified
(ib)	(3)–(11.4), 1:4–8	
	John's appearance	place: in wilderness as predicted
		time: unspecified, but after Isaiah and before Jesus
(ii)	(12)–(17.2), 1:9–11	
	Jesus' baptism	place: at Jordan (in wilderness)
		time: unspecified but while John is still active
(iii)	(18)–(22), 1:12–13	
	Jesus' testing	place: in the wilderness
		time: subsequent to his baptism by John
(iv)	(23)–(26.4), 1:14–15	
	Beginning of Jesus' activity	place: Galilee
		time: subsequent to the imprisonment of John[9]

10. *Spatial markers.* Isaiah's prediction anticipates the locale of John's activity: "the voice of one crying in the wilderness" (2.3). This locale is the scene of John's preaching ("appeared in the wilderness," (4)). The Jordan river must

8. RSV: "In those days," i.e., while John was doing what is narrated in 1:4–8.
9. After John's days; cf. 1:9.

be located in or near the wilderness, since Judeans and Jerusalemites come out to hear him and are then baptized in the Jordan (5)–(7). We thus have the geographical link: wilderness/Jordan.[10]

In the next segment, Jesus also comes out from Galilee and is baptized by John in the Jordan (1:9–11). Jesus is then driven out into the wilderness by the spirit for a period of testing (1:12–13). This sequence suggests that the wilderness is a space that differs from the Jordan, yet the connection of the two places in vss 4–5 indicates that the two spaces are proximate to each other. In Mark's geography, moreover, the wilderness and the Jordan are clearly distinguished from both Judea and Jerusalem, on the one hand, and from Galilee, on the other.

The setting of segments ib, ii, and iii is the wilderness/Jordan; this setting binds the three segments together. An unequivocal change in locale separates 1:4–13 from 1:14ff; there is a clear spatial change, in other words, that sets segment iv off from what precedes.

11. Participants. Isaiah is not a participant in the drama. John the Baptist is, however, and he is the *agent* of the principal actions in 1:4–8 and 1:9–11. Jesus does not appear in 1:4–8, and in 1:9–11 he is the patient (something happens to him). He continues as the patient in 1:12–13, where the spirit, Satan, and the angels are agents. He does not assume a role as agent until he returns to Galilee in 1:14. Thus, with respect to participant roles, viewed grammatically, Jesus does not become the "subject" (viz., the agent) of the story until he begins to preach in Galilee. Prior to that point, John is the "subject" or the agent. There is thus another decisive narrative grammatical shift at 1:14.

12. Summary of narrative markers. By assembling the narrative markers we are in a position to come to a clear and decisive narrative segmentation of the beginning of Mark's gospel. Verse 1 is a title. Verses 2–13 constitute an INTRO to the gospel as a whole, while 1:14–15 provide the INTRO to the body of the narrative in which Jesus assumes the principal role. We are able, moreover, to analyze the narrative into smaller segments and indicate their relation to each other. These segments and relationships were outlined in §9.9 and indicated in figure 21.[11]

13. Modes of narrative discourse. The preliminary narrative analysis of the INTRO to Mark is confirmed by another set of formal narrative observations. These observations have to do with modes of narrative discourse. The four modes were treated in §6.1–17; they may be reviewed briefly here.

In the first mode, which we termed *enactment*, the narrator takes the reader

10. In considering spatial notices we are dealing with the geography of the text and not physical geography. It is not our intention in this context to ask whether Mark's geographic sense squares with the physical realities.

11. The formal grammatical analysis thus confirms the pioneering work of Petersen on Mark 1:1–15 in his work *Literary Criticism for New Testament Critics*, 50–54.

(listener) to the scene and allows him or her to look on and listen in.[12] The narrator brings the scene into focus and invokes the reader's senses directly. The account of the Lame Man in Acts 3:1–10 was cited as an example of a narrative segment predominantly in the mimetic mode. In the second mode, the narrator *recounts* what happened without focusing the scene; the reader is dependent on the narrator's word or report. Since the reader is dependent upon a report for narrative information, this mode involves mediation: the narrator intervenes between event and reader. There are two kinds of recounting. In one kind, the events reported are singular events; the mode is accordingly termed the singulative mode. In a second type, the events reported happened more than once; the mode is thus iterative.

Gospel of Mark

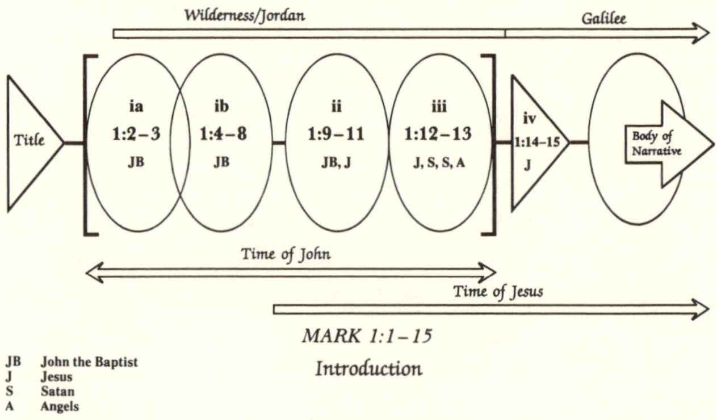

Figure 21

The distinction between enacting and recounting is by no means absolute. Enactment will contain some recounting, however minimal, and recounting is often mixed with enactment, especially in the form of direct discourse inserted into scenes that are basically recounted. This is only to say that the narrator regularly intrudes to some degree on the story being told, but only rarely makes that intrusion absolute.

The fourth mode, discussed in §6.11–17, is description. In description, the narrator focuses on either participant or setting, in the absence of action. Pure description involves a narrative pause. Unlike the INTRO to Shane, the INTRO to Mark lacks pure description.

14. Recounting in both the singulative and the iterative modes is typical of narrative openings for one of two reasons: (a) the narrator often wants to

12. Characteristics of enactment are sketched in §6.3–5.

recapitulate in brief a series of events belonging to story time and leading up to the particular events constituting the body of the narrative; for this purpose, recounting in the singulative mode is appropriate. (b) The narrator may wish to depict characteristic actions or facets of leading participants as a means of defining character and establishing expectations; for this purpose, recounting in the iterative mode is useful. The two types of recounting may, of course, be combined and usually are.

15. Recounting in the introduction to Mark. The verbs in Mark 1:4–8 indicate that the narrator is summarizing the activities of John the Baptist that lead up to the appearance of Jesus on the scene and which characterize John in fulfillment of Isaiah's prediction and identify him as the forerunner. The verbs in Greek are either iterative (or descriptive) imperfects or participles.[13] The segment is thus clearly iterative; it does not depict or enact a particular event or events, but generalizes on the activity of John as a way of characterizing John and setting the stage. In the analysis of Mark 1:1-15, we have therefore labelled statements with iterative verbs in them as *iter*.

The narrative function of this passage can perhaps best be captured by underscoring the iterative or descriptive character of the language in a translation designed for that purpose:

> [4]There was John out in the wilderness proclaiming a baptism of repentance for the forgiveness of sins. [5]And the entire populations of Judea and Jerusalem made the pilgrimage out to him at one time or another, and they regularly allowed themselves to be baptized by him after confessing their sins. [6]Now John habitually wore camel's hair and a leather girdle about his waist; his diet consisted of locusts and wild honey. [7]And this was the message he used to preach. . . .

There is not a single aorist in this passage, apart from the initial formulaic *ἐγένετο*, "John appeared" or "It came to pass that. . . ."[14] It is thus clear that the activities of John prior to the appearance of Jesus on the scene are introductory: they prepare the way for the narrative proper. For that reason they are cast in a descriptive or iterative mode.

The first action aorists appear in 1:9 (*ἦλθεν*, "Jesus came"; *ἐβαπτίσθη*, "he was baptized") and 1:10 (*εἶδεν*, "he saw"). The mini-scene in 1:9–11 is partly recounted, partly enacted: the reader is permitted to see the dove and hear the voice from heaven with Jesus.

In the next mini-scene, however, the narrator resorts to the iterative mode

13. In vs 4, *κήρυσσων*, "preaching"; in vs 5, *ἐξεπορεύετο*, "used to come out"; *ἐβαπτίζοντο*, "used to be baptized"; *ἐξομολογούμενοι*, "confessing": vs 6, *ἦν . . . ἐνδεδυμένος*, "was habitually clothed"; *ἐσθίων*, "used to eat"; vs 7, *ἐκήρρυσεν*, "used to preach"; *λέγων*, "saying."

14. This verb is employed in Greek merely to indicate the continuation of the narrative. See Bauer, s.v. *γίνομαι*, 3f.

once again (present and imperfects in Greek) as he recounts and generalizes on a forty-day period. We may once again represent the verbs and participles in translation:

> [12]And the spirit immediately makes him go out into the wilderness. [13]And he spent forty days in the wilderness, being tempted all the while by Satan; and he kept company with wild beasts; and the angels took care of him.[15]

The mini-scenes represented by 1:9–11 and 12–13 are transitional: the iterative mode continues to dominate; the stage is still being set, although the principal actor is now on the scene. The formal marks of recounting in the iterative mode support the view that these scenes are introductory; they thus confirm the evidence supplied by participant sets and the grammatical relation of participants to the action, as sketched earlier.

15. Vs 12: ἐκβάλλει, "makes him go out" (present); vs 13: ἦν, "was" (imperfect), πειραζόμενος, "being tempted all the while" (participle), ἦν, "kept company" (imperfect), διηκόνουν, "kept ministering" (imperfect).

·10·

Passion Narratives

Chapter 26, Death of Little Eva

INTRODUCTION

Eva's bedroom was a spacious apartment, which, like all the other rooms in the house, opened on to the broad verandah. The room communicated, on one side, with her father and mother's apartment; on the other, with that appropriated to Miss Ophelia. St. Clare had gratified his own eye and taste, in furnishing this room in a style that had a peculiar keeping with the character of her for whom it was intended. The windows were hung with curtains of rose-colored and white muslin, the floor was spread with a matting which had been ordered in Paris, to a pattern of his own device, having round it a border of rosebuds and leaves, and a centre-piece with full-blown roses. The bedstead, chairs, and lounges, were of bamboo, wrought in peculiarly graceful and fanciful patterns. Over the head of the bed was an alabaster bracket, on which a beautiful sculptured angel stood, with drooping wings, holding out a crown of myrtle-leaves. From this depended, over the bed, light curtains of rose-colored gauze, striped with silver, supplying that protection from mosquitos which is an indispensable addition to all sleeping accommodation in that climate. The graceful bamboo lounges were amply supplied with cushions of rose-colored damask, while over them, depending from the hands of sculptured figures, were gauze curtains similar to those of the bed. A light, fanciful bamboo table stood in the middle of the room, where a Parian vase, wrought in the shape of a white lily, with its buds, stood, ever filled with flowers. On this table lay Eva's books and little trinkets, with an elegantly wrought alabaster writing-stand, which her father had supplied to her when he saw her trying to improve herself in writing. There was a fireplace in the room, and on the marble mantel above stood a beautifully wrought statuette of Jesus receiving little children, and on either side marble vases, for which it was Tom's pride and delight to offer bouquets every morning. Two or three exquisite paintings of children, in various attitudes, embellished the wall. In short, the eye could turn nowhere without meeting images of childhood, of beauty, and of peace. Those little eyes never opened in the morning light, without falling on something which suggested to the heart soothing and beautiful thoughts.

scene i

INTRODUCTION

The deceitful strength which had buoyed Eva up for a little while was fast passing away; seldom and more seldom her light footstep was heard in the verandah, and oftener and oftener she was found reclined on a little lounge by the open window, her large, deep eyes fixed on the rising and falling waters of the lake.

NUCLEUS

It was towards the middle of the afternoon, as she was so reclining,—her Bible half open, her little transparent fingers lying listlessly between the leaves,—suddenly she heard her mother's voice, in sharp tones, in the verandah.

"What now, you baggage!—What new piece of mischief! You've been picking flowers, heh?" and Eva heard the sound of a small slap.

"Law, Missis—they's for Miss Eva," she heard a voice say, which she knew belonged to Topsy.

"Miss Eva! A pretty excuse!—you suppose she wants *your* flowers, you good-for-nothing nigger? Get along off with you!"

In a moment, Eva was off from her lounge, and in the verandah.

"O, don't, mother! I should like the flowers; do give them to me; I want them!"

"Why, Eva, your room is full now."

"I can't have too many," said Eva. "Topsy, do bring them here."

Topsy, who had stood sullenly, holding down her head, now came up and offered her flowers. She did it with a look of hesitation and bashfulness, quite unlike the eldrich boldness and brightness which was usual with her.

"It's a beautiful bouquet!" said Eva, looking at it.

It was a rather a singular one,—a brilliant scarlet geranium, and one single white japonica, with its glossy leaves. It was tied up with an evident eye to the contrast of color, and the arrangement of every leaf had carefully been studied.

Topsy looked pleased, as Eva said,—"Topsy, you arrange flowers very prettily. Here," she said, "is this vase I haven't any flowers for. I wish you'd arrange something every day for it."

"Well, that's odd!" said Marie. "What in the world do you want that for?"

"Never mind, mamma; you'd as lief as not Topsy should do it,—had you not?"

"Of course, anything you please, dear! Topsy, you hear your young mistress;—see that you mind."

Topsy made a short curtsey, and looked down; and, as she turned away, Eva saw a tear roll down her dark cheek.

"You see, mamma, I knew poor Topsy wanted to do something for me," said Eva to her mother.

"O, nonsense! it's only because she likes to do mischief. She knows she mustn't pick flowers, so she does it; that's all there is to it. But if you fancy to have her pluck them, so be it."

"Mamma, I think Topsy is different from what she used to be; she's trying to be a good girl."

"She'll have to try a good while before *she* gets to be good," said Marie, with a careless laugh.

"Well, you know, mamma, poor Topsy! everything has always been against her."

"Not since she's been here, I'm sure. If she hasn't been talked to, and preached to, and every earthly thing done that anybody could do;—and she's just so ugly, and always will be; you can't make anything of the creature!"

"But, mamma, it's so different to be brought up as I've been, with so many friends, so many things to make me good and happy; and to be brought up as she's been, all the time, till she came here!"

"Most likely," said Marie, yawning,—"dear me, how hot it is!"

"Mamma, you believe, don't you, that Topsy could become an angel, as well as any of us, if she were a Christian?"

"Topsy! what a ridiculous idea! Nobody but you would ever think of it. I suppose she could, though."

"But, mamma, isn't God her Father, as much as ours? Isn't Jesus her Saviour?"

"Well, that may be. I suppose God made everybody," said Marie. "Where is my smelling-bottle?"

"It's such a pity,—oh! *such* a pity!" said Eva, looking out on the distant lake, and speaking half to herself.

"What's a pity?" said Marie.

"Why, that any one, who could be a bright angel, and live with angels, should go down, down, down, and nobody help them!—oh, dear!"

"Well, we can't help it; it's no use worrying, Eva! I don't know what's to be done; we ought to be thankful for our own advantages."

"I hardly can be," said Eva, "I'm so sorry to think of poor folks that haven't any."

"That's odd enough," said Marie;—"I'm sure my religion makes me thankful for my advantages."

"Mamma," said Eva, "I want to have some of my hair cut off,—a good deal of it."

"What for?" said Marie.

"Mamma, I want to give some away to my friends, while I am able to give it to them myself. Won't you ask aunty to come and cut it for me?"

Marie raised her voice, and called Miss Ophelia, from the other room.

The child half rose from her pillow as she came in, and shaking down her long golden-brown curls, said, rather playfully, "Come, aunty, shear the sheep!"

"What's that?" said St. Clare, who just then entered with some fruit he had been out to get for her.

"Papa, I just want aunty to cut off some of my hair;—there's too much of it, and it makes my head hot. Besides, I want to give some of it away."

Miss Ophelia came, with the scissors.

"Take care,—don't spoil the looks of it!" said her father; "cut underneath, where it won't show. Eva's curls are my pride."

"O, papa!" said Eva, sadly.

"Yes, and I want them kept handsome against the time I take you up to your uncle's plantation, to see Cousin Henrique," said St. Clare, in a gay tone.

"I shall never go there, papa;—I am going to a better country. O, do believe me! Don't you see, papa, that I get weaker, every day?"

"Why do you insist that I shall believe such a cruel thing, Eva?" said her father.

"Only because it is *true*, papa; and if you will believe it now, perhaps you will get to feel about it as I do."

St. Clare closed his lips, and stood gloomily eyeing the long, beautiful curls, which, as they were separated from the child's head, were laid, one by one, in her lap. She raised them up, looked earnestly at them, twined them around her thin fingers, and looked, from time to time, anxiously at her father.

"It's just what I've been foreboding!" said Marie; "it's just what has been preying on my health, from day to day, bringing me downward to the grave, though nobody regards it. I have seen this, long. St. Clare, you will see, after a while, that I was right."

"Which will afford you great consolation, no doubt!" said St. Clare, in a dry, bitter tone.

Marie lay back on a lounge, and covered her face with her cambric handkerchief.

Eva's clear blue eye looked earnestly from one to the other. It was the calm, comprehending gaze of a soul half loosed from its earthly bonds; it was evident she saw, felt, and appreciated, the difference between the two.

She beckoned with her hand to her father. He came, and sat down by her.

"Papa, my strength fades away every day, and I know I must go. There are some things I want to say and do,—that I ought to do; and you are so unwilling to have me speak a word on this subject. But it must come, there's no putting it off. Do be willing I should speak now!"

"My child, I *am* willing!" said St. Clare, covering his eyes with one hand, and holding up Eva's hand with the other.

"Then, I want to see all our people together. I have some things I *must* say to them," said Eva.

"*Well,*" said St. Clare, in a tone of dry endurance.

Miss Ophelia despatched a messenger, and soon the whole of the servants were convened in the room.

Eva lay back on her pillows; her hair hanging loosely about her face, her crimson cheeks contrasting painfully with the intense whiteness of her complexion and the thin contour of her limbs and features, and her large, soul-like eyes fixed earnestly on everyone.

The servants were struck with a sudden emotion. The spiritual face, the long locks of hair cut off and lying by her, her father's averted face and Marie's sobs, struck at once upon the feelings of a sensitive and impressible race; and, as they came in, they looked one on another, sighed, and shook their heads. There was a deep silence, like that of a funeral.

Eva raised herself, and looked long and earnestly round at every one. All looked sad and apprehensive. Many of the women hid their faces in their aprons.

"I sent for you all, my dear friends," said Eva, "because I love you. I love you all; and I have something to say to you, which I want you always to remember. . . . I am going to leave you. In a few more weeks, you will see me no more—"

Here the child was interrupted by bursts of groans, sobs, and lamentations, which broke from all present, and in which her slender voice was lost entirely. She waited a moment, and then, speaking in a tone that checked the sobs of all, she said,

"If you love me, you must not interrupt me so. Listen to what I say. I want to speak to you about your souls. . . . Many of you, I am afraid, are very careless. You are thinking only about this world. I want you to remember that there is a beautiful world, where Jesus is. I am going there, and you can go there. It is for you, as much as me. But, if you want to go there, you must not live idle, careless, thoughtless lives. You must be Christians. You must remember that each one of you can become angels, and be angels forever. . . .If you want to be Christians, Jesus will help you. You must pray to Him; you must read—"

The child checked herself, look piteously at them, and said, sorrowfully,

"O, dear! you *can't* read,—poor souls!" and she hid her face in the pillow and sobbed, while many a smothered sob from those she was addressing, who were kneeling on the floor, aroused her.

"Never mind," she said, raising her face and smiling brightly through her tears, "I have prayed for you; and I know Jesus will help you, even if you can't read. Try all to do the best you can; pray every day; ask Him to help you, and get the Bible read to you whenever you can; and I think I shall see you all in heaven."

"Amen," was the murmured response from the lips of Tom and Mammy, and some of the elder ones, who belonged to the Methodist church. The younger and more thoughtless ones, for the time completely overcome, were sobbing, with their heads bowed upon their knees.

"I know," said Eva, "you all loved me."

"Yes; oh, yes! indeed we do! Lord bless her!" was the involuntary answer of all.

"Yes, I know you do! There isn't one of you that hasn't always been very kind to me; and I want to give you something that, when you look at, you shall always remember me. I'm going to give all of you a curl of my hair; and, when you look at it, think that I loved you and am gone to heaven, and that I want to see you all there."

It is impossible to describe the scene, as, with tears and sobs, they gathered round the little creature, and took from her hands what seemed to them a last mark of her love. They fell on their knees; they sobbed, and prayed, and kissed the hem of her garment; and the elder ones poured forth words of endearment, mingled in prayers and blessings, after the manner of their susceptible race.

As each one took their gift, Miss Ophelia, who was apprehensive for the effect of all this excitment on her little patient, signed to each one to pass out of the apartment.

At last, all were gone, but Tom and Mammy.

"Here, Uncle Tom," said Eva, "is a beautiful one for you. O, I am so happy, Uncle Tom, to think I shall see you in heaven,—for I'm sure I shall; and Mammy,—dear, good, kind Mammy!" she said, fondly throwing her arms around her old nurse,—"I know you'll be there, too."

"O, Miss Eva, don't see how I can live without ye, nohow!" said the faithful creature, " 'Pears like it's just taking everything off the place to oncet!" and Mammy gave way to a passion of grief.

Miss Ophelia pushed her and Tom gently from the apartment, and thought they were all gone; but, as she turned, Topsy was standing there.

"Where did you start up from?" she said, suddenly.

"I was here," said Topsy, wiping the tears from her eyes. "O Miss Eva, I've been a bad girl; but won't you give *me* one, too?"

"Yes, poor Topsy! to be sure, I will. There—every time you look at that, think that I love you, and wanted you to be a good girl!"

"O Miss Eva, I *is* tryin'!" said Topsy, earnestly; "but, Lor, it's so hard to be good! 'Pears like I an't used to it, no ways!"

"Jesus knows it, Topsy; He is sorry for you; He will help you."

Topsy, with her eyes hid in her apron, was silently passed from the apartment by Miss Ophelia; but, as she went, she hid the precious curl in her bosom.

All being gone, Miss Ophelia shut the door. That worthy lady had wiped away many tears of her own, during the scene; but concerned for the consequence of such an excitement to her young charge was uppermost in her mind.

St. Clare had been sitting, during the whole time, with his hand shading his eyes, in the same attitude. When they were all gone, he sat so still.

"Papa!" said Eva, gently, laying her hand on his.

He gave a sudden start and shiver; but made no answer.

"Dear papa!" said Eva.

"I *cannot,*" said St. Clare, rising, "I *cannot* have it so! The Almighty hath dealt *very bitterly* with me!" and St. Clare pronounced these with a bitter emphasis, indeed.

"Augustine! has not God a right to do what He will with his own?" said Miss Ophelia.

"Perhaps so; but that doesn't make it any easier to bear," said he, with a dry, hard, tearless manner, as he turned away.

"Papa, you break my heart!" said Eva, rising and throwing herself into his arms; "you must not feel so!" and the child sobbed and wept with a violence which alarmed them all, and turned her father's thoughts at once to another channel.

"There, Eva,—there, dearest! Hush! hush! I was wrong; I was wicked. I will feel any way, do any way,—only don't distress yourself; don't sob so. I will be resigned; I was wicked to speak as I did."

Eva soon lay like a wearied dove in her father's arms; and he, bending over her, soothed her by every tender word he could think of.

Marie rose and threw herself out of the apartment into her own, when she fell into violent hysterics.

CONCLUSION

"You didn't give me a curl, Eva," said her father, smiling sadly.

"They are all yours, papa," said she, smiling,—"yours and mamma's; and you must give dear aunty as many as she wants. I only gave them to our poor people myself, because you know, papa, they might be forgotten when I am gone, and because I hoped it might help them remember. . . .You are a Christian, are you not, papa?" said Eva, doubtfully.

"Why do you ask me?"

"I don't know. You are so good, I don't see how you can help it."

"What is being a Christian, Eva?"

"Loving Christ most of all," said Eva.

"Do you, Eva?"

"Certainly, I do."

"You never saw Him," said St. Clare.

"That makes no difference," said Eva. "I believe Him, and in a few days I shall *see* Him"; and the young face grew fervent, radiant with joy.

St. Clare said no more. It was a feeling which he had seen before in his mother; but no chord within vibrated to it.

INTERLUDE

Eva after this, declined rapidly; there was no more any doubt of the event; the fondest hope could not be blinded. Her beautiful room was avowedly a sick room; and Miss Ophelia day and night performed the duties of a nurse,—and never did her friends appreciate her value more than in that capacity. With so well-trained a hand and eye, such perfect adroitness and practice in every art which could promote neatness and comfort, and keep out of sight every disagreeable incident of sickness,—with such a perfect sense of time, such a clear, untroubled head, such exact accuracy in remembering every prescription and direction of the doctors,—she was everything to him. They who had shrugged their shoulders at her little peculiarities and setnesses, so unlike the careless freedom of southern manners, acknowledged that now she was the exact person that was wanted.

Uncle Tom was much in Eva's room. The child suffered much from nervous restlessness, and it was a relief to her to be carried; and it was Tom's greatest delight to carry her little frail form in his arms, resting on a pillow, now up and down her room, now out into the verandah; and when the fresh sea-breezes blew from the lake,—and the child felt freshest in the morning,—he would sometimes walk with her under the orange-trees in the garden, or, sitting down in some of their old seats, sing to her their favorite old hymns.

Her father often did the same thing; but his frame was slighter, and when he was weary, Eva would say to him,

"O, papa, let Tom take me. Poor fellow! it pleases him; and you know it's all he can do now, and he wants to do something!"

"So do I, Eva!" said her father.

"Well, papa, you can do everything, and are everything to me. You read to me,—you sit up nights,—and Tom has only this one thing, and his singing; and I know, too, he does it easier than you can. He carries me so strong!"

The desire to do something was not confined to Tom. Every servant to the establishment showed the same feeling, and in their way did what they could.

Poor Mammy's heart yearned towards her darling; but she found no opportunity, night or day, as Marie declared that the state of her mind was such, it was impossible for her to rest; and, of course, it was against her principles to let any one else rest. Twenty times in a night, Mammy would be roused to rub her feet, to bathe her head, to find her pocket-handkerchief, to see what the noise was in Eva's room, to let down a curtain because it was too light, or to put it up because it was too dark; and, in the daytime, when she longed to have some share in the nursing of her pet, Marie seemed unusually ingenious in keeping her busy anywhere and everywhere all over the house, or about her own person; so that stolen interviews and momentary glimpses were all she could obtain.

"I feel it my duty to be particularly careful of myself, now," she would say, "feeble as I am, and with the whole care and nursing of that dear child upon me."

"Indeed, my dear," said St. Clare, "I thought our cousin relieved you of that."

"You talk like a man, St. Clare,—just as if a mother *could* be relieved of the care of a child in that state; but, then, it's all alike,—no one ever knows what I feel! I can't throw things off, as you do."

St. Clare smiled. You must excuse him, he couldn't help it,—for St. Clare could smile yet. For so bright and placid was the farewell voyage of the little spirit,—by such sweet and fragrant breezes was the small bark borne towards the heavenly shores,—that it was impossible to realize that it was death that was approaching. The child felt no pain,—only a tranquil, soft weakness, daily and almost insensibly increasing; and she was so beautiful, so loving, so trustful, so happy, that one could not resist the soothing influence of that air of innocence and peace which seemed to breathe around her. St. Clare found a strange calm coming over him. It was not hope,—that was impossible; it was not resignation; it was only a calm resting in the present, which seemed so beautiful that he wished to think of no future. It was like that hush of spirit which we feel amid the bright, mild woods of autumn, when the bright hectic flush is on the trees, and the last lingering flowers by the brook; and we joy in it all the more, because we know that soon it will all pass away.

scene iia

INTRODUCTION

The friend who knew most of Eva's own imaginings and foreshadowings was her faithful bearer, Tom. To him she said what she would not disturb her father by saying. To him she imparted those mysterious intimations which the soul feels, as the cords begin to unbind, ere it leaves its clay forever.

NUCLEUS

Tom, at last, would not sleep in his room, but lay all night in the outer verandah, ready to rouse at every call.

"Uncle Tom, what alive have you taken to sleeping anywhere and everywhere, like a dog for?" said Miss Ophelia. "I thought you was one of the orderly sort, that liked to lie in bed in a Christian way."

"I do, Miss Feely," said Tom mysteriously. "I do, but now—"

"Well, what now?"

"We mustn't speak loud; Mas'r St. Clare won't hear on't; but, Miss Feely, you know there must be somebody watchin' for the bridegroom."

"What do you mean, Tom?"

"You know it says in Scripture, 'At midnight there was a great cry made. Behold, the bridegroom cometh.' That's what I'm spectin' now, every night, Miss Feely,—and I couldn't sleep out o' hearin', no ways."

"Why, Uncle Tom, what makes you think so?"

"Miss Eva, she talks to me. The Lord, he sends his messenger in the soul. I must be thar, Miss Feely; for when that ar blessed child goes into the kingdom, they'll open the door so wide, we'll all get a look in at the glory, Miss Feely."

"Uncle Tom, did Miss Eva say she felt more unwell than usual to-night?"

"No; but she telled me this morning, she was coming nearer,—thar's them that tells it to the child, Miss Feely. It's the angels,—'it's the trumpet sound before the break o' day,'" said Tom, quoting from a favorite hymn.

This dialogue passed between Miss Ophelia and Tom, between ten and eleven, one evening, after her arrangements had all been made for the night, when, on going to bolt her outer door, she found Tom stretched along by it, in the outer verandah.

segment iib

She was not nervous or impressible; but the solemn, heartfelt manner struck her. Eva had been unusually bright and cheerful that afternoon, and had sat raised in her bed, and looked over all her little trinkets and precious things, and designated the friends to whom she would have them given; and her manner was more animated, and her voice more natural, than they had know it for weeks. Her father had been in, in the evening, and had said that Eva appeared more like her former self than ever she had done since her sickness; and when he kissed her for the night he said to Miss Ophelia,—"Cousin, we may keep her with us, after all; she is certainly better"; and he had retired with a lighter heart in his bosom than he had had there for weeks.

scene iic

INTRODUCTION

But at midnight,—strange, mystic hour!—when the veil between the frail present and the eternal future grows thin,—then came the messenger!

NUCLEUS

There was a sound in that chamber, first of one who stepped quickly. It was Miss Ophelia, who had resolved to sit up all night with her little charge, and who, at the turn of the night, had discerned what experienced nurses significantly call "a change." The outer door was quickly opened, and Tom, who was watching outside, was on the alert, in a moment.

"Go for the doctor, Tom! lose not a moment," said Miss Ophelia; and, stepping across the room, she rapped at St. Clare's door.

"Cousin," she said, "I wish you would come."

These words fell on his heart like clods upon a coffin. Why did they? He was up and in the room in an instant, and bending over Eva, who still slept.

What was it he saw that made his heart stand still? Why was no word spoken between the two? Thou canst say, who hast seen that same expression on the face dearest to thee;—that look indescribable, hopeless, unmistakable, that says to thee that thy beloved is no longer thine.

On the face of the child, however, there was no ghastly imprint,—only a high and almost sublime expression,—the overshadowing presence of spiritual natures, the dawning immortal life in that childish soul.

They stood there so still, gazing upon her, that even the ticking of the watch seemed too loud. In a few moments, Tom returned, with the doctor. He entered, gave one look, and stood silent as the rest.

"When did this change take place?" said he, in a low whisper, to Miss Ophelia.

"About the turn of the night," was the reply.

Marie, roused by the entrance of the doctor, appeared, hurriedly, from the next room.

"Augustine! Cousin!—O!—what!" she hurriedly began.

"Hush!" said St. Clare, hoarsely; "*she is dying!*"

Mammy heard the words, and flew to awaken the servants. The house was soon roused,—lights were seen, footsteps heard, anxious faces thronged the verandah, and looked tearfully through the glass doors; but St. Clare heard and said nothing,—he saw only *that look* on the face of the little sleeper.

"O, if she would only wake, and speak once more!" he said; and, stooping over her, he spoke in her ear,—"Eva darling!"

The large blue eyes unclosed,—a smile passed over her face;—she tried to raise her head, and to speak.

"Do you know me, Eva?"

"Dear papa," said the child, with a last effort throwing her arms about his neck. In a moment they dropped again; and, as St. Clare raised his head, he saw a spasm of mortal agony pass over the face,—she struggled for breath and threw up her little hands.

"O God, this is dreadful!" he said, turning away in agony, and wringing Tom's hand, scarce conscious what he was doing. "O Tom, my boy, it is killing me!"

Tom had his master's hands between his own; and, with tears streaming down his dark cheeks, looked up for help where he had always been used to look.

"Pray that this may be cut short!" said St. Clare,—"this wrings my heart."

"O, bless the Lord! it's over,—it's over, dear Master!" said Tom; "look at her."

CONCLUSION

The child lay panting on her pillows, as one exhausted,—the large clear eyes rolled up and fixed. Ah, what said those eyes, that spoke so much of heaven? Earth was past, and earthly pain; but so solemn, so mysterious, was the triumphant brightness of that face, that it checked even the sobs of sorrow. They pressed around her, in breathless stillness.

"Eva," said St. Clare, gently.

She did not hear.

"O Eva, tell us what you see! What is it?" said her father.

A bright, a glorious smile passed over her face, and she said, brokenly,—"O! love,—joy,—peace!" gave one sigh, and passed from death unto life!

"Farewell, beloved child! the bright eternal doors have closed after thee; we shall see thy sweet face no more. O, woe for them who watched thy entrance into heaven, when they shall wake and find only the cold gray sky of daily life, and thou gone forever!"

• 10 •

UNCLE TOM'S CABIN: CHAPTER 26, "DEATH"

1. Summary. Harriet Beecher Stowe narrates the death of Little Eva in her famous novel, *Uncle Tom's Cabin,* in two scenes, with recounted material covering an indefinite span of days connecting them. In the first scene Eva says goodbye to all the members of the household and gives a lock of hair to each of the principals. The second scene is the deathbed scene.

Scene i (lines 32–279)[1] is set in Little Eva's bedroom. The time is during her declining days, on a mid-afternoon of one of those days. The participants are: Eva, her mother (Marie), Topsy (a servant girl), Ophelia (an aunt from New England), Eva's father (St. Clare), and the household servants, including Tom and Mammy, who, along with Topsy, are sometimes singled out from the larger group of servants.

Scene ii (342–446) is also set principally in Eva's bedroom. It is days later than scene i, during Eva's declining days, and specifically on one of those days between ten and eleven in the evening. The participants are Tom, Ophelia, St. Clare, Marie, Mammy, and the servants.

The same participants appear in the interlude of recounted material that connects the two scenes (280–341).

2. The Introduction. The first full paragraph of the chapter functions as the introduction to the whole (1–31); to distinguish it from the introductions to specific scenes, we shall refer to it as the general introduction.

The general INTRO consists of three types of narrative material:

(a) Descriptions of the physical setting: Eva's bedroom and its appointments;
(b) Portrayal of items in the setting that involve repeated events (recounting in the iterative mode);
(c) Portrayal of one event out of the past that contributes to the present setting (recounting in the singulative mode).

We may now particularize these types.

The narrator begins with the physical layout of the relevant part of the house (1–4). Eva's bedroom is joined on one side by the apartment of her father and mother, and on the other by that of Ophelia, her solicitous New England aunt. A broad verandah stretches across all three spaces on the inner

1. Since the text of chapter 26 is lengthy, it has been printed as a continuous text. We will make use of traditional line numbers in this section rather than employ numbered narrative statements.

court of the house, as is typical of New Orleans houses of this period. These are all descriptive statements related to setting; they are actionless.

The narrator then depicts the decoration of the bedroom of Eva as St. Clare conceived it (4–31). Aside from the statements to be examined momentarily, these, too, are descriptive statements concerned with setting. Stowe's general INTRO is substantial; and, like the INTRO to *Shane*, it is rich in descriptive material.

There are three statements that involve repeated events:

(1) On a bamboo table stood a Parian vase, . . . *ever filled with flowers* (18–21);
(2) On the mantel stood marble vases, . . . *for which it was Tom's pride to offer bouquets every morning* (24–26);
(3) Images of childhood, of beauty, and of peace filled Eva's room: *those little eyes never opened in the morning light, without falling on something which suggested to the heart soothing and beautiful thoughts* (29–31).

Someone filled the Parian vase repeatedly; Tom put bouquets in the marble vases on the mantel each morning; and every morning, when Eva opened her eyes, she saw images of childhood, beauty, and peace.

The scene is brought together in a general way: the narrator does not depict particular occasions or particular times, but repeated actions by unspecified agents or customary or habituated actions by a specific participant. The reader is given a fairly full picture of the room before the action opens.

The room also contains an alabaster writing-stand. This stand goes back to an event of the past: this stand *her father had supplied to her when he saw her trying to improve herself in writing* (21–23). The occasion on which her father had presented the writing-stand to her is unspecified. It is only located at some point in the past—outside the present scene or sequence of scenes; it is therefore an analepsis. It is already an accomplished fact and makes up part of the furniture of her room. This is the only item in the setting of the room about which the narrator chooses to relate how it got there. In the midst of iterative statements the narrator chooses to insert a recounted event in the singulative mode.

The general INTRO deals primarily with spatial setting. The INTRO to scene i will provide the temporal setting.

3. Scene i. The second paragraph of the chapter (32–36) provides the INTRO to scene i. Three iterative events leading up to the first action are narrated:

(a) Eva's strength ebbs
(b) She goes out on the verandah less frequently
(c) She reclines more frequently on her lounge

Then, on one such occasion, when she is reclining on her lounge, the second scene opens (37–40).

The NUC begins with the third paragraph (37ff.). The *ts* is toward the middle of the afternoon; the *ls* is Eva reclining on her lounge, her Bible open, her fingers listless on the page. It is to be noted that the space is narrowed down finally to her fingers on the page of the book. Suddenly she hears her mother's voice on the verandah outside her door (*f¹:perc*): what Eva hears brings the reader's hearing to the same focal point. The voices of Marie and Topsy on the verandah are the focalized and Eva is the focalizing agent; hearing a sound is the focalizing device.

Eva listens to an exchange between her mother and Topsy, which disturbs her (41–46). So she rises and joins them on the verandah (47). That movement constitutes an *arrival* and is a second focalizing element (*f²:arr*). We could say that the scene is focalized twice: once by hearing and once by arriving. In actuality, the two work in tandem in focalizing a single scene. Eva has now joined Marie and Topsy on the verandah; the dialogue continues.

4. Locus in scene i. Special notice should be taken of the spatial markers in scene i.

The scene opens just outside Eva's bedroom on the verandah, as noted above. This is also the case with scene ii. However, in scene i it is not easily possible to divide the scene into subscenes, whereas scene ii is readily separable into three subscenes. The reason for this difficulty in scene i is that the narrator does not explicity move the locale from the verandah back into Eva's bedroom, where most of the scene obviously takes place.

When Eva mentions the vase to Topsy during the conversation about the flowers, we may already be back in the bedroom (60ff.). But the narrator has not told us so. We are not concerned with locale as readers until Marie calls Ophelia, who is in the next room, and Eva is again reclining on her pillow (111f.): *pillow* is reinforced by *lounge*, and eventually the *room* is mentioned with the arrival of the house servants (156ff.). The bulk of the scene is thus set in the bedroom, with the opening moments transpiring on the verandah outside Eva's door.

5. Participants in scene i. The scene is relatively complicated from the standpoint of the participants. At the opening Eva is alone on her lounge. Marie and Topsy are heard in conversation on the verandah; Eva joins them. Topsy then exits (67f.) and we are back to two participants. A little later, Marie calls Ophelia (111), who arrives (112), and St. Clare enters at about the same time (115f.). Now the participants number four. The servants are sent for at Eva's request (156f.). When they arrive the number of active participants is raised to five, which is a substantial number to handle in a focused scene.

After the locks of hair are handed out, the undifferentiated group of servants departs (213–15). Mammy and Tom, who have been singled out from the larger group, but now function as a smaller group, depart next

(216–25); then Topsy departs (225–36). The servants thus depart in ascending order of importance.[2]

With the departure of the servants, St. Clare, Ophelia, and Marie are left with Eva: we are back to four (237ff.). Marie quits the room next (261f.) and the scene closes with St. Clare and Ophelia alone with Eva (263–79). Or is that the case? The narrator does not notify us that Ophelia departs, and yet Eva's remark, *you must give dear aunty as many* [curls] *as she wants* (265), suggests that Aunt Ophelia is no longer present. But we cannot be sure.

In this scene, then, participants are gathered one or several at a time until the whole household is present. They are then made to depart, not precisely in reverse order, but something like that: father remains until last, as he does in the death scene, scene ii, although he does not arrive first.

To summarize:

pos	Eva	
arr	Topsy	
arr	Marie	
	Topsy	*dep*
arr	Ophelia	
arr	St. Clare	
arr	servants	
	most servants	*dep*
	Tom and	
	Mammy	*dep*
	Topsy	*dep*
	Marie	*dep*
	[Ophelia]	*dep*
	St. Clare	
pos	Eva	

6. The Conclusion to scene i. Scene i is concluded with Eva and her father, and perhaps Ophelia, still in view. Eva has a terminal dialogue with her father about whether he is a Christian (*constop*)(267ff.).

Eva anticipates her own departure (death): *in a few days I shall see Him* [Christ] (*dep*)(276).

Eva is radiant with joy (*termf*)(277).

St. Clare falls silent (*a:term*)(278).

Eva's feeling recalls that of St. Clare's mother: he was unable to resonate with it then and is unable to do so now (278f.). We thus have a *termf* now cast

2. Ordinarily Tom would rank first among the servants. After all, this is his story. Yet in this scene, Topsy appears to have the temporary ascendancy. In scene ii, Tom's first rank reasserts itself.

back into the past, focused on his mother. In a sense the scene is doubly defocalized: in his mother's radiant joy and in Eva's.

7. *The interlude.* The interlude contains a number of iterative statements. Because they are iterative, they are, of course, also unfocused. We may simply list them (providing a kind of narrative summary):

(1) Eva declines rapidly (280f.).

(2) Ophelia performs the duties of a nurse night and day (282–91).

(3) Uncle Tom was often in Eva's room; he carries her about, *now up and down in her room, now out onto the verandah . . . he would sometimes walk with her . . . or, sitting down . . . , sing to her . . .* (292–98).

(4) *Her father often did the same thing. . . . When he was weary Eva would say to him . . .* (299–306). That is, she would say something like this on various occasions; in this technique, quoted speech is typical speech.[3] What Eva would say was: Tom carries me and sings; you read to me and sit up nights. Such statements refer not to one particular occasion but to plural particular occasions. The events were repeated and the mode of discourse is thus the iterative.

(5) Every servant *desired* to do something for Eva (307f.).

(6) Mammy *yearned* to help Eva, but Marie required her services (309–19): *Twenty times a night, Mammy would be roused to* (there follows a list of actions Mammy had to perform); *Marie seemed unusually ingenious in keeping her busy anywhere and everywhere all over the house* (she was kept busy all the time and everywhere: strongly iterative).

(7) Marie *would say* (i.e., habitual though quoted speech): *I feel it my duty to be particularly careful of myself. . . .* St. Clare's reply was one in kind: a typical reply (320–27).[4]

(8) On such occasions, St. Clare *smiled.* Then the implied author addresses the implied reader: *You must excuse him, he couldn't help it . . . .* The narrator attempts to dictate how the reader views the story at these points where she breaks out of the narrative framework (328f.).[5]

(9) The conclusion to the interlude is provided by a description of Eva: she is taking the *voyage of the little spirit,* which is *bright and placid*; *heavenly breezes* bear her *small bark towards the heavenly shores.* Death is approaching and Eva breathes an air of innocence and peace (329–40).

(10) Finally, St. Clare found a *strange calm coming over him.* This calm was *like that hush of the spirit which we feel amid the bright, mild woods of autumn.* It was also the mood that suggests: *It will all pass away* (340–46).

In the interlude, the narrator notes that Eva continues to decline; this is by way of introduction and links the interlude to scene i. Then she passes the

3. This phenomenon is the pseudo-iterative discussed in §6.44.

4. Again the pseudo-iterative: §6.44.

5. This phenomenon has been labelled *com* for commentary. This feature is discussed in §5.47.

members of the household in review, indicating what each did, or wished to do, during this period, to help little Eva. The interlude concludes by returning to Eva and renewing the introductory theme; this renewal initiates the conclusion to the interlude. The narrator then turns to Eva's father, St. Clare: he is being prepared for the death scene to follow, where he will also play the concluding role; the death of Eva will be recorded through his eyes, voice, and sensibilities. It is worth noting that St. Clare closes scenes i and ii, as well as the interlude: he is given a very prominent position in this sequence of the larger story.

8. Scene ii. Scene ii may be divided into three segments and an INTRO and CON.

The INTRO (342–45) depicts the closeness of Tom and Eva: she tells him things she would not say to her father and to him she imparts intimations of her imminent departure. This catapults Tom onto the same level with Eva's father. The intimation to Tom of her death sets the stage for scene iia.

Other elements of an "introduction" are reserved for the end of scene iia; these will be considered below.

9. Scene iia. The NUC of this scene is set on the outer verandah. Tom had taken to sleeping there to be ready to respond to Eva's call (346f.). It is there that Ophelia stumbles on him after arrangements had already been made for the night (368–71). In the ensuing dialogue (348–67), Tom tells Ophelia that "the bridegroom cometh" at midnight. He has received this message from Eva herself. Eva had told Tom so just that morning (365). We thus have a retrospective event of the morning inserted into a dialogue that takes place between ten and eleven that evening.[6] The setting is given, in part, at the close of the scene (368–71) rather than at the beginning.

Scene iia, then, consists of Tom and Ophelia as participants; the time is between and ten and eleven one evening, and the place is on the outer verandah. The action consists entirely of dialogue between Tom and Ophelia.

The depiction of the relationship of Eva to Tom in the INTRO telegraphs the climactic event of scene iic: Eva's death. But for scene iia, Tom is in *position* on the verandah. Ophelia *arrives* when she goes to bolt her outer door and finds Tom stretched out there. The initial action is the question addressed to Tom by Ophelia.

Scene iia is opened and closed with material that theoretically belongs to the INTRO; the INTRO is broken apart, so to speak, and made to function as both INTRO and CON.

10. Segment iib (interlude). Segment iib is actually another interlude in which events are recounted: the current action stops momentarily during Ophelia's

6. This is another example of analepsis, §§8.3–7.

reverie. In that reverie, Ophelia recounts events and impressions of the afternoon—items that are immediately related to the demeanor of Tom in the immediately preceding dialogue (scene iia): Tom's "solemn, heartfelt manner struck her." The events that Ophelia recounts to herself are two: (1) Eva had been bright and cheerful *in the afternoon*; her manner was more animated, her voice more natural. (2) *In the evening*, Eva's father had come in: Eva appeared more her former self to him; he thought perhaps Eva would not die and tells Ophelia so; he retires with a much lighter heart.

The events recounted in segment iib thus *reach* back to the afternoon and early evening.[7] The narrator has decided that these moments from earlier in the day will be more effective when narrated analeptically, or retrospectively, probably because she wanted to place them as near the final scene as possible.

The INTRO to this scene consists of the statement that Tom's manner struck Ophelia: she is thrown into a reverie in that way. The CON is achieved by having St. Clare retire with lighter heart (*dep*). The NUC consists of the two events, one in the afternoon, the second in the early evening, that the narrator recounts through Ophelia's reverie.

The interlude is designed, of course, to contribute to the mood: hope arising in the face of certain doom.

11. Scene iic.

> Time: midnight
> Place: bedroom of Little Eva
> Participants: all

The "messenger" arrives at midnight—a symbolic hour (*f:arr*). There is a sound in Little Eva's bedroom, that of the step of Ophelia, who had decided to sit up all night: her step is a *f:percprec*. Tom hears it and hurries in (*f:arr*[2]). The focalizing process is complex: the arrival of the "messenger" and the *ts* (at midnight) are announced first. Then the step of Ophelia functions as a focalizing sound, precipitating the appearance of Tom, who has been on watch outside on the verandah.

Once the scene has been brought into focus, the narrator presents a succession of events involving all the participants known heretofore in the chapter, in addition to the doctor. These actions may be summarized:

(1) Ophelia sends Tom for the doctor
(2) Ophelia summons St. Clare from the adjoining room;
St. Clare arrives
[The narrator addresses the reader directly]

7. Genette calls the temporal distance to which an analepsis returns from the present moment in the narrative its reach: *Narrative Discourse*, 48. In this instance, the narrator reaches, via Ophelia's reverie, from late evening back to the afternoon and early evening. Earlier, in scene iia, Tom had reached from late evening back to that same morning. Reach is discussed in §8.7.

(3) The doctor arrives with Tom
A dialogue ensues between the doctor and Ophelia
(4) Marie arrives, having been roused by the arrival of the doctor
(5) Mammy hears St. Clare declare that Eva is dying
[we are not told when Mammy arrived] and summons the servants
(6) St. Clare now knows that Eva is dying: he *sees* the look on her face. This functions as the focalizing device for the conclusion.

The participants of the CON, which occupies lines 433–46 of the chapter, are Eva, St. Clare, and Tom. The strong defocalizer is of course the death of Eva, supported by her father's farewell. In what is perhaps unusual order, a *departure* is thus followed by a *dismissal*.

The formal structure of the entire sequence is diagrammed in figure 22.

Uncle Tom's Cabin

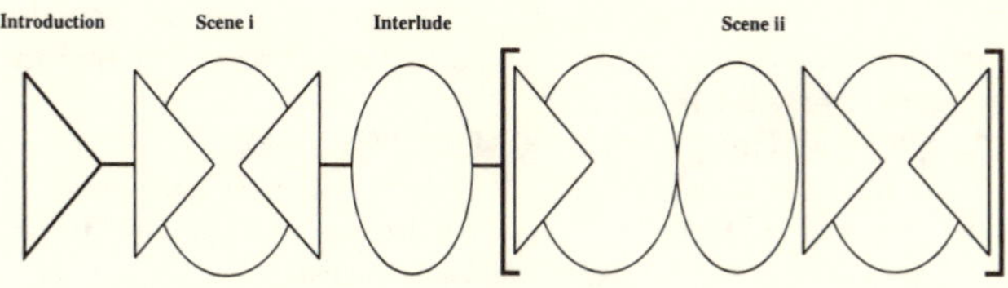

CHAPTER 26

Formal Structure of the Death of Little Eva

Figure 22

Passion Narrative

INTRODUCTION

Mark 14:1–2

[1]It was now two days before the Passover and the feast of Unleavened Bread. And the chief priests and the scribes were seeking how to arrest him by stealth, and kill him; [2]for they said, "Not during the feast, lest there be a tumult of the people."

Mark 14:3–9

[3]And while he was at Bethany in the house of Simon the leper, as he sat at table, a woman came with an alabaster flask of ointment of pure nard, very costly, and she broke the flask and poured it over his head. [4]But there were some who said to themselves indignantly, "Why was the ointment thus wasted? [5]For this ointment might have been sold for more than three hundred denarii, and given to the poor." And they reproached her. [6]But Jesus said, "Let her alone; why do you trouble her? She has done a beautiful thing to me. [7]For you always have the poor with you, and whenever you will, you can do good to them; but you will not always have me. [8]She has done what she could; she has anointed my body beforehand for burying. [9]And truly, I say to you, wherever the gospel is preached in the whole world, what she has done will be told in memory of her."

Mark 14:10–11

[10]Then Judas Iscariot, who was one of the twelve, went to the chief priests in order to betray him to them. [11]And when they heard it they were glad, and promised to give him money. And he sought an opportunity to betray him.

THE PASSOVER MEAL

Mark 14:12–16

[12]And on the first day of Unleavened Bread, when they sacrificed the passover lamb, his disciples said to him, "Where will you have us go and prepare for you to eat the passover?" [13]And he sent two of his disciples, and said to them, "Go into the city, and a man carrying a jar of water will meet you; follow him, [14]and wherever he enters, say to the householder, 'The Teacher says, Where is my guest room, where I am to eat the passover with my disciples?' [15]And he will show you a large upper room furnished and ready; there prepare for us." [16]And the disciples set out and went to the city, and found it as he had told them; and they prepared the passover.

Mark 14:17–21

[17]And when it was evening he came with the twelve. [18]And as they were at table eating, Jesus said, "Truly, I say to you, one of you will betray me, one who is eating with me." [19]They began to be sorrowful, and to say to him one after another, "Is it I?" [20]He said to them, "It is one of the twelve, one who is dipping bread into the dish with me. [21]For the Son of man goes as it is written of him, but woe to that man by whom the Son of man is betrayed! It would have been better for that man if he had not been born."

Mark 14:22–25

[22]And as they were eating, he took bread, and blessed, and broke it, and gave it to them, and said, "Take; this is my body." [23]And he took a cup, and when he had given thanks he gave it to them, and they all drank of it. [24]And he said to them, "This is my blood of the covenant, which is poured out for many. [25]Truly, I say to you, I shall not drink again of the fruit of the vine until that day when I drink it new in the kingdom of God."

EVENTS IN GETHSEMANE

Mark 14:26–31

26 And when they had sung a hymn, they went out to the Mount of Olives. 27 And Jesus said to them, "You will all fall away; for it is written, 'I will strike the shepherd, and the sheep will be scattered.' 28 But after I am raised up, I will go before you to Galilee." 29 Peter said to him, "Even though they all fall away, I will not." 30 And Jesus said to him, "Truly, I say to you, this very night, before the cock crows twice, you will deny me three times." 31 But he said vehemently, "If I must die with you, I will not deny you." And they all said the same.

Mark 14:32

32 And they went to a place which was called Gethsemane; and he said to his disciples, "Sit here, while I pray."

Mark 14:33–34

33 And he took with him Peter and James and John, and began to be greatly distressed and troubled. 34 And he said to them, "My soul is very sorrowful, even to death; remain here, and watch."

Mark 14:35–36

35 And going a little farther, he fell on the ground and prayed that, if it were possible, the hour might pass from him. 36 And he said, "Abba, Father, all things are possible to thee; remove this cup from me; yet not what I will, but what thou wilt."

Mark 14:37–38

37 And he came and found them sleeping, and he said to Peter, "Simon, are you asleep? Could you not watch one hour? 38 Watch and pray that you may not enter into temptation; the spirit indeed is willing, but the flesh is weak."

Mark 14:39

39 And again he went away and prayed, saying the same words.

Mark 14:40

40 And again he came and found them sleeping, for their eyes were very heavy; and they did not know what to answer him.

Mark 14:41–42

41 And he came the third time, and said to them, "Are you still sleeping and taking your rest? It is enough; the hour has come; the Son of man is betrayed into the hands of sinners. 42 Rise, let us be going; see, my betrayer is at hand."

Mark 14:43–52

43 And immediately, while he was still speaking, Judas came, one of the twelve, and with him a crowd with swords and clubs, from the chief priests and the scribes and the elders. 44 Now the betrayer had given them a sign, saying, "The one I shall kiss is the man; seize him and lead him away under guard." 45 And when he came, he went up to him at once, and said, "Master!" And he kissed him. 46 And they laid hands on him and seized him. 47 But one of those who stood by drew his sword, and struck the slave of the high priest and cut off his ear. 48 And Jesus said to them, "Have you come out as against a robber, with swords and clubs to capture me? 49 Day after day I was with you in the temple teaching, and you did not seize me. But let the scriptures be fulfilled." 50 And they all forsook him, and fled.

51 And a young man followed him, with nothing but a linen cloth about his body; and they seized him, 52 but he left the linen cloth and ran away naked.

THE TRIAL BEFORE THE COUNCIL AND THE DENIAL OF PETER

Mark 14:53–54

53 And they led Jesus to the high priest; and all the chief priests and the elders and the scribes were assembled. 54 And Peter had followed him at a distance, right into the courtyard of the high priest; and he was

sitting with the guards, and warming himself at the fire.

Mark 14:55–65

55 Now the chief priests and the whole council sought testimony against Jesus to put him to death; but they found none. 56 For many bore false witness against him, and their witness did not agree. 57 And some stood up and bore false witness against him, saying, 58 "We heard him say, 'I will destroy this temple that is made with hands, and in three days I will build another, not made with hands.'" 59 Yet not even so did their testimony agree. 60 And the high priest stood up in the midst, and asked Jesus, "Have you no answer to make? What is it that these men testify against you?" 61 But he was silent and made no answer. Again the high priest asked him, "Are you the Christ, the Son of the Blessed?" 62 And Jesus said, "I am; and you will see the Son of man seated at the right hand of Power, and coming with the clouds of heaven." 63 And the high priest tore his garments, and said, "Why do we still need witnesses? 64 You have heard his blasphemy. What is your decision?" And they all condemned him as deserving death. 65 And some began to spit on him, and to cover his face, and to strike him, saying to him, "Prophesy!" And the guards received him with blows.

Mark 14:66–68

66 And as Peter was below in the courtyard, one of the maids of the high priest came; 67 and seeing Peter warming himself, she looked at him, and said, "You also were with the Nazarene, Jesus." 68 But he denied it, saying, "I neither know nor understand what you mean." And he went out into the gateway.

Mark 14:69–70

69 And the maid saw him, and began again to say to the bystanders, "This man is one of them." 70 But again he denied it.

Mark 14:70–72

70 . . . And after a little while again the bystanders said to Peter, "Certainly you are one of them; for you are a Galilean." 71 But he began to invoke a curse on himself and to swear, "I do not know this man of whom you speak." 72 And immediately the cock crowed a second time. And Peter remembered how Jesus had said to him, "Before the cock crows twice, you will deny me three times." And he broke down and wept.

TRIAL BEFORE PILATE

Mark 15:1–5

1 And as soon as it was morning the chief priests, with the elders and scribes, and the whole council held a consultation; and they bound Jesus and led him away and delivered him to Pilate. 2 And Pilate asked him, "Are you the King of the Jews?" And he answered him, "You have said so." 3 And the chief priests accused him of many things. 4 And Pilate again asked him, "Have you no answer to make? See how many charges they bring against you." 5 But Jesus made no further answer, so that Pilate wondered.

Mark 15:6–15

6 Now at the feast he used to release for them one prisoner for whom they asked. 7 And among the rebels in prison, who had committed murder in the insurrection, there was a man called Barabbas. 8 And the crowd came up and began to ask Pilate to do as he was wont to do for them. 9 And he answered them, "Do you want me to release for you the King of the Jews?" 10 For he perceived that it was out of envy that the chief priests had delivered him up. 11 But the chief priests stirred up the crowd to have him release for them Barabbas instead. 12 And Pilate again said to them, "Then what shall I do with the man whom you call the King of the Jews?" 13 And they cried out again, "Crucify him." 14 And Pilate said to them, "Why, what evil has he

done?" But they shouted all the more, "Crucify him." 15 So Pilate, wishing to satisfy the crowd, released for them Barabbas; and having scourged Jesus, he delivered him to be crucified.

THE CRUCIFIXION

Mark 15:16–20

16 And the soldiers led him away inside the palace (that is, the praetorium); and they called together the whole battalion. 17 And they clothed him in a purple cloak, and plaiting a crown of thorns they put it on him. 18 And they began to salute him, "Hail, King of the Jews!" 19 And they struck his head with a reed, and spat upon him, and they knelt down in homage to him. 20 And when they had mocked him, they stripped him of the purple cloak, and put his own clothes on him. And they led him out to crucify him.

Mark 15:21

21 And they compelled a passer-by, Simon of Cyrene, who was coming in from the country, the father of Alexander and Rufus, to carry his cross.

Mark 15:22–32

22 And they brought him to the place called Golgotha (which means the place of a skull). 23 And they offered him wine mingled with myrrh; but he did not take it. 24 And they crucified him, and divided his garments among them, casting lots for them, to decide what each should take. 25 And it was the third hour, when they crucified him. 26 And the inscription of the charge against him read, "The King of the Jews." 27 And with him they crucified two robbers, one on his right and one one his left. 29 And those who passed by derided him, wagging their heads, and saying, "Aha! You who would destroy the temple and build it in three days, 30 save yourself, and come down from the cross!" 31 So also the chief priests mocked him to one another with the scribes, saying, "He saved others; he cannot save himself. 32 Let the Christ, the King of Israel, come down now from the cross, that we may see and believe." Those who were crucified with him also reviled him.

Mark 15:33–41

33 And when the sixth hour had come, there was darkness over the whole land until the ninth hour. 34 And at the ninth hour Jesus cried with a loud voice, "Eloi, Eloi, lama sabachthani?" which means, "My God, my God, why hast thou forsaken me?" 35 And some of the bystanders hearing it said, "Behold, he is calling Elijah." 36 And one ran and, filling a sponge full of vinegar, put it on a reed and gave it to him to drink, saying, "Wait, let us see whether Elijah will come to take him down." 37 And Jesus uttered a loud cry, and breathed his last. 38 And the curtain of the temple was torn in two, from top to bottom. 39 And when the centurion, who stood facing him, saw that he thus breathed his last, he said, "Truly this man was the Son of God!"

40 There were also women looking on from afar, among whom were Mary Magdalene, and Mary the mother of James the younger and of Joses, and Salome, 41 who, when he was in Galilee, followed him, and ministered to him; and also many other women who came up with him to Jerusalem.

THE BURIAL

Mark 15:42–47

42 And when evening had come, since it was the day of Preparation, that is, the day before the sabbath, 43 Joseph of Arimathea, a respected member of the council, who was also himself looking for the kingdom of God, took courage and went to Pilate, and asked for the body of Jesus. 44 And Pilate wondered if he were already dead; and summoning the centurion, he asked him whether he was already dead. 45 And when he learned from the centurion that he was dead, he granted the body to Joseph. 46 And

he bought a linen shroud, and taking him down, wrapped him in the linen shroud, and laid him in a tomb which had been hewn out of the rock; and he rolled a stone against the door of the tomb. [47] Mary Magdalene and Mary the mother of Joses saw where he was laid.

THE EMPTY TOMB

Mark 16:1–8

[1] And when the sabbath was past, Mary Magdalene, and Mary the mother of James, and Salome, bought spices, so that they might go and anoint him. [2] And very early on the first day of the week they went to the tomb when the sun had risen. [3] And they were saying to one another, "Who will roll away the stone for us from the door of the tomb?" [4] And looking up, they saw that the stone was rolled back—it was very large. [5] And entering the tomb, they saw a young man sitting on the right side, dressed in a white robe; and they were amazed. [6] And he said to them, "Do not be amazed; you seek Jesus of Nazareth, who was crucified. He has risen, he is not here; see the place where they laid him. [7] But go, tell his disciples and Peter that he is going before you to Galilee; there you will see him, as he told you." [8] And they went out and fled from the tomb; for trembling and astonishment had come upon them; and they said nothing to any one, for they were afraid.

THE MARKAN PASSION NARRATIVE, 14:1–16:8

12. Segments and sequences. The passion narrative in Mark falls into eight sequences, with sixteen segments and scenes, as follows:[8]

S1	Introduction, 14:1–11	
		Plot to Kill Jesus, 14:1–2
	Scene i	Anointing Beforehand, 14:3–9
		Judas Makes a Deal, 14:10–11
S2	The Passover Meal, 14:12–25	
	Scene ii	Preparation, 14:12–16
	Scene iiia	The Traitor, 14:17–21
	Scene iiib	The Last Supper, 14:18–25

8. This segmentation underlies the organization of the material in *New Gospel Parallels*, vol. 1, and, along the analysis to follow, is justification for that organization.

S3 Events in Gethsemane, 14:26–52
  Scene iv Jesus Predicts Peter's Denial, 14:26–31
  Scene v The Prayers, 14:32–42
  Scene vi The Arrest, 14:43–52

S4 Trial Before the Council and Denial of Peter, 14:53–72
  Introduction, 14:53–54
  Scene vii Trial Before the Council, 14:55–65
  Scene viii Denial of Peter, 14:66–72

S5 Trial Before Pilate, 15:1–15
  Scene ix Pilate Interrogates Jesus, 15:1–5
  Scene x Pilate Condemns Jesus, 15:6–15

S6 The Crucifixion, 15:16–41
  Scene xi The Mocking, 15:16–20
  Scene xii Simon of Cyrene, 15:21
  Scene xiii The Crucifixion, 15:22–32
  Scene xiv The Death, 15:33–41

S7 The Burial, 15:42–47

S8 The Empty Tomb, 16:1–8

The outline reveals that there are twenty segments and scenes grouped into eight sequences. Each sequence has at least two segments, except for the last two, which consist of a single segment each. Segmentation and grouping are unequivocal in most instances; it is difficult, however, to know precisely how to construe the final two segments treating the burial and empty tomb, for reasons to be examined below.

In the narrative analysis it will be our purpose to examine the clues to be found in the text itself, as it presently stands, without resort to textual, source, and form criticism. That restriction does not mean that questions of text, source, and form are not relevant; it only means that, methodologically, narrative analysis must first of all address the text as it stands, and only then, in restrospect, raise questions arising out of narrative lapses. To use Petersen's way of stating the matter, our first task is to ascertain whether the narrative text sets out "a self-coherently intelligible world that displays traces of its having been plotted." Petersen goes on to argue that the Gospel of Mark displays such "traces" and offers evidence of such a "world." Were narrative analysis to turn up extensive lapses in coherence and sequence, Petersen's thesis will have been falsified. Such lapses, as he indicates, will then become the focus of textual, source, form, and redaction criticism.[9]

The first step in narrative analysis is to justify in detail the segmentation proposed above. In so doing, we shall raise other questions attendant upon narrative analysis. In view of the length of the text, we have once again not

9. *Literary Criticism for New Testament Critics*, 49 and n. 2.

resolved it into numbered narrative statements; the analysis will make use instead of chapter and verse numbers.

13. The Introduction (Mark 14:1–11). The passion narrative opens "two days before the Passover and the feast of Unleavened Bread" (14:1). The events narrated in 14:1–11 take place in the interval between this time and "the first day of Unleavened Bread," which marks the beginning of the next sequence (14:12).[10]

During this period, Jesus is evidently located outside the city, in Bethany, at the house of Simon the leper (14:3), although we are told of matters that may well have transpired in the city, or partly in the city (14:1–2, 14:10–11). Indeed, Jesus remains outside the city through 14:12–16, the first segment of the following sequence. Jesus sends two disciples into the city in the next sequence (14:13), and later enters the city himself with the others (14:17).

14. The narrator initiates three themes that anticipate subsequent events.

The chief priests and scribes were looking for a way to arrest Jesus by stealth and put him to death. But they hesitated to do so during the feast because they feared a tumult of the people (14:1–2). The INTRO thus provides motivation for events unfolding as rapidly as they do. In addition, the theme of the conspiracy, which is to reappear subsequently, is introduced. This first brief segment is recounted in the iterative mode: "they kept seeking to arrest him."[11]

The anointing at Bethany anticipates the anointing of Jesus' body for burial (14:8). It thus forecasts the burial and relieves the narrator of any motivation to relate an anointing later.[12] Jesus and the anonymous woman are the principal participants in the enacted scene; those who protest, to themselves, and then reproach the woman, are not identified. Simon the leper, in whose house they were dining, is not otherwise known.

The scene now shifts to Judas and the chief priests (14:10–11); the latter had already figured in the first segment. In the diegetic mode, the narrator tells the reader that Judas made a deal, with which the authorities were pleased. The reader will learn more about this agreement subsequently (14:44). Meanwhile, another narrative imperfect indicates that Judas is constantly on the lookout for the right moment to effect the betrayal: "And he kept seeking an opportunity . . ." (14:11).[13]

15. The three themes have now been set:

10. Statements of this order are of course based on the text. In making such statements, the analysis is not making a historical claim; questions like the date of the last supper and its relation to the Passover meal are simply not being addressed.

11. Here the Greek imperfect combines the iterative with the conative.

12. An anointing appears to be in the offing in 16:1, however. That anointing is frustrated, of course, by the absence of the body of Jesus.

13. Again, the imperfect combines the iterative and the conative.

(1) The chief priest and scribes are looking for a way to seize and kill Jesus; this may be called the conspiracy;

(2) An anonymous woman anoints Jesus' body in advance for his burial: the anointing;

(3) Judas makes a deal with the chief priests to betray Jesus: the betrayal.

It will be necessary to inquire eventually whether these themes contribute significantly to the coherence and consistency of the passion narrative.

16. The Passover Meal. The time is the first day of Unleavened Bread, the day on which the Passover lamb was sacrificed (and eaten)(14:12). Jesus sends two disciples into the city to prepare a room where they may eat together (14:13–16). That evening (14:17), Jesus comes with the twelve. During the meal, Jesus indicates one of the group will betray him (14:18–21); this account continues the story begun in 14:10–11. In a second segment devoted to the supper, Jesus breaks the bread and blesses the cup, apparently in instituting the Lord's Supper (14:22–25).

The narrative of the Passover meal consists of three segments: 14:12–16, 17–21, and 22–25. The first introduces and prepares for the meal; the second and third are subscenes during the meal, each of which is introduced by a comparable phrase: "as they were [at table] eating. . . ." The first segment is a mixture of recounting and enactment; it is, however, a well-formed segment, with clear focalizing and defocalizing features. The second and third are made up almost entirely of direct discourse; they lack formal focalizers and defocalizers.

17. Many critics argue that the account of the supper given in 14:22–25 is not that of a Passover supper.[14] Vernon Robbins, in particular, cites two reasons for this judgment: bitter herbs are not mentioned and there is no liturgy related to the eating of the Passover lamb. He also suggests that a common bowl (14:20), as opposed to individual bowls, is not characteristic of the Passover meal, although he admits that the practice of individual bowls for this period cannot be established. His conclusion is as abrupt as some of the transitions he identifies in the narrative: if there ever was an account of the Passover meal, no traces of it have been preserved in Mark.[15] This is a case, of which there are numerous instances in the commentary literature, where historical judgments simply override the data in the narrative text. It may well be that the meal depicted in 14:22–25 is not a Passover meal in the light of the historical evidence we can garner. That is simply irrelevant to the questions the reader naturally puts to the narrator. The narrator understands

14. Cf., for example, the analysis of Martin Dibelius, *From Tradition to Gospel*, 121, 181f. Dibelius holds the view that 14:12–16 (preparation for the supper in the upper room) was not a part of the original passion story. On the other hand, the account of the last supper, since it was not identified as the Passover meal, was integral to the earliest version of the passion narrative.

15. *The Passion in Mark*, 25 and nn. 11 and 12.

the meal as a Passover meal, rightly or wrongly, historically or fictively, as the introduction unequivocally demonstrates. However, one form of the question Robbins raises, along with many other scholars, is whether the description of the meal in 14:22–25 goes together with the introduction in 14:12–16 and the account of the traitor in the next segment, 14:17–21. This question can be addressed on the grounds of narrative coherence, although it may not be answered definitively on those grounds.

The depiction, in 14:17–21, of the prediction of the betrayal continues the narrative theme announced in 14:10–11. This binds the second sequence to the first. The temporal marker in 14:12 connects up with the one in 14:1. And the two markers together indicate that the meal Jesus is about to eat with his disciples is the Passover meal. The narrator has charted a clear course. On the other hand, the double introduction to direct discourse in the two subscenes (14:18 and 22) may suggest that the second subscene, the account of the breaking of bread, is intrusive in the flow of the narrative. It is quite possible to read from 14:21 directly to 14:26 without feeling a break in the story. That is to say, the course of the narrative does not require that a meal be narrated, and there has been no thematic preparation for it in the introduction. If there was an earlier version of the passion narrative than the one before us in the Gospel of Mark, it is conceivable that it lacked the account of the meal proper. Against this view is the fact that the account of the meal that is given may well be a Christianized version of that meal Jesus was thought to have eaten with his disciples. In that case, it need not be considered intrusive, although it may not belong to the primary story line, which appears to concern conspiracy, betrayal, and Jesus' death.[16]

18. Events in Gethsemane, 14:26–52. The next sequence is comprised of three principal scenes; the middle scene has seven subscenes.

Jesus and the twelve end the Passover meal by singing a hymn. They then depart the upper room (14:15) and go to the Mount of Olives (14:26), a departure and an arrival ending the previous segment and opening the new one. Perhaps on the way to the Mount of Olives, or after they arrive, Jesus predicts that the twelve (carry-over from 14:17) will all desert him (14:27). He forecasts, further, that he will be raised up and will precede them to Galilee (14:28; cf. 16:7). Peter rejects the idea that he will desert Jesus. Jesus is very specific about Peter's threefold denial (14:29–31; cf. 14:66–72).

19. On the Mount of Olives, presumably, they enter a place called Gethsemane (14:32). Jesus first withdraws from the larger group with Peter, James, and John (14:33–34), forming the first subscene. Next, Jesus withdraws from the three and prays alone (14:35–36), forming the second subscene. Three

16. The reference to the blood that is poured out for many, in 14:24, may provide an adequate thematic link with death. In that case, there is a link, although perhaps an oblique one.

times he leaves and returns to the trio only to find them sleeping (14:37, 40, 41); each of these movements creates a minature subscene. The betrayer and authorities arrive at this moment and the final subscene draws to a close (14:41–42). The narrator has not made provision in the sequence for the return of Jesus and the three to the larger group prior to the close of the sequence (cf. 14:32, 33). However, his narrative sense probably dictated that he not drag the sequence out by the addition of a meaningless detail. Since the seven subscenes are so terse and their organization so tightly conceived, they are represented in the diagram as a series of overlapping ovals (figure 23).

20. In the next subscene (14:43–52), Judas arrives with a crowd as messengers of the authorities (*f:arr*, 14:43). The locale has not changed, but there is now a new participant set. The reader learns an additional detail about the agreement between Judas and the authorities made earlier (14:10–11): a kiss will identify Jesus (14:44). Judas arrives on the scene, then he goes up to Jesus (*f:arr*^{2}), addresses him as "Rabbi" (*f:attn*), then kisses him (*f:perc*, 14:45). Jesus is betrayed, defended, and rashly defended (14:45–58). Jesus then reminds them that they could have taken him at any moment during the period when he taught daily in the temple. This is evidently a reference to events that transpired earlier, during passion week (11:15–13:37), and hence a link to the preceding narrative. All his followers forsake him (*def:dep*).

As an extended conclusion, the story of the young man who followed them after the arrest is also related (14:51–52). He also flees, leaving his linen cloth behind (*def:dep*). The scene is predominantly enacted.

21. The trial before the Council and Peter's denial (14:53–72). The scene now shifts from the Mount of Olives and Gethsemane to the place where the chief priest, elders, and scribes are assembled before the high priest (14:53). Peter has been following along and is in the courtyard of the high priest (sequence: place of the high priest, courtyard of the high priest, from larger to narrower space), warming himself at the fire of the guards (14:54). It is the same day, but the hour is presumably late (cf. 14:17 and 15:1). These two notices serve as the INTRO to the two scenes that follow (14:55–65; 66–72). They are recounted.

22. The first scene is the trial before the Council (14:55–65). The participants are Jesus, anonymous witnesses, the high priest, the guards, and the council. Jesus is of course condemned. The scene is a mixture of recounting and enactment.

The second scene has three subscenes, again relatively terse and tightly conceived, 14:66–68, 69–70a, and 70b–72; they are also represented in the diagram (figure 23) as overlapping ovals. The three subscenes represent each of Peter's three denials. In the first two, a maid of the high priest accuses Peter; the locale shifts in the second subscene from the courtyard to the gateway (14:68). In the third, a bystander accuses Peter, "after a little while" (i.e., there is a temporal shift). The narrator thus uses a combination of spatial and temporal changes and modifications in the participant sets to discriminate the three brief scenes.

23. The trial before Pilate, 15:1–15. A temporal change marks the beginning of the trial before Pilate: it is now the next morning (15:1; cf. 14:17). Jesus has been bound and led away and delivered to Pilate: a locale change (15:1). Pilate is of course a new participant, so the P*set* has also been modified. Pilate apparently interrogates Jesus initially in private. The private interrogation constitutes the first scene in this sequence (15:1–5).

The scene then shifts to a public hearing, which involves Pilate and the crowd (15:8ff.); the chief priests are also indirectly involved (15:11). Owing to the fact that a new situation is about to develop, the narrator inserts two verses of introductory material (15:6–7): the reader learns of the tradition of releasing a prisoner of public choice at the feast, and the reader is informed of the incarceration of Barabbas for murder and insurrection. The crowd calls for the release of Barabbas and the crucifixion of Jesus. Pilate releases the former (a dismissal), and turns Jesus over to be crucified (another dismissal: 15:15).

The two trials and the scenes depicting Peter's denial form a continuous narrative (14:53–15:15), although the INTRO in 14:53–54 anticipates only the first sequence. The diagram has accordingly been designed to show two sequences combined into a hierarchy (indicated by the bracket beneath the line in figure 23) within the larger narrative.

24. The crucifixion, 15:16–41. The next sequence is comprised of four scenes devoted to the mocking and crucifixion. The first scene takes place inside the palace, in the praetorium (15:16), the second en route to the crucifixion (15:21), and the third and fourth at Golgotha (15:22). The time of the scene in the praetorium follows immediately upon that of the trial before Pilate, and the march to Golgotha comes immediately after. It is the third hour when they crucify Jesus (15:25), the sixth hour when darkness covers the land (15:33), and the ninth hour when he cries out and gives up the ghost (15:34). The trial before Pilate and the crucifixion thus all take place in the span of time from "morning" (15:1) to the ninth hour (mid-afternoon: 15:34). The sequence beginning with the eating of the Passover meal to the death of Jesus covers the time from the previous evening to the next afternoon. The narrative is temporally tight.

25. In the first scene, 15:16–20, the soldiers who lead Jesus away from Pilate call together the whole battalion (15:16). Jesus, of course, is the continuity participant. The scene is not formally focused: the soldiers function as a group, now this one, now that one responsible for the action. The narrator attributes the action to "they," even when he quotes them directly. The scene is thus recounted, with traces of enactment. It is defocalized by their departure, with Jesus in tow (15:20).

En route to the place of crucifixion, a certain Simon of Cyrene is compelled to carry the cross for Jesus (15:21): this mini-segment is set off by the introduction of a new participant and by a change in locale.

The soldiers play a role in the third scene as well, although they are not specifically mentioned ("they brought him, . . ." "they offered him, . . ." "they crucified him, . . ." are all actions of the soldiers: 15:22ff.). The narrator again brings some individuals forward out of the crowd and has them revile Jesus: passersby (15:29), chief priests (15:31f.), and those crucified with Jesus (15:32). The participant set in segment 3 thus varies from that in the first segment. The narrative mode is again recounting, with elements of enactment.

26. The soldiers as a group have disappeared from the fourth segment; all that is left of them is a single centurion (15:39), who is to serve as a narrative link with the next segment (15:44). Out of the crowd milling around the cross, the narrator brings forward three other participants. The first consists of bystanders (15:35), followed by one of the bystanders (a change in scope: 15:36), and finally the women (15:40–41); the women are a further link with succeeding narrative segments.

The fourth segment is focalized by means of the darkness that covers the land (*f:percprec*) and the cry of Jesus. The scene is defocalized with the death of Jesus (*def:dep*). It is thus mostly enacted, again mixed with elements in a recounting mode (e.g., the remark concerning the curtain of the temple, 15:38). The identification of the women at the close of the scene is the displacement of introductory material, a phenomenon that is not uncommon in narrative discourse.

27. The burial, 15:42–47. The burial takes place on the evening of the same day (15:42: *tchg*); it is still the day of preparation, the day before the sabbath (15:42: *ts*). A new participant, Joseph of Arimathea, is introduced (15:43); he goes to Pilate and asks for the body of Jesus. Pilate sends for and consults the centurion (15:44f.). When it is confirmed that Jesus is dead, Pilate grants the body to Joseph. Joseph then buries Jesus in a rock-cut tomb, and rolls a stone against the door (15:46: *def:termf*). The two Marys again observe (15:47; cf. 14:40–41).

The scene is recounted: the setting begins with the place of Pilate and then shifts to the site of the tomb, without notice. There are no formal focalizers.

28. The empty tomb, 16:1–8. The sabbath has now passed (16:1) and it is early on the first day of the week (16:2: *tchg* and *ts*). The setting is again the tomb of the preceding scene. The P*set* has changed from Joseph, Pilate, and the centurion to the women, who have been mentioned on two previous occasions (16:1; cf. 15:40f., 15:47), and the young man dressed in a white robe (16:5). The scene is focalized by the arrival of the women at the tomb (*arr*: 16:2) and by their visual contact with the open tomb (*f:perc*: 16:4). A second set of focalizers is found in 16:5: they enter the tomb (*f:arr*) and see the young man (*f:perc*). The scene is defocalized, of course, by their departure (*def:dep*: 16:8). There are also other defocalizers: their trembling and astonishment are a *def:termf* (16:8), and their fear prompts them to remain silent (*def:constop*, 16:8). The scene is predominantly enacted.

29. Narrative continuity and coherence. In §§10.13–28 the attempt has been made to justify the segmentation and sequencing of the passion narrative as evidenced in §10.12 and figure 23. It will now be our purpose to examine linkages that provide for narrative coherence over longer stretches of text and suggest the hierarchical arrangement of some sequences. References will be to numbered scenes and segments, as indicated in figure 23.

Gospel of Mark

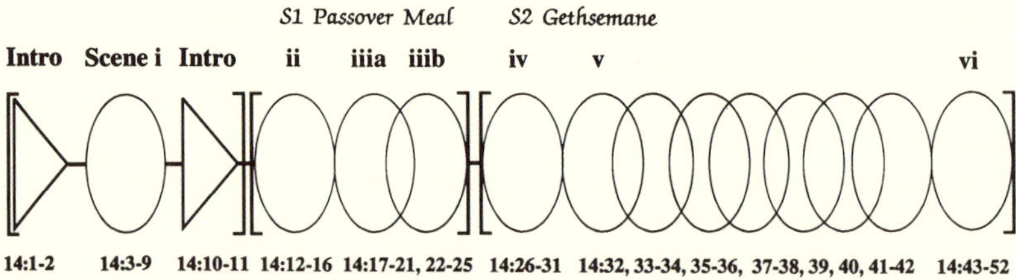

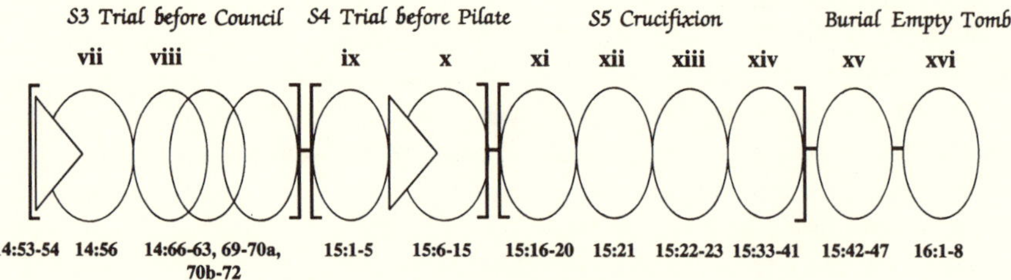

MARK 14:1–16:8

Formal Structure of Passion Narrative

Figure 23

In the INTRO, 14:1–11, the narrator introduces three themes: the conspiracy, the anointing, and the betrayal, as discussed in §10.14. The reach of each of these themes will give the narrative a certain amount of coherence. The conspiracy is announced in 14:1–2 as INTRO and then is connected, in 14:10–11, with the betrayal of Judas, as a instrument of its fulfillment. The narrator does not come back to the conspiracy until 14:43, when he recalls the P*set*, chief priests and scribes (in this instance, with elders), in connecton with the arrest. The same P*set* is announced in 14:53 (also with elders), in anticipation of the trial before the council. That trial itself belongs to the conspiracy (scene vii, 14:55–65). Further, at the trial before Pilate, the chief priests accuse Jesus (15:3–4), and at the public hearing following (scene x, 15: 6-15), they stir up the crowd against Jesus and for Barabbas (15:10–11). The chief priests and the scribes are present at the crucifixion as well: they mock him along with others (15:31). The condemnation and crucifixion are, of course, the culmination of the conspiracy. Even Joseph of Arimathea is identified as a member of the council (15:43), to which the chief priests, scribes, and elders also presumably belong. The conspiracy thus reaches from 14:1 through scene xiii and by means of Joseph even into scene xv. This theme provides a substantial amount of coherence to the narrative as a whole, except for the scene at the empty tomb.

30. The betrayal on the part of Judas is linked, as was suggested, to the conspiracy. However, the role of Judas is a distinctive theme in the narrative and may be plotted separately.

The Judas theme is introduced in 14:10–11 and renewed in the opening scene at the last supper, in scene iii, 14:17–21. It is taken up again in the final scene in the garden of Gethsemane, scene v, 14:41–42. The betrayal culminates in the arrest in scene vi, 14:43–52. Judas then exits the narrative.

The falling away or the denial of the other disciples (other members of the "twelve") is introduced in scene iv and linked to the betrayal and arrest in scene vi, especially 14:50–52. In any case, the falling away comes to be focused in Peter's denial in scene viii, 14:66–72, which was introduced by the note in 14:54. The falling away and denial culminate in Peter's weeping in 14:72. Peter drops from the narrative at this point, never to reappear, except in forecast (16:7).

The reach of the betrayal theme with Judas as the antagonist extends to 14:52; that of the denial theme extends to 14:72. These two themes combine to give the first half of the passion narrative additional continuity and coherence.

31. An undifferentiated crowd plays a significant role in the middle section of the passion narrative. A crowd appears with Judas to make the arrest in the garden in scene vi, 14:43–53. A crowd leads Jesus to the council in 14:53, at the opening of sequence 3. Persons out of the crowd are presumably those who offer false testimony at the trial (14:55–60) and then later mock him (14:65), although we cannot be sure of this identification. The crowd also plays a role in the second scene of the trial before Pilate (scene x, 15:6-15): they call for the release of a prisoner according to custom and then request Barabbas rather than Jesus (16:8ff.). The passersby in 15:29 and the bystanders in 15:35f. are also a part of the crowd. In sum, the crowd is a more or less constant feature of the narrative from the arrest in scene vi through the death of Jesus in scene xiv.

Pilate as a participant connects sequence 4, scenes ix and x, with the burial, scene xv. The centurion is present at the death of Jesus (15:39) and is queried in the segment treating the burial (15:44). These linkages afford some coherence to seven scenes (including those sandwiched between the death and the burial).

The women, specified as the two Marys and Salome, are present at the death of Jesus (scene xiv), observe the burial (scene xv), and are the principal participants in the scene at the empty tomb (xvi). Since the women overlap with Pilate and the centurion, the three together provide coherence for the last third of the passion narrative.

32. It was noted earlier that the anointing theme, announced in scene i, 14:3–9, anticipates the anointing of the body of Jesus after his death (cf. 16:8). This theme provides a linkage enclosing the outer limits of the passion story. Another connection is formed by the prediction of the resurrection and the transfer to Galilee in 14:28 and its repetition in the announcement of the young man at the tomb in 16:6, 7.

33. Repeating and completing analepses. There are still other kinds of narrative linkages. One kind, the repeating analepsis—so dubbed by Genette—is illustrated by the statement in 15:44:

> (1) And Pilate wondered if he were already dead; and summoning the centurion, he asked him whether he was already dead.

This statement recalls the preceding scene in which Jesus dies (14:37). However, Pilate was evidently not present on that occasion and had not received information about it. The narrator accordingly recalls the scene and allows Pilate to rectify his lack of knowledge—knowledge the reader already has. References of this type are simple "recalls."[17] Another example is found in 14:72 where Peter recalls Jesus' prediction that he will deny him three times before the cock crows twice (14:30). In a third example, we have what Genette calls a "completing analepsis": a reference to an event that was narrated earlier in the text but with an additional detail. In 14:10–11, the narrator informed the reader of Judas' bargain with the authorities to betray Jesus. Then, in 14:44, the narrator supplies an additional bit of information that actually belongs to the earlier segment: "Now the betrayer had given them a sign, saying, 'The one I shall kiss is the man; seize him and lead him away safely.'" An analepsis of this order provides more than mere thematic continuity; it supplies a strong, direct narrative link.

34. Other analepses. There are other kinds of analepses, which are not as significant for coherence within the passion narrative. References to earlier

17. See chap §§8.3–7. on analepses in general.

events in the first narrative and within its chronological limits, are called "homodiegetic analepses."[18] The type discussed in §33 are homodiegetic analepses; however, the three examples given were limited to the chronological limits of the passion narrative itself. If we go beyond those limits, but stay with the Gospel of Mark, there are additional examples. In 14:49, Jesus asks them why they did not arrest him while he was teaching daily in the temple. That is a reference to his activities during the passion week, as indicated above, §10.20. In a similar vein, the maid remarks to Peter, in 14:67, that he had been with "the Nazarene, Jesus." That evidently is a reference to the association of the two men earlier in the narrative. Analepses of this order provide continuity and coherence for the larger text.

There are also interesting "heterodiegetic analepses."[19] Heterodiegetic means that the item in question belongs to another narrative line, to another story. In 15:43, Joseph of Arimathea is described as "a respected member of the council, who was also himself looking for the kingdom of God." The story of Joseph's quest for the kingdom is another story; Mark does not weave it into his account of Jesus, except in this oblique way. The reference to Barabbas in 15:6–7 is a kindred example: Barabbas had committed murder in connection with an insurrection; the reader learns no more about him other than that fact. His story is also another story. Heterodiegetic analepses provide a narrative with social breadth (other things were going on at the same time) and temporal depth (other interesting things transpired long before).

35. The anointing at Bethany. The question has often been raised whether the story of the anointing at Bethany belonged originally to the passion narrative, or whether Mark added it. Perhaps the question could be restated as: does the account of the anointing contribute to or detract from narrative continuity and coherence? In choosing to address this question, we are also asking whether narratology has anything to contribute to source and redaction criticism.

Dibelius holds that the story does not belong to the passion narrative because (1) it is an isolated narrative, and (2) it interrupts the flow of the introduction (14:1–2, 10–11).[20] Are there narrative reasons to support that judgment?

The account of the anointing is an enacted scene, sandwiched between two pieces of INTRO that are recounted. It is rare to find an enacted scene as part of an INTRO, and even rarer to find one enclosed in two pieces of recounting to which it is tenuously related at best. Although we treated the segment as an integral part of the narrative earlier (§§10.13–14), its thematic connection with the rest of the narrative is thin, in contrast to 14:1–2 and 10–11, where

18. Genette, *Narrative Discourse*, 51.
19. Genette, *Narrative Discourse*, 50.
20. *From Tradition to Gospel*, 178, 181.

the thematic connections are robust. It does anticipate that Jesus will be buried without being anointed (14:8); nevertheless, the enacted scene, 16:1–8 anticipates an anointing—the women come prepared with spices for that purpose—although in the end that process is frustrated for want of a corpse. Has the narrator taken that into account in placing 14:3–9 where he has? In other words, how subtle was Mark? The answer to that question will depend on how the Markan narrative as a whole is read. It is also unusual for an enacted scene to lack temporal and spatial connections with the surrounding narrative terrain. There are other examples of this in Mark, the story of the cleansing of the leper, for example (1:40–45). The two taken together suggest that the judgment of Dibelius has strong narrative support: the anointing, like the cleansing of the leper, is an independent narrative segment, without strong narrative ties to its present context. In spite of these qualifications, it is the responsibility of narrative analysis, in the first instance, to read the segment as a part of the sequence to which it belongs in the present text. Only in that connection is it legitimate to raise questions of coherence and continuity. However, a fully developed narrative grammar may well provide us with more precise tools for addressing problems of textual, source, and tradition criticism.

—·11·—

Hänsel and Gretel

INTRODUCTION

Near a large forest
lived a poor woodcutter
with his wife
and two children.
The boy's name was Hänsel
and the girl's Gretel.
The woodcutter had little to eat,
and once when a great famine swept the country,
he was no longer able to earn even their daily bread.

ACT I

scene ia (A+B/in bed/evening)

One evening
when he was lying in his bed
tossing about
and worrying,
he sighed
and said to his wife,
"What's to become of us?
How can we feed our poor children
when there's nothing left for ourselves?"
"Do you know what, husband,"
answered the wife,
"the first thing tomorrow morning
we'll take the children out into the densest part of the forest.
There we'll kindle them a fire
and give each a little piece of bread;
then we'll go about our work
and leave them there alone;
they won't find the way back home,
and we'll be rid of them."
"No, wife,"
said the man,
"that I won't do.
How could I have the heart to leave my children alone in the forest;
the wild animals would soon come
and tear them to pieces."
"O you fool,"
she said,
"then all four of us will starve to death;
you might as well start planing the boards for our coffins,"
and she gave him no peace
until he agreed.
"But all the same I'm sorry for the poor children,"
said the man.

scene ib1 (C^1+C^2/in bed/evening)
The two children hadn't been able to get to sleep, either,
because they were hungry
and heard what their stepmother said to their father.
Gretel wept bitter tears,
and said to Hänsel,
"Now it's all up with us."
"Be quiet, Gretel,"
said Hänsel,
"Don't worry,
I'll get us out of this, of course."

scene ib2 (C^1outside/night)
And when his mother and father had fallen asleep,
he got up,
put on his jacket,
opened the lower half of the door,
and crept out of the house.
The moon was shining bright,
and the white pebbles
which were in front of the house
gleamed like so many new silver coins.
Hänsel stooped down
and put as many of them
as he could
in his jacket pocket.

scene ib3 (C^1+C^2/in bed/night)
Then he went back
and said to Gretel,
"Don't worry, sister dear,
and just go to sleep;
God won't forsake us."
Then he went to bed again.

scene ii (B+C/at home/next morning)
When day dawned, even before sunrise
the mother came
and woke the children up,
saying,
"Get up,
you lazybones,
we're going into the forest to fetch wood."
Then she gave each a piece of bread,
saying,
"Here's something for your dinner,
but don't eat it beforehand;
you're not getting anything else."
Gretel put the bread in her apron

because Hänsel had the stones in his pocket.
Then they all set out together for the forest.

scene iii (C^1+A+B/way to forest/later)
When they'd been walking a little while,
Hänsel stopped
and looked back toward the house
and did so again and again.
The father said,
"Hänsel,
what are you looking at there,
and why are you lagging behind?
Watch out
or you'll be forgetting your legs."
"Oh Father,"
said Hänsel,
"I'm looking at my white kitten;
it's sitting on top of the roof
and wants to say good-bye to me."
The woman said,
"You fool,
that's not your kitten;
it's the morning sun shining on the chimmey."
But Hänsel hadn't been looking at the cat
but was ever tossing one of the white pebbles from his pocket onto the path.

scene iva (A+B+C/middle of forest/later)
When they reached the middle of the forest,
the father said,
"Now gather some wood,
children.
I'll make a fire for you
so you won't get cold."
Hänsel and Gretel gathered brush, quite a pile of it.
The brush was kindled,
and when the fire was blazing,
the wife said,
"Now lie down by the fire,
children,
and take a rest.
We're going into the forest to cut wood;
when we're finished,
we'll come back and fetch you."

scene ivb (C/middle of forest/noon)
Hänsel and Gretel sat by the fire
and when it was noon
they ate their piece of bread.

And because they heard the blows of the ax,
they thought their father was near by.
But it wasn't the ax;
it was a branch he'd tied to a dead tree,
which the wind was banging back and forth.
When they'd been sitting for a long time,
their eyes closed from weariness,
and they fell fast asleep.

scene ivc (C^2+C^1/middle of forest/night)
When they finally woke up,
it was already pitch-dark.
Gretel began to weep
and said,
"How shall we get out of the forest now?"
But Hänsel consoled her,
saying,
"Just wait a bit till the moon's up;
then we'll easily find our way."

scene v (C^1+C^2/way out/night)
When the full moon had risen,
Hänsel took his sister by the hand
and followed the pebbles,
which glittered like new silver coins
and showed them the way.
They kept walking all night

scene vi (C+B+A/home/daybreak)
and at daybreak
were back at their father's house.
They knocked at the door,
and when the wife opened it
and saw Hänsel and Gretel,
she said,
"You naughty children,
why did you sleep so long in the forest?
We thought you weren't coming back at all."
But the father was glad,
for he was sorry he'd left them.

ACT II
scene viia (C+A+B/in bed/at night)
Not long after that,
there was again a famine everywhere,
and one night
the children heard their mother say in bed to their father,
"Everything's been eaten up again;
we've only got a half a loaf of bread left

and then we'll be at the end of our rope.
The children must be sent away.
Let's take them deeper into the forest to make sure they won't find the way out again.
There's no other salvation for us."
With heavy heart the man thought,
"It'd be better to share our last morsel with your children,"
but the woman would listen to nothing he said,
scolded him,
and since he'd given in the first time,
he had to the second, also.

scene viib (C^1+C^2/in bed/later at night)
The children, however, were still awake
and heard the conversation.
When the mother and father were asleep,
Hänsel again got up
and was going out to pick up pebbles as before,
but the wife had locked the door,
and Hänsel couldn't get out.
Nevertheless, he consoled his sister,
and said,
"Don't weep,
Gretel,
and just go to sleep;
the dear Lord will surely help us."

scene viii (B+C/at home/next morning)
Early in the morning
the wife came
and got the children out of bed.
They received their piece of bread,
but it was even smaller than last time.

scene ix (C^1+A+B/way to forest/later)
On their way to the forest
Hänsel crumbled it up in his pocket
and, stopping often,
scattered the crumbs on the ground.
"Hänsel,
why are you stopping
and looking around?"
said his father;
"go ahead."
"I'm looking at my pigeon;
it's sitting on the roof
and wants to say good-bye to me,"
answered Hänsel.

"You fool,"
said the woman,
"that's not your pigeon;
it's the morning sun shining on the chimney."
Nevertheless, Hänsel gradually scattered all the bread crumbs along the path.

scene xa (A+C/middle of forest/later)
The woman led the children still deeper into the forest
where they'd never been in all their lives.
Then a big fire was again made,
and the mother said,
"Just sit there,
children,
and if you feel tired,
you can take a little nap.
We're going into the forest to cut wood
and this evening when we're finished,
we'll come
and fetch you."

scene xb (C^1+C^2/middle of forest/later)
When it was noon,
Gretel shared her bread with Hänsel,
who'd scattered his piece along the way.
Then they fell asleep,
and the evening passed,
and no one came to get the poor children.

scene xc (C^1+C^2/middle of forest/night)
They didn't wake up till it was pitch-dark,
and Hänsel consoled his sister,
saying,
"Just wait,
Gretel,
till the moon's up;
then we'll see the bread crumbs I scattered.
They'll show us the way home."

scene xi (C^1+C^2/wandering/night+)
When the moon rose,
they set out
but didn't find any bread crumbs,
for the thousands of birds that fly about in forest and field had pecked them all up.
Hänsel said to Gretel,
"We'll surely find the way,"
but they didn't find it.

They walked all night
and still another day from morning till evening,
but didn't get out of the forest.
And they were very hungry,
for they had nothing but a few berries that were on the ground,
and because they were so tired that their legs wouldn't carry them any farther,
they lay down under a tree
and fell asleep.

ACT III

INTRODUCTION

By now it was already the third morning since they'd left their father's house.
They began walking again
but kept getting deeper and deeper into the forest,
and unless help came soon,
they were doomed to die of exhaustion.

scene xii (C+bird/forest/noon)

When it was noon,
they saw a pretty snow-white bird perched on a branch;
it sang so beautifully that they stopped
and listened to it.
And when it had finished,
it flapped its wings
and flew ahead of them;
they followed it
until they came to a cottage.

scene xiiia (C^1+C^2+D/cottage/later)

There it lighted on the roof,
and when they got quite near,
they saw that the cottage was made of bread with a cake roof and that the windows were made of sugar candy.
"Let's make for it,"
said Hänsel,
"and have a fine meal.
I'll eat a piece of the roof,
and, Gretel,
you may eat some of the window;
that's sweet."
Hänsel reached up and broke off a little piece of the roof for himself to see how it tasted,
and Gretel took her place at the windowpanes
and nibbled at them.
Then a shrill voice called out from the living room,
"Nibble, nibble, nibble!

Who's nibbling at my cottage?"
The children answered,
"The wind, the wind,
The Heavenly Child,"
and went on eating
without being put off.
Hänsel, who quite liked the taste of the roof,
pulled down a large piece,
while Gretel took out a whole round windowpane,
sat down,
and ate it with relish.

scene xiiib (C+D/cottage/later)
Then suddenly the door opened,
and a very old woman leaning on a crutch came slinking out.
Hänsel and Gretel were so frightened
that they dropped what they had in their hands.
But the old woman shook her head
and said,
"Well, well,
you dear children,
who brought you here?
Come right in
and stay with me;
no harm will befall you."
She took them both by the hand
and led them into her cottage.
They were served a good meal with milk, pancakes and sugar, apples and nuts.
Then she made up two pretty beds with white sheets,
and Hänsel and Gretel lay down in them
and thought they were in Heaven.

INTRODUCTION *(continued)*
The old woman was, however, only pretending to be kind;
as a matter of fact, she was a wicked witch
who lay in wait for children
and who'd built the cottage of bread just to lure them to her.
Once she got a child in her power,
she'd kill it,
cook it,
and eat it,
and that would be a red-letter day for her.
Witches have red eyes
and can't see far,
but they've a keen sense of smell, just like animals,
and scent the approach of human beings.

scene xiiic (C+D/near the cottage/same as 13a)
As Hänsel and Gretel were getting near her,
she laughed wickedly
and mockingly said,
"I've got them!
they shan't get away from me again!"

scene xiv (D+C^1+C^2/in cottage/next morning)
Early in the morning
before the children were awake,
she was already up
and seeing them both sleeping so sweetly with their full rosy cheeks,
muttered to herself,
"That'll be a fine snack."
Then with her withered hand she seized Hänsel
and carried him to a little pen
and shut him up behind a grilled door.
No matter how hard he cried,
it did him no good.
Then she went to Gretel,
shook her till she woke up,
and said,
"Get up,
you lazybones,
fetch some water
and cook something good for your brother;
he's outside in the pen
and must be fattened up.
Once he's fat,
I'll eat him."
Gretel began to weep bitterly,
but it was no use:
she had to do what the wicked
witch ordered her.

scene xv (D+C^1+C^2/at cottage/generalized)
Now the best food was cooked for poor Hänsel,
but Gretel got nothing but crab shells.
Every morning the old woman would slink out to the pen
and cry,
"Hänsel!
stick out your fingers
so I can feel whether you'll be fat soon."
But Hänsel stuck out a little bone,
and the old woman,
whose eyesight was poor,
couldn't see it
and thought it was one of Hänsel's fingers
and was surprised he didn't get fat.

scene xvi (D+C^2/at cottage/next morning)
When four weeks had passed
and Hänsel still stayed thin,
she got impatient
and wouldn't wait any longer.
"Come on,
Gretel!"
she called out to the girl,
"hurry up!
bring some water!
whether Hänsel's fat or lean,
I'm going to kill him tomorrow
and cook him."
Oh, how the poor little sister cried out
when she had to carry the water,
and how the tears rolled down her cheeks!
"Dear Lord,
please help us,"
she cried;
"if only the wild animals in the forest had devoured us,
then at least we should have died together."
"Just stop your whining,"
said the old woman,
"it won't do you any good at all."

scene xvii (D+C^2/at the cottage/next morning)
Early in the morning
Gretel had to go out
and hang up the kettle full of water
and kindle the fire.
"First let's do some baking,"
said the old woman,
"I've already heated up the oven
and kneaded the dough."
She pushed poor Gretel out to the oven,
from which big flames already were leaping.
"Crawl in!"
said the witch,
"and see whether it's properly hot,
so we can put the bread in."
Once Gretel was in,
she intended to shut the oven
and roast Gretel in it
and then she was going to eat her up, too.
But Gretel saw what she was up to
and said,
"I don't know how to.
How do I get in?"

"Stupid goose,"
said the old woman,
"the opening's big enough.
Why, I could get in myself,"
and she waddled up
and stuck her head in the oven.
Then Gretel gave her a shove
so that she slid way in,
shut the iron door,
and shot the bolt.
My!
then she began to howl—something horrible!
But Gretel ran away,
and the wicked witch burned to death miserably.

scene xviii (C^2+C^1/at the cottage/later)
Then Gretel went straight to Hänsel,
opened his pen,
and called,
"Hänsel,
we're saved!
The old witch is dead!"
Then Hänsel jumped out like a bird from its cage
when the door's opened.
How happy they were!
They fell on each other's necks,
skipped about,
and kissed one another,
and because they didn't need to be afraid any more,
they went into the witch's house,
where there were chests of pearls and jewels in every nook and corner.
"These are even better than pebbles,"
said Hänsel,
filling his pockets as full as he could,
while Gretel said,
"I want to bring something home, too,"
and filled her apron.
"Now let's be off,"
said Hänsel,
"and get out of this enchanted forest."

scene xixa (C^1+C^2+white duck/water/hours later)
But when they'd been walking for a couple of hours,
they reached a big body of water.
"We can't get across,"
said Hänsel;
"I don't see any plank or bridge."
"And there isn't any boat here,

answered Gretel,
"but there's a white duck.
I'll ask it,
it'll help us across."
Then she called out,
"Duck, duck!
Here's Hänsel and Gretel.
There's no plank or bridge;
Take us on your white back."
As a matter of fact, the duck did come up,
and Hänsel got on it
and told his sister to sit down beside him.
"No,"
answered Gretel,
"it'll be too heavy for the duck;
it had better carry us over one at a time."
The good creature did so,
and when both were safely across

scene xixb (C+A/near and at home/later)
and had gone a short distance,
the forest kept getting more and more familiar to them,
and finally they spied their father's house from afar.
Then they began to run
and rushed into the living room
and fell on their father's neck.
The man hadn't had a single happy hour
since he'd left his children alone in the forest.
The wife, however, had died.
Gretel shook out her apron,
and the pearls and jewels bounced about in the room,
and Hänsel threw one handful after the other from his pocket.
Then all their troubles were at an end,
and they lived most happily together.

EPILOGUE

My tale's done.
There runs a mouse;
whoever catches it may make a great big cap out of its fur.

• 11 •

THE STRUCTURE OF "HÄNSEL AND GRETEL"

1. The narrative stretches submitted to analysis have grown steadily longer. As a crowning exercise, it is appropriate to consider a narrative sufficiently long to encompass an entire story, and yet not a story of the short, short variety. As a folktale of incomparable power and beauty, "Hänsel and Gretel" commends itself for this purpose. "Hänsel and Gretel" affords a strong, clear structure, about the general lineaments of which there can be little debate. At the same time, it offers ample opportunity to observe an abundance of narrative markers and to explore curious and interesting wrinkles in the telling.

2. "Hänsel and Gretel" is organized in three major sequences, which we shall call "acts" on the analogy of drama. The first two acts are parallel; the second does not end, of course, with the return of the children to their home, as does the first, but rather with their being lost in the woods. In the third act they stumble upon the gingerbread house of the old witch, learn how to cope successfully with her, escape, and finally make their way safely home. The return that is anticipated but aborted in the second act is thus consummated in the third act. By comparison with the first two long sequences, the third act is unique.

ACT I

3. Segments and sequences in Act I. Act I is made up of twelve segments grouped in six scenes and an INTRO. In discussing these segments and their hierarchical arrangement, constant reference will be made to the text by numbered line and to the graphic representation in figure 24.

The participants in Act I are the father (A), the mother (B), and the two children (C). The children sometimes function as a single participant, hence the common designation (C). When they act separately, they are designated as (C^1), Hänsel, and (C^2), Gretel.

The three participants of Acts I and II are presented in the INTRO (lines 1–9), which functions to introduce both Acts. Act III has its own INTRO (254–58; 313–25). The scene is set near a large forest (the father is a woodcutter); the time is during a great famine. The family is destitute.

4. It will be illuminating, in considering longer narrative stretches as wholes, to examine locale and temporal markers as they bear on hierarchy and coherence, and to view the modification of P*sets* in the same light.

In Act I, scenes i and ii are set at the home of the woodcutter and his family.

At the conclusion of scene ii, the family sets out for the forest: scenes iii–v take place on the way to the forest, while they are there, and on the way back. With scene vi the family is again at home.

Hänsel & Gretel

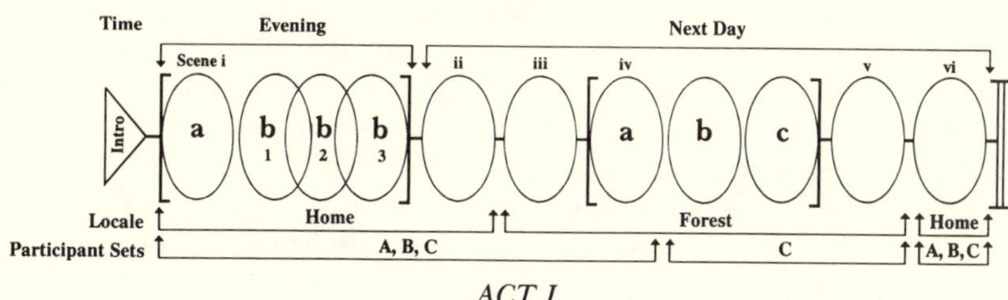

ACT I

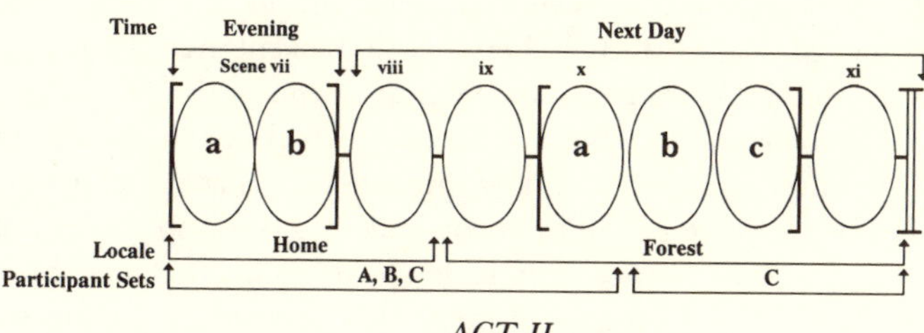

ACT II

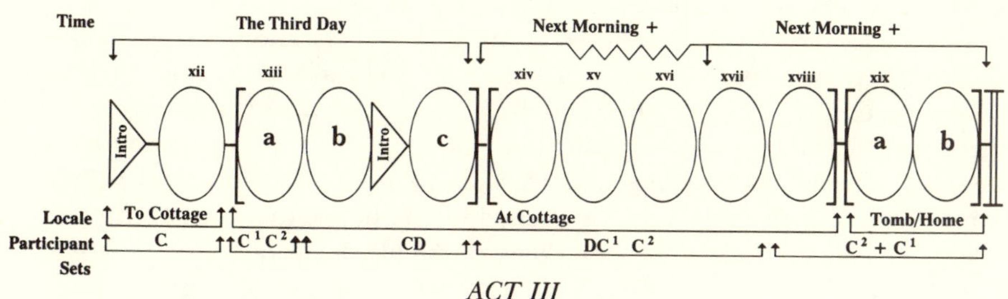

ACT III

Narrative Analysis

Figure 24

Temporal markers indicate that the several parts of scene i take place during that first evening and night (10; cf. 53, 71). Scene ii opens the next morning (72). There is thus a nocturnal pause between scenes i and ii. Nevertheless, the two scenes are both set in the same locale, home. We have here an example of the simplest marks of segmentation being employed simultaneously as linking devices: the locale, home, links scenes i and ii, while temporal diversity separates them.

Scenes iii through v occur, as indicated, on the way to the forest (iii), during the stay in the forest (iv), and on the way home (v). In scene vi, Hänsel and Gretel are again back home. The temporal continuum begins, however, with scene ii, the next morning, and extends through that night and to daybreak the next morning (vi). The continous time of scenes ii through vi links those scenes together, even though they are divided spatially: scenes i and vi = home; scenes ii–v =forest. These relationships are indicated in figure 24.

When we now add the shifts in P*sets* to the locale and temporal markers, we discover further combinations. The P*set* A, B, C dominates through scene iva, when the set is reduced to C^1 and C^2. But when the children return home, the full set is restored (scene vi). The first modification in the P*set* thus does not coincide with either the first temporal break or the first shift in local. This, again, provides a certain amount of cohesiveness for the narrative. The second spatial shift and the return to the full P*set* do coincide at the end of scene v, but the temporal line runs without break. Indeed, the end of scene v and the beginning of vi are tightly linked in a single sentence (149f.).

5. *Scene i* is divided into two parts. In the first, scene ia, the woodcutter and his wife have a conversation in bed; in iib, the two children are the participants. The scenes are very closely linked, however, in that the children, who are in their own bed, overhear their parents talk and respond accordingly. In scene ia, the woodcutter is in position, so to speak, in his bed, and his wife is beside him (both are *f:pos*), so that an arrival is unnecessary. The scene is focalized by the sigh of the woodcutter (14: *f:attn*, under these circumstances, an attention-getter). It is defocalized by an agreement (40), which is a *termf*, and by the father's proleptic sorrow for his children (41), another *termf*. Scene ib has three subparts, which are labelled b1, b2, and b3 in the graphic representation. The two children are also in position in their bed (43ff.); from there they hear their parents talking (45: *f:perc*), to which Gretel responds by weeping bitter tears (46: *f:attn*). Hänsel replies with reassurances (49ff.). This constitutes scene ib1. Scene ib2 is opened by the notice that the parents fall asleep (53), which is a temporal marker (*tc*), but also a curious kind of departure which helps defocalize the previous segment (*dep*). At this signal Hänsel gets out of bed and goes outdoors (54–57); this constitutes a *lchg* and an *arr*. The moon shining on the pebbles is the visual focalizer (58–61: *f:percprec*). Hänsel fills his jacket pocket with the pebbles. Scene ib3' is opened with Hänsel's return to his room (66: *lchg, f:arr*), which also functions to close the previous scene (*dep*). The third subscene is closed when they fall asleep—a departure (a *def:dis* appears in 69: Hänsel tells Gretel to go to sleep; that they both do so is implied but not stated in 71).

Scenes ia and ib1 overlap temporally: the children hear, in ib1, the parents talk in ia. This has the effect of connecting the two scenes closely. In addition, scenes ib1 and ib3 serve as an envelope structure to enclose scene ib2. In the second Hänsel reminds Gretel essentially of what he had already told her in the earlier scene. For this reason, the three sub-subscenes are represented as overlapping ovals in figure 24.

6. Scenes ii–vi. Scene ii is focalized by the mother's arrival at the children's bed (73), the next morning (*tc*), even before dawn (72: *ts*). It is defocalized when the family sets out for the forest (86: *def:dep*).

Scene iii is marked by the iterative (Hänsel stops repeatedly and looks back toward the house; he drops a white pebble on each such occasion: 89f., 107) and by pseudo-iterative quoted speech (91–105).[1]

Scene iv is segmented into three parts. The place is the middle of the forest (108), sometime later in the same day. In iva, the family builds a fire and the children are admonished to lie down and rest. The parents depart to cut wood. It is still morning. At noon—scene ivb (124–34)—the children eat their piece of bread, think they hear their parents chopping wood, and then fall asleep from weariness (*def:dep*). When they wake up, it is dark (scene ivc: 135–43). Hänsel once again consoles Gretel and admonishes her to wait.

Scene iv consists of the three episodes—related to three periods during the day, morning, noon, and night—devoted to their sojourn in the middle of the forest. Scene ii represents the outward journey to that locale, scene v the return home. The movement embodied in these three scenes corresponds to the locale, designated "forest" in figure 24. "Hänsel and Gretel" works as a fairy tale, in part, because this movement arouses the expectation, as Act II unfolds, that the same trajectory will be repeated. Of course, it is not, or not in the same fashion. Act III takes up at the end of Act II with the children lost in the forest—their initial effort to return is frustrated—and provides them with the occasions to mature, so that, in the end, they are able to make it back home. The repetition of Act I in Act II is first frustrated and then consummated, and that tension-laden circuit gives palpable narrative body to the process of growing up evidenced by the content of the narrative. Narrative duration and frustration, in other words, contribute materially to the theme of the story.

ACT II

7. The scenes and subscenes of Act II correspond to those of Act I in large part. The correlations with notes on the differences will serve as narrative commentary on Act II.

Scene viia corresponds to ia, and viib to ib, except that viib (177–89) is not divided into the three parts of its correlary. This modification in structure suggests that the frustration of movement has begun: Hänsel cannot get outside at night in order to collect white pebbles. This frustration telegraphs

1. The pseudo-iterative is discussed in §6.44.

his later frustration in being unable to find his way back home; that frustration is reflected in scene construction.

Scene viii is parallel to ii, except that viii (190–94) is shortened and entirely in the recounting mode. Scene ix (195–212), like its counterpart, scene iii, is again iterative, with pseudo-iterative speech. The tripartite structure of scene iv is retained in scene x (213–38), with reference to the three periods of the day. Scene xi (239–53) corresponds to scene v, and there is, of course, no corollary in Act II to scene vi. Because scene xi brings Act II to a close, it is elaborately defocalized. First of all, the activity of the children is extended:

(246) They walked all night *def:ae*

and so is the time during which it takes place:

(247) and still another day from morning till evening *def:te*

Finally, they become so tired,

(252) they lay down under a tree
(253) and fell asleep. *def:termf/dep*

which is a *termf* or another form of *dep*. The elaboration of the defocalizing process suggests that the narrative has arrived at a major pause.

8. It is again worth observing the use of temporal and locale markers, and the modification of P*sets*, to achieve both segmentation and coherence.[2]

Scene vii with its two subscenes takes place at night, while the parents and children are in bed. Scenes viii through xi are set the next day, with the exception of the strong defocalizers at the end of xi, which extend the activity of the children an additional day. There is thus a temporal break in the form of a nocturnal pause between vii and viii (see figure 24 for a graphic representation of these features). The setting of scenes vii and viii is the home. The first change in locale does not come until the end of viii, when the family departs for the forest. Locale thus binds viii to vii, while a temporal break separates them. Again, the structure of the narrative both segregates the units and causes them to cohere. The shift in P*set* does not come until the end of xa: in the first part of the Act, (A), (B), and (C) are all present; in the second part the children are alone. The shift in P*set* does not coincide with either a major local or temporal break.

ACT III

9. The Introduction and scene xii. Acts III opens with a brief INTRO designed to link up with Act II and set the story in motion again after the nocturnal pause that comes between the two. The time is the third morning (254); all

2. Cf. §11.4 for the discussion of these features in connection with Act I.

important things happen on the third day. The children have started walking again and are getting deeper and deeper into the forest (255f.), as only an omniscient narrator will know. They are on the point of exhaustion (258). The INTRO is of course recounted.

Scene xii opens at noon (259: *tc*); they are deep in the forest (inferred from the INTRO). A snow-white bird perched on a branch attracts their attention, both visually (260: *f:perc*) and aurally (261f.: *f:percprec*). The bird leads them to the cottage (263–67). This constitutes a departure (*def:dep*) and a fresh arrival, to open the next scene.

10. *Scene xiii.* The next scene is made up of three subscenes and a block of recounted and descriptive material. This cluster offers some interesting features. These features are graphically represented in figure 24, as are the other features of this act.

In scene xiiia, Hänsel and Gretel act individually ($C^1 + C^2$), and the witch (D) appears only in a preliminary, unidentified form (her voice appears from offstage, so to speak). The door pops open with xiiib, however, and she greets the children as a friendly old woman (295f.). In this scene, Hänsel and Gretel act as one, owing to their fear (297). Since the witch was not introduced at the beginning of Acts III, and since she appears in scene xiiib to be something other than what she is, the narrator inserts another piece of INTRO, as it were, and presents the wicked witch (313–25). Then in scene xiiic, the narrator reverts to the time of xiiia and narrates the same scene from her standpoint; earlier the narrator had told the story exclusively from the perspective of the children. In the earlier version, they had acted individually, now (xiiic) they are represented as a single participant. The third subscene is what Genette calls a *completing analepsis*: the narrator returns to an earlier point in the story and fills in something that was omitted. The analepsis involving the witch is, however, a special kind of completing analepsis; it does not actually fill in a gap, or an ellipsis, in the narrative, but supplements the information provided at the earlier stage by adding what was sidestepped or deliberately avoided, for narrative reasons. This kind of "lateral ellipsis" or sidestepping Genette calls a "paralepsis."[3] This is not unlike the paralepsis in John 5:9: the reader learns for the first time that the day on which the healing was performed was the sabbath. That bit of new information explains the fuss that follows.[4]

In effect, the insertion of the new block of INTRO and the narrating of scene xiiic, which is actually contemporaneous with xiiia, prompts the reader to stop and reconsider the import of the story as narrated up to the end of xiiib: everything related at the beginning—the friendly bird, the cake and candy house—appears not friendly and sweet, but ominous. The narrative takes on a fresh seriousness. Indeed, if the Freudian reading of this story is not wide of

3. *Narrative Discourse,* 51–53. In §§8.3–7 we discussed analepsis in more general terms.
4. This point is elaborated in §7.15, although it is not there referred to as a paralepsis.

the mark, the threat posed by the stepmother at the outset of the story is the same threat now posed by the old witch. That migration of roles is supported by the narrative fact that when the children eventually return home, the stepmother is dead; the children had, of course, killed the ogre of the cake house.

11. Scenes xiv–xviii. Scenes xiv–xviii are best considered together. These five segments take place after the true colors of the witch have been revealed and before the children depart for home. Scene xiv is enacted. Segment xv is recounted in the iterative mode (357–60, 364–69), with pseudo-iterative quoted speech (361–63). Scenes xvi–xviii are again enacted.

Scene xiv is set in and at the cottage (events take place both inside and outside, e.g., 349), the time is early the next morning after the children arrive (331). The participants are the witch (D) and the two children acting independently (C^1, C^2). The witch "sees" the children sleeping sweetly (334: *f:perc*) and congratulates herself. She then deals with each child separately. As a consequence, there are separate scenes within the scene. Lines 340f. defocalize the first by means of *def:ae* (Hänsel cries repeatedly, but it does him no good), while 355f. defocalize the second (Gretel must carry out the various orders given her by the witch), also *def:ae*.

12. Scene xv is recounted in the iterative mode and is designed to cover the four-week interval indicated by 370. Lines 357f. depict what each child was given to eat during the period, while 359ff. describe the morning ritual of the witch. The quoted speech is once again pseudo-iterative: every morning she said something like this, of which the words quoted are one realization.[5] Since the segment is recounted in the iterative mode, it is neither focalized nor defocalized. However, it is clearly set off by the preceding and following scenes.

13. In scenes xvi and xvii, Gretel and the witch appear without Hänsel; there is thus a shift in the P*set*. The time of xvi is four weeks later; xvii opens early the next morning (393). At the end of xvi, Gretel is told to stop her whining (390ff.: *constop*). Scene xvii is defocalized by the death of the witch (428: *termf* and *dep*).

The P*set* shifts back to (C^1) and (C^2) in scene xviii; the witch is of course dead. It is later the same day and the locale is still in and around the cottage. The scene opens with the arrival of Gretel at Hänsel's cage (429ff.: *f:arr*), closes with Hänsel's "dismissal" (450ff.: *def:dis*).

14. This block of scenes (xiv–xviii) constitutes the heart of the sequence at the cottage: scene xiii is an introductory sequence with its three subscenes and block of introductory material; scene xix, on the other side, forms the CON to Act III and functions as the CON to the narrative as a whole.

15. The Conclusion: scene xix. The reader learns, at the close of scene xviii,

5. Cf. the discussion of the pseudo-iterative in §6.44.

that the forest in which the children have been wandering, is enchanted (452). That is good reason to quit it at the earliest possible moment. They set out and come immediately to a large body of water (454: *f:arr*). The events at the lake form subscene xixa. Gretel advises Hänsel that they are now mature enough to act separately,[6] so the white duck carries one at a time across the pond. The scene is defocalized when they complete the crossing and leave the lake (*def:dep*).[7]

Hänsel and Gretel spy their father's house from afar (479: *f:perc*); they arrive quickly (480–482: *f:arr*) and fall on their father's neck. These features signal the beginning of scene xixb. Two powerful defocalizers bring the narrative to a conclusion. Hänsel and Gretel exhibit the riches they had found in the witch's cottage (486ff., cf. 443ff.: a *termf* like winning a major lottery), which brings their poverty to an end. As a consequence, they live happily together (490: *def:ae*). As an epilogue, the narrator addresses the reader directly. If the narrative is structured well, the reader does not need to be informed that the tale is at an end. Yet it is a convention, as often in cinema, to break the spell with "THE END."

6. As a matter of fact, they have been acting individually since scene xiv; their experience with the white duck confirms their new maturity.

7. Implied by 477.

—·12·—

The Unwritten

• 12 •

INTRODUCTION

1. The focus of this study has thus far been what stands written in the narrative text. Insofar as narrator, narratee, reader, and even story have come into view, they have been considered primarily in relation to the traces they leave in the discourse. In sum, this investigation has gone in pursuit of clues explicitly planted in the text; the aim has been to concentrate intensely on what stands written.

In the brief consideration given to story, narrator, narratee, and reader, we took notice of much that was unwritten, inexplicit, to be inferred. Among these were traces of the narrator's presence in the text, evidences left by the participation, potential and realized, of the narratee or reader, and the various levels of story, which in its ultimate form is always unwritten. These elements lie beyond the textual surface, but are implicit in it. While it will not be possible, within the limits of this study, to pursue the investigation of these items in detail, it is appropriate to suggest lines along which they could be pursued and to develop, once again in a preliminary fashion, the conceptual framework within which that work might be carried out.

The subject of this final chapter, in a word, is the unwritten.

FACETS OF THE UNWRITTEN

2. Story. The first sense in which the unwritten can be understood is story. Story, it will be recalled, is taken to form a continuous stream of events, of which the narrative discourse reflects a selection (§2.35). The experience of events and relationships among humankind is "chaotic": their number is overwhelming because they form an unbroken sequence, and they are disorganized because they lack segmentation and plot. The primary fiction created by the storyteller is the organization of the chaos of experience: the narrator selects, segments, sequences, and in so doing disengages the particular story from all other stories, those that precede, follow, and are lateral to the story as narrated.[1]

3. Frame of reference. A second sense of the unwritten Hrushovski calls the "frame of reference" (*fr*). A frame of reference may be defined as any continuum, in time or space, or in theme or ideas, "that can accommodate a number of referents."[2] A narrative scene located in a particular time and place is such a *fr*, as is a particular theory of narrative, or the guild of biblical

1. Cf. Petersen, *Rediscovering Paul*, 10, 15f., for a perceptive statement of this point.
2. *Segmentation and Motivation*, 13.

scholars, or the local chamber of commerce. Another form of a *fr* is the person or character appearing in a narrative text. The essential aspect of a *fr* is that when speaking or writing about it or them, one may draw on the listener's knowledge of that *fr* to supply certain things left unsaid. The frame of reference itself is unwritten; but the text contains clues that point to the *fr*. For example, the narrator posits a character, whose established traits become a resevoir upon which both the narrator and the reader draw in filling in subsequent scenes or rereading earlier ones.

The concept of the frame of reference may be illustrated by comparing the narration of a scene with a photograph or representational painting.[3]

What the storyteller says and what he or she leaves unsaid become evident in the comparison. The painter and the photographer frame their pictures. The frame means that they limit what is represented to what is inside the frame and say nothing about what is outside.[4] What is represented within the frame, however, is depicted in explicit detail: the painter cannot fail to be specific in representational painting.[5] Verbal representation, on the other hand, is unable to depict scenes in the same detail; it must be content to provide a few details and permit the reader to infer the rest. A viewer can return to a painting or photograph repeatedly and examine further details; the amount of detail offered by the narrative is limited. As a consequence, the continuum of a scene is not manifested. The narrative depiction might be infinitely long, but it would still not provide the detail of a photograph.

4. A field of reference (FR), according to Hrushovski, is "a theoretical continuum of a large number of frames of reference."[6] In a work of fiction, for example, an author may provide a limited number of *frs*, spanning a period of thirty years. The *frs* actually made explicit will consist of a few points or periods of shorter or longer duration along that decades-long spectrum, but from the *frs* provided the reader is prompted to infer the entire period, or shall we say the *FR*. The *fr*, it was said above, consists of clues designed to suggest the whole, although the whole is inexplicit. The *FR* is likewise a construction of the author and reader, based on clues provided by a series of *frs*. Neither the *fr* nor the *FR* are therefore explicit or written.

To speak of America and things American is to draw on a huge contemporary resevoir of the taken-for-granted. If one fails to limit the period to modern America, or nineteenth-century America, or the antebellum South,

3. I am indebted to Chatman, *Story and Discourse*, 29ff., for his suggestive discussion of the differences.

4. There are some interesting exceptions to this generalization that cannot be pursued here. For example, a photograph or painting may imply things or activities outside the frame. In this respect, visual representation is like verbal.

5. Non-representational painting, of course, is another matter.

6. *Segmentation and Motivation*, 13. Field of reference is abbreviated *FR* (caps) to distinguish it from *fr* (frame of reference).

the *FR* is even larger and less well defined, encompassing as it does the entire history of the country, along with its prospective future.

5. World as field of reference. "World" is the name for an all-encompassing field of reference. World may be defined in this context as the way things hang together for individuals and society when they are not thinking consciously about them. The *FR* as world is all-encompassing for an individual, for a piece of narrative fiction, for a historical period, for a people, etc. Things hang together in an *FR* in both temporal and spatial dimensions. That is another way of saying that world has both diachronic and synchronic aspects. Translated into the terms of a narrative text, world has dimensions that are both syntagmatic and paradigmatic. Once again, world or *FR* is not made explicit in the text; it is left to be inferred and is therefore unwritten along with story and frame of reference.

6. The internal field of reference and the external field of reference. It is necessary, further, to distinguish two broad types of field of reference (*FRs*). A narrative text creates an internal field of reference (*IFR*), which may also be referred to as the narrative or story world. Petersen succinctly defines this *FR*:

> The narrative world is that reality which the narrator bestows upon his actors and upon their actions, a reality into which he authoritatively invites his audience, whether he is telling a fairy tale, a spy story, or a great novelistic adventure.[7]

Within this fictive world, or *IFR*, the reader knows only what the text presents; it is out of the material provided by the text that the narrative world is to be constructed; it is illegitimate to go beyond the information provided by the text to inquire whether the author is telling the truth. Within the *IFR*, it is illegitimate, for example, to inquire whether the places in Thomas Hardy's novels are real places on the English countryside, whether Merlin in the works of Mary Stewart was a historical person, or whether Captain Ahab once actually sailed a whaling ship. The narrative creates its own *frs* and *IFR*, and it is to these that the reader refers all sentences in the narrative text.

7. To say that the *IFR* governs the story world of narrative fiction is not to say that such texts draw exclusively on an *IFR*. Indeed, fictive texts draw freely on a second type of *FR*, viz., the *external field of reference* (*ExFR*). When Luke opens his gospel with "In the days of Herod . . . ," he is referring to a royal figure in the world external to the text (Luke 1:5). In sketching the duties of priests connected with the Jerusalem temple, he is alluding to social arrangements in the *ExFR*. Many other statements in the Gospels refer to customs and practices of the world contemporary with the events depicted in the narrative, such as sabbath observance, sowing and reaping, exorcisms, and the like. Similarly, Tolstoy refers to the situation in Europe in 1805 in his

7. *Rediscovering Paul*, 7.

War and Peace as the *ExFR* for the *IFR* of the narrative text, and the author assumes that the two *FRs* are continuous, as Hrushovski has shown.[8]

Historical narration differs from fiction in one important respect: historical narrative presumably refers principally to events and persons in the *ExFR*, and so one of the considerations in evaluating historical narrative is whether it represents data in the *ExFR* accurately. One does so, of course, by consulting other records and reports which also allegedly report data from the *ExFR*. The *ExFR* is thus available via storied accounts, and those storied accounts are also framed by their own *IFR*. Testing takes place, in other words, by testing one story against another.

8. Multiple fields of reference. It is now necessary to complicate the matter even further. Petersen points out, in the discussion of text and context, that the relevant context for a text is "the time in which and for which" it was written, whereas we spoke above of the *ExFR* as the world external to the events to which the narrative refers. From the latter *ExFR* is now to be discriminated from that *ExFR* to which Petersen refers: that of the narrator and the narrator's text. Moreover, the narrator's *ExFR* is to be distinguished from his or her own *FR*, inasmuch as a person is also a continuum and inhabits a world that in some respects, at least, differs from the ordinary, everyday *ExFR*.

If we add one reader to the picture, the number of *FRs* grows again, since the reader brings a second private *FR* to the text, along with an *ExFR* that may or may not overlap with the *ExFR* of the narrator. In any case, just how the reader admits his or her own *FR* and *ExFR* into the interpretative process will differ in large or small ways from the same process under the jurisdiction of the narrator. For every additional reader, other *FRs* come into the picture. These complexities are summarized in figure 25.

To make all these discriminations may seem unduly complicating. Yet they are essential, particularly where time and place of the narrative, narrator, and reader are widely divergent. This applies especially to texts written in late antiquity and read by modern readers. There are examples, of course, of narrative texts where the divergence is much narrower, but in no case will the *FRs* of narrative, narrator, and reader absolutely coincide.

LANGUAGE AS SYSTEM AND WORLD

9. It will prove illuminating to link the discussion of frames of reference or world to the Saussurean concept of language as system, on the view that the two are homologous.

Ferdinand de Saussure was a Swiss linguist who lived around the turn of the century. His views have been tremendously influential, shaping as they have

8. *Segmentation and Motivation*, 18.

linguistics, formalism, structuralism, and now deconstructionism from his time to the present. In brief, Saussure maintained that knowledge of the world was inextricably bound up with language. He held that signs of which language consists are purely arbitrary. There is, he insisted, no natural or common sense link between the word and that for which the word allegedly stands: the referent in the external world. Language consists of a system of signs, the value and meaning of which is determined by relationships and oppositions between and among signs within the system, signs which have no connection with the "real" world.

Multiple Frames of Reference

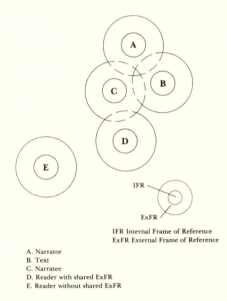

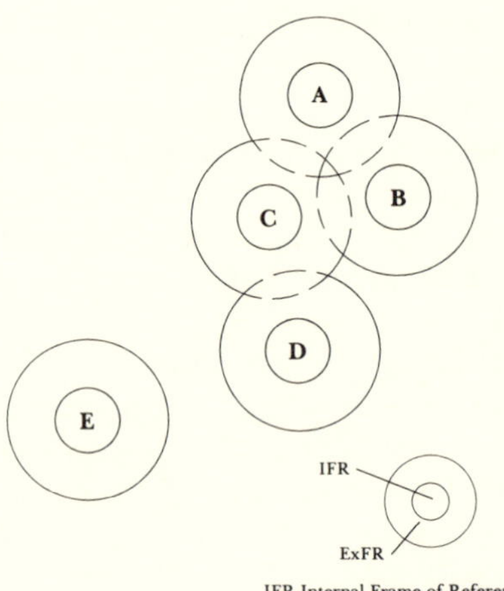

A. Narrator
B. Text
C. Narratee
D. Reader with shared ExFR
E. Reader without shared ExFR

Figure 25

A sign, according to Saussure, consists of a signifier (a sound, a word) and a signified (an idea, a concept). Thus, not only do the signifiers of language constitute a system internal to language, so also does the system of signifieds or referents: they, too, are constructs within the language system and not entities outside language. Saussure's view entails a relativity of thought and meaning: there is only language; language is divorced from its referents; indeed, it is divorced in large measure from the control of its human users, which are dependent on the system already in place.

10. Saussure's synchronic system of oppositions or differences as a description of language is structurally homologous to "world" understood as a circumspective totality or network of significations. This network of significations is either identical with, or closely akin to, the frame of reference described by Hrushovski. Indeed, "world" may turn out to be the same thing as Saussure's network of signifieds.

It is impossible to describe language as a network of signifieds in concrete terms because the network as a whole never manifests itself; it is unwritten. Rather, it constitutes something like a "horizon." A horizon represents the limits of a system of meaning, of a world. Since the user cannot get beyond the horizon or behind the system, it is impossible to comprehend the constellation as a whole. To employ a favorite term of Jacques Derrida, the meaning of the network as a whole is always deferred: the shape and content of the whole is always outstanding. To say that something is outstanding is to suggest that the time may come when it will become instanding: in that case, however, the temporal flow will stop and the system will have ceased to develop and hence function.

11. What users comprehend of the system are pieces, fragments, and satellite spheres of significance. Speakers of natural languages get "glimmers" or "glimpses" of the whole through "facets." When a sufficient number of facets of the configuration combine to illuminate each other at some unspecified and unspecifiable point, the system of language or world jumps into view, momentarily, providing a passing glimpse of the horizon.

A facet—a face that reflects light—is an insight from the perspective of the viewer; an insight is apprehending a thing in one of its facets. Synonyms of facet are phase, aspect, side, angle. It may be said, "That facet of the problem stood out in bold relief." A facet is thus an insight into one aspect of a thing that gives a new name to the whole: the facet is used to characterize the whole. A facet is therefore metonymy, a change in name, the substitution of the name of a new aspect for the whole.

To return now to the subject of narrative and frames of reference, it may be said that a narrative is a selected series of insights linked together in a chain of events involving one or more characters: the narrative text is a chain of insights that provokes or suggests a frame of reference, a world, which is itself unwritten, indeed, ineffable.[9]

STORY, FIELDS OF REFERENCE, AND PLAUSIBILITY

12. Story and fields of reference as the ordering of experience. It has been argued that story and fields of reference are unwritten in the sense that, although they are implied by the text, they cannot, by the nature of the case, be made explicit by it. At most, the text affords glimpses, facets of the story, and *FRs*. Nevertheless, the unwritten plays a fundamental role in storytelling, in

9. One might even venture to say that narrative is a metonymic equivalent of metaphor, where metaphor is understood as a paradigmatic glimpse of a new horizon.

narrative discourse, whether of a so-called historical or a fictive sort: the unwritten services what may be called plausibility, also termed recuperation, naturalization, motivation, verisimilitude. In essence, story and the *FRs* prompt the reader to suspend disbelief and enter the narrative world by making the narrative plausible. Why this is so and how it functions are to be explored next.

13. The human mind is predisposed to turn raw sensation into ordered perception.[10] An isolated, unrelated sensation is a rare experience. When it occurs, it induces fear or panic if one is unable to give that sensation a plausible frame of reference: an unidentified sound in the night, especially in a strange setting, precipitates anxiety until one is able to "locate" the source and provide the sound with a rational explanation. The frame of reference for such explanations is derived from previous experiences that have been categorized and codified, that is, from a world or field or reference already inhabited and therefore habituated. Humankind, accordingly, is prone to treat unusual sensations—if it is now appropriate to generalize—the same way they process normal average sensations: one claims them for spheres of domesticated experience and meaning without thinking. The process is subconscious. The field of reference into which such sensations are taken is called "life world" by Heidegger and Alfred Schutz, which they define as a circumspective totality of significations of the ready-to-hand that governs the way one perceives things in their everydayness.[11]

14. Related to the proclivity to order sensations is the inclination to connect divergent events into a temporal chain, to turn almost any set of events into a story. A pure "chronicle," a listing of isolated events with no connection between them, would be very difficult to achieve. For example,

> She withdrew money from the bank
> She left Chicago

are likely to be taken as related events if they appear proximate to each other in a list or chronicle. Even if one were to draw up a list of unrelated events, readers would be provoked to find some connection, real or imagined, among the items listed. There seems to be no limit to the capacity of the human mind to assert connecting links.

15. Plausibility. What is the basis of this tendency to provide a frame of reference for sensations, to connect events of the most disparate sort? In a

10. Chatman, *Story and Discourse,* 46. Chatman's discussion of the notion of plausibility and verisimilitude extends from 45–53. The basic discussion is provided by Culler, *Structuralist Poetics,* 131–60. Todorov has also published a sketch of the concept: *Poetics of Prose,* 80–88. See also Rimmon-Kenan, *Narrative Fiction,* 122–25. A phenomenological account of the concept is afforded by Martin Heidegger, *Being and Time,* especially 91–148 and 149–68, and by Alfred Schutz, *Structures of the Life-World.*

11. The formulation is Heidegger's: *Being and Time,* 95–107.

general way it may be said that the human mind ingests present experience into the stomach of ordered memories: the known, the plausible, the credible are retained as nourishment, while the unknown, the implausible, the incredible are sloughed off as waste. Or so it seems primarily and for the most part.

Ordered memories are (1) memories shared with contemporaries and those who inhabit the same social space, and (2) memories shared with predecessors and thus inherited as tradition. The latter are transmitted culturally and received as a common legacy. The former are what passes for the acceptable in thought, expression, and behavior, for the plausible in a given time and place, for the regnant reality.[12] Ordered memories are the "texts" of appropriate response to experience and the norms of behavior of society at large. Such "texts" are in fact an ill-defined corpus of the commonly understood, the opinion of the "they say" that constitutes what deconstructionists call "intertextuality." Such texts are intersubjective: the fund of common experience on which all members of a given society draw in making everyday, routine decisions without having to give attention to them. They also make for rigidity among those who would prefer the comfort of decisions made for them.

Plausibility is the translation of the French term *vraisemblablisation*: verisimilitude, having the appearance of truth. It encompasses the process that goes by several different labels in recent criticism: recuperation, naturalization, motivation, verisimilitude. The Russian Formalists preferred the term motivation; Culler is inclined to naturalization; the translation of Todorov employs versimilitude because of its relation to the French term. Plausibility is not burdened with previous technical use and so is available for duty; it also points to the broadest of the categories, the verisimilar.

16. Types of plausibility. Todorov and Culler list four (five) types of plausibility.[13] In the list to follow I have redefined and reordered their lists. The first type (1) is the naive meaning, "to be consistent with reality, with the real world" (Culler). Both Todorov and Culler dismiss this type, since they will not admit of any connection between things and events in the external world and the sea of intertextuality.[14] However, the problem of the relation of narrative to history deserves more than a casual dismissal. It will be taken up below (§§12.19–24). The second meaning (2) is the correspondence of the text to a generalized text which may be designated "public opinion" or "they say." This broad category may be referred to as the received world; the terminology employed earlier was the external field of reference.

A third sense (3) is the narrativized world, or the internal field of reference. The term narrative world was used earlier and that is a good term, provided it

12. Cf. the remarks of Chatman, *Story and Discourse*, 49.
13. *Poetics of Prose*, 80–88; *Structuralist Poetics*, 141f.
14. Cf. Saussure's view of language, §§12.9–11.

is understood as the world that has already been storied, reduced to narrative, and passed on and around. Of course, much of the received world is carried along in narrative, so that categories (2) and (3) overlap to a certain degree. The fourth type (4) consists of ploys and strategies employed by the author to make the reader think that the text conforms to reality, when in fact it is violating other forms of plausibility. An example would be: "If I were writing a novel, at this point the hero would have to . . . , but since I am telling the truth, here is what really happened." The fifth and final form (5) consists of authorial commentary or direct appeal to the reader. In this instance the author interferes in the narrative in order to assure the reader that the norms of behavior or feature are quite plausible, appearances to the contrary notwithstanding.

These types of plausibility are intertwined. Together they form the pool of intertextuality of which deconstructionists love to speak. Authors, readers, and the texts they create and consume are immersed in the same atmosphere, from which they draw their sustenance and in relation to which they are defined as as specific instances of expression or interpretation.

17. Plausibility and the text. The creator of narrative discourse appeals to the received world in order to make the story plausible. By so doing, the author cuts down on the amount of detail to be narrated: one need only "suggest" certain things and the reader will supply the background or field of reference out of a common stock, or the reader will fill in the gaps in the narrative. To be affective at this strategy, the author must make the narrative seem "natural": the narrative induces the reader to forget the narrative technique, which is artificial, and invest the narrative with plausibility or reality. In so doing, the reader adjusts events and characters to his or her own life world and creates a coherent whole out of the parts, by the reader's own standards. From the standpoint of the author, one cannot anticipate entirely what a reader will make out of a text: everything depends on how well it is crafted. From the standpoint of the reader, one can fault an author for being too explicit and therefore not very interesting, or for calling on a received world that is alien, fractured, or unrecognizable. Too much plausibility weakens a narrative; too much implausibility wrecks it.

18. The only requirement is plausibility. Implausible acts are permitted if they are given proper "motivation," if they are accounted for in some "plausible" way. This can be achieved by providing a slightly or greatly modified field of reference (a new lived world) for the narrative as a whole. Such a fictional world would be an implied or putative life world, either unknown or forgotten, or belonging to some indeterminate future or alien space. Or, the author can insert "commentary" into the narrative in order to argue for the plausibility of the aberrations by the appeal to some general truth or by the appeal to the axiom that life is stranger than fiction.

When novels began to be "implausible" themselves, as in France in the late nineteenth and early twentieth centuries, it was because the lived world was experienced as "implausible," without ultimate rhyme or reason. Implausibility became a new form of plausibility.

The implausible and improbable are introduced into narrative, both fiction and history, as a means of keeping the story interesting. A static life world would be uninteresting; a chaotic life world would be intolerable; a deviant life world is interesting, exciting, intriguing. In inserting the implausible, however, the expectations associated with narrative are also gradually modified. Interesting narratives in the sense just defined puts the habituated world in fine imbalance: perceptions of the real are made to shift imperceptibly.

FICTION AND NON-FICTION

19. The two great categories of narrative texts in the publishing and library worlds are fiction and non-fiction. The narrative text may have as its referents its story, a fiction, some imagined series of events. In that case, its story lacks an objective basis in the world of lived experience, although it will also perforce appeal to an external frame of reference that draws upon that lived world for its plausibility. Or, the narrative may be about "real" events, events taken actually to have occurred, apart from particular interpretations. In this case, the discourse presumably has history as its referent. In everyday parlance, native speakers and writers of English tend to distinguish story as fiction from the kind of story called history, although both are story in the technical sense in which we have defined the term. Nevertheless, history is also storied, as it were, and exists only or primarily in that form.

From a naive perspective, narrators may be said (1) to refer to events or objects as having been experienced or encountered (corresponding to what we have defined as mimetic discourse, creating the illusion that the reader or listener is present at the events being narrated); or, they may be said (2) to report events or objects as having been experienced or encountered (corresponding to what was termed recounting, in which the narrator overtly mediates between events and reader); or, the narrator may be said (3) to refer to objects or events remembered as having been experienced or encountered. The direct encounter reflected in (1) is illusory, as we have indicated, since events and objects enter narrative only as reports and, hence only as (2), recounting. The third category is distinguished from the first two only by virtue of the distance the narrator puts between himself or herself and the events being reported, whether based on the narrator's own experience or on reports of memories of others.

20. Like other constraints of narration, the story is external to the text, as observed earlier (§§2.29–37). Whether in the form of imagined objects and events, or in the form of history, the story—again in the technical sense—brings "pressure" to bear on the narrator: the testimony of storytellers is nearly universal to the effect that they are relating a tale that has its own life, a tale that is beyond them, that tells itself, so to speak.

21. Biblical scholarship is perhaps at a major crossroads in its modern development as regards the nature of biblical narratives. It has been difficult to decide whether biblical narratives are about real or fictive events. This problem has been at the center of historical criticism since its rise in the Enlightenment, although a tendency has recently emerged among literary critics, both secular and biblical, and among new wave pietists, to dismiss it preemptorily and take the canonical texts in their received form as the object of investigation. Structuralists and deconstructionists, on the other hand, have also belittled the historical issue as false, for something like opposite reasons. They hold that texts, historical as well as fictive, are ensnared in the endless play of differences of which language consists. Historical critics of traditional persuasions, understandably, have been at a loss in these cross currents, since their methodological paradigm is being discredited on both fronts. In spite of these trends, the problem will not go away. It belongs to the modern mind, along with a greatly heightened consciousness and a conviction that science has uncovered the really real world. Scholars may vacate their responsibilities in this regard, either out of a false sense of piety, or out of a beleaguered cynicism. Nevertheless, both those inside and those outside the circle of faith deserve, and will demand, a clear scholarly assessment of the nature of the texts. All want to know what is the real external field of reference for this or that piece of tradition. Clearing away the rubble of fact could be a most salutary experience for current fundamentalisms, which are based on appeals to ignorance and fear, just as clarity regarding the nature of narrative might prove liberating for biblical scholarship, which has tended to go in exclusive quest of the holy land of historical fact.

22. The distinction between history and fiction does not seem to affect the question of how story (in the technical sense) brings pressure to bear on the narrative process. It does not seem possible, in principle, to distinguish fictive and historical narration on the basis of formal markers in the narrative text. I do not share the conviction of Rimmon-Kenan that one can discriminate the two on the basis of formal properties,[15] although I would agree that claims to be one or the other are often discernible. But that is something quite different from segregating texts that are genuinely historical from those that are predominantly fictive.

23. It is patent nonsense, in historical narration, to claim that there is no relation between the historical events to which the text refers and the narrative text. But it is equally nonsensical to claim that the relationship is univocal. We may agree with Petersen that

15. *Narrative Fiction*, 3.

> to be sure, there is something out there outside of us and apart from our knowledge of it, but it is not a "world" apart from what we know about it. In this respect, therefore, "worlds" are like "histories." As we saw in our discussion of history as story, there are events "out there" in the past, but they are not "history" until we compose a story about them. "Histories" are authorial constructions and "worlds" are social constructions.[16]

Histories are a kind of world, as defined in this study, but that does not mean that all historical narratives are fictitious in the same sense. The relationship between actual occurrences and the narratives that report them is subtle. We do not know precisely how "the facts"—the facets of objects and events—influence the telling of a story, yet there is some influence, more or less, to a greater or lesser degree. We shall explore this subtle pressure momentarily. Meanwhile, it should be said that humankind cannot afford to do without the distinction between fact and fiction. To do so is to open oneself and society to demonic stories, such as the one on which Nazism was based. Moreover, all our sciences rest on the distinction, as fictive as that distinction may be.

24. This issue arises against the background of current structuralist and post-structuralist claims that historical objects and events enter the narrative transaction only via sedimented experience already encoded in the network of differences of which language consists. This claim rests on two "rigorous structuralist principles," to quote Frank Lentricchia, which are: (1) "that the self is an intersubjective construct formed by cultural systems over which the individual person has no control; and (2) that the text is a kind of formless space whose shape is imposed by structured modes of reading."[17] The two principles are at bottom one, in that "the structured modes of reading" brought to the text and the formative cultural systems over which the individual has no control vest in the network of differences of which language consists. Viewed this way, it follows that unknown objects and events, as well as items with uncoded properties, cannot enter the network; they are excluded by virtue of the limits imposed on experience by the system. Now the linguistic network, according to these same interpreters, is passed on, transmitted, from one person to another, from one generation to another, as a form of verisimilitude or plausibility already sedimented in "writing." In other words, the basis of the transmission is intersubjective or intertextual.

Deconstructionists hold that interpreters are caught, inevitably and perpetually, in the eternal play of texts; that they cannot hope to penetrate the text to something more durable, more satisfying, beyond; that they are ensnared in a rhetorical will to power, of the dimensions of original sin.

16. *Rediscovering Paul*, 29. We might quibble with Petersen that histories are always authorial and stories always social. It seems that some histories are social and some worlds private. That is because both individuals and societies have constructs that are both syntagmatic and paradigmatic.

17. *After the New Criticism*, 108.

I share the conviction that the interplay of texts is inevitable and perpetual, but I am also convinced that humankind, on rare occasions, catches glimpses of reality aborning, of fellow men and women without disguises, of the "beyond" of texts. Tellers of stories reach that beyond by continuing to cross over from received preconceptions, from habituated illusions, from rhetorical ploys, to what is "there," outside and beyond, outside and beyond language. Mortals are destined to perish before crossing into that far land; they will never possess it. But that land is the only haven of humanity against its own propensity to mistake its perceptions of the real for the real itself.

And so, the question is: How does the unique, the uncoded, manage to break into the network against the overpowering odds that oppose it, the habituated, the conventional, the staunchly plausible?

OLD AND NEW HORIZONS

25. The concept of an all-encompassing field of reference, or life world, is the very means of explicating how such novelty may be introduced into the network.[18] The "text" of the natural attitude of a society requires no justification; it is the fundamental and paramount reality of men and women within society. It requires no justification because it seems to derive from the structures of the real world as they are experienced. Among the things assumed by the natural attitude, according to Alfred Schutz, are the following: (1) I take the existence of other persons like myself for granted; (2) I assume those other persons are endowed with consciousness as I am; (3) I assume that objects and events in the "outer" world are the same for them as for me (that is, I assume that for them, as for me, the natural world is made up of well-circumscribed objects with determinate properties); (4) I assume that I can enter into relations with my fellowmen, as they can with me and with each other; (5) I assume that I can make myself understood to them, to a greater or lesser degree (put to the test frequently in the classroom); (6) I further take it for granted that the stratified social and cultural world is pregiven for them as for me, and that it serves as the frame of reference for their explications of the world, as it does for me; I also assume that the status of the social and cultural world is comparable to the status of the natural world; (7) I conclude that my situation is only to a small extent determined by me, and I draw the same conclusion about my fellowmen.

26. How does one think within the framework of the natural attitude, given the assumptions just sketched? My thinking about the world and my place within it (1) is based on a "stock of previous experiences," both those I have had directly and those mediated to me by my parents, my teachers,

18. The remarks that follow are derived chiefly from Schutz, *Structures of the Life-world*, especially 1–40.

others about me, and by my entire tradition. (2) All of these experiences are incorporated into a kind of unity that serves as "a reference schema" for my interpretation of the world. (3) The sum of my experiences is integrated into this reference schema as a network of typifications, or, to put the matter in other terms, as a network of signifieds. (4) As I think about this organized fund of experience, I come to trust its reliability, and I assume that it will continue to be valid. (5) Accordingly, I am prepared to base my actions upon that knowledge and assume, as as consequence, that I can repeat actions that have been successful in the past.[19]

27. As a rule, individuals do not question the validity of the everyday life world. Being parsimonious of thought and action, humankind tend to routinize action so that conscious attention to decision-making is limited to the more significant reaches of existence. Nevertheless, an individual's life world does not constitute a closed, logically articulated system. It will be recalled that language as a system is never fully manifested and cannot even be fully articulated, as the efforts of the linguists to do so demonstrate.[20] Neither is story fully told: there is always something further than can be said. In any case, the agreements and coherence between and among the components of my network, shared with my fellows, are not absolute. They are surrounded by uncertainty. There is co-given with my interpretative scheme something like a horizon that is indeterminate in character; while that horizon encloses my everyday world, it is always open to question. My everyday world consists of a network of determinacies against a backdrop of indeterminacy.

28. How may this network be interrupted or modified? Interruption occurs, or may occur, when something comes within my purview that does not fit with my organized stock of experiences. The network of typifications that constitute my received world is thus challenged. The challenge calls my attention to the horizon itself, i.e., to the reach and organization of my network. I must now adjust the content of my world to accommodate the novel experience, or I am obliged to put that unique experience "on hold" until further notice.[21] But if I accommodate the new and the novel, I must then check my reference schema against those of my fellows. Should the social context support the accommodation, I have a new recipe for understanding experience.[22]

29. The "pressure" on the narrator predominantly and for the most part is the received world, the everyday, what society already knows. The same predominant pressures are also on the reader and interpreter, adjusted, of

19. The summary of thinking in the natural attitude is found in Schutz, *Structures of the Life-world*, 6f.

20. Cf. the discussion of world and language as system in §§12.9–11.

21. Cf. the earlier discussion of ordered memories, §§12.12–15.

22. See Schutz, *Structures of the Life-world*, 8–15, for a discussion of the notion of interruption.

course, for his or her time and place. But there is also the subtle pressure of the "interruption," from the glimpse, the facet, that may provoke a slight or marked deformation of the received story. The twin poles of the transaction are story and narrative: there is a residue of the unexpressed on both sides: there is always more (story) to tell; a modified genre, or narrative grammar, or language, or plausible world will admit of new perspectives, plots, characters, setting, encompassing the same or different events.

As Frank Kermode reminds us by way of Kafka's parable of the Doorkeeper, the interpreter will never manage to slip by the guardian of the door into the shrine of the single sense.[23] But interpreters will keep trying. They must. For all must attend the pressure of the "interruption," the glimpse, the facet whose glimmer awakens to new horizons. We must do so for that is what keeps the network alive, what causes it to change into nothing other than itself, but with new configurations. To allow the network to crystallize is like having frozen language: neither will serve a living, vibrant world.

Truth and meaning arise as blips on the network, as the unwritten, struggling to find expression in some minor poem, some little told story. Truth is always outstanding. Its "there" is some field of reference, without which the facts or facets would lack coherence, lack cogency. The facts are meaningless unless held in solution in some narrative or paradigm, some configuration that makes them hang together, cohere.

IDOLATRIES OF THE TEXT

30. Certainties about the nature of reality, about the ultimate, come in large and small doses. The biblical writers, both the older and the later ones, had a large dose, perhaps an extra large dose. In making their claims, as a consequence, they succumbed to the temptation to conflate their readings—their emerging texts—with what they were speaking and writing about. Their text could not be disinguished from its "about," their tale from its told, so strong was their conviction. Yet strength of conviction does not guarantee truth; it doesn't even guarantee meaning. Strength of conviction, on the contrary, tends to be directly proportional to the level of illusion.

There appears to be a correction in certain portions of the scriptures that functions as an antidote to this certainty born of conflation. One form of it is in the prophetic warning against overindulgence in received forms of piety; another is the mystery, or the parable, of God's presence to the chosen people, which obscures as well as announces. These antidotes suggest that it is always prudent to distinguish our narratives from their stories, to hold open the future to vistas as yet unglimpsed.

We could posit that the structure of our narratives mirrors the structure of

23. *Genesis of Secrecy*, 122f. Kafka, *Parables and Paradoxes*, 61–79.

our lived world: reality presents itself to us in glimpses, one, or at most two, facets at a time, and we are left to supply the balance. That is subtle pressure on the part of the real, but no less telling for that. Yet the effect is illusory: what we see, taste, touch, feel, hear, and smell is not enough to create a world, a circumspective totality of significations; we must take what we get and imagine, invent the whole.

Our ultimate—or perhaps we should hedge and say our penultimate—situation is ironic: the certitudes we strive for turn out to be illusory, while the illusions we seek to escape turn out to be real. Things are never what they seem.

Why that is so is the ultimate subject of a narrative poetics.

Glossary

References are to primary discussions, by chapter and paragraph number.

Anachrony: the narration of any event out of chronological order. The story order is the natural chronological order. When the discourse order violates the story order, it is an anachrony (§§8.1–2, 13–32). Prolepses and analepses are anachronies.

Anachrony, external: if an anachrony occurs outside the temporal boundaries of the first narrative, it is external (§8.7).

Anachrony, internal: if an anachrony occurs within the temporal boundaries of the first narrative, it is internal (§8.7).

Analepsis: any event narrated belatedly, i.e., at some point in the narrative order later than when it occurred in story time (§§8.1–2, 3–7). In film an analepsis is called a "flashback." Cf. prolepsis.

Analepsis, completing: the narrator returns to an earlier point in the story and fills in something that was omitted (§8.6; 11.10).

Analepsis, heterodiegetic: analepses that belong to a story outside the first or primary narrative (§8.5). Contrast homodiegetic analepses.

Analepsis, homodiegetic: analepses that belong to the same story line as the first or primary narrative (§8.5). Contrast heterodiegetic analepses.

Analepsis, repeating: the narrator repeats a detail or event narrated earlier in the story (§8.6).

Conclusion (CON)***:*** the final part of a narrative segment in which the defocalizing process takes place (§§3.23–31, 32).

Diegesis: refers to the unfocused narrative presentation in which the narrator reports what has transpired without permitting the reader to witness events directly or immediately. In diegesis the narrator recounts rather than enacts, tells rather than shows (§§6.1–2, 6–7, 25–30). Cf. mimesis, diegetic.

Diegetic: the Greek term, *diegesis,* literally means the narrative. It technically refers to the first or primary narrative. Intradiegetic refers to a narrative within the primary narrative. In this sense, diegetic concerns narrative levels (§2.7). Diegetic is also used to denote the recounting narrative mode as contrasted with the mimetic mode. Cf. diegesis, mimesis.

Ellipsis: a temporal gap in the chronological baseline of the first narrative.

Enact, enactment, s. mimesis.

Extent: the period or duration of a proleptic or analeptic event (§8.7).

Event: a cluster of actions or happenings that advance the story (§1.43; Narrative Diagramming §1).

First narrative: refers to the temporal baseline of the primary narrative. Cf. Second narrative.

Focalizer: any narrative device that prompts the reader where to focus the senses, where to look for the action about to take place (§§1.46; 3.7–19; 5.1–24).

Focalizing process: the narrator focuses the narrative by bringing a finite set of participants together in a specific time and particular place (§§1.46; 3.7–19; 5.1–24).

Defocalizer: any narrative device that reverses the focalizing process and brings the story to narrative rest (§§1.47; 3.29; 5.25–48).

Defocalizing process: reverses the focalizing process by dispersing the participants, expanding the space, lengthening the time frame, or introducing a terminal function (§1.47; 3.29; 5.25–48).

Heterodiegetic: a narrator or narratee that falls outside the first or primary narrative is said to be heterodiegetic (belonging to another narrative) (§2.9).

Homodiegetic: a narrator or narratee that appears within the first or primary narrative is said to be homodiegetic (belonging to the same narrative) (§2.9).

Hyperdiegetic: the narrative level or layer "above" the first or primary narrative. A hyperdiegetic narrator is immediately "superior" to the first narrative. The narrator always belongs to the level "above" the tale being narrated. Cf. intradiegetic, hypodiegetic. All three terms concern the narrative levels to which narrators belong (§2.7).

Hypodiegetic: the narrative level or layer "below" the first narrative. A hypodiegetic narrator appears within a story that is within the first narrative and narrates a story at a third level (§2.7). Cf. hyperdiegetic and intradiegetic.

Introduction (INTRO)***:*** the first part of a narrative segment in which two or more participants are brought together in a common time or place (§§3.6, 7–19, 32; Narrative Diagramming §2).

Iterative: events that happen more than once or repeatedly are customarily narrated in the iterative mode. Cf. singulative.

Intradiegetic: refers to the level or layer of the first narrative. An intradiegetic narrator appears in the first narrative and narrates a story within the first narrative (§2.7). Cf. hyperdiegetic and hypodiegetic.

Mimesis, mimetic: refers to the focused scene in which events are enacted rather than recounted, shown rather than told (§§6.1–2, 3–5, 25–30). Cf. diegesis.

Narratee: the second party to the narrative transaction: the one who reads or listens to the story (§1.6).

Narrative discourse: the linguistic vehicle of the story (§1.1).

Narrative statement: narrative statements are of two types: (1) those that express an action or happening; (2) those that express the status of a participant or other element. The first type consists of "do" statements; the second of "is" statements (§1.39).

Narrative text: the linguistic vehicle of the story; a synonym for narrative discourse.

Narratology: a subdivision of poetics; treats the formal properties of narrative texts (§1.8). Synonym: narrative poetics.

Nucleus (NUC)*:* a narrative segment consisting of a cluster of actions or happenings that constitute an event (§§1.48 and n. 42; 3.20–22, 32; Narrative Diagramming §3).

Paradigmatic: refers to thematic and other cohesive elements within the narrative that do not depend on sequential arrangement (§1.38). Cf. syntagmatic.

Paralepsis: the narrator supplies what was avoided or deliberately sidestepped earlier in the narrative. Literally, "a leaving aside."

Participant: any entity that is the agent of an action or to which something happens (§§1.38; 3.8).

Participant, continuity: the participant or group of participants that provides cohesiveness for the narrative as a whole (§§1.38; 3.8).

Participant, theme: the participant or group of participants that is the "subject" of a narrative segment or sequence (§§1.38; 3.8). The theme participant is customarily the participant in focus.

Poetics: treats the formal properties of literary texts (§1.8).

Pre-focalizer: any narrative device that prepares the way for or anticipates a focalizer (§5.4).

Prolepsis: any event narrated prematurely, i.e., at some point prior to the time it occurred in story chronology. Cf. analepsis.

Pseudo-iterative: a narrative statement to the effect that an identical something happens everyday, when in fact that something varies from day to day (§6.44).

Reach: the temporal distance from the present moment in the narrative to the moment of the proleptic or analeptic event (§8.7).

Recount, s. diegesis.

Second narrative: an anachrony, whether an analepsis or prolepsis, constitutes a second narrative in relation to the temporal order of the first narrative.

Segment: a cluster of actions that constitute an event. A segment has an INTRO, NUC, & CON (§§1.43, 48 and n. 42; Narrative Diagramming §§1, 3).

Sequence: consists of two or more narrative segments arranged in a hierarchical structure (§1.43; Narrative Diagramming §§5–8).

Showing, s. mimesis.

Singulative: in the ordinary narrative mode, what happens once is narrated once. This is the singulative mode. A neologism coined by Genette. Cf. iterative.

Story: a series of events, real or fictive, that are the content or the referents of a narrative text (§1.2).

Stretch: a chronological period covered by a narrative (§2.24).

Syntagmatic: refers to the sequential arrangement, the before/after movement, of the narrative (§1.38). Cf. paradigmatic.

Telling, s. diegesis.

Works Consulted

Abrams, M. H., *The Mirror and the Lamp: Romantic Theory and The Critical Tradition.* New York: W. W. Norton & Co. Inc., 1958 (original publication, 1953).

Alter, Robert, *The Art of Biblical Narrative.* New York: Basic Books, Inc., 1981.

——, *The Art of Biblical Poetry.* New York: Basic Books, Inc., 1985.

Auerbach, Erich, *Mimesis. The Representation of Reality in Western Literature.* Eng. Trans. W. R. Trask. New York: Doubleday, 1957.

Bal, Mieke, *Narratologie. Essais sur la signification narrative dans quatre romans modernes.* Paris: Klincksieck, 1977.

——, "Notes on Narrative Embedding." *Poetics Today* 2,2 (1981): 41–60.

——, "The Laughing Mice, or: on Focalization." *Poetics Today* 2,2 (1981): 202–10.

Barthes, Roland, *Mythologies.* Trans. Annette Lavers. New York: Hill and Wang, 1972 (original publication, 1957).

Bauer, Walter, *A Greek-English Lexicon of the New Testament and Other Early Christian Literature.* 2nd ed. Trans., rev., and augmented by William F. Arndt, F. Wilbur Gingrich, and Frederick W. Danker. Chicago: University of Chicago Press, 1981.

Blass, F., and Debrunner, A., *A Greek Grammar of the New Testament and Other Early Christian Literature.* Trans. and revised by Robert W. Funk. Chicago: University of Chicago Press, 1961.

Booth, Wayne, *The Rhetoric of Fiction.* Chicago: University of Chicago Press, 1961.

——, *A Rhetoric of Irony.* Chicago: University of Chicago Press, 1974.

Chatman, Seymour, "New Ways of Analyzing Narrative Structure, with an Example from Joyce's *Dubliners.*" *Language and Style* 2 (1969): 3–36.

——, ed., *Literary Style: A Symposium.* London and New York: Oxford University Press, 1971.

——, "On the Formalist–Structuralist Theory of Character." *Journal of Literary Semantics* 1 (1972): 57–79.

——, *Story and Discourse. Narrative Structure in Fiction and Film.* Ithaca: Cornell University Press, 1978.

Crites, Stephen, "The Narrative Quality of Experience." *Journal of the American Academy of Religion* 39 (1971): 291–311.

Crossan, John Dominic, *The Dark Interval. Towards a Theology of Story.* Sonoma: Polebridge Press, 1988 (original publication, 1975).

Culler, Jonathan, *Structuralist Poetics. Structuralism, Linguistics and the Study of Literature.* Ithaca: Cornell University Press, 1975.

——, *On Deconstruction: Theory and Criticism after Structuralism.* Ithaca: Cornell University Press, 1982.

Culpepper, R. Alan, *Anatomy of the Fourth Gospel: A Study in Literary Design.* Philadelphia: Fortress Press, 1983.

Derrida, Jacques, *Of Grammatology.* Trans. Gayatri Chakravorty Spivak. Baltimore and London: The Johns Hopkins University Press, 1976.

Dibelius, Martin, *From Tradition to Gospel.* New York: Charles Scribner's Sons, n.d.

Dobschütz, E. von, "Zur Erzählungskunst des Markus." *Zeitschrift für die neutestamentliche Wissenschaft* 27 (1928): 193–98.

Donahue, John R., *Are You the Christ? The Trial Narrative in the Gospel of Mark.* Missoula, Montana: Scholars Press, 1973.

Ducrot, Oswald and Todorov, Tzvetan, *Encyclopedic Dictionary of the Sciences of Language.* Trans. Catherine Porter. Baltimore and London: The Johns Hopkins University Press, 1979.

Faulkner, William, "That Evening Sun Go Down." In *Modern American Short Stories.* New York: Pocket Books, Inc., 1943.

Funk, Robert W., *A Beginning-Intermediate Grammar of Hellenistic Greek.* 3 Vols. Second ed. Missoula, Montana: Scholars Press, 1973.

_____, *Parables and Presence: Forms of the New Testament Tradition.* Philadelphia: Fortress Press, 1982.

_____, *New Gospel Parallels. Volume One, The Synoptic Gospels.* Philadelphia: Fortress Press, 1985 (Sonoma, CA: Polebridge Press, 1987).

Genette, Gérard, *Narrative Discourse. An Essay in Method.* Trans. Jane E. Lewin. Ithaca: Cornell University Press, 1980.

_____, *Figures of Literary Discourse.* Trans. Alan Sheridan. Introduction by Marie-Rose Logan. New York: Columbia University Press, 1982.

Greimas, Algirdas Julien, *Sémantique structurale.* Paris: Larousse, 1966.

_____, "Narrative Grammar: Units and Levels." *Modern Language Notes* 86 (1971): 793–806.

_____, "Elements of a Narrative Grammar." *Diacritics* 7 (1977): 23–40.

The Complete Grimm's Fairy Tales. Trans. Margaret Hunt. Rev. James Stern. New York: Random House, 1972.

Haenchen, Ernst, *The Acts of the Apostles.* Philadelphia: The Westminster Press, 1971.

Hawkes, Terence, *Structuralism and Semiotics.* Berkeley and Los Angeles: University of California Press, 1977.

Heidegger, Martin, *Being and Time.* Trans. John Macquarrie and Edward Robinson. London: SCM Press Ltd., 1962.

Hendricks, W. O., "The Structural Study of Narration: Sample Analyses." *Poetics* 3 (1972): 100–123.

_____, "Methodology of Narrative Structural Analysis." *Semiotica* 7 (1973): 163–84.

Hrushovski, Benjamin, *Segmentation and Motivation in the Text Continuum of Literary Prose. The First Episode of War and Peace.* Tel-Aviv: The Porter Institute for Poetics and Semiotics, n. d.

Iser, Wolfgang, *The Implied Reader. Patterns of Communication in Prose Fiction from Bunyan to Beckett.* Baltimore: The Johns Hopkins University Press, 1974.

_____, *The Act of Reading. A Theory of Aesthetic Response.* Baltimore: The Johns Hopkins University Press, 1978.

Jameson, Frederic, *The Prison-House of Language. A Critical Account of Structuralism and Russian Formalism.* Princeton: Princeton University Press, 1972.

Kafka, Franz, *Parables and Paradoxes.* New York: Schocken Books, 1961.

Kee, Howard Clark, *Community of the New Age: Studies in Mark's Gospel.* Philadelphia: The Westminster Press, 1977.

Kermode, Frank, *The Sense of an Ending: Studies in the Theory of Fiction.* London and New York: Oxford University Press, 1967.

_____, *The Genesis of Secrecy: On the Interpretation of Narrative.* Cambridge and London: Harvard University Press, 1979.

Lentricchia, Frank, *After the New Criticism.* Chicago: University of Chicago Press, 1980.
Lipski, John M., "From Text to Narrative: Spanning the Gap." *Poetics* 7 (1976): 191–206.
McKnight, Edgar V., *Meaning in Texts: The Historical Shaping of a Narrative Hermeneutics.* Philadelphia: Fortress Press, 1978.
———, *The Bible and the Reader: An Introduction to Literary Criticism.* Philadelphia: Fortress Press, 1985.
Mitchell, W. J. T., ed., *On Narrative.* Chicago: The University of Chicago Pess, 1981 (original publication, 1980).
Newman, Barclay M., Jr., "Discourse Structure." Pp. 237–41 in *The Interpreter's Dictionary of the Bible. Supplementary Volume.* Ed. Keith Crim. Nashville: Abingdon Press, 1976.
Nida, Eugene A. and Taber, Charles R., *The Theory and Practice of Translation.* Leiden: E. J. Brill, 1974.
Norris, Christopher, *Deconstruction: Theory and Practice.* London: Methuen, 1982.
Olsson, Birger, *Structure and Meaning in the Fourth Gospel. A Text-Linguistic Analysis of John 2:1–11 and 4:1–42.* Trans. Jean Gray. Coniectanea Biblica, New Testament Series 6. Lund: CWK Gleerup, 1974.
Ong, Walter J., *Orality and Literacy: The Technologizing of the Word.* London and New York: Methuen, 1982.
O'Toole, L. Michael, *Structure, Style and Interpretation in the Russian Short Story.* New Haven: Yale University Press, 1982.
Patte, Daniel, *What is Structural Exegeis?* Philadelphia: Fortress Press, 1976.
Petersen, Norman R., *Literary Criticsm for New Testament Critics.* Philadelphia: Fortress Press, 1978.
———, *Rediscovering Paul: Philemon and the Sociology of Paul's Narrative World.* Philadelphia: Fortress Press, 1985.
Prince, Gerald, "Notes Toward a Categorization of Fictional 'Narratees.'" *Genre* 4 (1971): 100–105.
———, *A Grammar of Stories: An Introduction.* The Hague: Mouton, 1973.
———, "Introduction à l'étude du narrataire." *Poétique* 14 (1973): 178–96.
———, "Aspects of a Grammar of Narrative." *Poetics Today* 1,3 (1980): 49–63.
Propp, Vladimir, *Morphology of the Folktale.* First edition trans. Laurence Scott. Second edition revised and edited by Louis A. Wagner. Austin: University of Texas Press, 1968.
Rimmon-Kenan, Shlomith, *Narrative Fiction: Contemporary Poetics.* London and New York: Methuen, 1983.
Robbins, Vernon K., "Last Meal: Preparation, Betrayal, and Absence." Pp. 21–40 in *The Passion in Mark.* Ed. Werner Kelber. Philadelphia: Fortress Press, 1976.
de Saussure, Ferdinand, *Course in General Linguistics.* Trans. Wade Baskin. Ed. Charles Bally and Albert Sechehaye in collaboration with Albert Riedlinger. New York: McGraw-Hill Book Company, 1966 (originally published, 1916).
Schaefer, Jack, *Shane.* Toronto: Bantam Books, 1980 (originally published, 1949).
Scholes, Robert, *Structuralism in Literature: An Introduction.* New Haven and London: Yale University Press, 1974.
———, *Semiotics and Interpretation.* New Haven and London: Yale University Press, 1982.
Schutz, Alfred and Luckmann, Thomas, *Structures of the Life-World.* Trans. Richard M. Zaner and H. Tristram Engelhardt, Jr. Evanston: Northwestern University Press, 1973.
Staley, Jeffrey Lloyd, *The Print's First Kiss: A Rhetorical Investigation of the Implied Reader*

in the Fourth Gospel. Doctoral dissertation, Graduate Theological Union, Berkeley, CA, 1985.

Stowe, Harriet Beecher, *Uncle Tom's Cabin*. Toronto: Bantam Books, 1981 (originally published, 1851–1852).

Todorov, Tzvetan, "Structural Analysis of Narrative." *Novel. A Forum on Fiction* 3 (1969–1970): 70–76.

——, "The Structural Analysis of Literature: The Tales of Henry James." Pp. 73–103 in *Structuralism: An Introduction*. Ed. David Robey. Oxford: Clarendon Press, 1973.

——, *The Fantastic. A Structural Approach to a Literary Genre*. Trans. Richard Howard. Ithaca: Cornell University Press, 1973.

——, *The Poetics of Prose*. Trans. Richard Howard. Ithaca: Cornell University Press, 1977.

——, *Introduction to Poetics*. Trans. Richard Howard. Minneapolis: University of Minnesota Press, 1981.

Webster's Third New International Dictionary of the English Language Unabridged. Springfield, MA: G. and C. Merriam, 1967.

Wister, Owen, *The Virginian*. New York: New American Library, 1979 (originally published, 1902).

Index of Modern Authors

References are to chapter and paragraph number.

Index of Primary Texts

References are to chapter and paragraph number.

Ancient Texts & Authors

Modern Texts & Authors

Index of Subjects

References are to chapter and paragraph number. Asterisks (*) indicate key passages.

Design & typesetting: Polebridge Press, Sonoma, California
Printing & binding: McNaughton & Gunn, Inc., Saline, Michigan
Display type: Baskerville and Zapf Chancery
Text type: Baskerville
Charts: Techart, San Francisco, California